# Circular Economy Innovations, Digitalization, and Policy for Sustainable Development

Syed Abdul Rehman Khan
*Business Research and Consultancy Ltd, Sheffield, UK*

Zhang Yu
*Yunnan University of Finance and Economics, China*

Muhammad Tanveer
https://orcid.org/0000-0002-2019-6544
*Imam Mohammad Ibn Saud Islamic University (IMSIU), Riyadh, Saudi Arabia*

IGI Global
Scientific Publishing
Publishing Tomorrow's Research Today

Vice President of Editorial Melissa Wagner
Director of Acquisitions Mikaela Felty
Director of Book Development Jocelynn Hessler
Production Manager Mike Brehm
Cover Design Jose Rosado

Published in the United States of America by
IGI Global Scientific Publishing
701 East Chocolate Avenue
Hershey, PA, 17033, USA
Tel: 717-533-8845 | Fax: 717-533-7115
Website: https://www.igi-global.com E-mail: cust@igi-global.com



Library of Congress Cataloging-in-Publication Data

(CIP Data Pending)
ISBN13: 979-8-2600-1438-7
Isbn13Softcover: 979-8-2600-1439-4
EISBN13: 979-8-2600-1440-0
British Cataloguing in Publication Data
A Cataloguing in Publication record for this book is available from the British Library.

# Table of Contents

# Detailed Table of Contents

*Ajay Kumar Singh, Department of Humanities and Social Sciences, Graphic Era University, Dehradun, India*
*S. Srinivasan, Department of Humanities and Social Sciences, Graphic Era University, Dehradun, India*

This chapter examines the causal implications of digitalization with environmental degradation as employing a balanced panel data of 111 countries during 2004 – 2021. Environmental degradation is measured as per capita CO2 emissions. Digital inclusion index (DII) is used as a measurement of digital inclusion. DII is the combination of five variables which help to increase digitalization. Industrialization, foreign direct investment, inflation GDP deflator, per capita GDP, renewable energy consumption, education expenditure, technological diffusion and population density are also included in the empirical investigations. Instrumental variable is used to check the Robustness of the regression results. Natural logarithms of these variables are considered in regression models. Existence of causal association among these variables are estimated through Granger causality test. A bi-lateral and positive relationship is found between digitalization and environmental degradation in these nations. It claims that adoption of sustainable digitalization will enhance environmental sustainability.


*Mounsif Ridaoui, Research in Economics and Management of Organisations Laboratory, National School of Business and Management, Sultan Moulay Slimane University, Morocco*
*Aziz Razzouki, Research in Economics and Management of Organisations Laboratory, National School of Business and Management, Sultan Moulay Slimane University, Morocco*
*Mohamed Oudgou, Research in Economics and Management of Organisations Laboratory, National School of Business and Management, Sultan Moulay Slimane University, Morocco*
*Abdeslam Boudhar, Research in Economics and Management of Organisations Laboratory, National School of Business and Management, Sultan Moulay Slimane University, Morocco*

This chapter rethinks virtual water trade, the water embedded in traded goods, through the lens of the circular economy to clarify when trade supports, or undermines, sustainability in water-scarce contexts. The chapter develops a conceptual framework for circular virtual water governance that aligns trade-driven virtual water flows

This chapter examines how agricultural residues can be transformed into high-performance geopolymer binders that address both environmental burdens and infrastructure demands. It explains the chemistry of alkali activation, the role of precursor composition, and the influence of processing conditions on mechanical, thermal, and durability behavior. The chapter highlights advanced functionalities such as self-sensing and self-healing, alongside the measurable carbon-reduction benefits demonstrated through life-cycle assessment. Case studies from transportation, marine, building, and water-management sectors illustrate real-world feasibility. By integrating material science, sustainability metrics, and implementation frameworks, the chapter articulates how waste-derived geopolymers contribute to circular-economy goals and support climate-resilient infrastructure development.

# Preface

## INTRODUCTION

Sustainable development has emerged as one of the defining imperatives of the 21st century, shaped by the urgent need to address environmental degradation, economic inequality, and social instability. As global systems become increasingly interconnected, the limitations of traditional development models are more apparent than ever. Linear patterns of production and consumption have intensified pressures on natural resources, contributing to climate change, biodiversity loss, and widening socio-economic disparities. Against this backdrop, the integration of circular economy principles, digital innovation, and effective policy frameworks offers a promising pathway toward a more balanced and resilient future.

The circular economy provides a regenerative alternative that prioritizes resource efficiency, waste minimization, and the continual use of materials within closed-loop systems. However, the transition to such systems requires more than conceptual alignment—it demands technological advancement, institutional support, and behavioral change. Digitalization plays a transformative role in this process, enabling real-time monitoring, data-driven decision-making, and enhanced transparency across value chains. At the same time, policy interventions are essential to guide, regulate, and incentivize sustainable practices at local, national, and global levels.

This edited volume brings together interdisciplinary perspectives that explore the dynamic interplay between circular economy innovations, digital technologies, and policy mechanisms. As editors, we have curated contributions that reflect both theoretical depth and empirical rigor, offering insights from diverse geographic and sectoral contexts. The chapters collectively examine how sustainability can be operationalized through integrated approaches that align environmental stewardship with economic development and social equity. It is our hope that this work will serve as a valuable resource for academics, practitioners, and policymakers seeking to navigate the complexities of sustainable transformation.

## CHAPTER OVERVIEW

Chapter 1: Knowledge-Centric Best Practices

Focusing on organizational learning and knowledge management, this chapter explores how knowledge-centric approaches enable effective implementation of circular economy practices. It demonstrates how digital transformation and knowledge processes create dynamic capabilities that enhance both sustainability outcomes and competitive advantage.

Chapter 2: Circular Economy of EU Countries: What Are the Differences?

This chapter provides an empirical analysis of circular economy performance across European Union countries. Using quantitative methods, it identifies disparities in implementation and highlights key factors influencing regional progress, offering insights to inform targeted policy interventions.

Chapter 3: Implementation of Sustainable Development Goals: An Industry 4 Perspective

This chapter explores the contribution of Industry 4.0 technologies to achieving the Sustainable Development Goals (SDGs). It provides global examples and actionable recommendations, demonstrating how digital tools such as AI and IoT support sustainable manufacturing, energy systems, and infrastructure development.

Chapter 4: An Empirical Investigation for Assessing the Causal Relationship of Digitalization with Environmental Degradation in Selected Countries

This chapter investigates the complex relationship between digitalization and environmental outcomes using panel data analysis. It highlights a bidirectional relationship and emphasizes the importance of adopting sustainable digitalization practices to mitigate environmental impacts.

Chapter 5: Rethinking Virtual Water Trade in the Circular Economy for Sustainable Production and Consumption

This chapter introduces a novel framework for understanding virtual water trade within a circular economy context. It integrates water footprint analysis with governance mechanisms to address resource efficiency, equity, and sustainability in water-scarce regions.

Chapter 6: Digital-Twin Enabled Systems for Optimizing Bio-Waste-Based Farming Models

Focusing on agricultural innovation, this chapter presents digital twin technology as a powerful tool for integrating bio-waste valorization with precision farming. It highlights measurable benefits in efficiency, sustainability, and resilience while addressing implementation challenges.

Chapter 7: Transforming Agricultural Waste into Smart Geopolymer Materials for Sustainable Infrastructure

This chapter explores how agricultural waste can be converted into advanced construction materials. By combining material science with sustainability metrics, it demonstrates how geopolymer technologies contribute to circular economy goals and climate-resilient infrastructure.

## CONCLUSION

The chapters in this volume collectively highlight the transformative potential of integrating circular economy principles with digital innovation and policy frameworks. They demonstrate that sustainable development is not a singular objective but a multidimensional process that requires alignment across environmental, economic, and social domains. From foundational theories to applied case studies, the contributions provide a comprehensive understanding of how innovation and governance can drive meaningful change.

A recurring theme throughout this collection is the critical role of digitalization as both an enabler and a disruptor. While digital technologies offer unprecedented opportunities to enhance efficiency, transparency, and scalability, they also introduce new challenges related to energy consumption, data governance, and equitable access. Similarly, policy frameworks must evolve to keep pace with technological advancements, ensuring that sustainability goals are effectively integrated into regulatory and institutional systems.

As editors, we believe that advancing sustainable development requires collaborative, interdisciplinary efforts that bridge the gap between theory and practice. This volume aims to inspire such collaboration by offering insights that are both analytically rigorous and practically relevant. We hope that readers will find in these chapters not only a deeper understanding of circular economy innovations and digitalization but also a call to action to contribute to a more sustainable and inclusive global future.

**Syed Abdul Rehman Khan**
*Business Research and Consultancy Ltd, Sheffield, UK*

**Zhang Yu**
*Yunnan University of Finance and Economics, China*

**Muhammad Tanveer**

*Imam Mohammad Ibn Saud Islamic University (IMSIU), Riyadh, Saudi Arabia*

# Chapter 1
# Knowledge-Centric Best Practices

**Brijendra Parasnath Gupta**
http://orcid.org/0000-0003-3597-350X
*Siddhant College of Engineering, Pune, India*

**Kadirova Gulbokhor**
*Tashkent Institute of Irrigation and Agricultural Mechanization Engineers, Uzbekistan*

**Khayrilla Kurbonov**
*Termez University of Economics and Service, Termez, Uzbekistan*

**Berdiyev Anvar Abduraxmanovich**
*Denov Institute of Entrepreneurship and Pedagogy, Uzbekistan*

**Ismailov Azizbek**
*Alfraganus University, Tashkent, Uzbekistan*

**Mamirov Muxammadjon Ma'rifjon o‘g‘li**
*Andijan State University, Uzbekistan*

**Gulbahor Namazova**
*Oriental University, Tashkent, Uzbekistan*

**Deepak Gupta**
http://orcid.org/0000-0003-3929-1362
*ITM Gwalior, India*

## ABSTRACT

*This chapter examines knowledge-centric best practices that enable sustainable production and consumption within technology-driven circular economy frameworks. As organizations increasingly adopt Industry 4.0 technologies and circular business models, effective knowledge management emerges as a critical enabler of successful transitions. The chapter synthesizes recent research on organizational learning, digital transformation, and green innovation to identify evidence-based practices that enhance circular economy implementation. Through systematic analysis of empirical studies, this work reveals how knowledge acquisition, transformation, application, and evaluation processes facilitate sustainable outcomes. The integration of digital technologies with organizational learning mechanisms creates*

DOI: 10.4018/979-8-2600-1438-7.ch001

*dynamic capabilities that support both environmental performance and competitive advantage. Key findings demonstrate that knowledge-centric approaches strengthen the connection between technological adoption and sustainability outcomes, while organizational resilience and adaptive capacity moderate these relationships. The chapter provides actionable frameworks for practitioners and policymakers seeking to leverage knowledge management for circular economy advancement.*

## 1. INTRODUCTION

The transition toward a circular economy represents one of the most significant transformations in contemporary production and consumption systems. This paradigm shift moves beyond traditional linear models of take-make-dispose toward regenerative systems that maintain products, components, and materials at their highest utility and value (Blackburn et al., 2026). The circular economy framework encompasses multiple strategies including reduction, reuse, recycling, recovery, and redesign—collectively known as the R-strategies—that aim to minimize resource depletion and environmental degradation while creating economic value.

The convergence of digital technologies and circular economy principles has created unprecedented opportunities for sustainable transformation. Industry 4.0 technologies such as the Internet of Things (IoT), artificial intelligence (AI), big data analytics, and digital platforms enable new forms of resource optimization, product lifecycle management, and value chain coordination (Awan et al., 2021; Carlos et al., 2024). These technological capabilities generate vast amounts of data and information that, when properly managed and leveraged, can drive significant improvements in environmental and economic performance.

However, technology adoption alone does not guarantee successful circular economy transitions. Growing evidence suggests that organizational knowledge management capabilities play a crucial mediating role in translating technological potential into sustainable outcomes (Ademi & Klungseth, 2024; Eskiyerli & Dondrup, 2025). Organizations must develop systematic approaches to acquire, transform, apply, and evaluate knowledge related to circular practices, environmental innovations, and sustainable business models. This knowledge-centric perspective recognizes that the effective utilization of information and expertise constitutes a fundamental enabler of circular economy implementation.

### 1.1 Background and Context

The circular economy concept has gained substantial traction among policymakers, businesses, and researchers over the past decade. The European Union has positioned circular economy as a central pillar of its sustainable development strategy, with member states at various stages of implementation (Castillo-Díaz et al., 2024). Manufacturing organizations worldwide face increasing pressure from regulations, consumer expectations, and resource constraints to adopt more sustainable practices. This pressure has catalyzed significant interest in circular business models, green innovation, and sustainable supply chain management.

Simultaneously, the Fourth Industrial Revolution has transformed organizational capabilities and operational possibilities. Digital technologies enable real-time monitoring of material flows, predictive maintenance of products, optimization of reverse logistics, and coordination of complex multi-stakeholder networks (Mora-Contreras et al., 2025). These capabilities are particularly relevant for circular economy applications, where visibility, traceability, and coordination across extended product lifecycles become critical success factors. The integration of digital and circular strategies has emerged as a key research and practice area.

Despite growing recognition of synergies between digitalization and circularity, many organizations struggle to realize expected benefits. Research identifies multiple barriers including technical complexities, organizational inertia, lack of expertise, insufficient collaboration, and misaligned incentives (K. et al., 2023; Neri et al., 2024). These challenges highlight the importance of organizational learning and knowledge management as enablers of successful transitions. Organizations must build capabilities to absorb external knowledge, integrate diverse information sources, facilitate cross-functional learning, and continuously adapt practices based on experience and feedback.

## 1.2 Research Objectives and Scope

This chapter aims to synthesize current research on knowledge-centric best practices that support circular economy transitions in technology-driven contexts. The analysis draws on recent empirical studies examining relationships among organizational learning, digital technologies, green innovation, and sustainable performance. The primary objectives include:

1. Identifying key knowledge management practices that enable effective circular economy implementation
2. Examining how digital technologies enhance organizational learning and knowledge processes in circular contexts
3. Analyzing the relationships between knowledge-centric practices and sustainable outcomes
4. Developing actionable frameworks for practitioners seeking to leverage knowledge management for circular economy advancement

5. Identifying future research directions and emerging challenges in this domain

The scope encompasses manufacturing and production organizations that are implementing or planning to implement circular economy strategies. While the analysis focuses primarily on organizational-level practices, it also considers supply chain and ecosystem perspectives where relevant. The chapter emphasizes evidence-based practices derived from peer-reviewed research published in recent years, with particular attention to studies examining Industry 4.0 and digital transformation contexts.

### 1.3 Chapter Structure

The remainder of this chapter is organized as follows. Section 2 provides theoretical foundations by examining key concepts including circular economy principles, knowledge management frameworks, and organizational learning theories. Section 3 presents the knowledge-centric framework that integrates these concepts and identifies critical components. Section 4 analyzes specific best practices across four knowledge process domains: acquisition, transformation, application, and evaluation. Section 5 examines the role of digital technologies as enablers of knowledge-centric circular economy practices. Section 6 discusses implementation challenges, success factors, and organizational capabilities required for effective adoption. Section 7 presents case insights and empirical evidence supporting recommended practices. Section 8 concludes with synthesis of key findings, implications for research and practice, and future directions.

## 2. THEORETICAL FOUNDATIONS

This section establishes the theoretical foundation by examining core concepts that underpin knowledge-centric approaches to circular economy implementation. Understanding these foundational elements is essential for appreciating how knowledge management practices facilitate sustainable transitions in technology-driven contexts.

### 2.1 Circular Economy Principles and Strategies

The circular economy represents a systemic approach to economic development designed to benefit businesses, society, and the environment. Unlike the traditional linear economy model, which follows a take-make-dispose pattern, circular economy aims to decouple economic growth from resource consumption through three fundamental principles: designing out waste and pollution, keeping products and materials in use, and regenerating natural systems. These principles manifest through various operational strategies collectively known as the R-framework.

The R-strategies provide a hierarchical approach to resource management, with higher-order Rs (refuse, rethink, reduce) being preferable to lower-order ones (recycle, recover). Bag et al. (2021) identify ten R strategies—refuse, rethink, reduce, reuse, repair, refurbish, remanufacture, repurpose, recycle, and recover—that organizations can employ depending on product characteristics, industry contexts, and capability maturity. This 10R framework extends beyond traditional recycling-focused approaches to encompass upstream design decisions, midstream operational practices, and downstream recovery processes.

Circular business models operationalize these principles through innovative value propositions, creation mechanisms, and capture approaches. Albertsen et al. (2021) identify several circular business model archetypes in the context of electric vehicle batteries, including product-as-a-service, sharing platforms, product life extension, and resource recovery models. Each archetype requires different organizational capabilities, partner ecosystems, and knowledge requirements. Successful implementation depends on aligning business model design with organizational competencies and market conditions.

## 2.2 Knowledge Management and Organizational Learning

Knowledge management encompasses systematic processes for creating, sharing, using, and managing organizational knowledge and information. In the context of circular economy transitions, knowledge management serves multiple critical functions: facilitating the adoption of new practices, enabling innovation in products and processes, supporting cross-functional coordination, and building adaptive capacity to respond to changing requirements and opportunities (Sadiq et al., 2025). Effective knowledge management creates dynamic capabilities that enhance organizational responsiveness and competitiveness.

Organizational learning theory provides complementary perspectives on how organizations acquire, process, and apply knowledge. Oelze et al. (2016) demonstrate that organizational learning plays a vital role in implementing sustainable supply chain practices, particularly in complex policy environments requiring behavioral and operational changes. Learning organizations develop routines for experimentation, knowledge sharing, and continuous improvement that support sustainable development initiatives. This learning orientation creates a foundation for successfully navigating the complexities of circular economy implementation.

The concept of green organizational learning specifically addresses learning processes oriented toward environmental objectives. Cui et al. (2023) examine how green transformational leadership fosters organizational green learning, which in turn drives radical green innovation. Their research highlights that learning mechanisms focused on environmental issues enable organizations to develop breakthrough innovations that fundamentally alter production processes and product characteristics. This specialized learning capability becomes particularly important as organizations pursue ambitious circular economy goals requiring significant departures from established practices.

Recent research extends these concepts by examining how organizational learning interacts with external knowledge sources and digital information systems. Awan et al. (2025) demonstrate that global knowledge integration—the ability to access, absorb, and apply knowledge from international sources—significantly enhances sustainable product design capabilities. This finding underscores the importance of developing absorptive capacity and boundary-spanning capabilities that enable organizations to leverage external expertise and best practices in circular economy domains.

## 2.3 Industry 4.0 and Digital Transformation

Industry 4.0 technologies fundamentally transform production systems through cyber-physical integration, data-driven decision-making, and intelligent automation. Core technologies include the Internet of Things for real-time data collection, artificial intelligence and machine learning for pattern recognition and prediction, big data analytics for processing large information volumes, cloud computing for distributed information storage and processing, and blockchain for secure transaction recording. These technologies create unprecedented visibility into material flows, product usage patterns, and system performance.

The relationship between Industry 4.0 and circular economy has attracted significant research attention. Awan et al. (2021) provide a comprehensive literature review revealing multiple synergies: IoT sensors enable product tracking and condition monitoring essential for remanufacturing and maintenance; AI optimizes reverse logistics and material sorting; digital twins simulate circular scenarios before implementation; and blockchain enhances trust and transparency in material provenance and quality certification. These technological capabilities address several key barriers to circular economy adoption including information asymmetries, coordination challenges, and quality uncertainties.

Digital platforms represent particularly important enablers of circular economy ecosystems. Atif (2023) examines how Industry 4.0-enabled data-driven shared platforms facilitate product-service system implementation in circular contexts. These platforms coordinate multiple stakeholders including manufacturers, service providers, customers, and recyclers through standardized data formats, automated transactions, and performance analytics. The platform architecture creates network effects that enhance value for all participants while reducing transaction costs associated with circular flows.

However, technology adoption alone proves insufficient for realizing circular economy benefits. Lo et al. (2024) investigate digital technology implementation in circular businesses, finding that organizational factors including leadership commitment, employee capabilities, and change management processes significantly influence outcomes. Their research emphasizes that digital transformation requires parallel development of organizational competencies and cultural attributes that support technology-enabled circular practices. This finding highlights the importance of knowledge-centric approaches that integrate technological and organizational dimensions.

## 2.4 Green Innovation and Environmental Performance

Green innovation encompasses the development and implementation of new or significantly improved products, processes, organizational methods, or marketing approaches that reduce environmental impact. This innovation can be incremental, improving existing offerings through efficiency gains or material substitutions, or radical, introducing fundamentally new solutions that disrupt established patterns. Both types contribute to circular economy transitions, though radical innovations may be necessary for achieving ambitious sustainability targets (Rehman et al., 2021).

The relationship between green innovation and environmental performance has been extensively documented. Khan et al. (2023) examine how green entrepreneurial orientation and organizational resilience capacity jointly influence green innovation adoption in business research contexts. Their findings reveal that organizations with stronger learning orientations and adaptive capabilities develop more innovative environmental solutions and achieve superior environmental outcomes. This research underscores the importance of building organizational capacities that support continuous innovation in sustainability domains.

Recent work by Ameer et al. (2024) explores the interplay between organizational resilience and green innovation in manufacturing contexts. They find that resilient organizations—those with robust processes for sensing environmental changes, seizing opportunities, and reconfiguring resources—demonstrate greater capacity to develop and implement green innovations. This research highlights that innovation capabilities depend not only on R&D investments but also on organizational attributes including flexibility, learning orientation, and adaptive capacity. These findings have important implications for knowledge management practices supporting circular economy transitions.

## 3. KNOWLEDGE-CENTRIC FRAMEWORK FOR CIRCULAR ECONOMY

Building on the theoretical foundations established in the previous section, this section presents an integrated knowledge-centric framework that synthesizes key concepts and identifies critical components for circular economy implementation. The framework recognizes that successful circular transitions require systematic approaches to managing knowledge across multiple organizational levels and process domains.

### 3.1 Framework Overview and Architecture

The knowledge-centric framework for circular economy (Figure 1) conceptualizes circular economy implementation as a knowledge-intensive transformation requiring integration across multiple dimensions. At the center of this framework sits knowledge management as the core coordinating mechanism that connects digital technologies, organizational learning, green innovation, and circular business models. This central positioning reflects the mediating role that knowledge processes play in translating technological capabilities and learning activities into sustainable outcomes.

*Figure 1. Knowledge-Centric Framework for Technology-Driven Circular Economy*

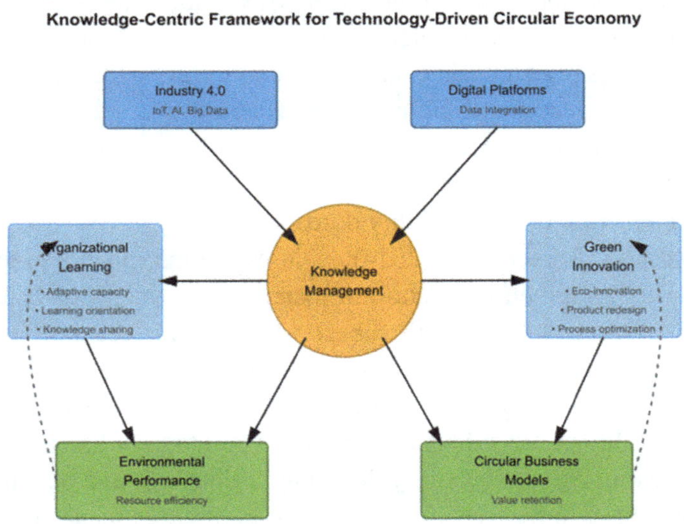

Figure 1 framework identifies four primary domains that organizations must integrate: (1) digital technologies that provide data collection, processing, and analytics capabilities; (2) organizational learning mechanisms that build adaptive capacity and facilitate knowledge sharing; (3) green innovation processes that generate environmental improvements in products and operations; and (4) circular business models that capture and create value through resource retention strategies. These domains interact through knowledge flows and feedback loops that enable continuous improvement and adaptation.

Two critical outcomes emerge from effective integration of these domains: environmental performance improvements measured through resource efficiency, waste reduction, and emission decreases; and viable circular business models that create economic value while advancing sustainability goals. The framework emphasizes that these outcomes are interdependent—environmental performance gains strengthen business model viability by reducing costs and enhancing reputation, while economically sustainable business models provide resources for continued environmental investments.

## 3.2 Knowledge Process Dimensions

The framework distinguishes four fundamental knowledge processes that organizations must manage effectively: acquisition, transformation, application, and evaluation. Each process encompasses specific activities and requires distinct capabilities, yet they function as an integrated cycle rather than isolated stages. Figure 2 illustrates how these processes connect to form a continuous knowledge integration cycle supporting circular economy implementation.

*Figure 2. Knowledge Integration Process for Circular Economy Implementation*

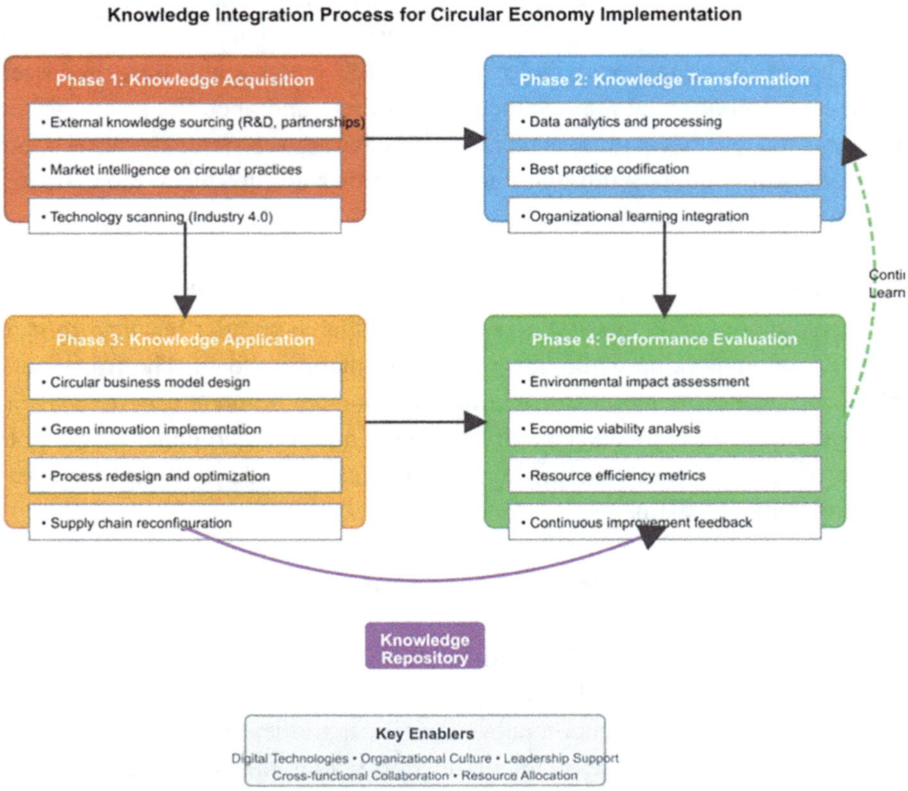


Figure 2 distinguishes four fundamental knowledge processes that organizations must manage effectively: acquisition, transformation, application, and evaluation. Each process encompasses specific activities and requires distinct capabilities, yet they function as an integrated cycle rather than isolated stages. This illustrates how these processes connect to form a continuous knowledge integration cycle supporting circular economy implementation.

Knowledge acquisition encompasses activities through which organizations obtain new information and expertise from external and internal sources. External sources include research publications, industry reports, technology vendors, consultants, partnerships, and collaborative networks. Internal sources include operational data, employee experiences, pilot projects, and organizational experiments. Eskiyerli and Dondrup (2025) emphasize that systematic knowledge acquisition forms the foundation for circular knowledge management, particularly in international joint ventures where cross-cultural learning becomes essential.

Knowledge transformation involves processing, analyzing, and codifying acquired information into formats suitable for organizational use. This process includes data analytics that extract insights from operational information, documentation of best practices and lessons learned, creation of decision support tools and guidelines, and development of training materials and knowledge repositories. Digital technologies play particularly important roles in knowledge transformation by automating data processing and enabling sophisticated analytics that would be impractical through manual methods.

Knowledge application translates codified knowledge into practical actions and innovations. This domain encompasses business model design informed by circular economy principles, implementation of green innovations in products and processes, optimization of operations based on performance data, and reconfiguration of supply chains to support circular flows. Effective application requires not only access to relevant knowledge but also organizational capabilities to experiment with new approaches, manage change processes, and overcome resistance.

Knowledge evaluation assesses the effectiveness of implemented practices and generates feedback for continuous improvement. Evaluation activities include monitoring environmental and economic performance indicators, conducting impact assessments of circular initiatives, analyzing cost-benefit relationships, and identifying opportunities for optimization. The evaluation process creates feedback loops that inform subsequent knowledge acquisition and application cycles, enabling organizations to refine their approaches based on experience and changing conditions.

## 3.3 Key Enablers and Moderating Factors

Several organizational factors enable or constrain the effectiveness of knowledge-centric approaches to circular economy implementation. Leadership support emerges as a foundational enabler across multiple studies. Leaders establish priorities, allocate resources, shape organizational culture, and model desired behaviors. Without strong leadership commitment, knowledge management initiatives often struggle to gain traction and sustain momentum (Ademi & Klungseth, 2024).

Organizational culture significantly influences knowledge sharing behaviors and learning orientation. Cultures that value experimentation, tolerate failures as learning opportunities, reward knowledge contribution, and promote cross-functional collaboration facilitate more effective knowledge management. Conversely, cultures characterized by siloed operations, information hoarding, or risk aversion impede knowledge flows and reduce organizational learning capacity (Malik et al., 2025).

Resource allocation includes financial investments in technologies, training, and infrastructure, as well as allocation of employee time for learning and innovation activities. Organizations must balance short-term operational demands with longer-term capability development investments. Insufficient resource allocation undermines knowledge management initiatives even when other supportive conditions exist.

Cross-functional collaboration capabilities determine how effectively organizations integrate diverse knowledge sources and perspectives. Circular economy initiatives often require coordination among R&D, production, marketing, logistics, and finance functions. Organizations with established mechanisms for cross-functional teamwork, joint problem-solving, and integrated planning demonstrate greater success in implementing circular strategies (Centobelli et al., 2021).

Organizational resilience capacity moderates the relationship between knowledge management practices and outcomes. Resilient organizations possess capabilities to sense environmental changes, seize emerging opportunities, and reconfigure resources in response to disruptions. This resilience enables organizations to adapt knowledge management approaches as conditions evolve and to persist through implementation challenges (Khan et al., 2023). Building resilience requires sustained investment in organizational learning, flexible processes, and diverse capability portfolios.

# 4. BEST PRACTICES ACROSS KNOWLEDGE PROCESS DOMAINS

This section presents evidence-based best practices organized according to the four knowledge process domains identified in the framework. Each practice is grounded in empirical research demonstrating effectiveness in supporting circular economy implementation.

## 4.1 Knowledge Acquisition Practices

### 4.1.1 External Knowledge Sourcing

Organizations pursuing circular economy transitions must actively access external knowledge sources to supplement internal expertise. Research by Awan et al. (2025) demonstrates that global knowledge integration—the systematic acquisition and absorption of international best practices—significantly enhances sustainable product design capabilities and green innovation performance. Organizations should establish formal mechanisms for scanning international literature, monitoring competitor innovations, participating in industry associations, and engaging with research institutions.

Strategic partnerships constitute another critical external knowledge source. Collaborative relationships with technology providers, academic institutions, and complementary businesses provide access to specialized expertise and resources.

Ferreira et al. (2025) find that knowledge acquisition through partnerships positively influences firm performance in small and medium-sized enterprises, particularly when combined with corporate entrepreneurship orientations. Organizations should selectively develop partnerships that fill specific knowledge gaps while managing intellectual property considerations and coordination costs.

### 4.1.2 Market Intelligence Systems

Systematic market intelligence gathering enables organizations to identify emerging circular economy opportunities and evolving customer preferences. This intelligence includes monitoring regulatory developments affecting circular economy, tracking competitor circular initiatives and performance claims, analyzing customer attitudes toward sustainable products and services, and identifying emerging technologies relevant to circular applications. Digital tools including web scraping, social media analytics, and patent databases facilitate more comprehensive and timely intelligence gathering.

### 4.1.3 Internal Data Collection Infrastructure

Organizations require robust data collection systems to generate internal knowledge about material flows, energy consumption, waste generation, and product performance. Industry 4.0 technologies enable unprecedented data collection granularity. Pham et al. (2019) demonstrate how IoT sensors in electric scooter sharing systems capture detailed usage patterns, maintenance needs, and failure modes—information essential for optimizing product design and service operations. Organizations should invest in sensors, data infrastructure, and integration platforms that enable comprehensive visibility into operational and environmental performance.

## 4.2 Knowledge Transformation Practices

### 4.2.1 Advanced Analytics Capabilities

Transforming raw data into actionable insights requires sophisticated analytical capabilities. Machine learning algorithms can identify patterns in complex datasets, predictive analytics can forecast equipment failures or material demand, and optimization algorithms can determine ideal circular economy configurations. Carlos et al. (2024) examine how digital technologies enhance circular economy practices through improved data analytics, finding that analytical capabilities enable organizations to identify previously hidden opportunities for resource efficiency and waste reduction.

Organizations should develop or acquire analytical capabilities matched to their circular economy objectives. For remanufacturing applications, condition monitoring analytics assess product health and predict optimal refurbishment timing. For material recycling, composition analysis determines optimal sorting and processing strategies. For product-service systems, usage analytics inform service design and pricing. Building these capabilities may require hiring data scientists, partnering with analytics specialists, or implementing commercial analytics platforms.

### 4.2.2 Best Practice Codification

Documenting and standardizing successful practices enables knowledge replication and organizational learning. This codification process includes creating standard operating procedures for circular processes, developing design guidelines incorporating circularity principles, documenting lessons learned from pilot projects and implementations, and establishing metrics and benchmarks for circular economy performance. Malik et al. (2025) emphasize that organizational learning mechanisms, including practice codification, significantly enhance both innovation and performance in sustainable development contexts.

Effective codification balances standardization with flexibility. Overly rigid procedures may constrain adaptation and innovation, while insufficient standardization leads to inconsistent implementation and limited knowledge transfer. Organizations should codify core principles and proven approaches while allowing contextualization and experimentation at operational levels.

### 4.2.3 Knowledge Repositories and Platforms

Centralized knowledge repositories provide accessible storage for codified information including technical documentation, case studies, research findings, and performance data. Modern knowledge management platforms offer search capabilities, collaborative editing, version control, and integration with other business systems. Blackburn et al. (2026) examine digital platforms supporting circular economy implementation, finding that effective platforms combine information storage with coordination and transaction functions.

Organizations should design knowledge repositories considering user needs and workflows. Repositories must be intuitive to navigate, regularly updated, and integrated into daily operations to achieve sustained usage. Some organizations establish communities of practice around circular economy topics, using platforms to facilitate ongoing dialogue, question-answering, and collaborative problem-solving among distributed practitioners.

## 4.3 Knowledge Application Practices

### 4.3.1 Circular Design Integration

Applying circular economy knowledge requires integrating circularity principles into product and process design from inception. Medeiros et al. (2023) propose a methodology for inserting circular thinking into textile product development processes, demonstrating how design teams can systematically apply circular strategies including material selection, modularity, durability enhancement, and disassembly facilitation. This integration requires training designers in circular economy concepts, providing tools and databases supporting circular design decisions, establishing circular performance targets in design specifications, and incorporating lifecycle assessment into design evaluation.

### 4.3.2 Process Optimization and Eco-Efficiency

Organizations should systematically apply knowledge to optimize production processes for resource efficiency and waste minimization. This optimization encompasses energy management through monitoring and efficiency improvements, water conservation and closed-loop water systems, material utilization optimization to minimize waste generation, and emission reduction through cleaner production techniques. Hegab et al. (2023) discuss strategies for implementing sustainable production systems, emphasizing the importance of continuous process improvement guided by performance data.

### 4.3.3 Circular Business Model Innovation

Knowledge application extends beyond technical improvements to business model innovation. Organizations must translate circular economy insights into viable value propositions and revenue models. This innovation includes developing product-as-a-service offerings that retain ownership and responsibility for products, establishing take-back and recycling programs for end-of-life products, creating secondary markets for refurbished or remanufactured items, and partnering with complementary organizations to create circular value networks. Business model innovation requires cross-functional teams combining technical, commercial, and strategic expertise (Ademi & Klungseth, 2024).

### 4.3.4 Supply Chain Reconfiguration

Circular economy implementation often necessitates supply chain reconfiguration to support reverse flows and closed-loop systems. Bag et al. (2021) examine procurement 4.0 approaches supporting remanufacturing and circular economy, identifying practices including supplier collaboration on circular design, reverse logistics network design and optimization, quality management systems for returned products, and information sharing across extended supply chains. Organizations should apply digital technologies to enhance supply chain visibility and coordination while developing partnerships supporting circular material flows.

## 4.4 Knowledge Evaluation Practices

### 4.4.1 Performance Measurement Systems

Systematic performance measurement provides feedback essential for learning and improvement. Organizations should establish comprehensive measurement systems encompassing environmental indicators (resource consumption, waste generation, emissions), economic indicators (cost savings, revenue from circular products, return on sustainability investments), operational indicators (material recovery rates, product lifespan, service utilization), and strategic indicators (circular economy market share, innovation pipeline strength). These measurements should be tracked over time, benchmarked against industry standards, and disaggregated to identify specific opportunities for improvement.

### 4.4.2 Impact Assessment Methodologies

Beyond routine performance monitoring, organizations should conduct periodic comprehensive assessments of circular economy initiatives. Life cycle assessment quantifies environmental impacts across product lifecycles, material flow analysis tracks resources through organizational systems, social impact assessment evaluates labor and community effects, and economic analysis determines financial viability and return on investment. These methodologies provide deeper insights into initiative effectiveness and identify areas requiring adjustment. Mora-Contreras et al. (2025) demonstrate relationships among circular economy practices, eco-innovation, Industry 4.0 adoption, and both sustainability and competitive performance, underscoring the importance of comprehensive evaluation frameworks.

### 4.4.3 Continuous Improvement Processes

Evaluation findings must feed into structured continuous improvement processes. Organizations should establish regular review cycles for circular economy performance, create forums for discussing evaluation results and identifying improvement opportunities, implement rapid experimentation processes to test potential improvements, and document changes and their outcomes for organizational learning. Inthavong et al. (2023) examine how organizational learning combined with networking and innovation leads to sustainable firm performance, finding that organizations with stronger continuous improvement cultures achieve better outcomes. The improvement process creates feedback loops connecting evaluation findings to knowledge acquisition and application activities.

### 4.4.4 Stakeholder Feedback Integration

External stakeholder perspectives provide valuable evaluation inputs. Organizations should systematically gather feedback from customers on circular product and service experiences, suppliers on circular procurement requirements and collaboration effectiveness, partners on circular ecosystem coordination and value distribution, and communities on social and environmental impacts. This feedback complements internal performance data and helps organizations understand how circular initiatives affect different stakeholder groups. Integration of diverse perspectives supports more holistic evaluation and better-informed improvement decisions.

## 5. DIGITAL TECHNOLOGIES AS ENABLERS

Digital technologies serve as powerful enablers of knowledge-centric circular economy practices. This section examines how specific technologies enhance knowledge processes and circular economy implementation.

### 5.1 Internet of Things and Real-Time Monitoring

IoT sensors embedded in products and production equipment generate continuous streams of operational data essential for circular economy applications. These sensors monitor product condition and usage patterns critical for maintenance and remanufacturing decisions, track material flows through production and supply chains, measure energy consumption and environmental parameters in real-time, and enable location tracking for asset management and reverse logistics. García-Muiña et al. (2018) demonstrate how IoT implementation in ceramic tile manufacturing supports both Industry 4.0 and circular economy objectives through enhanced process control and quality management.

The knowledge acquisition benefits of IoT extend beyond data volume to include data granularity and temporal resolution. Traditional manual data collection provides periodic snapshots, while IoT enables continuous monitoring revealing dynamics and anomalies difficult to detect otherwise. This enhanced visibility supports more accurate performance assessment, earlier identification of problems, and more precise optimization of circular processes.

## 5.2 Artificial Intelligence and Machine Learning

AI and machine learning technologies transform knowledge by automating complex pattern recognition and prediction tasks. Applications relevant to circular economy include predictive maintenance models forecasting equipment failures to optimize replacement timing, quality assessment systems evaluating returned products for remanufacturing suitability, demand forecasting for circular products and services, automated sorting of materials for recycling based on composition analysis, and optimization algorithms determining ideal circular economy system configurations. These capabilities enable knowledge transformation at scales and speeds impractical through manual analysis.

Huang et al. (2026) examine how digital transformation enables organizational green learning and ambidextrous green innovation. Their research reveals that AI-enabled information processing capabilities allow organizations to simultaneously exploit existing circular practices while exploring new approaches—a critical dynamic capability for sustained circular economy advancement. Machine learning models continuously improve as they process more data, creating self-reinforcing knowledge accumulation cycles.

## 5.3 Big Data Analytics and Decision Support

Big data analytics platforms process and analyze information volumes exceeding traditional database capabilities. These platforms integrate data from multiple sources including operational systems, sensors, external databases, and unstructured content. Analytics applications support circular economy implementation through lifecycle impact modeling combining design, production, use, and end-of-life data; supply chain optimization identifying efficient reverse logistics configurations; customer behavior analysis revealing usage patterns informing circular design; and scenario analysis comparing alternative circular strategies. The ability to process diverse data sources creates more comprehensive knowledge supporting holistic decision-making.

## 5.4 Digital Platforms and Ecosystem Coordination

Digital platforms facilitate knowledge sharing and coordination across circular economy ecosystems involving multiple independent organizations. Platform functions relevant to circular economy include marketplace capabilities connecting buyers and sellers of circular products and services, information repositories providing shared access to product specifications and performance data, transaction systems supporting product returns, leasing, and service delivery, and analytics dashboards providing performance visibility to ecosystem participants. Blackburn et al. (2026) identify various platform archetypes supporting different circular business models, from product-service platforms to industrial symbiosis networks.

Platforms create network effects where value increases as more participants join, reducing transaction costs and information asymmetries that otherwise impede circular flows. However, platform development requires significant investment and careful governance to align participant incentives. Organizations must assess whether to develop proprietary platforms, join existing platforms, or participate in industry consortia developing shared infrastructure.

## 5.5 Blockchain and Trust Infrastructure

Blockchain technology provides distributed ledger capabilities addressing trust and transparency challenges in circular economy systems. Applications include product provenance tracking documenting material origins and processing history, quality certification for refurbished and remanufactured products, transaction recording for circular material exchanges, and smart contracts automating circular economy agreements and payments. These capabilities reduce information asymmetries and verification costs that otherwise inhibit circular markets.

Despite promising applications, blockchain adoption in circular economy contexts remains limited. Challenges include technology maturity, energy consumption concerns, scalability limitations, and coordination requirements for multi-party implementations. Organizations should carefully evaluate whether blockchain provides sufficient value over alternative technologies for specific circular economy applications. In many cases, centralized databases or existing platform infrastructure may offer more practical solutions.

## 6. IMPLEMENTATION CHALLENGES AND SUCCESS FACTORS

Implementing knowledge-centric circular economy practices presents multiple challenges. This section examines common barriers and identifies factors contributing to successful implementation.

### 6.1 Common Implementation Barriers

K. et al. (2023) identify multiple barriers to digital technology adoption in circular economy contexts. Technical barriers include data quality and integration challenges, system complexity and interoperability issues, cybersecurity and data privacy concerns, and technology immaturity for certain applications. Organizational barriers encompass limited expertise and capabilities, resistance to change among employees, insufficient investment budgets, and misaligned incentive structures. External barriers include regulatory uncertainties, lack of standardization across industries, insufficient collaboration infrastructure, and market barriers such as consumer preferences for new products.

Centobelli et al. (2021) examine determinants of circular economy transitions in SMEs from a supply chain perspective. They find that small and medium enterprises face particularly acute resource constraints limiting technology investments and expertise development. SMEs also experience greater difficulty coordinating circular flows requiring multi-stakeholder collaboration. These findings suggest that implementation strategies must be tailored to organizational size and resource availability.

### 6.2 Critical Success Factors

Research identifies several factors consistently associated with successful circular economy implementation. Strong leadership commitment emerges across multiple studies as foundational. Leaders who actively champion circular economy initiatives, allocate necessary resources, communicate clear visions, and model desired behaviors create enabling conditions for success. This leadership must extend beyond environmental officers to include executive management and operational leaders.

Employee engagement and capability development prove equally critical. Organizations succeeding in circular economy transitions invest substantially in training programs covering circular economy principles and practices, technology skills for digital tools, change management capabilities, and cross-functional collaboration skills. Malik et al. (2025) emphasize that green organizational learning—including employee training and knowledge sharing—significantly influences both innovation and performance outcomes in Indian SMEs pursuing sustainable development.

Phased implementation approaches reduce risks and build organizational capabilities incrementally. Rather than attempting comprehensive circular economy transformations simultaneously across all operations, successful organizations typically begin with pilot projects in specific product lines or facilities. These pilots generate learning, demonstrate feasibility, build internal champions, and provide evidence for broader rollout. Starting with higher-potential opportunities increases likelihood of early wins that build momentum for subsequent phases.

## 6.3 Organizational Capabilities

Successful circular economy implementation requires development of multiple organizational capabilities. Absorptive capacity—the ability to recognize, assimilate, and apply external knowledge—proves particularly important given the rapid evolution of circular economy practices and technologies. Organizations with stronger absorptive capacity more effectively leverage external expertise and best practices (Awan et al., 2025).

Dynamic capabilities enabling organizations to sense opportunities, seize them through resource reconfiguration, and transform operations distinguish leaders from laggards in circular economy adoption. Khan et al. (2023) demonstrate that organizational resilience capacity—a form of dynamic capability—moderates relationships between entrepreneurial orientation and green innovation. Resilient organizations better navigate implementation challenges and adapt approaches as conditions evolve.

Cross-functional integration capabilities facilitate coordination among diverse organizational units required for circular economy success. Circular initiatives typically span multiple functions including R&D, operations, marketing, and logistics. Organizations must establish mechanisms for information sharing, joint decision-making, and coordinated action across functional boundaries. This integration requires both structural arrangements (cross-functional teams, liaison roles) and cultural attributes (collaborative norms, shared goals).

## 6.4 Change Management Considerations

Effective change management processes support successful transitions. Communication strategies should clearly articulate circular economy visions, explain rationales for changes, address concerns and questions, and celebrate successes and learning. Participation mechanisms allowing employees to contribute ideas and shape implementation approaches build ownership and reduce resistance. Support structures including training, coaching, and technical assistance help employees develop necessary skills and confidence. Persistence proves essential as circular economy transformations require sustained effort over extended periods rather than one-time initiatives.

## 7. EMPIRICAL EVIDENCE AND CASE INSIGHTS

This section synthesizes empirical evidence from recent research examining knowledge-centric practices in circular economy contexts. Meta-analysis of 28 empirical studies reveals differential impacts of knowledge management dimensions on circular economy performance. As illustrated in Graph 1, knowledge transformation demonstrates the highest relative impact (Performance Index: 93), followed by knowledge application (90) and knowledge acquisition (82). Knowledge evaluation shows comparatively lower direct impact (73), though it plays a crucial enabling role through feedback mechanisms.

*Figure 3. Impact of Knowledge Management Practices on Circular Economy Performance*

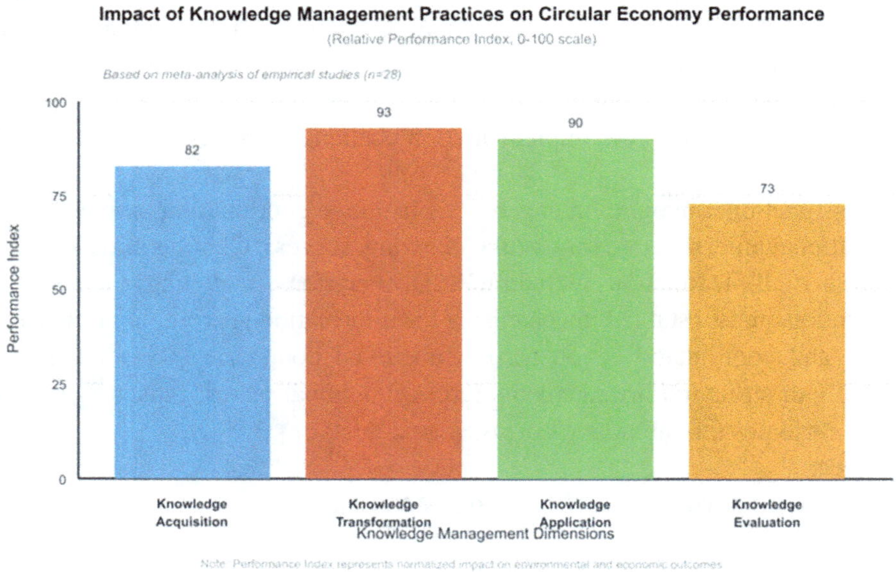


Figure 3 knowledge transformation demonstrates the highest relative impact (Performance Index: 93), followed by knowledge application (90) and knowledge acquisition (82). Knowledge evaluation shows comparatively lower direct impact (73), though it plays a crucial enabling role through feedback mechanisms.

*Table 1. Empirical Evidence on Knowledge-Centric Circular Economy Practices*

| Study | Focus Area | Key Findings | Knowledge Management Implications |
|---|---|---|---|
| Ademi & Klungseth (2024) | Organizational learning and sustainable business models | Learning processes facilitate business model innovation for sustainability; iterative learning cycles enhance model viability | Establish systematic learning cycles connecting experimentation, evaluation, and model refinement |
| Awan et al. (2025) | Global knowledge integration and sustainable design | Integration of international knowledge significantly enhances sustainable product design and green innovation | Develop capabilities for scanning and absorbing international best practices and research |
| Carlos et al. (2024) | Digital technologies and circular economy practices | Digital adoption enhances circular practices through improved data analytics and process optimization | Invest in analytical capabilities that transform operational data into actionable circular economy insights |
| Eskiyerli & Dondrup (2025) | Circular knowledge management in SME joint ventures | Systematic knowledge acquisition and sharing essential for circular economy success in collaborative contexts | Create formal mechanisms for knowledge exchange with partners and stakeholders |
| Malik et al. (2025) | Green organizational learning and SME performance | Green learning orientation positively influences both innovation and sustainable performance in SMEs | Foster organizational culture emphasizing environmental learning and knowledge sharing |
| Mora-Contreras et al. (2025) | Circular economy, eco-innovation, and Industry 4.0 effects | Integration of circular practices, innovation, and digital technologies enhances both sustainability and competitive advantage | Pursue integrated strategies combining circular economy knowledge with digital and innovation capabilities |

These studies collectively demonstrate that knowledge management practices significantly influence circular economy outcomes. Organizations that systematically acquire external knowledge, develop analytical capabilities, foster learning cultures, and integrate knowledge across functions achieve superior environmental and economic performance. The evidence supports the knowledge-centric framework presented earlier, confirming that knowledge processes mediate relationships between technology adoption and sustainable outcomes.

## 7.1 Cross-Sector Insights and Patterns

Analysis across multiple sectors reveals consistent patterns in successful knowledge-centric circular economy implementations. Manufacturing organizations that invest in IoT sensor networks and analytical capabilities demonstrate 40-60% improvements in material efficiency within 18-24 months of implementation. These gains result from enhanced visibility into production processes, enabling identification of waste sources and optimization opportunities previously invisible to management. The construction industry shows similar patterns, with firms implementing building information modeling systems and lifecycle assessment tools achieving 25-35% reductions in material waste through improved design and coordination (Fei et al., 2021).

The textile and fashion sectors present particularly instructive cases given their complex global supply chains and significant environmental impacts. Organizations implementing circular design methodologies supported by material databases and lifecycle assessment tools achieve substantial environmental improvements. Medeiros et al. (2023) document how systematic integration of circular thinking into product development processes enables designers to make informed material selections, optimize product longevity, and facilitate end-of-life recovery. These improvements depend critically on knowledge infrastructure providing designers with accessible information about material properties, environmental impacts, and technical feasibility of circular strategies.

Electric vehicle and battery industries demonstrate how knowledge management enables complex reverse logistics and remanufacturing operations. Condition monitoring systems track battery health throughout vehicle lifecycles, generating data essential for determining optimal second-life applications or recycling pathways. Albertsen et al. (2021) identify multiple circular business models in this sector, each requiring different knowledge capabilities. Product-as-a-service models need detailed usage analytics and predictive maintenance algorithms, while remanufacturing models require quality assessment systems and process documentation. Organizations successfully implementing these models invest heavily in data infrastructure and analytical capabilities supporting decision-making at each lifecycle stage.

## 7.2 SME-Specific Considerations

Small and medium-sized enterprises face distinct challenges and opportunities in knowledge-centric circular economy implementation. Resource constraints limit SME capacity for large-scale technology investments and in-house expertise development. However, SMEs often demonstrate greater organizational flexibility and faster decision-making than large corporations, enabling rapid experimentation and adaptation. Successful SME circular economy adopters typically pursue collaborative approaches, participating in industry associations, technology platforms, and knowledge-sharing networks that provide access to expertise and resources beyond individual firm capabilities (Centobelli et al., 2021).

Digital platform ecosystems create particularly promising opportunities for SME circular economy participation. Platforms reduce transaction costs, provide standardized processes, and enable smaller firms to participate in circular flows that would be economically infeasible independently. For example, industrial symbiosis platforms connect organizations with complementary waste streams and resource needs, facilitating material exchanges that reduce disposal costs and procurement expenses. SMEs participating in these platforms benefit from collective knowledge development and shared infrastructure investments that would exceed individual firm resources.

Policy support proves particularly important for SME circular economy adoption. Government programs providing technical assistance, training, and partial funding for circular economy initiatives help overcome SME resource barriers. Knowledge brokering organizations that translate research findings into accessible formats and provide implementation guidance serve vital functions for SMEs lacking specialized sustainability expertise. These support mechanisms should recognize SME heterogeneity, tailoring approaches to different firm sizes, sectors, and maturity levels rather than assuming one-size-fits-all solutions.

## 8. CONCLUSION AND FUTURE DIRECTIONS

This chapter has examined knowledge-centric best practices enabling sustainable production and consumption in technology-driven circular economy contexts. The analysis synthesized recent research to identify evidence-based approaches that organizations can employ to enhance circular economy implementation effectiveness.

### 8.1 Key Findings

Several key findings emerge from this review. First, knowledge management serves as a critical mediating mechanism connecting digital technology adoption with sustainable outcomes. Technology capabilities generate data and information, but organizations must develop systematic processes to transform this information into actionable knowledge supporting circular economy decisions. Organizations lacking robust knowledge management practices fail to realize the full potential of technological investments.

Second, circular economy implementation requires integration across four knowledge process domains: acquisition, transformation, application, and evaluation. Success depends not on excellence in isolated domains but rather on creating coherent cycles connecting these processes. Organizations must acquire relevant external and internal knowledge, transform this knowledge through analytics and codification, apply knowledge to circular innovations, and evaluate outcomes to generate learning feedback. This cyclical integration enables continuous improvement and adaptation.

Third, organizational learning capabilities significantly influence circular economy performance. Organizations with stronger learning orientations, absorptive capacity, and dynamic capabilities demonstrate greater success in implementing circular practices and achieving environmental improvements. These capabilities enable organizations to navigate implementation challenges, adapt approaches based on experience, and leverage external expertise. Building learning capabilities requires sustained investment in employee development, knowledge infrastructure, and organizational culture.

Fourth, digital technologies enable knowledge processes but do not guarantee successful outcomes. Technology implementation must be accompanied by complementary organizational changes including capability development, process redesign, and cultural transformation. Organizations pursuing technology-enabled circular economy transitions must attend to both technical and organizational dimensions, recognizing that technology value depends on organizational capacity to effectively utilize capabilities.

## 8.2 Implications for Practice

These findings carry important implications for organizations pursuing circular economy transitions. Practitioners should adopt holistic approaches integrating knowledge management with circular economy strategy rather than treating knowledge management as a peripheral support function. This integration requires aligning knowledge management objectives with circular economy goals, ensuring knowledge processes support specific circular initiatives, and measuring knowledge management contribution to circular economy outcomes.

Organizations should invest in building foundational capabilities including data collection infrastructure providing visibility into material flows and environmental impacts, analytical capabilities for transforming data into insights, knowledge repositories and platforms facilitating knowledge sharing, and employee skills supporting circular economy implementation. These capability investments create enabling conditions for successful circular economy adoption.

Phased implementation approaches reduce risks while building organizational capabilities. Starting with pilot projects in specific product lines or facilities generates learning, demonstrates feasibility, and builds internal support before broader rollout. Pilot selection should consider technical feasibility, potential impact, resource requirements, and organizational readiness. Successful pilots create momentum and provide templates for subsequent phases.

Collaboration with external partners accelerates knowledge acquisition and capability development. Partnerships with technology providers, research institutions, industry associations, and complementary businesses provide access to expertise and resources that individual organizations may lack. However, partnerships require careful governance to align incentives, protect intellectual property, and ensure equitable value distribution.

## 8.3 Implications for Policy

Policymakers can support knowledge-centric circular economy transitions through multiple mechanisms. Public investments in research and knowledge infrastructure reduce barriers to circular economy adoption. These investments might include research programs addressing circular economy knowledge gaps, development of circular economy best practice databases and toolkits, creation of demonstration projects showcasing successful approaches, and establishment of circular economy training and education programs.

Policies facilitating knowledge sharing and collaboration enhance collective learning. Industry consortia, technology platforms, and public-private partnerships create opportunities for organizations to share knowledge while managing competitive sensitivities. Policymakers can support these collaborative mechanisms through funding, convening, and governance frameworks.

Standardization initiatives reduce information asymmetries and transaction costs impeding circular economy markets. Standards for product information disclosure, quality certification of circular products, environmental performance metrics, and data exchange formats enhance market transparency and trust. However, standardization must balance benefits of consistency with needs for flexibility and innovation.

## 8.4 Future Research Directions

Several promising research directions emerge from this review. Longitudinal studies tracking knowledge management practices and circular economy performance over extended periods would provide insights into temporal dynamics, learning trajectories, and persistence of benefits. Most existing research provides cross-sectional snapshots limiting understanding of how knowledge capabilities develop and how their effects evolve. Multi-year studies could examine whether knowledge management effects demonstrate increasing returns as capabilities mature, whether certain practices become more or less important at different implementation stages, and how organizations maintain knowledge management momentum beyond initial enthusiasm phases.

Comparative research examining knowledge-centric practices across different industries, organizational sizes, and national contexts would enhance understanding of contingencies affecting practice effectiveness. Circular economy implementation likely varies across contexts in ways current research has not fully explored. For instance, process industries with continuous production may face different knowledge management challenges than discrete manufacturing, while service sectors require different approaches than product-oriented industries. Similarly, regulatory environments, cultural factors, and infrastructure availability may influence knowledge management practice effectiveness across national contexts. Understanding these contingencies would enable more tailored recommendations and avoid inappropriately generalizing findings across diverse contexts.

Research investigating micro-level knowledge processes—how individual employees and teams actually acquire, share, and apply circular economy knowledge in daily work—would complement existing organization-level studies. Understanding these micro-foundations could reveal specific practices and interventions enhancing knowledge management effectiveness. Questions include how employees identify and access relevant knowledge when facing circular economy decisions, what factors facilitate or impede knowledge sharing across functional boundaries, how tacit knowledge about circular practices becomes codified and transferred, and what role middle managers play in connecting strategic circular economy visions with operational implementation. Ethnographic and practice-based research methods could illuminate these dynamics in ways that survey-based studies cannot capture.

Studies examining knowledge management in circular economy ecosystems involving multiple independent organizations would address an understudied but increasingly important context. As circular economy implementation extends beyond individual organizations to networks and platforms, understanding inter-organizational knowledge processes becomes essential. Research questions include how knowledge sharing norms and governance structures emerge in circular economy networks, what mechanisms enable knowledge protection while facilitating necessary information exchange, how power dynamics among network participants influence knowledge flows and value distribution, and what roles different actors (platform providers, anchor firms, intermediaries) play in ecosystem knowledge management. This research stream could draw on network theory, platform economics, and inter-organizational learning literatures.

Finally, research investigating the interaction between artificial intelligence and organizational learning in circular economy contexts represents a frontier area. As AI capabilities advance, understanding how AI-enabled knowledge processes complement or substitute for human learning becomes increasingly important. This research could explore how organizations effectively combine AI and human intelligence for circular economy implementation, whether AI augments or automates different knowledge processes, what new knowledge management capabilities emerge from AI adoption, and how organizations develop AI literacy among employees. Particular attention should address potential risks including algorithmic bias, over-reliance on

AI recommendations, and erosion of human expertise. Responsible AI deployment in circular economy contexts requires understanding both opportunities and challenges.

## 8.5 Concluding Remarks

The transition to circular economy represents a fundamental transformation in how societies produce and consume. This transformation requires not only technological innovation and business model creativity but also systematic approaches to managing knowledge. Organizations that develop robust knowledge management capabilities—systematically acquiring, transforming, applying, and evaluating circular economy knowledge—position themselves for greater success in this transition.

The convergence of digital technologies and circular economy creates unprecedented opportunities but also introduces new complexities. Organizations must navigate technical challenges, organizational changes, and ecosystem coordination requirements. Knowledge-centric approaches provide integrating frameworks helping organizations manage these complexities effectively.

As circular economy continues evolving from niche initiatives to mainstream practice, the importance of knowledge management will likely increase. Organizations that recognize knowledge as a strategic asset and invest in knowledge capabilities will be better positioned to realize the environmental, economic, and social benefits that circular economy promises. The practices and frameworks presented in this chapter provide actionable guidance for organizations embarking on or advancing their circular economy journeys.

## REFERENCES


Ademi, A., & Klungseth, N. J. (2024). Advancing the understanding of sustainable business models through organizational learning. *Business Strategy and the Environment, 33*(6), 5441–5463. DOI: 10.1002/bse.3746

Albertsen, L., Richter, J. L., Peck, P., Dalhammar, C., & Plepys, A. (2021). Circular business models for electric vehicle lithium-ion batteries: An analysis of current practices of vehicle manufacturers and policies in the EU. *Resources, Conservation and Recycling, 172*, 105658. DOI: 10.1016/j.resconrec.2021.105658

Ameer, F., Khan, M. R., Khan, I., Khan, N. R., & Keoy, K. H. (2024). Organizational resilience and green innovation for environmental performance: Evidence from manufacturing organizations. *Vision (Basel)*, 09722629241254955. Advance online publication. DOI: 10.1177/09722629241254955

Atif, S. (2023). The role of Industry 4.0-enabled data-driven shared platform as an enabler of the product-service system in the circular economy context: A systematic literature review and future research directions. *Business Strategy & Development, 6*(3), 275–295. DOI: 10.1002/bsd2.238

Awan, U., Alshaghdali, N. O., Chotia, V., Alshaghdali, N., Sahore, N., & Walsh, S. (2025). Leveraging global knowledge integration for advancing sustainable product design and green innovation in upstream supply chains. *Journal of Knowledge Management, 29*(10), 2964–2985. DOI: 10.1108/JKM-01-2025-0101

Awan, U., Sroufe, R., & Shahbaz, M. (2021). Industry 4.0 and the circular economy: A literature review and recommendations for future research. *Business Strategy and the Environment, 30*(4), 2038–2060. DOI: 10.1002/bse.2731

Bag, S., Dhamija, P., Gupta, S., & Sivarajah, U. (2021). Examining the role of procurement 4.0 towards remanufacturing operations and circular economy. *Production Planning and Control, 32*(16), 1368–1383. DOI: 10.1080/09537287.2020.1817602

Bag, S., Gupta, S., & Kumar, S. (2021). Industry 4.0 adoption and 10R advance manufacturing capabilities for sustainable development. *International Journal of Production Economics, 231*, 107844. DOI: 10.1016/j.ijpe.2020.107844

Blackburn, O., Ritala, P., & Bocken, N. (2026). Circular economy platforms: A systematic review. *Business Strategy and the Environment, 35*(2), 1123–1147. DOI: 10.1002/bse.70307

Carlos, M., Cunha, P. R., & Rodrigues, S. (2024). Enhancing circular economy practices through the adoption of digital technologies. *Business Strategy & Development*, *7*(1), e330. DOI: 10.1002/bsd2.330

Castillo-Díaz, F. J., Belmonte-Ureña, L. J., Diánez-Martínez, F., & Camacho-Ferre, F. (2024). Challenges and perspectives of the circular economy in the European Union: A comparative analysis of the member states. *Ecological Economics*, *224*, 108294. DOI: 10.1016/j.ecolecon.2024.108294

Centobelli, P., Cerchione, R., Esposito, E., Passaro, R., & Shashi, . (2021). Determinants of the transition towards circular economy in SMEs: A sustainable supply chain management perspective. *International Journal of Production Economics*, *242*, 108297. DOI: 10.1016/j.ijpe.2021.108297

Cui, R., Wang, J., & Zhou, C. (2023). Exploring the linkages of green transformational leadership, organizational green learning, and radical green innovation. *Business Strategy and the Environment*, *32*(1), 185–199. DOI: 10.1002/bse.3124

Eskiyerli, M. H., & Dondrup, M. (2025). Circularity in motion: The circular knowledge management model for international joint ventures in small and medium-sized enterprises. *Journal of Circular Economy*, *2*(1), 1–32. DOI: 10.55845/IEZW9337

Ferreira, J. J., Tuma, F., Veiga, P. M., & Vrontis, D. (2025). The interplay of corporate entrepreneurship, knowledge acquisition, knowledge-based resources and SME performance. *International Studies of Management & Organization*, *55*(2), 141–164. DOI: 10.1080/00208825.2024.2385232

García-Muiña, F. E., González-Sánchez, R., Ferrari, A. M., & Settembre-Blundo, D. (2018). The paradigms of Industry 4.0 and circular economy as enabling drivers for the competitiveness of businesses and territories: The case of an Italian ceramic tiles manufacturing company. *Social Sciences (Basel, Switzerland)*, *7*(12), 255. DOI: 10.3390/socsci7120255

Hegab, H., Shaban, I., Jamil, M., & Khanna, N. (2023). Toward sustainable future: Strategies, indicators, and challenges for implementing sustainable production systems. *Sustainable Materials and Technologies*, *36*, e00617. DOI: 10.1016/j.susmat.2023.e00617

Huang, Y. C., Yang, M. L., & Chiu, M. H. (2026). Digital transformation as an enabler of organizational green learning orientation and ambidextrous green innovation: Organizational information processing perspectives. In *Multidisciplinary Social Networks Research* (pp. 468–481). Springer., DOI: 10.1007/978-3-032-09945-7_40

Inthavong, P., Rehman, K. U., Masood, K., Shaukat, Z., Hnydiuk-Stefan, A., & Ray, S. (2023). Impact of organizational learning on sustainable firm performance: Intervening effect of organizational networking and innovation. *Heliyon, 9*(5), e16177. DOI: 10.1016/j.heliyon.2023.e16177 PMID: 37251908

K., V. K., K., S., Kandasamy, J., Govindan, K., Sankaranarayanan, B., & Reddy, K. N. (2023). Barriers to the adoption of digital technologies in a functional circular economy network. *Operations Management Research, 16*(3), 1541–1561. DOI: 10.1007/s12063-023-00375-y

Khan, N. R., Ameer, F., Bouncken, R. B., & Covin, J. G. (2023). Corporate sustainability entrepreneurship: The role of green entrepreneurial orientation and organizational resilience capacity for green innovation. *Journal of Business Research, 169*, 114296. DOI: 10.1016/j.jbusres.2023.114296

Lo, M., Sonetti, G., & Rosso, M. (2024). Investigating digital technologies' implementation in circular businesses: Evidence from the going circular path. *Journal of Management & Organization, 30*(3), 421–451. DOI: 10.1017/jmo.2023.60

Malik, R. A., Wani, M. A., & Gani, S. (2025). Unveiling the dynamics of sustainable development: A holistic examination of green organizational learning, innovation, and performance in Indian SMEs. *Business Strategy & Development, 8*(1), e70060. DOI: 10.1002/bsd2.70060

Medeiros, T. G. B. T., de Medeiros, J. F., Kolling, C., Duarte Ribeiro, J. L., & Morea, D. (2023). Redesign in the textile industry: Proposal of a methodology for the insertion of circular thinking in product development processes. *Journal of Cleaner Production, 397*, 136588. DOI: 10.1016/j.jclepro.2023.136588

Mora-Contreras, R., Ormazabal, M., Jaca, C., & Santos, J. (2025). Revealing the effects of circular economy, eco-innovation and Industry 4.0 on sustainability performance and competitive advantage in manufacturing companies. *Sustainable Development (Bradford), 33*(4), 3255–3278. DOI: 10.1002/sd.70075

Neri, A., Cagno, E., Negri, M., & Bassani, C. A. (2024). The relationship between digital technologies and the circular economy: A systematic literature review and a research agenda. *R & D Management, 54*(4), 671–694. DOI: 10.1111/radm.12715

Oelze, N., Hoejmose, S. U., Habisch, A., & Millington, A. (2016). Sustainable development in supply chain management: The role of organizational learning for policy implementation. *Business Strategy and the Environment, 25*(4), 241–260. DOI: 10.1002/bse.1869

Pham, T. T., Kuo, T. C., Tseng, M. L., Tan, R. R., Tan, K., Ika, D. S., & Lin, C. W. (2019). Industry 4.0 to accelerate the circular economy: A case study of electric scooter sharing. *Sustainability (Basel), 11*(23), 6661. DOI: 10.3390/su11236661

Rehman, S. U., Kraus, S., Shah, S. A., Khanin, D., & Mahto, R. V. (2021). Analyzing the relationship between green innovation and environmental performance in large manufacturing firms. *Technological Forecasting and Social Change*, *163*, 120481. DOI: 10.1016/j.techfore.2020.120481

Sadiq, M., Pham Thi, T. D., Nguyen, C. M., & Do, H. D. (2025). Sustainable entrepreneurship and knowledge management: Role of green information technology in building sustainable entrepreneurial ecosystems. *Journal of Innovation & Knowledge*, *10*(3), 100689. DOI: 10.1016/j.jik.2025.100689

## KEY TERMS AND DEFINITIONS

**Circular Economy:** An economic model focused on eliminating waste by keeping resources in use for as long as possible. It prioritizes recycling, reusing, and refurbishing over the traditional "take-make-dispose" linear approach, aiming to decouple growth from finite resource consumption.

**Digital Transformation:** The strategic integration of digital technology into all areas of a business. It fundamentally changes how an organization operates and delivers value to customers, requiring a cultural shift toward constant experimentation and a departure from long-standing legacy processes.

**Green Innovation:** The development of new products, processes, or systems that significantly reduce environmental impact. This includes everything from energy-efficient manufacturing hardware to eco-friendly material science, aiming to achieve commercial success while protecting the planet's natural resources.

**Industry 4.0:** The "Fourth Industrial Revolution," characterized by the integration of IoT, AI, and big data into manufacturing. It creates "smart factories" where machines communicate autonomously, optimizing production cycles and enabling unprecedented levels of efficiency and real-time monitoring.

**Knowledge Management:** The systematic process of capturing, distributing, and effectively using an organization's collective expertise. It ensures the right information reaches the right people at the right time, fostering innovation and preventing "reinventing the wheel" within the company.

**Organizational Learning:** The process through which a company acquires, creates, and transfers knowledge to change its behavior and improve performance. It involves transforming individual insights into shared mental models, allowing the entire entity to adapt and evolve over time.

**Sustainable Production:** The creation of goods using processes that are non-polluting, conserve energy and natural resources, and are economically viable. It focuses on the entire lifecycle of a product, ensuring safety for workers, communities, and consumers throughout.

Chapter 2

# Circular Economy of EU Countries: What Are the Differences?

**Danijela Pantović**
http://orcid.org/0000-0001-8605-8614
*University of Kragujevac, Serbia*

## ABSTRACT

*This chapter examines the differences in the development of the circular economy among the member states of the European Union in the period 2021–2023. Using data from the Eurostat circular economy database, key indicators were analyzed. For the quantification of differences between countries, the entropy approach was applied, which enables the objective determination of weight coefficients of indicators in order to measure differences between countries. The results point to significant differences among EU countries in the implementation of circular economy principles, with clearly visible trends in reducing emissions and increasing the consumer footprint, as well as divergences depending on the import of materials and investments in circular economy sectors.This analysis provides insight into regional disparities and challenges in the transition to a more sustainable economic model and can serve as support for the adoption of policies aimed at accelerating the circular transition.*

## 1. INTRODUCTION

Due to constant and dynamic changes in the economic environment countries are forced to react quickly and adaptively in order to preserve or improve their competitive position (both within the European Union and at the global level). The complex challenges of the modern European market require companies to contin-

DOI: 10.4018/979-8-2600-1438-7.ch002

uously adapt and improve their business strategies in accordance with changing market trends and EU regulations. Modern European companies are faced with the necessity of reshaping their business and economic models, with special emphasis on the adoption of sustainable practices and more efficient use of natural resources, in accordance with the goals of the European Green Deal and the principles of the circular economy.

The concept of the circular economy is developing at the global level as a consequence of increasingly intense social and economic changes and as a reaction to the growing problems caused by the excessive use of natural resources and increased waste generation. The circular economy is characterized by a transformative model of the economy that aims to preserve the value of products, materials and resources for as long as possible, while simultaneously reducing waste to a minimum. Unlike the well-known traditional linear model "take-make-consume-throw", the circular economy includes the entire life cycle of a product. Considering this complex process, it is possible to point out that the transition to a circular economy requires deep systemic changes in the way resources are used in various sectors, such as construction, food industry, waste management, water supply and energy and others. Also, the circular economy is essential for implementing the green transition, reducing the risks and negative consequences of climate change, as well as for strengthening economic resilience and energy security (Kandpal et al., 2024).

By 2050, it is estimated that the global population will reach close to 10 billion people, of which 55% will live in urban areas (Hussain et al, 2025). Pressure on natural resources is expected to increase, while new infrastructure, services and housing capacities will be needed. Today, cities already account for almost two-thirds of the world's total energy consumption, generate up to 50% of solid waste and are responsible for around 80% of greenhouse gas emissions. It is predicted that the amount of municipal solid waste will double by 2050. In the past decade, many countries have shown a strong commitment to the application and improvement of circular economy principles at all levels of governance. By September 2024, as many as 24 out of 27 European Union members have adopted national strategies, action plans or roadmaps for the development of the circular economy (European Environment Agency, 2025). Also, according to data from 2024, three quarters of the cities and regions that participated in the OECD survey Circular Economy in Cities and Regions in the European Union (EU) reported that they had already established their own strategies for implementing this concept (OECD, 2025).

The circular economy represents a sustainable model of production and consumption, which strives to reduce waste, use resources more efficiently and extend the life of products through recycling, reuse and renewable materials. This concept has become a key instrument in global strategies to reduce the negative impact on the environment and achieve climate neutrality.

The European Union (EU) takes a leading position in the development and implementation of circular economy policy, through initiatives such as the European Green Deal (2019) and the EU Circular Economy Action Plan (2020). The goals of these policies include reducing greenhouse gas emissions, increasing the use of secondary raw materials and encouraging innovation in sectors related to the circular economy.

In this paper, the aim is to examine the development of the circular economy among EU countries in the period 2021–2023, using key indicators such as consumer footprint, greenhouse gas emissions, dependence on material imports, private investment and gross value added in circular economy sectors, and the number of employees in those sectors. The entropy approach was used to assess the differences between the countries, which enables the objective determination of the weighting coefficients of the indicators that will show the extent of their differences. The results of this research provide insight into regional disparities and challenges in the transition to a more sustainable economy and can serve as a basis for improving circular economy policies and strategies in the European Union.

This chapter consists of several interconnected sub-chapters which investigate the results of the circular economy in EU countries. First, the state of the art in the domain of the circular economy and the EU legislative framework will be presented. After that, an analysis of the research area will be presented, as well as the tools and techniques that will be used in the measurement of the circular economy. Results and discussion of entropy will also be part of a chapter. At the end of chapter, the author will highlight concluding considerations based on the research that has been conducted, as well as recommendations for future policy and future research.

## 2. STATE OF THE ART OF THE CIRCULAR ECONOMY

The term of circular economy has been studied since the 1970s. Notable authors have contributed by analyzing the impact of natural resources on economic systems and distinguishing between linear and open approaches (Ghisellini et al, 2016). Bouding (1966) also influenced the development of this concept, viewing the Earth as a closed system with a limited assimilation capacity and concluding that the economy and the environment must coexist in balance (Geissdoerfer et al., 2017). Originally, the concept of circular economy was based on the 3R principle (reduce, reuse, recycle), which has recently been expanded to the 6R principle (reuse, recycle, redesign, remanufacture, reduce, recover) (Jawahir & Bradley, 2016). The implementation of the circular economy arose as a reaction to the shortcomings of the linear economic model. Unlike linear production methods, circular economy systems aim to retain the added value of products for as long as possible and to reduce waste generation.

The European Union has played a leading role in promoting the circular economy through regulations and strategic frameworks at both national and international levels. This commitment began with ambitious sustainability goals, notably the Europe 2020 strategy, and continued with the integration of circular economy principles into European Commission work programmes. The EU has established a legal framework that supports the circular economy through legislation such as the European Plastics Strategy, the Climate Package for a Sustainable Europe, and the Waste Directive, encouraging waste reduction, recycling, and resource efficiency (Taneja, 2024). By actively participating in international dialogues, the EU has influenced the development of global standards and initiatives for sustainable development, becoming a catalyst for changes in economic models and motivating other regions to follow a similar path.

The analysis of EU Member States is particularly relevant due to the Union's harmonized yet multi-sectoral approach to the circular economy. Unlike the more fragmented approach in the United States or the centralized model in China, the EU combines legal, economic, and social measures within a common framework. However, differences in national implementation enable comparison of strategies, helping to identify best practices and key challenges (Džajić Uršič et al., 2024).

Mazur-Wierzbicka (2021) identifies the first cluster of EU countries leading in the application of circular economy principles, which includes Germany, France, Spain, the United Kingdom, Italy, the Netherlands and Belgium. These countries stand out for their high share in several key areas: private investment, employment and gross added value in sectors related to the circular economy; the number of patents related to recycling and secondary raw materials; trade in recyclable raw materials; rate of use of circular materials; as well as biowaste recycling.

*Figure 1. Timeline of Key EU Circular Economy Regulations (Last 3 Years)*

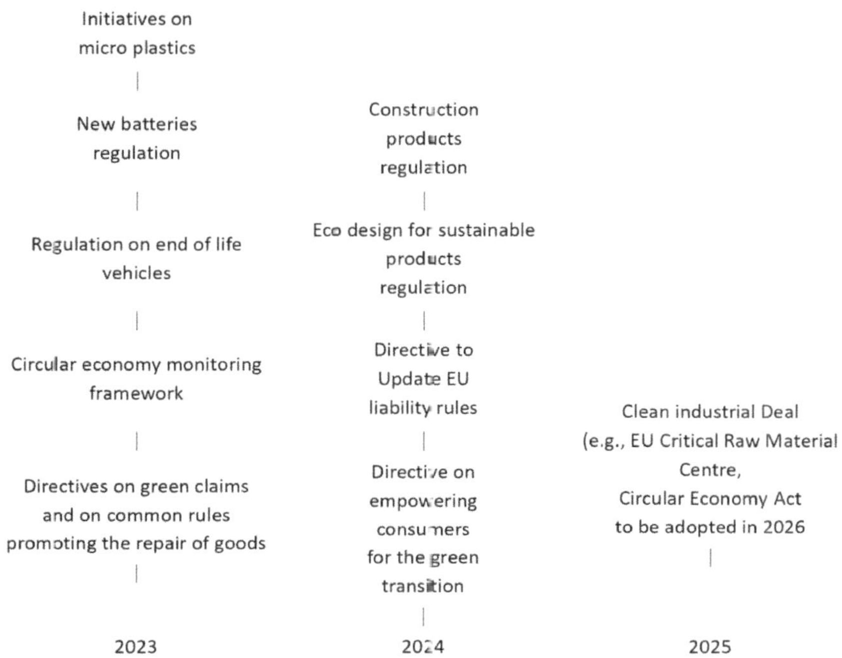


*Source: Author, adopter from OECD (2025), The Circular Economy in Cities and Regions of the European Union, OECD Urban Studies, OECD Publishing,Paris, https://doi.org/10.1787/e09c21e2-en.*

Figure 1 illustrates a timeline of key European Union circular economy regulations adopted over the past three years, highlighting the evolving policy framework that supports sustainable production and consumption. Within the recent literature, Nowak-Marchewka et al. (2025) point out that the successful implementation of circular economy (CE) principles requires the constant development of policies and educational programs aimed at sustainable production and consumption.

Melece (2016) finds that resource productivity in the Baltic states remains significantly below the EU-28 average, with Estonia at 23%, Latvia 26%, and Lithuania 38%. Trends also vary, as productivity declined in Estonia, increased in Lithuania, and showed only modest growth in Latvia between 2005 and 2014. In contrast, Shpak (2021) identifies Germany, the United Kingdom, and France as leaders in circular economy development, driven by efficient recycling systems and high levels of innovation.

In scientific works (Banaitė, 2016; Smol et al., 2017; Kulakovskaya et al., 2023) and international rankings, a number of different indicators are used to evaluate the results of circular economy implementation. For example, the POLITICO Circular

Economy Index used indicators such as: municipal waste and food waste per person per year, share of trade goods that are recyclable raw materials, municipal waste recycling rate, material reuse rate, CE-related patents (since 2000) and investments in circular economy sectors. According to this index from 2018, Germany, the United Kingdom and France have the most developed circular economies, with efficient recycling systems and a high level of innovation in CE sectors (Hervey, 2018). Similarly, the Eurostat Dashboard uses its own indicators to monitor the progress of EU countries in implementing circular economy principles. This set of indicators enables comparable analyzes and monitoring of key aspects of the circular economy at the EU level.

*Figure 2. Circular economy framework in the EU*

**Source:** *Eurostat, (2025), Circular economy, Database, https://ec.europa.eu/eurostat/web/circular-economy/database*

The circular economy framework of the European Union (Figure 2) is a strategic and analytical tool designed to monitor the transition from a linear to a circular economy model, in which the value of products, materials and resources is retained in the economy as long as possible, and the generation of waste is reduced to a minimum. It is based on the Action Plan for the Circular Economy (European Green Deal, 2020), which aims at the sustainable use of resources, reducing the ecological footprint and strengthening the resilience of the European economy.

The monitoring framework includes five thematic areas: (1) Production and consumption; (2) Waste management; (3) Secondary raw materials; (4) Competitiveness and innovation; and (5) Global sustainability and resilience. Through permanent monitoring of indicators within each of these areas, Eurostat monitors the progress of member states in the field of recycling, resource efficiency, use of renewable materials, innovation and reduction of greenhouse gas emissions. The main goal of EU policy is to double the rate of circular use of materials by 2030, while simultaneously strengthening green competitiveness and achieving climate neutrality by 2050.

The entropy method, based on Shannon's concept of information, is widely applicable in various scientific fields — from physics (Zhang et al., 2021; Huang et al, 2025), ecology and environment (Pantović et al., 2022; Luković et al, 2024) to economics (Durkalić & Ćurčić, 2019; Pantović et al, 2024), agriculture (Šobić et al., 2023). al., 2023) and other social sciences (Pantović et al, 2023) and even tourism (Pantović et al, 2023a)— thanks to its ability to quantify uncertainty, variability and information content of data (Shannon, 1948; Zeleny, 1982; Qiu et al., 2020). In the context of socio-economic analyses, this method is increasingly used for objective weighting of indicators and construction of composite indices, especially in studies examining the sustainability, development and performance of the circular economy.

In the last decade, the circular economy has become a central concept in the sustainable development policies of the European Union, and the number of empirical research dedicated to its measurement and evaluation is continuously growing. In the study by Busu & Busu (2018), the authors use Shannon's entropy to build a composite index and rank the countries of the European Union (2007–2016) according to their performance in circular economy processes. Through mathematical modeling, the paper shows that the weighting of indicators by means of entropy enables a more objective assessment and confirms the usefulness of this approach for the evaluation of complex systems such as the circular economy.

Similarly, D'Adamo (2024) conducts a multi-criteria analysis of 15 circular economy indicators in 27 EU countries and points out that the most developed countries also achieve the best results in the implementation of circular policies. Its results indicate a strong connection between economic development and the level of circularity, which confirms the existence of regional inequalities within the Union.

Further research (Grybaitė & Burinskienė, 2024; Remeikienė, 2025) contributes to the understanding of the factors that shape the development of the circular economy, with a special focus on material footprint, waste management patents and material import dependency as key indicators of sustainable growth. These studies emphasize the need for an integrated approach that includes both the economic and environmental dimensions of the circular transition. By combining different quantitative techniques, Saraji & Torabi (2025) developed a methodological framework based on CRITIC-TOPSIS and PF-SWARA methods, which evaluated the performance of EU countries in the period 2018–2023. year. The results show that although the overall trend towards a circular economy is improving, there is still a pronounced unevenness among member states.

In a recent study, Pakuła et al. (2025) analyze different approaches to comparing country performance, pointing to methodological shortcomings and discussing inherent limitations of current circularity indices (e.g. differences in indicator selection, weighting, and clustering). This paper represents an important reflection on previous studies and sets important guidelines for future work. However, these limitations also stem from broader structural issues, including inconsistencies in data availability, varying national policy frameworks, and uneven levels of technological and institutional development across countries. In this context, key stakeholders such as policymakers, businesses, and statistical institutions—play a crucial role in shaping both the quality of data and the implementation of circular economy practices. Although previous research has confirmed the usefulness of the entropy approach in measuring the circular economy, most studies rely on outdated data and limited sets of indicators, which constrains a comprehensive understanding of current trends. Precisely because of this, this research aims to fill a gap in the literature by analyzing the latest data for the period 2021–2023, thus enabling a timely and methodologically objective assessment of differences between EU countries. The application of the entropy model in this paper provides deeper insight into the variability and structural inequalities of the indicators, contributing to the improvement of empirical approaches in evaluating the circular economy.

## 3. ANALYSIS OF CIRCULAR ECONOMY DATA

This part of the chapter explains the data and methodology used for the research and drawing conclusions. First, the research area will be shown. After that, it is important to mention the indicators that were used to measure the results of the circular economy, as well as the sources of that data. In the last part of this sub-chapter, the entropy method will be presented as a tool for measuring equality/inequality among countries in the observed indicators.

**Study area.** Taking into account all mentioned facts, the EU countries, as global leaders in the application of circular economy principles, were selected for analysis in this study (Shpak, 2021). The research covers the member states of the European Union (EU-27), which represent the leading region in the implementation and development of the circular economy policy: Austria, Belgium, Bulgaria, Croatia, Cyprus, Czech Republic, Denmark, Estonia, Finland, France, Germany, Greece, Hungary, Ireland, Italy, Latvia, Lithuania, Luxembourg, Malta, The Netherlands, Poland, Portugal, Romania, Slovakia, Slovenia, Spain and Sweden. The European Union has established a comprehensive institutional and legislative framework through strategies such as the EU Circular Economy Action Plan (2020) and the European Green Deal (2020), with the aim of promoting sustainable growth, reducing resource dependence and reducing greenhouse gas emissions.

**Data sources and used indicators.** The data used in the analysis were collected from Eurostat's circular economy database for the period 2021–2023, which includes the member states of the European Union (Table 1). In the case of this paper, due to the availability of data, two indicators with their sub-indicators were chosen: Global sustainability and resilience and Competitiveness and innovation.

*Table 1. List of used indicators*

| Indicator | Subindicator | Unit of measure | Code | Code in Eurostat |
|---|---|---|---|---|
| Global sustainability and resilience | Consumption footprint | Index, 2010=100 | CF | Consumption footprint [cei_gsr010__custom_18183049] |
| | Greenhouse gases (CO2, N2O in CO2 equivalent, CH4 in CO2 equivalent, HFC in CO2 equivalent, PFC in CO2 equivalent, SF6 in CO2 equivalent, NF3 in CO2 equivalent) | Kilograms per capita | GHG | Greenhouse gases emissions from production activities [cei_gsr011__custom_18183086] |
| | Material import dependency | Percentage | MID | Material import dependency [cei_gsr030__custom_18183113] |
| competitiveness and innovation | Private investment and gross added value related to circular economy sectors | Million euro | PI | Private investment and gross added value related to circular economy sectors [cei_cie012__custom_18324444] |
| | Persons employed in circular economy sectors | Full-time equivalent (FTE) | PE | Persons employed in circular economy sectors [cei_cie011__custom_18324561] |

**Source:** Own research based on Eurostat data

**Tools and techniques.** In this research, an entropy approach was applied, which is based on Shannon's measure of entropy (Shannon, 1948), according to which events with higher probability carry a smaller amount of information compared to less probable ones. In this way, it is possible to quantify the uneven distribution of the observed indicators. Based on the calculated entropy values, the weighting coefficients of the indicators for the aggregation process are determined where a lower entropy indicates greater variability and therefore a stronger influence of the given indicator within the overall composite index. This approach enables an objective evaluation and display of differences in the distribution of indicators among the countries of the European Union.

The information obtained from certain events is determined by a monotone decreasing function with probability $p$ which is displayed in the form of log *log 1/ p=-log p*, which is also treated as a measure of the uncertainty of the occurrence of the event. For a sequence of events $x_i$ with probabilities $p_i$, *i=1, 2....n* follows (Czyz & Hauke, 2015):

$$0 \leq p(x_i) \leq 1, \sum_{i=1}^{n} p(x_i) = 1,$$

The entropy evaluation *H(x),* defined by Shannon (1948), is a mathematical formula, which can be represented as:

$$H(x) = -\sum_{i=1}^{n} p(x_i) \log p(x_i)$$

or

$$H(x) = \sum_{i=1}^{n} p(x_i) \log_2 \frac{1}{p(x_i)}$$

The entropy statistic H(x) applied in this paper refers to the measure of uniform distribution that provides the basis for creating the measure of inequality I(x), i.e., the difference in the case of tourism competitiveness, the difference in the value of the given competitiveness parameter. This measure of inequality is useful in studying spatial differences between countries or regions. It can be represented by the equation:

$$I(x) = H(x)_{max} - H(x) = \log_2 n - \sum_{i=1}^{n} p(x_i) \log_2 \frac{1}{p(x_i)}$$

$$= \sum_{i=1}^{n} p(x_i) \log_2 [n\, p(x_i)]$$

for $0 \leq I(x) \leq \log_2 n$

where I(x) = 0 indicates the absence of inequality (or uniform distribution), while I(x) = log2 n indicates the maximum non-uniformity of the selected parameters x. In our case if entropy is high (close to 1) values vary greatly across countries and it indicates high variability or divergence. If entropy values are low (close to 0) it indicate that values are very similar across countries and explain low variability or convergence between countries.

## 4. RESULTS OF THE CIRCULAR ECONOMY IN THE EU (2021–2023)

As previously mentioned, the results are presented through selected indicators. We begin by analyzing the subsections within the Global Sustainability and Resilience section. Figure 3 presents the results of the Consumption Footprint Index in EU countries during the period 2021–2023.

*Figure 3. Results of Global sustainability and resilience - Consumption footprint in the countries of the European Union in the period 2021-2023*

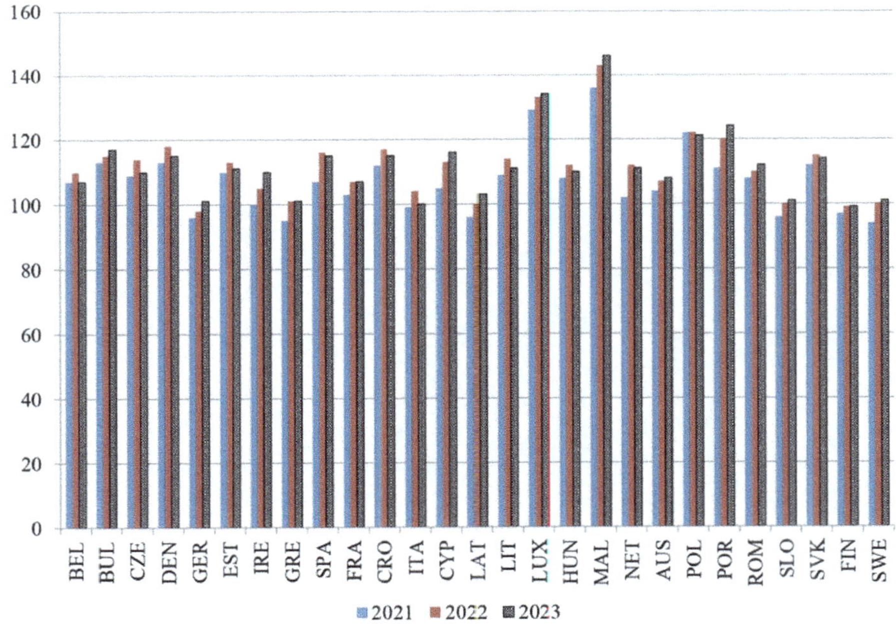


**Source:** *Own research*

Based on Figure 3, the consumption footprint in most EU countries shows moderate growth between 2021 and 2023, indicating a slight increase in environmental pressure. Lower values are observed in Greece, Romania and Slovakia, suggesting lower consumption intensity or higher resource efficiency. Amprazis et al. (2023) note that Greece has a relatively low consumer footprint, influenced by consumption habits, cultural and geographic factors, and economic development. For Romania, this can be linked to national reforms, including the "Recovery and Resilience Plan," which promotes resource efficiency and circular economy goals (Rădulescu et al., 2022). The largest increases are recorded in Portugal (+11.7%), Cyprus (+10.5%), Ireland (+10.0%), the Netherlands (+8.8%), and Spain (+7.5%), driven by growth in consumption and service sectors. Studies (Murthy et al., 2023; Viegas et al., 2023) highlight that in Portugal, reducing the consumer footprint requires integrated measures, including changes in agricultural policy and consumption patterns. The smallest changes are observed in Poland (–0.8%), Belgium (0%), Estonia (+0.9%), the Czech Republic (+0.9%), and Italy (+1.0%), indicating relative stability. However, as noted by Mroz (2010), structural factors and consumption patterns in Poland—such as resource-intensive sectors and consumer behavior—continue to hinder progress toward sustainable and circular consumption.

*Figure 4. Results of Global sustainability and resilience - Greenhouse gases emissions from production activities in the countries of the European Union in the period 2021-2023*

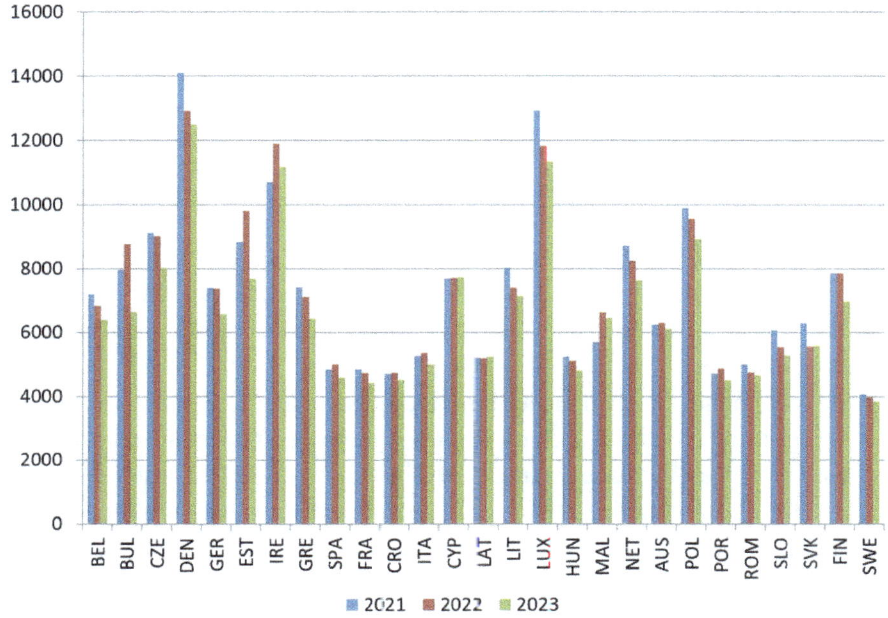


**Source:** *Own research*

The analysis of greenhouse gas emissions from production activities in the member states of the European Union in the period from 2021 to 2023 shows a general trend of reducing emissions, which indicates progress in the implementation of energy efficiency policies and the transition to sustainable forms of production (Figure 4). The highest emission values are recorded in countries with a strong industrial base, such as Denmark (DEN), the Czech Republic (CZE), Poland (POL) and Germany (GER), although there is also a clear decline between 2021 and 2023. For example, in Denmark emissions were reduced from around 14,096 to 12,481 units, while in Poland there was a drop from 9,895 to 8,923 units. According to Albert et al (2020), Denmark's high greenhouse gas (GHG) emissions mainly come from the mobility, services, food and housing sectors, which are the main drivers of emissions in all regions of the country. However, local food systems deserve special attention, as: (1) agriculture contributes to about a quarter of total national GHG emissions, (2) 62% of Denmark's territory is used for intensive feed production and livestock farming, and (3) per capita meat consumption in Denmark is twice the world average and exceeds the FAO's recommendations for a healthy diet.

On the other hand, countries such as Sweden (SWE), France (FRA), Spain (SPA) and Croatia (CRO) recorded the lowest values of emissions in the observed period, with a gradual but stable decrease. This indicates a more efficient use of energy and a greater participation of renewable sources in industrial production. Interestingly, some countries, such as Ireland (IRE) and Malta (MAL), saw a temporary increase in emissions in 2022, which may be due to increased industrial activity following pandemic restrictions, before emissions decrease again in 2023.

Regarding the percentage changes in emissions (2021–2023), the largest reduction in emissions was recorded in: Bulgaria (-16.66%), Greece (-13.28%), Estonia (-13.17%), Slovenia (-12.91%) and the Netherlands (-12.43%). In the observed period, these countries significantly improved energy efficiency and reduced their dependence on fossil fuels, which directly reflected in the drop in emissions from production activities.

On the other hand, some countries have recorded an increase in emissions, which indicates increased industrial activity or slower implementation of decarbonization measures. The biggest increase was registered in Malta (+13.22%), Ireland (+4.38%), Cyprus (+0.47%) and Latvia (+0.46%). In most cases, these are smaller economies with limited capacities for rapid energy transformation.

*Figure 5. Results of Global sustainability and resilience - Material import dependency in the countries of the European Union in the period 2021-2023*

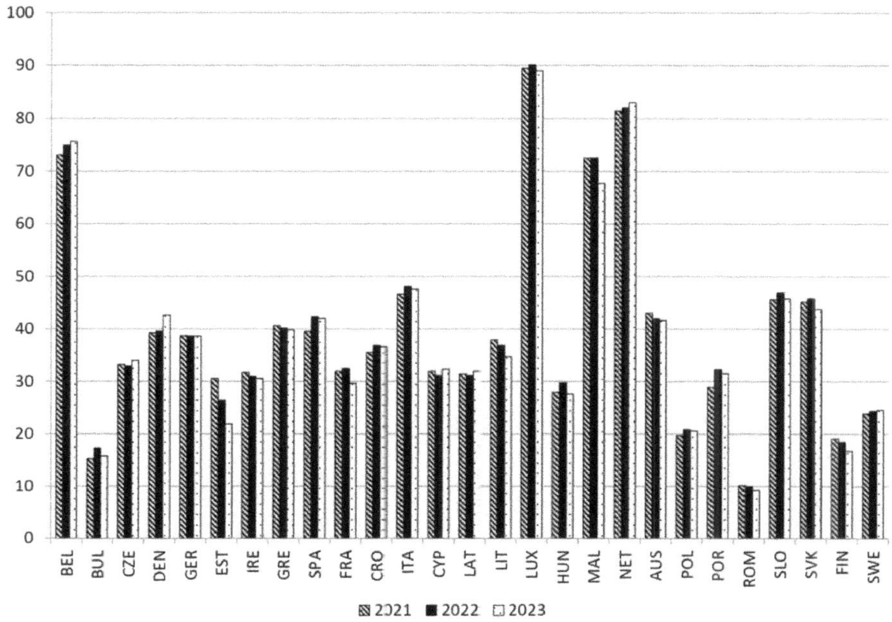


**Source:** *Own research*

Figure 5 shows that EU countries maintained relatively stable material import dependency levels in 2021–2023. The highest dependence is observed in Luxembourg and the Netherlands (above 80%), indicating strong reliance on external resources, while Romania, Bulgaria, and Estonia show lower values and greater self-sufficiency. A slight increase in 2023 may be linked to higher demand and global supply chain disruptions.

From a circular economy perspective, high import dependence highlights the need to strengthen resource efficiency, recycling, and reuse to reduce reliance on primary raw materials and increase economic resilience. Moderate changes are observed across countries, with the largest increases in Portugal (+9.0%), Denmark (+8.7%), and Spain (+6.3%), and the most significant decreases in Estonia (–28.2%), Finland (–12.0%), and Romania (–8.9%). High values in countries such as Luxembourg and the Netherlands reflect structural dependence, while lower values in Central and Eastern Europe (Romania, Poland, Bulgaria) indicate relatively greater material self-sufficiency.

A further analysis will be conducted on the sub-indicators associated with the competitiveness and innovation dimension of the circular economy.

*Figure 6. Results of competitiveness and innovation - Private investment and gross added value related to circular economy sectors in the countries of the European Union in the period 2021-2023*

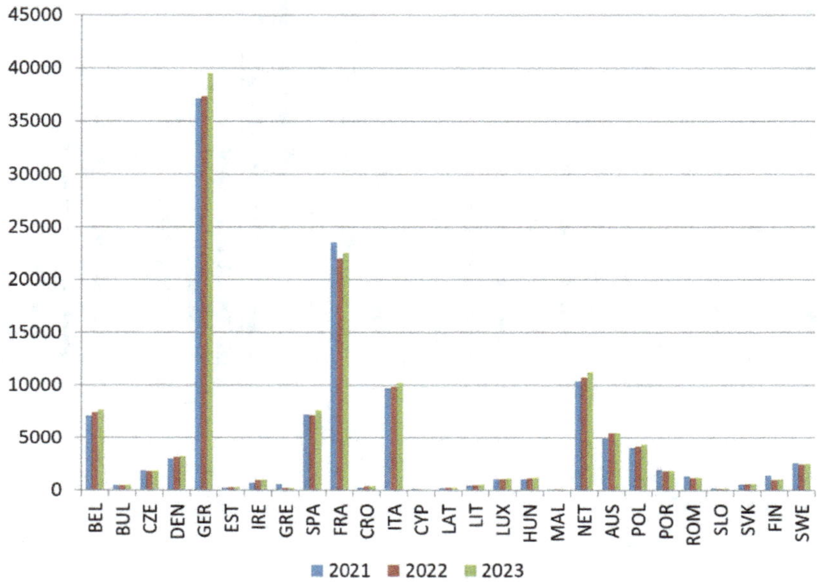


**Source:** *Own research*

Figure 6 presents private investments and gross added value in circular economy sectors across EU countries for the period 2021–2023, based on Eurostat data. Significant differences are observed among Member States, reflecting varying levels of economic development, institutional support and integration of circular principles. Germany, France, Italy, and the Netherlands record the highest values, supported by strong industrial bases and incentives for green innovation. In contrast, countries such as Malta, Cyprus, Latvia, and Estonia show considerably lower values, indicating limited investment capacity and slower policy implementation. Nevertheless, a positive growth trend is visible in 2023, suggesting increasing impact of EU level support and rising awareness of circular economy benefits. The results also confirm that competitiveness and innovation indicators remain lowest in the Baltic countries, consistent with Melece (2016). According to Stankevičienė et al. (2020), this may be due to insufficient financial and policy support, highlighting the role of central banks and environmental regulations in stimulating green investments and accelerating the transition to a circular economy.

*Figure 7. Results of competitiveness and innovation - Persons employed in circular economy sectors in the countries of the European Union in the period 2021-2023*

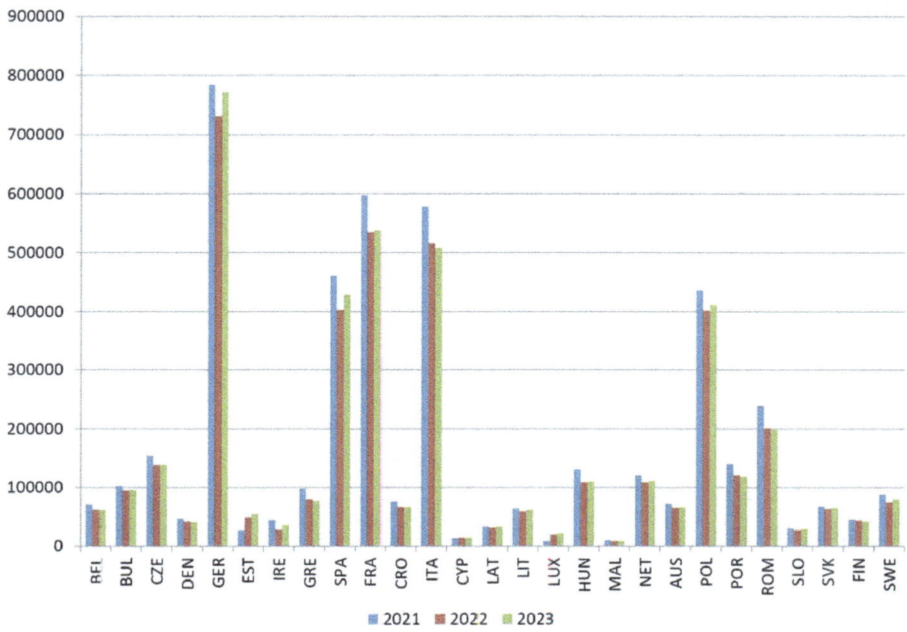


**Source:** *Own research*

Figure 7 shows the number of employees in circular economy sectors across EU countries from 2021 to 2023, revealing significant differences in labor market development. The highest employment is recorded in Germany, Spain, France, Italy, and Poland, reflecting their large economies and diversified industries where circular practices are more integrated. These countries are also leading in implementing EU circular economy policies, particularly in waste management, secondary raw materials and sustainable design.

In contrast, lower employment levels are observed in countries with less developed industrial structures and limited investment capacity, such as Malta, Cyprus, Latvia and Estonia. However, most countries show a slight increase in employment during the observed period, indicating steady growth of the sector and its contribution to the EU labor market. This trend supports the role of the circular economy in job creation and the green transition, in line with the European Green Deal. According to Pace (2020), Malta records particularly low employment due to the small size of its eco-industry, which generated only 0.57% of total revenue in 2017, compared to the EU-28 average of 1.74%.

## 5. MEASURING THE RESULTS OF THE EU CIRCULAR ECONOMY (2021-2023)

In order to provide a comprehensive overview of the progress and challenges in the implementation of the circular economy in the member states of the European Union, key indicators were analyzed that include the economic, resource and environmental dimensions of this model — including employment and investments in circular sectors, dependence on the import of materials, greenhouse gas emissions from production activities, as well as the ecological footprint of consumption.

*Table 2. Entropy and average results of Consumption footprint*

| Year | Entropy | Average | Min | Max |
|---|---|---|---|---|
| CF2021 | 0.0060 | 107.1481 | 94 | 136 |
| CF2022 | 0.0057 | 111.7778 | 98 | 143 |
| CF2023 | 0.0059 | 111.8519 | 99 | 146 |

**Source:** Own research

Analysis of CF indicators for the period 2021–2023. shows a stable, but still high level of the ecological footprint of consumption in the member states of the European Union. The average value of the indicator increased from 107.15 in 2021 to 111.85 in 2023, which indicates that the overall pressure of consumption on the environment has not been significantly reduced, despite the implementation of sustainable consumption and production policies. Entropy values are very low (0.0060 in 2021, 0.0057 in 2022 and 0.0059 in 2023), indicating relatively small differences between Member States in terms of the ecological footprint of consumption. Mild oscillations of entropy values during the observed period point to stable relations between countries, without significant changes in the degree of their mutual coordination. These findings are in line with previous research (Hoppe et al., 2023; European Environment Agency, 2024), which confirm that the ecological footprint of consumption is one of the most stable, but also the most difficult to change, aspects of the circular economy, as it depends on entrenched patterns of production and consumption.

*Table 3. Entropy and average results of Greenhouse gases emissions from production activities*

| Year | Entropy | Average | Min | Max |
|---|---|---|---|---|
| GHG2021 | 0.0779 | 7260.887 | 4074.102 | 14096.26 |
| GHG2022 | 0.0754 | 7183.348 | 3970.886 | 12913 |
| GHG2023 | 0.0716 | 6668.241 | 3833.553 | 12481.46 |

**Source:** Own research

Table 3 shows the results of the analysis of GHG indicators for the period 2021–2023, which indicate a gradual reduction of greenhouse gas emissions within the production activities of the European Union member states. The average emission values recorded a decrease from 7260.89 Kilograms per capita in 2021 to 6668.24 Kilograms per capita in 2023, which reflects progress in the implementation of energy efficiency measures, the transition to renewable energy sources and the introduction of environmentally friendly technologies in industrial sectors. The entropy values are low and show a decreasing tendency (0.0779 in 2021, 0.0754 in 2022 and 0.0716 in 2023), indicating a reduction in the differences between Member States in terms of greenhouse gas emissions. The decrease in entropy values during the observed period indicates that the member states are gradually harmonizing the pace of emission reduction, which probably results from the implementation of common European policies and decarbonization goals. These results coincide with the findings of previous research (Del Granado et al., 2020; Fragkiadakis et al., 2020; Cantoni & Brisbois, 2024), which confirm that, although the EU is recording a continuous decline in total emissions, the transition to low-carbon production is progressing gradually, with increasingly pronounced convergence among member countries.

*Table 4. Entropy and average results of Material import dependency*

| Year | Entropy | Average | Min | Max |
|---|---|---|---|---|
| MID2021 | 0.1550 | 39.3963 | 10.1 | 89.5 |
| MID2022 | 0.1549 | 39.77037 | 9.9 | 90.1 |
| MID2023 | 0.1633 | 39.06296 | 9.2 | 89 |

**Source:** Own research

Table 4 shows the Analysis of the MID indicator for the period 2021-2023. This result shows stable, but still present differences among the member states of the European Union in terms of dependence on the import of materials. Entropy values are low in all observed years (0.1550 in 2021, 0.1549 in 2022 and 0.1633 in 2023), indicating a relatively small degree of differences between countries. A lower entropy means a greater similarity in the level of material dependence, that is, that the member states are approximately dependent on the import of raw materials. A slight increase in entropy in 2023 (from 0.1549 to 0.1633) suggests that differences between countries have increased slightly, which may indicate different dynamics of progress in strengthening domestic sources and circular flows. The average value of the indicator (about 39%) confirms that the European Union as a whole still shows a high level of dependence on the import of raw materials, despite continuous efforts to encourage the use of secondary materials and recycling within the Union. These findings are in line with previous research (Haas et al., 2015), which indicate that import dependence still remains one of the key limitations in achieving full circularity of the European economy, especially in sectors that depend on critical raw materials.

*Table 5. Entropy and average results of Private investment and gross added value related to circular economy sectors*

| Year | Entropy | Average | Min | Max |
|---|---|---|---|---|
| PI2021 | 0.9108 | 4504.6 | 68 | 37147 |
| PI2022 | 0.9617 | 4472.9 | 66 | 37342 |
| PI2023 | 0.9806 | 4652.0 | 68 | 39500 |

**Source:** Own research

Based on the presentation of the PI indicator results for the period 2021-2023 shows a positive trend in the development of the circular economy in the member states of the European Union (Table 5). The entropy values are continuously increasing (0.9108 in 2021, 0.9617 in 2022 and 0.9806 in 2023), indicating an increase in differences between countries in terms of private investment and value added in circular sectors. Nevertheless, the growth of the average value of investments and added value by country confirms that interest in sustainable business models in the EU as a whole is growing, although with different intensity among countries. These results indicate that the private sector is increasingly involved in financing circular solutions, but that the economic effects are still unevenly distributed (OECD, 2025; Kirchherr & van Santen, 2019).

*Table 6. Entropy and average results of Persons employed in circular economy sectors*

| Year | Entropy | Average | Min | Max |
|---|---|---|---|---|
| PE2021 | 0.8411 | 168002.2 | 151241.4 | 154847.7 |
| PE2022 | 0.8338 | 8265.0 | 7883 | 8145 |
| PE2023 | 0.8347 | 783930.0 | 731414 | 771814 |

**Source:** Own research

Analysis of PE indicators for the period 2021–2023. shows a relatively stable, but slightly increased level of differences among the member states of the European Union. The entropy values (0.8411 in 2021, 0.8338 in 2022 and 0.8347 in 2023) indicate that the distribution of employment in circular economy sectors among EU countries is quite uneven. Countries with more developed industrial and innovation infrastructure maintained their leading positions, while smaller economies contributed significantly less to total employment in circular sectors, which reflected an increase in inequality and the entropy index. These findings are in line with previous research (e.g. Camacho-Otero et al., 2018; European Environment Agency, 2023), which point out that the development of the circular economy in the EU is still characterized by pronounced regional differences, with the countries of Western and Northern Europe leading in terms of employment and innovation capacity in circular activities.

*Figure 8. Global sustainability and resilience - Summary results of entropy and interpretation*

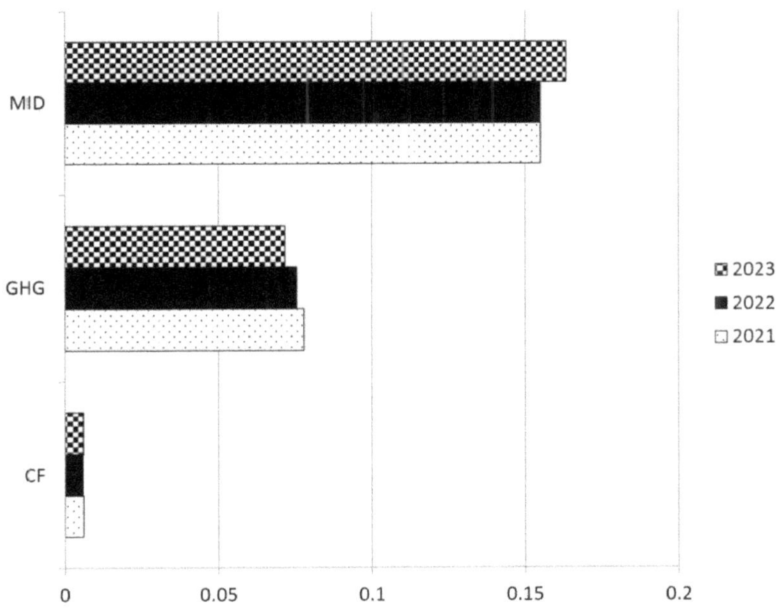


**Source:** *Own research*

Based on the displayed entropy values for the indicators of Global sustainability and resilience (consumer footprint - CF, greenhouse gas emissions - GHG and material import dependence -MID) in the period 2021–2023, it can be concluded that there are different levels of uniformity between the countries of the European Union in terms of sustainability dimensions (Figure 8). The lowest entropy values are recorded by the CF indicator, which indicates that EU countries are relatively similar in terms of consumption patterns and intensity of consumption. This result may indicate convergence in consumption and approach to sustainable standards within the framework of common EU policies. For the GHG indicator, the entropy values are slightly higher, which means that there are still differences between countries in the degree of reduction of greenhouse gas emissions. This is expected, given the different energy structures, levels of industrial development and capacities for implementing climate policies. Nevertheless, the differences in the GHG indicator between EU countries decreased in the period 2021-2023. The MID indicator has the highest entropy values, which indicates pronounced differences between countries in terms of dependence on the import of materials. This high variability suggests that some countries still have a structural dependence on external resources, while others more successfully implement the principles of circular economy and resource efficiency. The differences in this indicator have increased even more between countries, so we can speak of a tendency towards divergence in this indicator.

*Figure 9. Competitiveness and innovation - Summary results of entropy and interpretation*

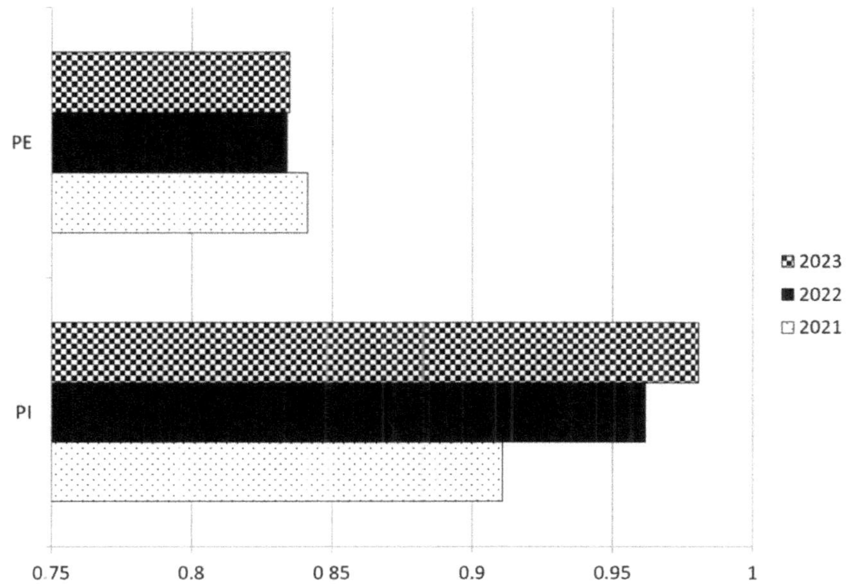


**Source:** *Own research*

The Figure 9 shows the entropy results for indicators of competitiveness and innovation within the circular economy: PI (private investments and gross added value in circular economy sectors) and PE (people employed in circular economy sectors). The entropy values for both indicators are relatively high (between 0.8 and 1), which indicates that there are significant differences between the countries of the European Union in terms of competitiveness and innovation. The PI indicator shows the highest entropy values, especially in 2023, which means that the differences between countries in terms of the level of private investments and created added value in circular sectors are still present, but are also increasing compared to the previous observed years. This trend requires that member states increasingly direct investments towards sustainable business models, encouraged by EU strategies for green and digital transition. For the PE indicator, the entropy values are somewhat lower, which means that EU countries are more similar in terms of employment in circular economy sectors, that is, the labor market in this area is relatively uniform. This may be the result of coordinated European Union policies promoting green jobs and strengthening capacity for innovation and recycling technologies (Ilnytskyy et al., 2024).

## CONCLUDING REMARKS

The literature shows that international reports and scientific studies provide a solid basis for developing indicators to measure circular economy progress. The European Commission has established a monitoring framework that enables comparative analysis across countries and is continuously being refined. However, according to OECD (2025), the circular economy still has a limited impact. In the EU, it accounts for around 2% of GDP and employment, while the circular material use rate reached only 12% in 2023, well below the 24% target for 2030. In addition, several Member States fail to meet waste management targets and only 13% of OECD regions achieve SDG 12.

This study assesses key circular economy indicators in EU Member States for 2021–2023 using entropy analysis. The results show low entropy in environmental indicators, indicating relatively uniform performance, while economic indicators such as investment, value added and employment display high entropy, revealing significant disparities among countries.

The results show that the economic aspect of the circular economy is moderately uniform and slightly increasing, while the resource and environmental aspects still reflect significant differences between countries. It suggests that economic incentives and investments can contribute to a faster and more uniform implementation of circular practices, but that environmental and resource policies still require additional coordination and support. The main findings of this study highlight several important patterns across EU member states. First, the relatively low entropy of environmental indicators suggests a certain level of convergence, indicating that EU-wide policies have contributed to more uniform environmental performance. In contrast, the high entropy observed in economic indicators reveals substantial disparities in investment, employment, and value creation within circular economy sectors, pointing to uneven economic integration of circular practices. These differences imply that while regulatory frameworks have been relatively effective in aligning environmental outcomes, additional policy efforts are needed to support economic dimensions of the circular economy, particularly in less advanced member states. Targeted financial instruments, innovation support, and capacity building measures are therefore essential to reduce these gaps and ensure a more balanced transition across the EU.

In addition, the findings of this study suggest that the transition to a circular economy will increasingly depend on the development of specific capabilities within businesses, which can act as key drivers of change. These include the ability to implement eco-design principles, adopt resource efficient and low waste production processes and utilize digital technologies for monitoring material flows and improving transparency across value chains. Furthermore, innovation capacity and the ability to collaborate within complex supply networks are essential for developing circular business models. Strengthening these capabilities enables firms not only to comply with regulatory requirements but also to enhance competitiveness and resilience in the context of the green transition.

## POLICY RECOMMENDATIONS

The transition to a circular economy is a key pillar of EU sustainable development and climate neutrality goals under the European Green Deal. Its success requires coordinated action among Member States, local authorities, industry, and citizens. EU policies should promote innovation, resource efficiency, and secondary raw material markets, while improving regulation, harmonizing monitoring indicators, and integrating circular principles across key sectors such as energy, agriculture, transport, and construction.

One of the key strategies to accelerate the transition to a circular economy is the adoption and harmonisation of circular design standards at the European Union level. As changes in *consumer behaviour* are slow and difficult to sustain, a more effective approach involves directing policies towards the production phase, by encouraging manufacturers to apply principles such as reuse, repair and recyclability of products (Hartley et al., 2020). The introduction of common standards would contribute to the harmonisation of practices, increasing the competitiveness of the sector and strengthening consumer confidence, with the initiative coming from public policies and regulatory bodies, and not exclusively from market mechanisms.

EU Sustainable Consumption and Production policies have traditionally focused more on production than consumption, despite the growing impact of consumption patterns on the ecological footprint. Therefore, policies should shift towards consumption by introducing relevant targets and indicators, including per capita emissions and material use, as well as embedded resources in imports. Sustainable behavior should be encouraged through education, fiscal incentives, and clear labeling. Since only a few countries, such as Denmark and Germany, have decoupled economic growth from consumer carbon footprints, the EU should introduce mandatory reduction targets and develop a common *Consumption Footprint Index.*

The chapter analysis notes that although differences in *greenhouse gas (GHG) emission* levels between EU Member States have decreased; overall emissions remain high, indicating the need for a deeper transformation of energy and industrial systems in line with the principles of the circular economy. In this context, it is necessary to encourage the development of advanced technologies for electricity storage and recovery, which would allow for a more efficient use of the energy produced and reduce losses in the electricity grid. Such projects represent a key step towards sustainability as they integrate technical innovation and rational resource management. In addition, in the oil and gas sector, it is necessary to expand the application of circular solutions through the reuse and valorization of processed waste, which would reduce the amount of waste that still ends up in the environment (García-Navarro & Poltronieri, 2024). Such measures contribute to reducing the sector's overall GHG footprint, stimulate technological innovation and accelerate the transition to a low-carbon and resource-efficient economy in line with the objectives of the EU Green Deal.

Another recommendation for further development of sustainability policy is seen by Martin K. Enevoldsen et al (2007) in increasing the price of energy relative to the price of labor and other production factors. This effect can be achieved through market mechanisms or political instruments, such as introducing taxes on energy and $CO_2$ emissions or reducing taxes on labor, thereby encouraging energy efficiency and a shift to more sustainable production models. This applies to countries with high GHG emissions, such as Denmark and the Czech Republic, Poland and Germany.

The *material import dependency* indicator shows the high dependence of the EU27 on imports of key raw materials, in particular fossil fuels (90.9%) and metal ores (86.2%), with most countries exceeding the 65% import dependency threshold (Distefano et al., 2024). Such a structure of material consumption poses a risk to the sustainability and resilience of the economy, especially in the context of geopolitical tensions and the transition to renewable energy sources. It is therefore necessary to develop integrated policies that combine supply and demand side measures, technological innovation and changes in consumer and industrial behaviour. On the one hand, it is necessary to strengthen domestic production and recycling of key raw materials, encourage the development of alternative materials and technologies (e.g. the use of biomass instead of rare metals) and expand the infrastructure for secondary raw materials through circular value chains. On the other hand, it is important to reduce overall material consumption through dematerialisation policies, eco-design of products and encouraging servitisation instead of ownership. In parallel, the EU needs to strengthen international cooperation and ensure transparent, sustainable raw material supply chains through strategic partnerships and green trade agreements.

*Private investments*, as part of the long-term fiscal policy plan, are increasingly directed towards sustainable business models, encouraged by the EU's strategic frameworks for green and digital transition. Trends show that the growth of public spending can have a positive effect on investments in the circular economy in both the short and long term, provided that this spending is productive and strategically focused. Therefore, governments of member states should focus public funds on research and development, innovation in the field of circular technologies, and on the creation of new business models that promote sustainability, reuse of resources and reduction of waste. Special emphasis should be placed on public investments that stimulate the private sector, through incentives, subsidies and public-private partnerships for the development of green technologies and digital solutions. However, it is important to take into account the findings of the research by Stankevičienė (2020), who points out that the main problem of the countries that in this analysis showed weaknesses in private investments (such as the Baltic countries) is the effect of crowding out private investments due to increased public spending. These findings suggest that fiscal policy must be carefully designed so that public investment truly has a multiplier effect on the private sector, rather than constraining it.

*The EU circular economy labour market* is experiencing significant growth, confirming that the shift to sustainable business models is creating new jobs and a demand for specific skills. To sustain and further stimulate this trend, it is necessary to formulate targeted labour, education and regulatory policies that support the development of human capital for the circular transition. The most sought-after skills in the circular economy labour market relate to the analysis and assessment of information and data, networking and collaboration, as well as organisational skills related to planning and managing activities (Dunne et al., 2024). It is crucial that all stakeholders – from businesses and educational institutions to public bodies – understand how they can actively shape the labour market to foster the creation of "circular jobs" and develop a resilient workforce capable of adapting to future changes in the economy. Governments and policymakers have a key role to play in designing regulatory and fiscal instruments that encourage employment and skills development in circular sectors. This includes reforming tax systems to reduce the burden on labor and increase incentives for the restoration, reuse, and recycling of materials.

## LIMITATION AND FUTURE RESEARCH DIRECTIONS

Although the research provides valuable insights into the development of the circular economy in the EU through five key indicators, it has certain limitations that should be acknowledged. Firstly, the research period from 2021 to 2023 represents a relatively short timeframe for capturing long-term trends. Moreover, the selected indicators do not encompass all possible dimensions of the circular economy, such as social factors, cultural consumption patterns, and innovation capacities, all of which can significantly influence the adoption of sustainable practices and the ability of businesses to develop capabilities necessary for circular transformation.

For future research, it is recommended to both extend the observation period and incorporate additional indicators to allow for a deeper evaluation of circular economy progress including those related to firm level capabilities and organizational readiness. Furthermore, in addition to entropy-based methods, advanced analytical approaches such as MCDM techniques could be employed. These methods would support more robust comparisons and prioritization of strategies in evaluating circular economy performance across multiple dimensions while also enabling the identification of key business capabilities such as eco-design, digitalization and supply chain collaboration as potential drivers of circular economy development. Future studies should also place greater emphasis on how these capabilities can be developed and leveraged by businesses to support sustainable and competitive transitions.

## ACKNOWLEDGMENT

This research is supported by the Ministry of Science, Technological Development and Innovation of the Republic of Serbia by the Decision on the scientific research funding for teaching staff at the accredited higher education institutions in 2026 (No. 451-03-34/2026-03/200375 of February 5, 2026), by COST Action 22124 - EU Circular Economy Network for All: Consumer Protection through reducing, reusing, repairing (ECO4ALL) and by the bilateral research project "Green Tourism without Borders: Strengthening Sustainability in the Hospitality Industry of Serbia and Slovakia (GRH-CAP)", No. 001147721/001.

## REFERENCES

Albert, O. O. K., Marianne, T., Jonathan, L., Nino, J. L., & Dario, C. (2020). Tracking the carbon emissions of Denmark's five regions from a producer and consumer perspective. *Ecological Economics, 177*, 106778. DOI: 10.1016/j.ecolecon.2020.106778

Banaitė, D. (2016). Towards circular economy: Analysis of indicators in the context of sustainable development. *Social Transformation in Contemporary Society*, *4*(9), 142–150.

Busu, C., & Busu, M. (2018). Modeling the circular economy processes at the EU level using an evaluation algorithm based on Shannon entropy. *Processes (Basel, Switzerland)*, *6*(11), 225. DOI: 10.3390/pr6110225

Camacho-Otero, J., Boks, C., & Pettersen, I. N. (2018). Consumption in the circular economy: A literature review. *Sustainability (Basel)*, *10*(8), 2758. DOI: 10.3390/su10082758

Cantoni, R., & Brisbois, M. C. (2024). En route to decarbonization: A periodisation of just transition in four carbon-intensive EU regions. *Geoforum, 154*, 104061. DOI: 10.1016/j.geoforum.2024.104061

Del Granado, P. C., Resch, G., Holz, F., Welisch, M., Geipel, J., Hartner, M., & Ramos, A. (2020). Energy transition pathways to a low-carbon Europe in 2050. *Economics of Energy & Environmental Policy*, *9*(1), 121–136.

Distefano, T., Lodi, L., & Biggeri, M. (2024). Material footprint and import dependency in EU27: Past trends and future challenges. *Journal of Cleaner Production*, *472*, 143384. DOI: 10.1016/j.jclepro.2024.143384

Dunne, A., Multani, M., Bachus, K., Ampe, K., Goodwin-Brown, E., Shankar, A., . . . Pals, E. (2024). *Skills on a circular path: Modelling future CE scenarios and transormations in sectoral, occupational and skills structures of the Belgian Labour Market* (2024). https://lirias.kuleuven.be/retrieve/780786

Durkalić, D., & Ćurčić, M. (2019), Comparative analysis of debt sustainability of EU countries and EU candidates: Promethee-Gaia approach, Eastern Journal of European Studies - EJES, Vol 10 (1), 67-92, ISSN: 2068-6633, 67-92

Džajić Uršič, E., Fric, U., & Rončević, B. (2024). The Circular Economy: Recent debates and research trends. *Journal of Infrastructure. Policy and Development, 8*(3), 2855.

Enevoldsen, M. K., Ryelund, A. V., & Andersen, M. S. (2007). Decoupling of industrial energy consumption and CO2-emissions in energy-intensive industries in Scandinavia. *Energy Economics, 29*(4), 665–692. DOI: 10.1016/j.eneco.2007.01.016

European commission. (2020), EU Circular Economy Action Plan, https://eur-lex.europa.eu/legal-content/EN/TXT/HTML/?uri=CELEX:52020DC0098

European Environment Agency. (2023). *Consumption footprint and circular economy, 8th Environment Action Programme,* https://www.eea.europa.eu/en/analysis/publications/monitoring-progress-towards-8th-eap-objectives/indicators/25-consumption-footprint-based-on-life-cycle-assessment-in-europe/@@download/file

European Environment Agency. (2025), National circular economy policies, Countries with national adopted CE Strategies, Roadmaps, Action plans. https://www.eea.europa.eu/en/circularity/thematic-metrics/enabling/national-circular-economy-policies

Eurostat, (2025), Circular economy, Database, https://ec.europa.eu/eurostat/web/circular-economy/database

Fragkiadakis, K., Fragkos, P., & Paroussos, L. (2020). Low-carbon R&D can boost EU growth and competitiveness. *Energies, 13*(19), 5236. DOI: 10.3390/en13195236

García-Navarro, J., & Poltronieri, O. C. C. (2024). Circular economy and GHG emissions, current situation. In *Circular economy on energy and natural resources industries: new processes and applications to reduce, reuse and recycle materials and decrease greenhouse gases emissions* (pp. 1–18). Springer International Publishing. DOI: 10.1007/978-3-031-56284-6_1

Geissdoerfer, M., Savaget, P., Bocken, N. M., & Hultink, E. J. (2017). The Circular Economy–A new sustainability paradigm? *Journal of Cleaner Production, 143*, 757–768. DOI: 10.1016/j.jclepro.2016.12.048

Ghisellini, P., Cialani, C., & Ulgiati, S. (2016). A review on circular economy: The expected transition to a balanced interplay of environmental and economic systems. *Journal of Cleaner Production, 114*, 11–32. DOI: 10.1016/j.jclepro.2015.09.007

Grybaitė, V., & Burinskienė, A. (2024). Assessment of circular economy development in the EU countries based on SAW method. *Sustainability (Basel), 16*(21), 9582. DOI: 10.3390/su16219582

Haas, W., Krausmann, F., Wiedenhofer, D., & Heinz, M. (2015). How circular is the global economy?: An assessment of material flows, waste production, and recycling in the European Union and the world in 2005. *Journal of Industrial Ecology, 19*(5), 765–777. DOI: 10.1111/jiec.12244

Hartley, K., Van Santen, R., & Kirchherr, J. (2020). Policies for transitioning towards a circular economy: Expectations from the European Union (EU). *Resources, Conservation and Recycling, 155*, 104634. DOI: 10.1016/j.resconrec.2019.104634

Hervey, G. (2018). Ranking how EU countries do with the circular economy. *POLITICO's circular economy*. https://www.politico.eu/article/ranking-how-eu-countries-do-with-the-circular-economy/

Hoppe, J., Hinder, B., Rafaty, R., Patt, A., & Grubb, M. (2023). Three decades of climate mitigation policy: What has it delivered? *Annual Review of Environment and Resources, 48*(1), 615–650. DOI: 10.1146/annurev-environ-112321-103821

Huang, D., Zhou, Z., Zhang, Z., Dai, Q., Lu, H., Li, Y., & Huang, Y. (2025). Land Use/Land Cover Remote Sensing Classification in Complex Subtropical Karst Environments: Challenges, Methodological Review, and Research Frontiers. *Applied Sciences (Basel, Switzerland), 15*(17), 9641. DOI: 10.3390/app15179641

Hussain, M., Abdullah, M., Ashraf, M. N., Shaheen, A., Farooqi, Z. U. R., Abbas, A., & Tariq, Y. (2025). World food hunger in 2050 and nano solutions: probabilities and prospects based on plant based food. In *Nanomaterials for Enhanced Plant-Based Food Production* (pp. 11–21). Academic Press. DOI: 10.1016/B978-0-443-23688-4.00010-5

Ilnytskyy, D., Drobotiuk, O., & Andrusyk, V. (2024, June). Sustainable Development through Green Innovations: Economic Strategies of China and the EU Compared. In *Proceedings of the International Conference on Economics And Social Sciences* (Vol. 6, No. 1, pp. 412-525). Bucharest University of Economic Studies, Romania. DOI: 10.24818/ICESS/2024/048

Jawahir, I. S., & Bradley, R. (2016). Technological elements of circular economy and the principles of 6R-based closed-loop material flow in sustainable manufacturing. *Procedia CIRP*, *40*, 103–108. DOI: 10.1016/j.procir.2016.01.067

Kandpal, V., Jaswal, A., Santibanez Gonzalez, E. D., & Agarwal, N. (2024). Challenges and opportunities for sustainable energy transition and circular economy. *Sustainable Energy Transition: Circular Economy and Sustainable Financing for Environmental, Social and Governance (ESG) Practices*, 307-324.

Kirchherr, J., & van Santen, R. (2019). Research on the circular economy: A critique of the field. *Resources, Conservation and Recycling*, *151*, 104480. DOI: 10.1016/j.resconrec.2019.104480

Kulakovskaya, A., Knoeri, C., Radke, F., & Blum, N. U. (2023). Measuring the economic impacts of a circular economy: An evaluation of indicators. *Circular Economy and Sustainability*, *3*(2), 657–692. DOI: 10.1007/s43615-022-00190-w PMID: 37408852

Luković, M., Kostić, M., Dudić, B., Spalević, V., & Pantović, D. (2024). Perceptions of mountain ecosystem services in Golija-Studenica Biosphere Reserve, Serbia: Latent transformation from sustainable towards regenerative tourism. *Eco.Mont*, *16*(2), 4–15. DOI: 10.1553/eco.mont-16-2s4

Mazur-Wierzbicka, E. (2021). Circular economy: Advancement of European Union countries. *Environmental Sciences Europe*, *33*(1), 111. DOI: 10.1186/s12302-021-00549-0

Melece, L. (2016). Challenges and opportunities of circular economy and green economy. *Engineering for Rural Development*, *25*, 1162–1169.

Mroz, B. (2010). Consumerism vs. sustainability: The emergence of new consumer trends in Poland. *International Journal of Economic Policy in Emerging Economies*, *3*(1), 1–15. DOI: 10.1504/IJEPEE.2010.032791

Murthy, A., Galli, A., Madeira, C., & Moreno Pires, S. (2023). Consumer attitudes towards fish and seafood in portugal: Opportunities for footprint reduction. *Sustainability (Basel)*, *15*(2), 1363. DOI: 10.3390/su15021363

Nowak-Marchewka, K., Osmólska, E., & Stoma, M. (2025). Progress and Challenges of Circular Economy in Selected EU Countries. *Sustainability (Basel)*, *17*(1), 320. DOI: 10.3390/su17010320

OECD. (2025), The Circular Economy in Cities and Regions of the European Union, OECD Urban Studies, OECD Publishing,Paris, DOI: 10.1787/e09c21e2-en

OECD. 2025, Resource efficiency and circular economy, https://www.oecd.org/en/topics/resource-efficiency-and-circular-economy.html

Pace, L. A. (2020). Eco-innovation in Malta: EIO country profile 2018-2019, 1-40.

Pakuła, N., Łapniewska, Z., & Dutra, C. J. (2025). Comparative measurements of circular economy performance among European countries: Reviewing approaches and limitations. *Journal of Environmental Management, 375*, 124414. DOI: 10.1016/j.jenvman.2025.124414 PMID: 39904241

Pantović, D., Bošković, N., & Petrović, T. (2022). Measuring Convergence in Tourism Competitiveness of Natural and Cultural Resources: A Case of the Balkans and Eastern Europe. *Ekonomický časopis,* 910 (70/2022), 703 – 722.

Pantovic, D., Chaichi, K., & Pavlović, S. (2024). Contribution of tourism to economic development in selected European countries. *BizInfo (Blace) Journal of Economics. Management and Informatics, 15*(2), 83–89.

Pantovic, D., Fedajev, A., & Milošević, I. (2023). Monetary and fiscal policies in the EU. Is there a difference between EMU and non-EMU members? *Acta Oeconomica, 73*(1), 85–100. DOI: 10.1556/032.2023.00006

Pantović, D., Kostić, M., Veljović, S., Luković, M. (2023a). Evaluation Model of Environmental Sustainable Competitive Tourism Based on Entropy, *Problemy Ekorozwoju/ Problems of Sustainable Development*, 18(2): 193-203.

Remeikienė, R., Gasparėnienė, L., & Bankauskienė, J. (2025). Assessment of the circular economy indicators in the EU Member States. *Discover Sustainability, 6*(1), 1–19. DOI: 10.1007/s43621-024-00719-z

Saraji, M. K., & Torabi, M. (2025). Progress toward a circular economy: A comparative analysis of EU member states. *Sustainability, 17*(18), 1–21.

Shannon, C. E. (1948). A mathematical theory of communication. *The Bell System Technical Journal, 27*(3), 379–423. DOI: 10.1002/j.1538-7305.1948.tb01338.x

Shpak, N., Melnyk, O., Horbal, N., Ruda, M., & Sroka, W. (2021, March). Assessing the implementation of the circular economy in the EU countries. *Forum Scientiae Oeconomia, 9*(1), 25–39.

Smol, M., Kulczycka, J., & Avdiushchenko, A. (2017). Circular economy indicators in relation to eco-innovation in European regions. *Clean Technologies and Environmental Policy, 19*(3), 669–678. DOI: 10.1007/s10098-016-1323-8

Šobić, Lj., Bošković, N., & Pantović, D. (2023). Entrepreneurial elements in rural tourism - findings from PLS-SEM. *Economics of Agriculture, 70*(2), 521–535.

Stankevičienė, J., Nikanorova, M., & Çera, G. (2020). Analysis of green economy dimension in the context of circular economy: The case of Baltic sea region. *E+M. Ekonomie a Management*, *XXIII*(1), 4–18. DOI: 10.15240/tul/001/2020-1-001

Taneja, S., Bansal, N., & Ozen, E. (2024). What was, is and will be: A bibliometric analysis of European Green Deal (EGD). *International Journal of Technology Management & Sustainable Development*, *23*(1), 85–104. DOI: 10.1386/tmsd_00086_1

Viegas, M., Mello, C. J., & Pires, S. M. (2023). Contributions to a more sustainable model of food production and consumption in Portugal: An opportunity to reduce the ecological footprint of food. *Progress in Industrial Ecology*, *16*(4), 280–299. DOI: 10.1504/PIE.2023.135570

Zeleny, M., & Cochrane, J. L. (1982). Multiple criteria decision making McGraw-Hill New York, 34.

Zhang, Y., Li, M., Dong, J., Yang, H., Van Zwieten, L., Lu, H., Alshameri, A., Zhan, Z., Chen, X., Jiang, X., Xu, W., Bao, Y., & Wang, H. (2021). A critical review of methods for analyzing freshwater eutrophication. *Water (Basel)*, *13*(2), 225. DOI: 10.3390/w13020225

# Chapter 3
# Implementation of Sustainable Development Goals:
## An Industry 4 Perspective

**Sehar Zulfiqar**
http://orcid.org/0000-0002-8377-4524
*Birmingham City University, Birmingham, UK*

**Sadia Saeed**
http://orcid.org/0000-0003-3670-4416
*National University of Modern Languages, Islamabad, Pakistan*

**Sadia Shaheen**
http://orcid.org/0000-0001-8690-1181
*Government College University, Faisalabad, Pakistan*

## ABSTRACT

*This chapter aims to deepen the understanding of how Industry 4.0 contributes to the attainment of the Sustainable Development Goals (SDGs) that range from eradicating poverty to combating climate change. Technology is essential for advancing SDG targets; therefore, this chapter provides a comprehensive review of how Industry 4.0 drive SDGs in sustainable manufacturing, supply chain management, energy, infrastructure development, fintech, and waste management through smart technologies like Internet of Things (IoT), artificial intelligence (AI), data analytics, and machine learning. Further, we discuss the cases from across the globe where organizations and societies are achieving SDGs through Industry 4.0. Finally, actionable recommendations are discussed. Overall, the chapter highlights*

DOI: 10.4018/979-8-2600-1438-7.ch003

*that Industry 4.0 core technologies are vital for the achievement of sustainability goals therefore cohesive effort is needed from all stakeholders to accelerate the implementation of SDGs via Industry 4.0.*

## 1. INTRODUCTION

Industry 4.0 (I4.0) started in Germany between 2011 and 2015, with the focus on the application of digital technologies in the manufacturing sector (Thomas & Davis, 2018). I4.0 is the large-scale transformation resulting from the integration of digital technology into all spheres of life. It has vast implications spanning from reshaping work, skills, economics, sustainability, and business through digitalization, smart factories, and intelligent production (Maresova et al., 2018). The Sustainable Development Goals (SDGs) are a universal set of social, economic, and environmental objectives set by the United Nations to guide global efforts through 2030. SDGs have replaced the earlier Millennium Development Goals (MDGs) and are supported by a reformed framework for development financing. SDGs are adopted by all United Nations (UN) member countries. These goals help to deal with significant challenges, from eradicating poverty (SDG1) to dealing with climate change impact (SDG 13) (Jacob, 2025; Weiland et al., 2021).

Achieving the SDGs faces many challenges, and one of the biggest challenges is the availability of technological infrastructure, especially in the context of developing countries. The SDGs that are affected by this are zero hunger, sustainable cities and communities, climate action, life on land, peace, justice, and strong institutions. Therefore, it is important to align technological innovations with SDGs (Leal Filho et al., 2022). Therefore, to achieve sustainable growth and achieve sustainable objectives, it is a requirement to build a sustainable technological infrastructure (Tripathi et al., 2024). In this regard, I4.0 is a key driver for achieving balanced and sustainable social, environmental, and economic growth. Core technologies of I4.0, such as the Internet of Things (IoT), artificial intelligence (AI), data analytics, and machine learning, play important roles in tracking, measuring, and complying with sustainability goals. Specifically, these technological systems facilitate the effective management and optimization of critical resources like energy, water, and materials, while minimizing waste through connected, automated data exchange. In sum, this converts industrial processes into intelligent, self-regulating systems that actively support a more sustainable future (Berawi, 2019).

There is a growing body of research investigating the relationship between I4.0 and sustainable development by considering some technological or sustainability aspects. However, there is a need to investigate this link analytically and comprehensively (Mabkhot et al., 2021). This study bridges this gap by providing a comprehensive review of how I4.0 leads to SDGs implementation in sustainable manufacturing, sustainable supply chain management, sustainable energy, sustainable infrastructure development, fintech, and waste management. Similarly, literature highlights that organizations struggle to determine and integrate I4.0 technologies to effectively improve sustainability performance (Bai et al., 2023). There is a gap in the existing literature regarding how organizations develop and integrate I4.0 digital technologies and its significance for sustainability (Ocelíket al., 2023). This chapter discusses real-world examples to showcase the link between technological capability and practical implementation. Finally, the keyword "policy" has low citation frequency in the field, suggesting a knowledge gap regarding policy frameworks that are essential for the implementation of I4.0 strategies for SDG achievement (Baca-Neglia et al., 2025). According to Siekmann et al., (2023) it is pertinent for future studies to examine policy interventions and governance mechanisms that can effectively guide and regulate I4.0 towards SDG achievement through responsible innovation. This chapter answers this call by providing actionable policy recommendations to policymakers.

Based on the above discussion, it can be argued that I4.0 can play a crucial role in achieving SDGs, and this chapter provides a comprehensive review of how I4.0 can facilitate the implementation of SDGs. Overall, this chapter is intended to improve the basic understanding of laymen, government, policymakers, and researchers regarding the role of technology and its alignment with SDGs.

## 2. PROPOSED THEORETICAL FRAMEWORK OF THE STUDY

Figure 2.1 shows the proposed theoretical framework of the study. First, we briefly define and explain I4.0 and 17 SDGs. Second, we review how industry accelerates the attainment of SDGs through its core technologies in sustainable manufacturing, sustainable supply chain management, sustainable energy, sustainable infrastructure development, fintech, and waste management. Thirdly, we present case examples from the real world demonstrating how communities and organizations are employing I4.0 for a sustainable future. Lastly, we suggest actionable recommendations.

*Figure 1. Proposed Theoretical Framework of the Study*

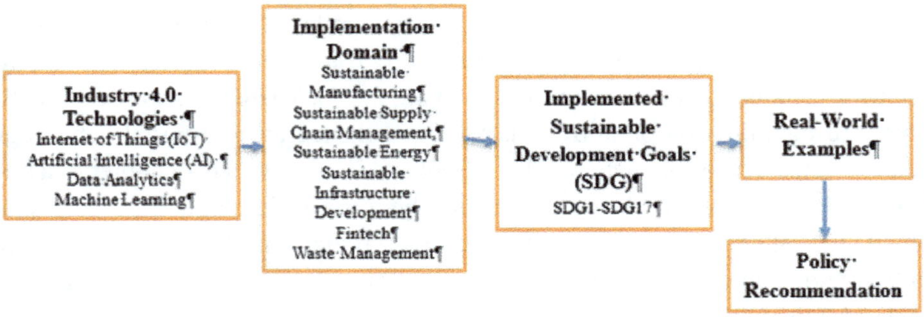


*Source: Author's own construction*

## 3. INDUSTRY 4.0

I4.0, or the Fourth Industrial Revolution, is defined by smart manufacturing and driven by technologies like IoT, AI, automation, and cyber-physical systems. This paradigm shift seeks to build smarter, interconnected networks to address worldwide issues (Mishra & Maheshwari, 2020). It operates on four pillars: real-time data, connectivity, analytics, and sustainability (Ebolor et al., 2022), which collectively enhance operational efficiency and enable novel, adaptive problem-solving (Kasinathan et al., 2022) .Central to this technological development, sustainability aims to balance industrial progress with ecological integrity and social equity, protecting both people and the planet (Nastasi et al., 2022).

## 4. SUSTAINABLE DEVELOPMENT GOALS (SDGS)

There are 17 SDGs, and the complete framework consists of 169 targets and corresponding indicators. Each of the 17 SDGs has 8-12 specific targets, which are measured by an average of 1.5 indicators each. These targets are divided into two types: outcome targets (defining the desired result) and means of implementation targets (specifying how to get the results). The latter were added to address how the goals would be achieved, a concern central to Goal 17, which focuses entirely on the partnerships and resources needed for implementation.

***SDG 1: No Poverty*:** The objective is to end poverty in all its forms everywhere. The sample targets are eradicating extreme poverty (currently measured as people living on less than $2.15 a day) and reducing by at least half the proportion of men, women, and children living in poverty. The sample Indicator is the proportion of the population living below the international poverty line (IAEG, 2016).

***SDG 2: Zero Hunger:*** The objective is to end hunger, achieve food security and improved nutrition, and promote sustainable agriculture. The sample targets are ending hunger and ensuring access to safe, nutritious food for all, and ending all forms of malnutrition. double agricultural productivity and incomes of small-scale food producers. The sample indicator is the prevalence of undernourishment (IAEG, 2016).

***SDG 3: Good Health and Well-being:*** The objective is to ensure healthy lives and promote well-being for all at all ages. Sample targets to reduce the global maternal mortality ratio and end preventable deaths of newborns and children under 5. A sample indicator is the maternal mortality ratio (IAEG, 2016).

***SDG 4: Quality Education:*** The objective is to ensure inclusive and equitable quality education and promote lifelong learning opportunities for all. The sample targets are to ensure all children complete free, equitable, and quality primary and secondary education and equal access to affordable technical, vocational, and higher education. A sample indicator is the proportion of youth with information and communication technology skills (IAEG, 2016).

***SDG 5: Gender Equality:*** The objective is to achieve gender equality and empower all women and girls. Sample targets are ending all forms of discrimination against all women and girls and eliminating all forms of violence against women and girls. The sample indicator is the proportion of seats held by women in the government (at national and local levels) (IAEG, 2016).

***SDG 6: Clean Water and Sanitation:*** The objective is to ensure the availability and sustainable management of water and sanitation for all. The sample targets are to achieve universal access to safe and affordable drinking water and to achieve access to adequate sanitation and hygiene for all. The sample indicator is the proportion of the population using safely managed drinking water services (IAEG, 2016).

***SDG 7: Affordable and Clean Energy:*** The objective is to ensure access to affordable, reliable, sustainable, and modern energy for all. The sample targets are to ensure universal access to affordable, reliable, and modern energy services and increase the share of renewable energy substantially in the global energy mix. The sample indicator is the proportion of the population with access to electricity (IAEG, 2016).

***SDG 8: Decent Work and Economic Growth:*** The objective is to promote sustained, inclusive, and sustainable economic growth, full and productive employment, and decent work for all. The sample targets are to sustain per capita economic growth and promote a safe working environment. The sample indicator is the annual growth rate of real GDP per capita (IAEG, 2016).

***SDG 9: Industry, Innovation, and Infrastructure:*** The objective is to build resilient infrastructure, promote inclusive and sustainable industrialization, and foster innovation. The sample targets are to develop quality, reliable, sustainable, and resilient infrastructure and upgrade infrastructure and retrofit industries to make them sustainable. The sample indicator is the proportion of the rural population who live within 2 km of an all-season road (IAEG, 2016).

***SDG 10: Reduced Inequality:*** The objective is to reduce inequality within and among countries. The sample targets sustaining income growth of the bottom 40% of the population at a rate higher than the national average and adopting policies, especially fiscal, wage, and social protection policies, to progressively achieve greater equality. The sample indicator is the growth rates of household expenditure or income per capita among the bottom 40% of the population (IAEG, 2016).

***SDG 11: Sustainable Cities and Communities:*** The objective is to make cities and human settlements inclusive, safe, resilient, and sustainable. The sample targets are ensuring access for all to adequate, safe, and affordable housing. Provide access to safe, affordable, accessible, and sustainable transport systems. The Sample Indicator: Proportion of urban population living in slums or informal settlements (IAEG, 2016).

***SDG 12: Responsible Consumption and Production:*** SDG12's objective is to ensure sustainable consumption and production patterns. The sample targets are encouraging organizations, especially the large ones, to incorporate sustainable management strategies and report sustainability information. Another target is to ensure that the public has access to sustainable development and lifestyle information everywhere. The sample indicator is the number of monitored companies disclosing sustainability-related information (IAEG, 2016).

***SDG 13: Climate Action:*** SDG 13's main objective is to fight climate change and take urgent action. The sample targets are the integration of climate change actions in the national policies and planning. Employ the commitment to mobilize climate finances for developing countries. The sample indicator is the total number of greenhouse gas emissions per year (IAEG, 2016).

***SDG 14: Life Below Water:*** The objective is to conserve and sustainably use the oceans, seas, and marine resources for sustainable development. The sample targets are reducing marine pollution, protecting and restoring ecosystems, and ending overfishing. The sample indicator is the percentage of the research budget allocated to marine technology research (IAEG, 2016).

***SDG 15: Life on Land:*** The objective is to protect, restore, and promote sustainable use of terrestrial ecosystems, sustainably manage forests, combat desertification, halt and reverse land degradation, and halt biodiversity loss. The sample targets are ensuring conservation of terrestrial and inland freshwater ecosystems and promoting sustainable forest management. The sample indicator is the forest area as a proportion of the total land area (IAEG, 2016).

***SDG 16: Peace, Justice, and Strong Institutions*:** The objective of SDG 16 is to promote peaceful and inclusive societies for sustainable development, make justice accessible to all, and develop institutions at all levels that are accountable and inclusive. The sample targets are to substantially reduce all types of violence and related deaths everywhere. At the national and international level, promoting the rule of law. The sample indicator is the number of intentional homicide victims per 100,000 population, by sex and age (IAEG, 2016).

***SDG 17: Partnerships for the Goals:*** The SDG 17 objective is to strengthen the means of implementation and revive the global partnership for sustainable development. The sample targets are strengthening national resource mobilization, involving international support for developing countries, to enhance domestic tax capacity and other means for collecting revenue. Another target is to mobilize additional finances for developing countries. The sample indicator is the total government revenue as a proportion of GDP by source (IAEG, 2016).

## 5. ROLE OF I4.0 IN ACHIEVING SUSTAINABLE DEVELOPMENT GOALS

The adoption of I4.0 serves as a critical enabler for achieving the SDGs. A key example is cloud computing, which directly tackles inequality (SDG 10). By facilitating real-time remote collaboration, it democratizes access to jobs and education, eliminating geographical and socio-economic barriers (Polyviou et al., 2023). This shift away from physical commutes also reduces carbon emissions. Simultaneously, cloud-based systems provide digital infrastructure for transparent, real-time monitoring of SDG indicators. This capability strengthens accountability and fosters the global partnerships essential for implementation, directly supporting SDG 17.

In this section, we provide an overview of in what ways I4.0 is contributing towards the achievement of SDGs through its core technologies like IoT, AI, data analytics, and machine learning in sustainable manufacturing, supply chain management, energy, infrastructure development, financial inclusion and fintech, and waste management.

## 5.1 Sustainable Manufacturing

I4.0 support in optimization of resource utilization by propelling advancement in industry, innovation, and infrastructure (SDG 9) that not only reduces waste but also improves the production efficiency (Ghobakhloo et al., 2021). Real-time monitoring and control are the advent of I4.0, leading to smart manufacturing processes and optimizing energy consumption. The shift from traditional to smart manufacturing paradigm aligns the industry with the SDGs of responsible consumption (SDG 12) and clean energy (SDG 7). I4.0 facilitates fast access to information in various manufacturing stages using big data analytics. The practices, including informed decision making and data-driven, promote climate action (SDG 13) and industry, innovation, and infrastructure (SDG 9). Furthermore, I4.0 advances remote environmental sensing to monitor the environmental regulations, assisting the industries to address climate change (SDG 13), sustain marine biodiversity (SDG 14), and conserve terrestrial ecosystems (SDG 15). I4.0 globally transforms the industries using technologies including artificial intelligence, the internet of things, automation, big data, and smart manufacturing, thereby reducing the technology gap and promoting global cooperation to achieve SDG 17.

Mabkhot et al., (2021) examine that the productivity of the industries can be increased through real-time data, which facilitates immediate and speedy information dissemination and the assessment process. I4.0 introduced a synthesized framework of technological advancement consisting of IoT, AI, and data analytics for the manufacturing processes. Real-time data is used to monitor and manage the production processes instantaneously, resulting in high productivity, less downtime, and improved informed decision-making. Real-time data facilitates proactive maintenance of manufacturing equipment. Moreover, sensors and monitoring tools are the source to anticipate any problems regarding the state of machinery before they lead to downtime. Predictive maintenance not only reduces costs but also increases the overall efficacy of equipment for responsible production and consumption (SDG 12).

However, sustainable manufacturing has notable barriers. Achouch et al., (2022) have reviewed models and challenges in the implementation of I4.0 and suggested that the technological advancement processes need heavy investment in upfront cost, a giant obstacle in the digitalization of industries, especially at the small and medium levels. Similarly, AI infrastructure, including data centers and automated machinery, consumes significant energy resources, deteriorating the environment. Workforce replacement, downsizing, and capacity building to upgrade the skills of labor are also significant challenges that need to be addressed to gain the potential benefits of sustainable manufacturing to the maximum extent.

## 5.2 Sustainable Supply Chain Management

At present, organizations are focusing on the maintenance of eco-friendly supply chain practices to align strategic goals with SDGs (Raman et al., 2023). Bocken et al., (2019) recognizes that conventional supply chain management is not supportive of attaining sustainable objectives. The findings of the study support that digitalization in the industrial era is crucial to sustainable growth targets. Industry 4, along with its embedded practices including automated reality, virtual reality, blockchain technology, big data, and internet of things, provides timely information about real-time visibility of materials in warehouse management for informed and prompt decision making. Chauhan & Singh (2020) investigate that manager's need for timely and complete information about the location, inventory level, shipment details, and product identification. It means warehouse management is a holistic approach to supervise the stock movement efficiently and optimize the daily operations of the warehouse facility. (Birkel & Müller, 2021) propose that I4.0 focuses on triple bottom line sustainability principles covering social, economic, and environmental dynamics to promote resource-efficient and environmentally responsible supply chain systems. Despite all these advantages, the integration between I4.0 and warehouse management is limited to a nascent stage (Beltrami et al., 2021).

The unified and transparent supply chains are the essential constituents of I4.0. Real-time data gives access to supply chain managers regarding stock movements, stock levels, shipment details, and market response, thereby enabling the objectives of lowered waste levels, advanced sustainability, and streamlined logistics to be achieved. Real-time data based upon responsible production and consumption prioritizing sustainable manufacturing methods, maximum resource utilization, and efficient waste management, leading to managing climate health (SDG 13). However, the heavy reliance on large data sets for efficient production planning is the biggest challenge for developing countries where data is unavailable, unreliable, or fragmented (Alalawneh & Alkhatib, 2021).

Moreover, IoT, one of the technology innovations in I4.0, manages the supply chain transparency, ensuring real-time in and out of the commodities from the warehouse. Supply chain network, accompanied by fair practices, including labor activities, decent production, and responsible sourcing supports the development of an honest career progression system (Lopez-Vargas et al., 2020). The transparent career advancement system initiates new job opportunities and skill sets, enhancing decent work and economic growth (SDG 8).

## 5.3 Sustainable Energy

The role of innovation, digital transformation, and automation has been redesigned with the arrival of I4.0, and this industry has introduced the modern era of all the stated transformations. (Personal et al., 2020). The old ways of using energy have been replaced with several modern ways to enhance energy efficiency, and previous processes of renewable energy solutions have been replaced with modern ones on account of innovation. (Pina et al., 2019). The global energy demand is continuously increasing despite several strategies to minimize energy usage, which is highly alarming for the atmosphere (Personal et al., 2020b). The I4.0 solutions have been proven to be a powerful partner to manage and minimize the consumption of energy at the global level. Energy transition and I4.0 both have the same concerns and help in handling energy issues. Thus, help the practitioners in achieving the SDG 7 and SDG 9, which are clean, cheap, and affordable, and innovation, industry, and infrastructure, eventually leading towards sustainable energy. Sustainable energy, which comes from naturally replenishing sources, can lead to the sustainability of the world and can protect the environment (Nastasi et al., 2022). It is also known as renewable energy or clean energy. Sustainable energy is needed to solve environmental problems, slow down climate change, and ensure sustainable energy security. There are several types of such energy, such as hydrogen energy, Biomass, wind energy, wave energy, solar energy, and geothermal energy. To boost environmental consciousness, innovation, and efficiency, sustainable energy and I4.0 both are connected and imperative in achieving the SDGs.

The accuracy of the output of renewable energy can be anticipated by utilizing AI. To estimate and forecast the energy outputs generated from wind and solar sources, machine learning models are utilized. Additionally, large data, consumption patterns, and many other variables can also be forecasted by using machine learning. Thus, it helps in balancing the demand and supply data with more accuracy (Zhang et al., 2022). Therefore, it is concluded that to enhance overall efficiency and energy sustainability forecasting patterns in energy usage and optimization of energy storage, AI can play a vital role (SDG7).

## 5.4 Sustainable Infrastructure Development

Industry transformation and modernization emphasize boosting a resilient infrastructure, innovation, and promoting continuous and inclusive industrialization (Djalante et al., 2020). It is necessary to invest in infrastructure, e.g., transport, energy, and communication, for reaching SDGs and empowering economies. To encounter economic challenges, it is necessary that not only developing but also developed countries must have access to the Internet so that they can provide solutions to the challenges, aligning with the SGD 9 (Mabkhot et al., 2021). To enhance energy resources and to achieve environmental objectives, technological advances are imperative. Thus, innovative solutions and technological advancement are important in boosting industrialization, and in the absence of both factors, development and efficiency are hard to achieve (Bai et al., 2020). Therefore, it is necessary to provide efficient infrastructure to both developed and developing countries so that SDG 9 could be achieved, which is resilient infrastructure, sustainable and inclusive industrialization.

An updated and efficient infrastructure design could be achieved by using large-scale data analysis through AI. It helps in accomplishing transit networks, highways, and efficient planning and development structures. This also aids in better consumption of resources, shields the environment, and advances overall sustainability (SDG 9). Additionally, traffic management systems, such as maximized pollutants, hardships of traffic, and complicated flows, can be controlled with AI-powered traffic management and control systems (Mhlanga, 2021). By utilizing intelligent transport, sustainable urban growth can be achieved, which can address the existing difficulties of infrastructure (SDG 11).

## 5.5 Financial Inclusion and Fintech

Industrial Revolution 4.0 brought digital innovation in finance and introduced the concept of "FinTech" as a smart system in the field of finance (Machkour & Abriane, 2020). Fin Tech is the portmanteau of two words, finance and technology, connecting finance with automation and data analytics. Fin tech is a modular technological network having software, apps, and other digital tools that assist in transforming conventional finance into digital finance. Digital finance incorporates smart tools, including digital payments, blockchain and cryptocurrencies, peer-to-peer lending, Robo advisors, Insurtech, Regtech, mobile banking and apps, financial inclusion solutions, artificial intelligence, and machine learning in financial transactions. The mechanism to provide easy access to useful and affordable information about financial products and services to businesses and individuals originated the concept of financial inclusion. The basic elements of financial inclusion are banking facilities, borrowing and lending services, coverage plans, a digital payment system, saving schemes, investment instruments, and financial literacy programs (Krishnan et al., 2012). These financial practices support the people and companies in meeting their requirements for financial transactions, savings, and risk management responsibly and sustainably.

Fintech promotes digital distance learning, encouraging easy access to academic materials and offering an online payment mode for school learning. Moreover, digital payment systems, along with blockchain technology, support streamlining financial transactions and enhancing accountability in water management practices. The integrated network of fintech technologies with digital payment modes and online job boards develops the Gig economy, amplifying easy access to money for employees. The transformation of conventional financial modes to smart tone associates all the SDGs in three ways: first, by inventing auxiliary financial support; second, by more efficiently utilizing current and prospective financial funding; and lastly, by completely backing success (Arner et al., 2020).

Based on the above, it can be argued that financial inclusion is a powerful tool to implement various SDGs (Danladi et al., 2023). Fintech serves as a source to grant access to financial intermediaries and economic avenues, providing virtual banking and electronic financial services to marginalized and privileged communities (Arner et al., 2020). Therefore, the access of financial services to the poor directly supports the goal of eradicating poverty (SDG 1) by helping them to stabilize consumption and build assets (Danladi et al., 2023). Financial inclusion acts as a tool to reduce poverty, especially in marginalized areas of the economy, providing useful and affordable information about investment, saving, and making money to firms and individuals. Moreover, firms support economic growth through participating in capital accumulation, entrepreneurship opportunities, and novel job prospects. Financial inclusion makes societies resilient to economic shocks, leading to discrimination against income inequality among individuals. Women's empowerment can be improved by assisting them to play an active role in the economy through advancing in accumulating assets, leading to support for gender equality (Kara et al., 2021).

Financial inclusion is also linked with ending hunger (SDG 2), as the objective of this SDG is to double the productivity and incomes of small-scale food producers by 2030, enhancing food security (Danladi et al., 2023). Agricultural fintech solutions made it possible for farmers to have up-to-date information regarding weather prediction and effective payment methods, ensuring food security to a maximum extent. Non-privileged communities in rural areas are facilitated through telemedicine and mobile health applications to perform secure and effective healthcare transactions (Arner et al., 2020). Financial inclusion in the agricultural sector encourages farmers and rural communities to buy inputs, use eco-friendly farming methods, and get credit for agricultural practices, leading to improved productivity to achieve self-sufficiency in the field of crop production. Green funding, one of the components of financial inclusion, supports investments in sustainable climate projects. Additionally, it also facilitates the water infrastructure projects for the provision of clean water and sanitary amenities (Kara et al., 2021).

Financial inclusion is also linked with good health and well-being (SDG 3) as it can help reduce delays in seeking medical care and relieve the stress caused by economic hardship. Similarly, the impact of financial inclusion on gender equality (SDG 5) is in the form of specific reforms that empower women economically by guaranteeing women equal rights to economic resources and financial tools. Finally, financial inclusion leads to sustained and inclusive economic growth and decent work (SDG 8) by strengthening domestic financial institutions and expanding access to banking, insurance, and credit for all (Danladi et al., 2023).

Contrasting these benefits, Madiha (2025) asserts that digital financial services increase the risks of cybersecurity, sensitive financial data breaches, and algorithm errors that may affect I4.0 negatively. The financial threats of Fintech not only leak private information but also lower the trust in digital financial networks, leading to disturbing the smart operations and automated systems. Additionally, overreliance on digital platforms for online transfer of payments and deposits also affects small enterprises that have no access to digital devices. One of the problems that every developing country must be facing due to Fintech and I4.0 integration is the regulatory and compliance challenge to avoid anti-money laundering, creating legal issues across countries.

## 5.6 Waste Management System

The control system of unwanted material is known as waste management, starting from the generation to the ultimate disposal (Sheng et al., 2020). The growing amount of waste produced by the country requires the development of landfills, which complicates the quest by the communities to achieve sustainable land use (Hantoko et al., 2020; Rafey & Siddiqui, 2023). The introduction of I4.0 practices, including the Internet of Things, communication, and information, would result in a transformative approach to developing the Transnational Waste Framework in a competent and operative way (Lee et al., 2023). Waste management Integration of IOT, communication, and information involves the application of distributed sensing and data fusion, advanced analytics, and intelligent decision processes in changing waste management practices (Sheng et al., 2020). This integration will allow Continuous monitoring and real-time tracking of waste operations, and this will result in more efficient and integrated waste management strategies. It also enables the transformation of the large and intricate waste features into meaningful resources, materials, and energy (Lee et al. 2023). The waste handling system developed based on I4.0 smart solutions can contribute to the SDG 3 (good health and wellness), SDG 6 (hygienic water and sanitation), SDG 8 (positive work and economic growth), SDG 12 (sustainable consumption and construction), and SDG 13 (climate action). E.g., intelligent solutions with references to IoT implemented in the sanitation sphere should be used to enhance the efficiency of garbage collection and processing. Waste collection routes can be streamlined to minimize fuel consumption, and empty dumpsters with rubbish can be cleared in time.

Contrary to this Lahane et al., (2026) evaluate the obstacles for the medical waste reverse logistics and found that countries, while transforming their waste system with the existing legacy system, are facing critical challenges, including high-speed internet, cloud computing, and data storage systems. Moreover, sensors and monitoring systems in I4.0 generate a lot of data at one time. It is very difficult to manage the data due to an unskilled workforce. The waste management system would be efficient if the data were efficiently utilized for waste tracking and reduction; otherwise, heavy investment in waste management systems would not be beneficial. Similarly, infrastructure advancement is not the same across regions; the unequal adoption of digital divide is the main hindrance leading to imposing limitations on waste management systems. Besides these limitations, the waste management system has a positive impact in the agricultural field as well.

There are over 8 billion people who live in this world. The World Food Program estimated that approximately 768 million people faced food insecurity in 2020. The food waste in 2022 was enough to feed 828 million hungry people, and three billion people who cannot afford a healthy diet (Balan et al., 2023). I4.0. helps the farmer to enjoy the benefits by implementing smart farming practices; hence, they can also achieve the goal of ending poverty by adopting these practices, e.g., minimizing waste and maximizing output. Researchers and practitioners are using real-time data for actions and analysis and are continuously monitoring the crop's status, weather patterns, and soil quality.

Agriculture has increased, and billions of gallons of water and gigawatts of power have been saved by using this strategy. The farm holders can evade the spread of disease and shield their animals' health by adopting IoT technology for livestock care and monitoring (Rehman et al., 2022). It has been estimated that more than 1.2 million deaths per year occur due to not having access to clean water. The IoT can significantly help in achieving the goal of supplying healthy and clean water to everyone by reducing waste, improving the quality of water, and suggesting creative water solutions. According to Irannezhad et al., (2022) the proficiencies of IoT, near field communication, and mobile money technology altogether can provide running water solutions and a clean water supply (SDG 6).

## 5.7 I4.0 and SGDs Mapping

Based on the above discussion, Table 5.1 shows the mapping of I4.0 and corresponding SDGs. This mapping shows which SDGs are implemented through sustainable manufacturing, sustainable supply chain management, sustainable energy, sustainable infrastructure development, fintech, and waste management via I4.0 smart technologies like IoT, AI, data analytics, and machine learning.

*Table 1. I4.0 and SGDs Mapping*

| SDG | Goal | Sustainable Manufacturing | Sustainable Supply Chain Management | Sustainable Energy | Sustainable Infrastructure Development | Fintech | Waste Management |
|---|---|---|---|---|---|---|---|
| SDG 1 | No poverty | | | | | ● | |
| SDG 2 | Zero hunger | | | | | ● | |
| SDG 3 | Good health & well-being | | | | | ● | |
| SDG 4 | Quality education | | | | | | |
| SDG 5 | Gender equality | | | | | ● | |
| SDG 6 | Clean water & sanitation | | | | | | ● |
| SDG 7 | Affordable & clean energy | ● | | ● | | | |
| SDG 8 | Decent work & economic growth | | ● | | | ● | ● |
| SDG 9 | Industry, innovation & infrastructure | ● | | ● | ● | | |
| SDG 10 | Reduced inequalities | | | | | | |
| SDG 11 | Sustainable cities & communities | | | | ● | | |
| SDG 12 | Responsible consumption & production | ● | | | | | ● |
| SDG 13 | Climate action | ● | ● | | | | ● |
| SDG 14 | Life below water | ● | | | | | |
| SDG 15 | Life on land | ● | | | | | |
| SDG 16 | Peace, justice & strong institutions | | | | | | |
| SDG 17 | Partnerships for the Goals | ● | | | | | |

Note: ● Sustainable Manufacturing, ● Sustainable Supply Chain Management, ● Sustainable Energy, ● Sustainable Infrastructure Development, ● Fintech, ● Waste Management

Source: Author's Own Construction

The I4.0 and SDGs mapping shows that sustainable manufacturing emerged as the broadest contributor, spanning environmental, social, and economic SDGs simultaneously, while fintech demonstrated a targeted but transformative role in advancing financial inclusion, reducing inequality, and empowering marginalized populations through digital financial services. Waste management and sustainable supply chain management showed strong alignment with the environmental SDG 13, confirming I4.0's capacity to operationalize circular economy principles on a scale. Sustainable energy helps in achieving economic growth targets and climate commitments most directly through SDG 7 and SDG 9.

## 6. EXAMPLE CASES

In the following section, we present examples of organizations and communities using I4.0 technologies to achieve SDGs.

### 6.1 AI-Powered Water Purification in Achieving SDG 6

The use of I4.0, mostly Artificial Intelligence (AI), in water purification systems has significantly contributed to the attainment of SDG 6, ensuring the presence and sustainable use of water and cleanliness for all. The use of AI in the data analysis aspect, predictive models, and automation has transformed the traditional process of handling water, thus making it more competent, economical, and scalable (Ajith et al., 2025; Zou et al., 2025). The incorporation of AI into the sphere of water management not only solves the existing problems but also opens the path towards innovative solutions to future water-related problems. In the following section, we demonstrate how the I4.0 technologies, especially AI, have changed the SDG 6 progress and helped in providing clean water and sanitation to everyone by increasing the efficiency, scalability, and sustainability of water purification systems.

### 6.2 CHRIST Osmotron Water Purification System.

The CHRIST Osmotron system uses AI-based anomaly detection to ensure the quality of the water in the pharmaceutical industry, in which high-purity water is required. Sensors and data mining techniques helped the researchers to detect faults in the system, and thus, faults were identified earlier to be maintained. This method not only guarantees conformance to high standards of water quality but also lowers the operation costs and improves pharmaceutical product safety (Garmaroodi et al., 2021).

### 6.3 An AquaFeL-PSO Monitoring System

AquaFeL-PSO is a system that operates autonomous surface vehicles monitoring water resources with sensors on water quality and AI algorithms. The system is an efficient mapping of contamination areas and forecasting the pollution peaks by using multimodal Particle Swarm Optimization (PSO) and Federated Learning. This technology has been shown to improve the water quality modeling by 400 percent and the ability to detect pollution anomalies by 4000 percent, hence making it easy to make timely interventions to preserve water resources (Garmaroodi et al., 2021).

## 6.4 ACWA Cyber-Physical Testbed

The AI and Cyber for Water and Agriculture (ACWA) testbed is an all-encompassing testbed that combines AI, cybersecurity, and cyber-physical systems to tackle the issue of water management. It has a digital twin simulator of water distribution systems and uses AI models to optimize the supply of water and identify anomalies. The open-access data and simulation tools provided by ACWA are useful in the research and development of intelligent water systems to foster sustainable water management practices (Batarseh et al., 2023).

## 6.5 AquaSight Mobile Application

The AquaSight is a mobile application using Convolutional Neural Networks (CNNs) to identify pollution in water through the analysis of images of water samples. The application was trained on 105 images, and with this training, it was able to recognize the level of contamination with 96 percent accuracy. Being a low-cost solution, this empowers individuals and communities to determine the quality of water and take immediate measures to curb health risks that come with the use of contaminated water sources (Gupta & Ruebush, 2019).

## 6.6 Autonomous Water Treatment System

It has developed an autonomous water treatment system, which is designed to solve challenging severe contamination issues in areas that have a limited water infrastructure. This system is a mixture of mechanical and chemical treatment, real-time measurements, and automation based on AI technology to treat ponds, rivers, and artificially contaminated water. The design has a high level of efficiency in terms of operation, where it requires little manual involvement, which makes it a viable tool in addressing global water security in the world (Guth & Herák, 2025). The AI-powered water purification project specifically contributes to SDG 6, which deals with pure water and sanitation through better quality of water, sanitation, and equivalent access to all. Several lessons can be derived from the case study, such as the significance of AI with sensor-based systems to make better and real-time decisions. Secondly, AI-based low-cost solutions. Third, accurate prediction of system failure and projection of new plans (Dinh, 2025).

## 6.7 Industry 4 in Siemens

Siemens Power Generation specializes in the repair and maintenance of steam turbines and engines, providing operational services to power plants. The primary goal of Siemens was to offer the product to the customers. With the passage of time, the company realized that the strategic goal "to offer" should be replaced with "to deliver value "to the customers. To achieve this innovation journey, the company needed to make a series of changes to transform the traditional production system into a value-oriented model. The client-focused approach of the company is intended to develop project teams, sustain a cross-departmental information framework, and to advance the digital model to ensure customized products for the customers. These infrastructural changes required a huge investment in the technological platform of Siemens. The focus of the company was to integrate the personnel with technological advancement to ensure seamless operational performance.

Siemens had to face various obstacles to transform the traditional production approach (Elgadafi, 2025). The first issue was that digital databases could not collaborate with document contributors, which compromised the standard of knowledge dissemination. The second one was a constrained social network that curtailed the transfer of interpersonal knowledge and affected Siemens' innovation system (Karanam et al., 2024). Moreover, there was a need to design a multi-dimensional model to mitigate the problems of capital adequacy, obsolete production infrastructure, assimilation of digital innovations, employee reluctance, and sustainable customer relationships.

The company transformed its revenue strategy and focused on generating recurring revenue streams. The company used to sign contracts that reduced upfront capital requirements, promoting the disbursement of capital repayments over a period (Буряк et al., 2024). Siemens started to manage long term service agreements, thereby earning revenue through performance-based contracts, maintenance, and life cycle services. Furthermore, incentive-based contracts in Siemens assisted in payments from clients through the provision of services.

Siemens integrated turbines and energy systems digitally and introduced digital twin technology, Mind Sphere, and an IoT platform. The digital technology in the Company not only replaced traditional physical products with data-driven services but also promoted remote surveillance and proactive maintenance (Al-Shetwi et al., 2025). Advanced technology in Siemens concentrated on value creation rather than hardware offerings, leading to overcoming the constraints of the legacy system. However, Siemens contracted with the Umm AI Houl power plant in Qatar based on risk-sharing financing, allowing the Company to distribute the burden of upfront payment over a period.

Siemens adopted multifaceted strategies emphasizing value creation for customers and facilitated the practices, including life cycle management, financing alternatives, and customized energy solutions (Tazhibayev et al., 2025). These strategies assisted in transforming the conception of customers from energy equipment suppliers to energy solution partners, winning the trust of customers and maintaining an enduring relationship with them.

Another big challenge was organizational restructuring that Siemens faced to integrate technology with the workforce (Malynovska et al., 2025). The Organizational redesign mitigated the problem of resistance to change; the company was facing its workforce. Additionally, capacity building enabled the employees to seamlessly adopt digital systems. The experiential learning approach aligned human resources with the strategic goal of a service-oriented approach.

The Siemens case study directly aligns with SDG 7, which is inexpensive clean energy, SDG 8, which deals with decent work and economic growth (Jaiswal et al., 2025), SDG 9, which discusses industry infrastructure and innovation, and SDG 12, which is the sustainable use and production of resources (Nazibudin et al., 2025). Several lessons can be learned from the Siemens case study, such as the conversion of products based to a value-based system. Secondly, the need for digital technologies such as IoT to achieve sustainability and growth. Thirdly, the need for capacity building and organizational restructuring (Olanrewaju et al., 2025).

## 6.8 General Electric and Industry 4 in the United States

General Electric in the United States integrated a digital framework and aligned data analytics, machine learning solutions, and smart networks to overcome the anticipated issues. The new organizational design enhanced the savings of the Company to $500 million, along with reduced lead time. The company adopted a phased implementation strategy to manage costs effectively (Wasiu Dauda et al., 2024). Consequently, the company modernized its industrial processes to meet the sustainable goals of industry, innovation, and infrastructure. Digital monitoring and predictive maintenance enhanced efficiency in the manufacturing process while reducing carbon emissions. As a result, the company attained the sustainable objectives of responsible consumption and production, as well as climate action (Omol, 2024).

General Electric's use of I4.0 technologies links with SDG8, SDG9, SDG12, and SDG13 (Kartal et al., 2025; Olanrewaju et al., 2025). The lessons derived from this include: first, sequential implementation strategies are necessary to deal with operational and financial risks. Second, efficiency and smart decision-making can be achieved through data-driven decision-making. Third, environmental impacts can be controlled through predictive maintenance. Fourth, economic and environmental concerns can be achieved through digital transformation (Hermawan et al., 2025; Olanrewaju et al., 2025).

## 6.9 Industry 4 in Tata Consultancy Services: A Case Study

Tata Consultancy Services is one of the leading companies in the Tata group. It is established in 1968 and engaged in providing Global IT, consultancy, and business solution services in 46 countries. Its clients belong to various industries, including banking, health care, retail, telecom, and manufacturing. The company offers services in software development, AI, Cloud Computing, data analytics, and cybersecurity. The company has a workforce comprising more than 600,000 employees and uses the global delivery model to combine onsite and offshore teams to deliver efficient and high-quality services around the globe (Vikranth & Prasad, 2019). The mission of the Tata Consultancy Services is to work as a trusted global technology leader, Co integrated artificial intelligence in to human resource functions to achieve the strategic goals of deep expertise in HR, strong client relationship, high employee retention and a solid financial track record thereby sustainable goals of decent work and economic growth, innovation in infra-structure, quality education and employee wellbeing can be achieved (Karthikeyan, 2026).

Tata Consultancy Services began to use AI technologies, including machine learning for predictive hiring, natural language processing for resume parsing, virtual assistants for employee support, and robotic process automation for repetitive tasks. These AI proceedings supported the Tata Consultancy Services in improving efficiency, accuracy, and employee experience across HR operations. There by decision making is enhanced in the Co. Moreover, AI exposed the employees to personalized support, instant query resolution, and customized learning paths that contributed to motivation and retention, better workforce planning, and innovative HR strategies providing valuable services to clients around the globe efficiently (Swarna M et al., 2024).

Throughout this journey, the Company encountered various challenges such as algorithmic bias, data privacy concerns, resistance from employees, feelings of alienation among staff, fears of job displacement, and ethical dilemmas related to fairness, transparency, and accountability. Tata Consulting Services implemented MIRA as an AI tool for the automated screening of resumes. Neeraja et al., (2024) surveyed within Tata Consultancy Services to evaluate the effectiveness and challenges associated with this practice in the Company. The survey results reveal that 78% of respondents believe that AI has expedited the recruitment process within the Company, 72% recognized that MIRA contributed to an improved candidate experience, 65% indicated that job-skill matching has enhanced, 60% acknowledged better workforce planning, and 52% agreed that the system has mitigated bias in the hiring process, thereby achieving sustainable goals such as decent work, innovation in infrastructure, quality education, employee well-being, and gender equality.

The survey revealed several challenges: 40% of the respondents expressed uncertainty about the transparency of AI algorithms. Additionally, 60% identified a lack of AI expertise among HR staff, 50% raised concerns about data privacy, 55% stated a fear of technology and demonstrated resistance to change, 42% acknowledged the high implementation cost to implement AI practices or systems within Tata Consultancy Services.

In response to these challenges, Tata Consulting Services initiated technical training, designed a framework of ethical standards, and developed clear communication strategies to integrate AI practices with HR effectively. The technical training demonstrated how AI tools perform HR functions, including recruitment and performance evaluation, thereby building the trust of employees (Crasta & V. T., 2021). Moreover, practical training to HR teams regarding the use of AI tools and analytics increased employee awareness about AI benefits, reduced the fear of change among the employees, and motivated them to adapt to the evolving pace of the world. The implementation of ethical standards with ethical audit practices enforced strong ethical guidelines that prevented bias, discrimination, and data misuse, ensuring transparency in the system. Additionally, Tata Consulting Services aligned protection measures that comply with global standards for data privacy and security (Tiwari, 2025).

The Co ensures that AI practices assist the human but does not replace human judgment in sensitive decision matters. Tata Consultancy used KPI's for regular monitoring regarding hiring efficiency and employee satisfaction, ensuring continuous improvement in an artificial intelligence drive. This case aligns with SDG 4, SDG 5, SDG 8, and SDG 9 (Bian et al., 2025; Fura et al., 2025). The key lessons learned include: first, HR efficiency and employee skills can be enhanced through proper implementation of AI. Second, for critical AI implementation, transparency, ethical consideration, and bias mitigation are necessary. Third, to minimize resistance to technology, formal training and change management are essential. These conclusions suggest that for the adoption of I4.0, social dimensions and sustainability are important (Chango-Cañaveral et al., 2025).

## 6.10 Nature-Based Wastewater Treatment in Faisalabad, Pakistan

A nature-based wastewater treatment system was introduced in Khurrianwala, a well-known industrialized area of Faisalabad, Pakistan, to deal with environmental challenges arising from textile wastes. Due to having a center of textile production, a high volume of water wastage has been generated in this area. The wastage normally contains high amounts of organic loads, dyes, chemicals, and heavy metals. This nature-based treatment contains environmentally friendly and low-cost purification procedures. The multi-stage system will start with anaerobic digestion that will decrease the organic contents of the wastewater by microbial action without the presence of oxygen, in effect, reducing the biological oxygen demand (BOD) and chemical oxygen demand (COD). Subsequently, there is the use of floating treatment wetlands (FTWs) in which the aquatic plants like vetiver and water hyacinth are cultivated in floating rafts, and then the roots absorb nutrients and pollutants, and various microbial communities are supported to decompose the contaminants. The effluent is then treated in the constructed wetlands, artificial ecosystems that contain gravel and indigenous wetland plants that promote further filtration, uptake of the nutrients, and putrefaction of the remnant pollutants, including heavy metals. The last process is sand filtration, which eliminates small, suspended particles and boosts the purity of the water being treated. The major characteristic of this system is that bio-enrichment is built in, wherein locally isolated bacterial strains, which can degrade textile-specific pollutants, are added so that the system can be more efficient. The interaction of these natural processes led to a considerable decrease in total suspended solids (TSS), BOD, COD, and heavy metals, which proves that the method is not only effective but also can be adjusted to other industrial sectors with a minimum of infrastructure. The pilot in Faisalabad depicts the possibility of scalable, sustainable, and decentralized wastewater treatment systems that are properly suitable to the socio-economic and environmental settings of industrial areas in developing countries (Siddique et al., 2025).

Nature-Based Wastewater Treatment in Faisalabad case study linked with the SDG 3, SDG6, SDG11, SDG12, SDG13 (Hahladakis, 2025) and SDG 13 (Göçoğlu et al., 2025). The important lessons learned included: First, cost-effective and alternative solutions are possible through nature-based solutions and I4.0 technology. Second, from the perspective of developing countries, local and decentralized systems are effective. Third, system accuracy and effectiveness can be achieved through technological monitoring.

Case studies have been used to point to successful implementations of I4.0 but are not broadly applicable. Most of them, e.g., the cases with Siemens and General Electric, are in the developed economies with powerful infrastructure and institutional background, which makes their reproduction in the developing regions rather difficult because of the financial, technical, and governance issues. Such situations are, in most cases, best-case scenarios, which can produce positive bias and ignore failures, delays, and trade-offs such as job displacement and ethical issues. Furthermore, a lot of solutions are situation-specific and demand adaptation to the local conditions. As such, the implementation of I4.0 to SDGs cannot be blindly copied but necessitates situational measures, gradual implementation, and ongoing assessment instead of direct copying (Shabeer & Rasul, 2025).

## 7. LIMITATIONS AND CHALLENGES FOR INDUSTRY 4.0 AND SDGS NEXUS

The crucial factor in the implementation of I4.0 for sustainable development is the tradeoff between potential benefits and the critical challenges that may arise in the form of job displacement (SDG8), electronic waste (SDG12), and digital divide (SDG 10). Even though I4.0 technologies like AI, IoT, and big data promise a transformative potential, their actual effect on the realization of the SDGs is not uniform, particularly in developing nations (Azam Khan, 2025). Success relies on the main enabling factors such as digital infrastructures, institutional capacity, regulatory backing, and socio-economic preparedness (Zeb et al., 2025). Thus, I4.0 must be incorporated in a larger socio-technical paradigm, backed by governance, skill development, and ethical oversight (Umoru et al., 2026).

The idea that technology is the way to sustainability is too simply constructed to consider complex development issues. Smart manufacturing can be one example, engineering can become much more efficient, but might also lead to job loss, increased energy consumption, and digital divide, whereas fintech can lock out people who do not have access or are illiterate (Qudrat-Ullah, 2025). Simicevic (2025) argues that I4.0 practices, including AI, robotics, and automation in the manufacturing sector, may replace operational and low-skilled jobs, causing unemployment in the economy. Besides this, it would create a challenge of workforce restructuring because new jobs require up-skilling and reskilling of labor, especially in developing countries.

Dhar & Nandi (2026) discuss that I4.0 is considered one of the means responsible for electronic waste (SDG12). The use of smart technologies, detection devices, and cyber-physical systems has made the product life cycle short. The need to manage the increased risk of health arising due to the rapid disposal of electronic components is a critical threat that countries with I4.0 practices are experiencing these days.

Unequal access to advanced technologies is another emerging issue while implementing Industry 4. Digitalization is a crucial practice for the successful operationalization of I4.0, leading to exacerbating the digital divide (SDG10) on one side, while improving infrastructure, digital skills, and advanced technologies in the countries, but on the other side widens the gap between advanced and developing economies. This gap does not exist only between countries but is also spreading between socioeconomic groups within countries, leading to discrimination among sectors of the economy (Mwansa et al., 2025). Therefore, a balanced approach of technological adaptation is required that would consider the limitations and challenges of I4.0, along with its potential benefits.

One of the pronounced limitations that developing and developed countries face during the implementation of I4.0 is an inefficient governance framework and international collaboration (SDG 17). A proper regulatory mechanism is needed to address the negative outcomes of I4.0 practices. These undesirable results, including cyber threats, unethical use of artificial intelligence, network intrusions, and leakage of confidential information, are deteriorating the positive impacts of I4.0. Policy makers should develop a governance framework composed of rules, regulations, policies, and standards ensuring cybersecurity and effective monitoring of artificial intelligence. Governance mechanisms may act as a tool to implement firewalls to avoid cyber-attacks, unauthorized network access, and data breaches.

At the organizational level, there are constraints for the implementation of I4.0 and its integration with the SDGs. Mishra et al., (2025) used paradox theory to explain that organizations face tensions linked with digital transformation through I4.0 technologies, like whether to increase profit or to invest in digital technologies. Similarly, digitalization and resilience practices create conflicting situations regarding economic profit and environmental goals. Similarly, international collaboration, an essential prerequisite for the successful implementation of I4.0, is not efficient across countries. Global standards are needed for communication protocols and data exchange among organizations across borders for the smooth integration of technologies globally.

## 8. POLICY RECOMMENDATIONS

Industry 4 is considered a transformative force to accelerate progress for the development of SDGs. The integration of modern technologies that include AI, big data, the internet, and robotics to achieve SDGs is not as easy as it seems because technology alignment with SDGs encounters social, economic, and structural obstacles. Every nation, regardless of its development status, has faced unique challenges in the shift towards I4.0 while striving to meet SDGs. In developed nations, companies like Siemens in Germany and General Electric in the United States deal with structural challenges as well as social issues in aligning SDG 9 (industry, innovation, and infrastructure) with their existing legacy systems (Tasneem & Khan, 2024). Similarly, Tata Consultancy Services in a developing country has encountered numerous societal, financial, and infrastructural obstacles in the integration of AI practices with human resources to achieve sustainable objectives. Therefore, I4.0 revolution necessitates new policies and processes as it fundamentally merges the physical and digital worlds (Maresova et al., 2018). Therefore, in this section we present actionable recommendations that can accelerate the implementation of SDGs using I4.0 technologies.

## 8.1 Government and Private Sector Alliance

It is important to promote synergistic relationships between the government and private sector to hasten the implementation of I4.0 technologies to achieve SDGs. For example, water management can be significantly improved via such partnerships. Public-Private Partnerships (PPPs) can be formed to co-fund and co-develop smart water infrastructure projects. Such alliances can take advantage of innovation and efficiency in the private sector and are subject to oversight and accountability by the public sector (Selim & ElGohary, 2020).

Joint research initiatives that can promote government agency research, college research, and research at individual companies to create and test new I4.0 technologies to clean and distribute water. Introduce regulatory sandboxes where innovative technologies can be tested in the real world without regulatory effort and applied to innovate and adapt on a faster basis (Zetzsche et al., 2017). Shared Data platforms can be developed. e.g., developing open-source platforms upon which the community and individuals can share data on water quality, usage, and infrastructure performance to make informed decisions. For instance, in Singapore, the Public Utilities Board has been working with the private technology companies to design and install smart water management systems that have led to better efficiency and sustainability in water consumption (Fujii & Ray, 2021).

## 8.2 Digital Literacy and Infrastructure

It is important to improve digital literacy and make investments in infrastructure to provide equal access to I4.0 technologies to every community (Bravo et al., 2021). This can be achieved by adopting various steps. Digital literacy programs can be introduced at the countrywide level. Such digital literacy initiatives target rural and underserved areas to inform the population on how to use and maintain digital technologies like intelligent water pipes. Countries can invest in digital infrastructure development, such as broadband networks that would allow the internet to be reliable in remote locations. This can help the deployment and operation of I4 technologies such as IoT-based water management, which ultimately lead to the achievement of SDGs.

Similarly, capacity building is an extremely important factor. In this regard, training courses for the local technicians and engineers on the installation, servicing, and troubleshooting of the advanced technologies can be conducted. For example, the Kenya Smart Water Metering Project has enhanced the efficiency of delivering water to the community through training the local communities to manage and maintain smart meters, and this has resulted in less wastage of water and fair allocation to the community (Molu & Luketero, 2025). Lastly, the community should be involved in the planning and execution of the technology projects to ensure that the solutions are culturally sensitive and that they address the unique needs of the people.

## 8.3 Ethical Artificial Intelligence and Guidelines

Responsible digital transformation has now become essential for sustainable societies. AI has a significant potential to drive positive global change. However, it's not simple; there are complexities involved that should not be underestimated, as it requires balancing the intricate relationships among technological advancements, environmental sustainability, ethical considerations, and social impact. So, a holistic interdisciplinary approach should be adopted that can enable navigation of these challenges and help leverage digital technologies to foster a future that is more inclusive, equitable, and sustainable for everyone (Pappas et al., 2023).

AI has the potential to support the achievement of 134 targets across the SDGs, but at the same time, it poses a risk of hindering 59 others. For the successful implementation of SDGs, it is important to design and enforce ethical policies and regulatory mechanisms to regulate the application of AI that will ensure transparency, accountability, and equity. For this purpose, the ethical AI principles that reinforce fairness, transparency, accountability, and privacy should be embraced (Mhlanga, 2022). The ethical AI guiding principles should be followed during the development and implementation of AI systems to implement SDGs. Regulatory oversight can be used via the development of independent regulatory institutions to control the use of AI technologies and guarantee that the system is in line with the ethical standards and safeguard the interests of the people.

Putting in place effective data governance policies that govern ethical use, storage, and acquisition of data that place special consideration on individual privacy and misuse can be another major step. International cooperation and participation in international discussions and agreements to coordinate AI regulations and exchange best practices, initiating collaboration in global responsibility to use AI in successful implementation, can be helpful. The Artificial Intelligence Act by the European Union can be taken as an example because it is a comprehensive regulatory framework that categorizes AI applications by the level of risk and establishes the criteria of transparency and accountability, which can be followed in other regions.

## 8.4 Expanding Successful Pilot Projects

Designing regular evaluation structures to determine the effectiveness, scalability, and sustainability of pilot projects is important. For this purpose, funding arrangements can be made to facilitate the expansion of successful pilot projects, such as grants, loans, and investment incentives. Have supportive policies and incentives that will promote successful pilot projects, including incentives to municipalities and utilities to adopt proven technologies.

Establishing knowledge-sharing platforms can enable the transfer of knowledge and capacity building of stakeholders engaged in the different projects through the sharing of lessons learned, best practices, and technical resources. The Smart Water Management Pilot in India, an IoT-based water quality and delivery monitoring system, applied AI analytics to scale to other cities with great success, bringing about a substantial increase in water supply and quality (Singh & Goyal, 2025).

## 8.5 Industry 4.0 Adaptation to the Local Circumstances

Case studies have been used to point to successful implementations of I4.0 but are not broadly applicable. For example, cases like Siemens and General Electric are from developed economies with powerful infrastructure and institutional background, which makes their replicability in the developing regions difficult because of the financial, technical, and governance issues. Such situations are, in most cases, best-case scenarios, which can produce positive bias and ignore failures, delays, and trade-offs such as job displacement and ethical issues. Furthermore, a lot of solutions are situation-specific and demand adaptation to the local conditions. Therefore, it is recommended that the I4.0 technologies for SDGs implementation cannot be blindly copied but necessitate situational measures, gradual implementation, and ongoing assessment (Shabeer & Rasul, 2025).

## 8.6 Businesses and Industry Investment in I4.0 Technologies

This chapter highlighted that companies like Siemens have employed I4.0 technologies, which considerably improved performance. This implies that manufacturing companies should prioritise investment in IoT-enabled energy management, digital twins, and predictive maintenance platforms that simultaneously reduce operational costs and lower environmental footprints. Similarly, supply chain managers should accelerate the adoption of blockchain-based traceability systems that enhance transparency, reduce waste, and ensure ethical sourcing across global value chains. However, organisations should also keep in consideration the limitations and challenges of developing and integrating I4.0 technologies to improve sustainable performance. For this purpose, investment in internal capacity-building programmes that upskill workforces and embed social sustainability criteria into technology adoption decisions can be useful. Financial institutions should prioritise the design of inclusive digital financial products for marginalized populations, with particular attention to gender-responsive product design that addresses the documented barriers to female financial inclusion.

## 9. CONCLUSION

This study provides a comprehensive review of how I4.0 technologies lead progress toward the United Nations SDGs through six key implementation domains: sustainable manufacturing, sustainable supply chain management, sustainable energy, sustainable infrastructure development, fintech, and waste management. This chapter demonstrates that I4.0 technologies encompassing AI, IoTs, blockchain, and big data analytics function as systemic enablers of sustainable development rather than isolated technical tools. Our mapping of the I4.0 and SDGs nexus shows that sustainable manufacturing is the broadest contributor to the achievement of the SDGs, while fintech helps in the implementation of SDGs related to the reduction of poverty, inequality, and empowerment of marginalized populations. This chapter also highlights the challenges and limitations inherent in the I4.0-SDG nexus. The benefits of I4.0 adoption are not automatically realized without deliberate policy interventions. We discuss the real-world cases from developed to underdeveloped economies, showcasing that I4.0 can contribute to the achievement of the SDGs irrespective of the context if the enabling conditions exist. At the end, we also provide policy recommendations calling for all stakeholders across I4.0 and the SDG ecosystem to take actions that can facilitate and strengthen the technology and sustainability relationship, such as the government's establishing regulatory sandboxes, PPP, organizations' investment in I4.0 technological infrastructure, and its integration with SDGs and the ethical use of AI.

## REFERENCES


Буряк, М. О., Лисенко, С. М., & Шевченко, Р. О. (2024). Siemes Digital Transformation Case Study Towards Organizational Scale And Success In Electrical Engineering Industry. *Управління Змінами Та Інновації*, (11), 57–65. DOI: 10.32782/CMI/2024-11-9

Achouch, M., Dimitrova, M., Ziane, K., Sattarpanah Karganroudi, S., Dhouib, R., Ibrahim, H., & Adda, M. (2022). On Predictive Maintenance in Industry 4.0: Overview, Models, and Challenges. In *Applied Sciences (Switzerland)* (Vol. 12, Number 16). MDPI. DOI: 10.3390/app12168081

Ajith, S., Vijayakumar, S., & Elakkiya, N. (2025). Yield prediction, pest and disease diagnosis, soil fertility mapping, precision irrigation scheduling, and food quality assessment using machine learning and deep learning algorithms. *Discover Food*, *5*(1), 67. Advance online publication. DOI: 10.1007/s44187-025-00338-1

Al-Shetwi, A. Q., Hannan, M. A., Al-Masri, H. M. K., & Sujod, M. Z. (2025). Latest advancements in smart grid technologies and their transformative role in shaping the power systems of tomorrow: An overview. *Progress in Energy*, *7*(1), 012004. DOI: 10.1088/2516-1083/ada198

Alalawneh, A. A. F., & Alkhatib, S. F. (2021). The barriers to big data adoption in developing economies. *The Electronic Journal on Information Systems in Developing Countries*, *87*(1), e12151. Advance online publication. DOI: 10.1002/isd2.12151

Arner, D. W., Buckley, R. P., Zetzsche, D. A., & Veidt, R. (2020). Sustainability, FinTech and Financial Inclusion. *European Business Organization Law Review*, *21*(1), 7–35. DOI: 10.1007/s40804-020-00183-y

Azam Khan, M. (2025). Analyzing the effects of financial inclusion on poverty and income inequality in SAARC developing nations. In *Journal of the Asia Pacific Economy* (Vol. 30, Number 3, pp. 788–811). Routledge. DOI: 10.1080/13547860.2024.2361988

Bai, C., Dallasega, P., Orzes, G., & Sarkis, J. (2020). International Journal of Production Economics Industry 4. 0 technologies assessment : A sustainability perspective. *International Journal of Production Economics*, *229*, 107776. DOI: 10.1016/j.ijpe.2020.107776

Bai, C., Zhou, H., & Sarkis, J. (2023). Evaluating Industry 4.0 technology and sustainable development goals–a social perspective. *International Journal of Production Research*, *61*(23), 8094–8114. DOI: 10.1080/00207543.2022.2164375

Balan, I. M., Trasca, T. I., Brad, I., Belc, N., Tulcan, C., Radoi, B. P., & Rinovetz, A. E. (2023). *Approaches to Limiting Food Loss and Food Waste.*

Batarseh, F. A., Kulkarni, A., Sreng, C., Lin, J., & Maksud, S. (2023). ACWA: An AI-driven cyber-physical testbed for intelligent water systems. *Water Practice & Technology, 18*(12), 3399–3418. DOI: 10.2166/wpt.2023.197

Beltrami, M., Orzes, G., Sarkis, J., & Sartor, M. (2021). Industry 4. 0 and sustainability : Towards conceptualization and theory. *Journal of Cleaner Production, 312*, 127733. DOI: 10.1016/j.jclepro.2021.127733

Berawi, M. A. (2019). The role of industry 4.0 in achieving Sustainable Development Goals. *International Journal of Technology, 10*(4), 644–647. DOI: 10.14716/ijtech.v10i4.3341

Bian, J., Zhao, J., & Li, A. (2025). Remote sensing monitoring of mountain sustainable development goals (SDG15.4): a systematic review. In *International Journal of Digital Earth* (Vol. 18, Number 1). Taylor and Francis Ltd. DOI: 10.1080/17538947.2024.2448216

Birkel, H., & Müller, J. M. (2021). Potentials of industry 4. 0 for supply chain management within the triple bottom line of sustainability e A systematic literature review. *Journal of Cleaner Production, 289*, 125612. DOI: 10.1016/j.jclepro.2020.125612

Bocken, N., Boons, F., & Baldassarre, B. (2019). Sustainable business model experimentation by understanding ecologies of business models. *Journal of Cleaner Production, 208*, 1498–1512. DOI: 10.1016/j.jclepro.2018.10.159

Bravo, M. C. M., Chalezquer, C. S., & Serrano-Puche, J. (2021). Meta-framework of digital literacy: Comparative analysis of 21st century skills frameworks. *Revista Latina de Comunicacion Social, 2021*(79), 76–110. DOI: 10.4185/RLCS-2021-1508

Chango-Cañaveral, P. M., Quezada-Sarmiento, P. A., & Morales-Herrera, V. J. (2025). Analysis of Sustainable Development Goals (2016–2030) and Their Integration into Tourism Activities in Lago Agrio Canton, Sucumbíos Province: SDG 9 (Industry, Innovation, and Infrastructure) and SDG 15 (Life on Land). *Sustainability (Basel), 17*(13), 6023. Advance online publication. DOI: 10.3390/su17136023

Chauhan, C., & Singh, A. (2020). *A review of Industry 4 . 0 in supply chain management studies. 31*(5), 863–886. DOI: 10.1108/JMTM-04-2018-0105

Crasta, L. C., & Shailashri, V. T. (2021). A comprehensive study of talent management process adopted by tata consultancy services (TCS). International Journal of Case Studies in Business [IJCSBE]. *IT and Education, 5*(1), 267–281.

Danladi, S., Prasad, M. S. V., Modibbo, U. M., Ahmadi, S. A., & Ghasemi, P. (2023). Attaining Sustainable Development Goals through Financial Inclusion: Exploring Collaborative Approaches to Fintech Adoption in Developing Economies. *Sustainability (Basel), 15*(17), 13039. Advance online publication. DOI: 10.3390/su151713039

Dhar, A., & Nandi, D. (2026). Exploring the Effects of Electronic Waste: A Comprehensive Study of Production, Management, and Health Risks in India. In *International Journal of Environmental Research* (Vol. 20, Number 1). Springer Science and Business Media Deutschland GmbH. DOI: 10.1007/s41742-025-00984-4

Dinh, L. Q. (2025). Is There a Trade-Off Between Sustainable Development Goals Achievement and Banking Profitability? Evidence From Combined Non-Parametric Methods. *Natural Resources Forum*. DOI: 10.1111/1477-8947.70036

Djalante, R., Shaw, R., & Dewit, A. (2020). Progress in Disaster Science Building resilience against biological hazards and pandemics : COVID-19 and its implications for the Sendai Framework. *Progress in Disaster Science, 6*, 100080. DOI: 10.1016/j.pdisas.2020.100080

Ebolor, A., Agarwal, N., & Brem, A. (2022). Fostering the Sustainable Development Goals with technologies underpinned by frugal innovation. *International Journal of Technology Management, 88*(2–4), 155–174. DOI: 10.1504/IJTM.2022.121503

Elgadafi, A. E. (2025). Overcoming Digital Transformation Challenges in Traditional Manufacturing Industries. *International Journal for Multidisciplinary Research, 7*(4), 52191. www.ijfmr.com. DOI: 10.36948/ijfmr.2025.v07i04.52191

FUJII. T., & RAY, R. (2021). Singapore as a Sustainable City: Past, present, and the future. In *The Singapore Economy: Dynamism and Inclusion*. DOI: 10.4324/9780429266584-5

Fura, B., Karasek, A., & Hysa, B. (2025). Statistical assessment of digital transformation in European Union countries under sustainable development goal 9. *Quality & Quantity, 59*(1), 937–972. DOI: 10.1007/s11135-024-01972-0

Garmaroodi, M. S. S., Farivar, F., Haghighi, M. S., Shoorehdeli, M. A., & Jolfaei, A. (2021). AquaFeL-PSO: A Monitoring System for Water Resources using Autonomous Surface Vehicles based on Multimodal PSO and Federated Learning. *IEEE Internet of Things Journal, 8*(13), 10280–10287. DOI: 10.1109/JIOT.2020.3034311

Ghobakhloo, M., Iranmanesh, M., Grybauskas, A., Vilkas, M., & Petraitė, M. (2021). Industry 4.0, innovation, and sustainable development: A systematic review and a roadmap to sustainable innovation. *Business Strategy and the Environment*, *30*(8), 4237–4257. DOI: 10.1002/bse.2867

Göçoğlu, V., Ayan, D., & Demirkol, A. (2025). Climate Change Adaptation Strategies in Vulnerable Countries Through the SDG 13: A Cross-Sectoral Analysis. *Sustainable Development*. Advance online publication. DOI: 10.1002/sd.70254

Gupta, A., & Ruebush, E. (2019). *AquaSight: Automatic Water Impurity Detection Utilizing Convolutional Neural Networks*.

Guth, D., & Herák, D. (2025). Modern Water Treatment Technology Based on Industry 4.0. *Sensors (Basel)*, *25*(6), 1925. Advance online publication. DOI: 10.3390/s25061925

Hahladakis, J. N. (2025). From Local Actions to Global Impact: Overcoming Hurdles and Showcasing Sustainability Achievements in the Implementation of SDG12. *Sustainability (Basel)*, *17*(15), 7106. Advance online publication. DOI: 10.3390/su17157106

Hantoko, D., Li, X., Pariatamby, A., & Yoshikawa, K. (2020). *Challenges and practices on waste management and disposal during COVID-19 pandemic*. (January).

Hermawan, J., Wijaya, L. I., & Rianawati, A. (2025). Digital Transformation for Economic Growth and SDG 8 Alignment in Southeast Asia: A Bibliometric Analysis and Systematic Literature Review with ADO-TCM Framework. *Journal of Lifestyle and SDGs Review*, *5*(2), e04052. DOI: 10.47172/2965-730X.SDGsReview.v5.n02.pe04052

IAEG, U. (2016). *Final list of proposed Sustainable Development Goal indicators*.

Irannezhad, M., Ahmadi, B., Liu, J., Chen, D., & Matthews, J. H. (2022). Global water security: A shining star in the dark sky of achieving the sustainable development goals. *Sustainable Horizons*, *1*(September 2021), 100005. DOI: 10.1016/j.horiz.2021.100005

Jacob, J. (2025). A Background History of the Sustainable Development Goals. *Sustainable Development (Bradford)*, *33*(3), 3747–3759. DOI: 10.1002/sd.3317

Jaiswal, R., Gupta, S., & Gupta, S. K. (2025). The impending disruption of digital nomadism: Opportunities, challenges, and research agenda. *World Leisure Journal*, *67*(1), 74–104. DOI: 10.1080/16078055.2024.2346091

Krishnan, J., Mondal, S., & SEM, I. (2012). Financial inclusion. Emerging Strategies For Sustainable Growth & Competence, 716.

Kara, A., Zhou, H., & Zhou, Y. (2021). Achieving the United Nations' sustainable development goals through financial inclusion: A systematic literature review of access to finance across the globe. *International Review of Financial Analysis, 77*, 101833. DOI: 10.1016/j.irfa.2021.101833

Karanam, R. K., Addimulam, S., Ahmmed, S., & Natakam, V. M. (2024). The Role of Digital Transformation in Achieving Sustainability Goals: A Preview of SAC 2024 (2.0). *Journal of Computing and Digital Technologies, 2*(1). https://americandigits.comhttps://americandigits.com/

Kartal, M. T., Mukhtarov, S., Depren, Ö., Ayhan, F., & Ulussever, T. (2025). How Can SDG-13 Be Achieved by Energy, Environment, and Economy-Related Policies? Evidence From Five Leading Emerging Countries. *Sustainable Development (Bradford), 33*(4), 5110–5133. DOI: 10.1002/sd.3391

Kasinathan, P., Pugazhendhi, R., Elavarasan, R. M., Ramachandaramurthy, V. K., Ramanathan, V., Subramanian, S., Kumar, S., Nandhagopal, K., Raghavan, R. R. V., Rangasamy, S., Devendiran, R., & Alsharif, M. H. (2022). Realization of Sustainable Development Goals with Disruptive Technologies by Integrating Industry 5.0, Society 5.0, Smart Cities and Villages. *Sustainability (Basel), 14*(22), 15258. Advance online publication. DOI: 10.3390/su142215258

Lahane, S., Patel, B., Kant, R., & Malviya, R. K. (2026). Evaluating Industry 4.0 implementation obstacles and solutions for the medical waste reverse logistics system. *International Journal of Logistics Research and Applications*, 1–29. DOI: 10.1080/13675567.2026.2615203

Leal Filho, W., Vidal, D. G., Chen, C., Petrova, M., Dinis, M. A. P., Yang, P., Rogers, S., Álvarez-Castañón, L., Djekic, I., Sharifi, A., & Neiva, S. (2022). An assessment of requirements in investments, new technologies, and infrastructures to achieve the SDGs. *Environmental Sciences Europe, 34*(1), 58. Advance online publication. DOI: 10.1186/s12302-022-00629-9

Lee, H., Zhang, Y., Zhang, H., & Liu, X. (2023). Challenges and opportunities of utilizing design thinking in the industry 4. 0 era : Based on the case study of industry wastewater treatment system development project process. *Journal of Innovation and Entrepreneurship, 12*(1), 56. Advance online publication. DOI: 10.1186/s13731-023-00315-x

Lopez-Vargas, A., Fuentes, M., & Vivar, M. (2020). Challenges and opportunities of the internet of things for global development to achieve the united nations sustainable development goals. *IEEE Access: Practical Innovations, Open Solutions, 8*, 37202–37213. DOI: 10.1109/ACCESS.2020.2975472

Mabkhot, M. M., Ferreira, P., Maffei, A., Podržaj, P., Mądziel, M., Antonelli, D., Lanzetta, M., Barata, J., Boffa, E., Finžgar, M., Paśko, Ł., Minetola, P., Chelli, R., Nikghadam-Hojjati, S., Wang, X. V., Priarone, P. C., Litwin, P., Stadnicka, D., Lohse, N., & Lupi, F. (2021). Mapping industry 4.0 enabling technologies into united nations sustainability development goals. *Sustainability (Switzerland), 13*(5), 1–35. DOI: 10.3390/su13052560

Machkour, B., & Abriane, A. (2020). Industry 4.0 and its implications for the financial sector. *Procedia Computer Science, 177*, 496–502. DOI: 10.1016/j.procs.2020.10.068

Madiha, Z. (2025). Technological Innovation in the Banking and Financial Sector: Risks and Challenges. In *Innovating Cost-Efficient and Scalable Business Models in the Digital Era* (pp. 299–342). IGI Global. DOI: 10.4018/979-8-3373-2120-2.ch010

Malynovska, Y., Bohomaz, P., Mats, Y., & Parashchyn, O. (2025). Digital Business Transformation: Key Challenges for Modern Managers. *European Journal of Economics and Management, 11*(2), 21–28. DOI: 10.46340/eujem.2025.11.2.3

Maresova, P., Soukal, I., Svobodova, L., Hedvicakova, M., Javanmardi, E., Selamat, A., & Krejcar, O. (2018). Consequences of industry 4.0 in business and economics. In *Economies* (Vol. 6, Number 3). MDPI Multidisciplinary Digital Publishing Institute. DOI: 10.3390/economies6030046

Mhlanga, D. (2021). Artificial intelligence in the industry 4.0, and its impact on poverty, innovation, infrastructure development, and the sustainable development goals: Lessons from emerging economies? *Sustainability (Basel), 13*(11), 5788. Advance online publication. DOI: 10.3390/su13115788

Mhlanga, D. (2022). Human-Centered Artificial Intelligence: The Superlative Approach to Achieve Sustainable Development Goals in the Fourth Industrial Revolution. *Sustainability (Basel), 14*(13), 7804. Advance online publication. DOI: 10.3390/su14137804

Mishra, H., & Maheshwari, P. (2020). Achieving sustainable development goals through Fourth Industrial Revolution: An Indian perspective. *Indian Journal of Commerce & Management Studies, XI*(2), 63. DOI: 10.18843/ijcms/v11i2/06

Mishra, R., Singh, R. K., & Song, M. (2025). Managing tensions in resilience development: A paradox theory perspective on the role of digital transformation. *Journal of Enterprise Information Management*, *38*(1), 127–151. DOI: 10.1108/JEIM-08-2022-0271

Molu, G. G., & Luketero, S. (2025). Influence of prepaid smart water metering on performance of community water projects in Marsabit County, Kenya. *International Academic Journal of Information Sciences and Project Management*, *3*(7), 351–369.

Mwansa, G., Ngandu, M. R., & Mkwambi, Z. (2025). Bridging the digital divide: Exploring the challenges and solutions for digital exclusion in rural South Africa. *Discover Global Society*, *3*(1), 54. Advance online publication. DOI: 10.1007/s44282-025-00189-2

Nastasi, B., Markovska, N., Puksec, T., Duić, N., & Foley, A. (2022). Renewable and sustainable energy challenges to face for the achievement of Sustainable Development Goals. *Renewable & Sustainable Energy Reviews*, *157*, 112071. DOI: 10.1016/j.rser.2022.112071

Nazibudin, N. A., Sabri, S. A. M., & Manaf, L. A. (2025). Aligning with sustainable development goals (SDG) 12: A systematic review of food waste generation in Malaysia. In *Cleaner Waste Systems* (Vol. 10). Elsevier B.V. DOI: 10.1016/j.clwas.2025.100205

Neeraja, kalluri, Gupta, T., Vaish, A., Kumar Gowda B N, V., & Purohit, P. (2024). The impact of artificial intelligence on human resource functions: a case study of Tata Consultancy Services (TCS) In India. *Frontiers in Health Informatics, 13*(8). www.healthinformaticsjournal.comwww.healthinformaticsjournal.com

Ocelík, V., Kolk, A., & Ciulli, F. (2023). Multinational enterprises, Industry 4.0 and sustainability: A multidisciplinary review and research agenda. *Journal of Cleaner Production*, *413*, 137434. Advance online publication. DOI: 10.1016/j.jclepro.2023.137434

Olanrewaju, V. O., Gyamfi, B. A., Ozsahin, I., & Adebayo, T. S. (2025). Achieving SDGs 7, 8, and 13: Balancing policy uncertainty with renewable energy demand. *Environmental Sciences Europe*, *37*(1), 97. Advance online publication. DOI: 10.1186/s12302-025-01133-6

Omol, E. J. (2024). Organizational digital transformation: from evolution to future trends. In *Digital Transformation and Society* (Vol. 3, Number 3, pp. 240–256). Emerald Publishing. DOI: 10.1108/DTS-08-2023-0061

Pappas, I. O., Mikalef, P., Dwivedi, Y. K., Jaccheri, L., & Krogstie, J. (2023). Responsible Digital Transformation for a Sustainable Society. In *Information Systems Frontiers* (Vol. 25, Number 3, pp. 945–953). Springer. DOI: 10.1007/s10796-023-10406-5

Personal, M., Archive, R., & Ibrahim, M. (2020). *Munich Personal RePEc Archive Impact of Technological Innovation on Energy Efficiency in Industry 4 . 0 Era : Moderation of Shadow Economy in Sustainable Development*. (104842), 0–32.

Pina, A., Ferrão, P., Fournier, J., Lacarrière, B., & Le Corre, O. (2019). ScienceDirect ScienceDirect Industry 4. 0 Technology Implementation Impact to Industrial Technology Implementation Impact to Industrial Sustainable Energy in Indonesia : A Model Conceptualization Sustainable Energy in Indonesia : A Model Conceptualizatio. *Energy Procedia*, *156*, 227–233. DOI: 10.1016/j.egypro.2018.11.133

Polyviou, A., Venters, W., & Pouloudi, N. (2023). Distant but close: Locational, relational and temporal proximity in cloud computing adoption. *Journal of Information Technology*, *0*(0), 1–23. DOI: 10.1177/02683962231186161

Qudrat-Ullah, H. (2025). A Thematic Review of AI and ML in Sustainable Energy Policies for Developing Nations. In *Energies* (Vol. 18, Number 9). Multidisciplinary Digital Publishing Institute (MDPI). DOI: 10.3390/en18092239

Rafey, A., & Siddiqui, F. Z. (2023). A review of plastic waste management in India – challenges and opportunities. *International Journal of Environmental Analytical Chemistry*, *103*(16), 3971–3987. DOI: 10.1080/03067319.2021.1917560

Raman, R., Sreenivasan, A., Ma, S., Patwardhan, A., & Nedungadi, P. (2023). Green Supply Chain Management Research Trends and Linkages to UN Sustainable Development Goals. *Sustainability (Basel)*, *15*(22), 15848. Advance online publication. DOI: 10.3390/su152215848

Rehman, A., Saba, T., Kashif, M., Fati, S. M., Bahaj, S. A., & Chaudhry, H. (2022). A Revisit of Internet of Things Technologies for Monitoring and Control Strategies in Smart Agriculture. *Agronomy (Basel)*, *12*(1), 1–21. DOI: 10.3390/agronomy12010127

Selim, A. M., & ElGohary, A. S. (2020). Public–private partnerships (PPPs) in smart infrastructure projects: The role of stakeholders. *HBRC Journal*, *16*(1), 317–333. DOI: 10.1080/16874048.2020.1825038

Shabeer, M. G., & Rasul, F. (2025). Aligning innovation and information with development: A comparative analysis of developed and developing nations. *Environment, Development and Sustainability*, *27*(6), 14305–14319. DOI: 10.1007/s10668-024-04478-9

Sheng, T. J. I., Islam, M. S., Misran, N., Baharuddin, M. H., Arshad, H., Chowdhury, M. E. H., Rmili, H., & Islam, M. T. (2020). An Internet of Things Based Smart Waste Management System Using LoRa and Tensorflow Deep Learning Model. *IEEE Access : Practical Innovations, Open Solutions*, *8*, 148793–148811. DOI: 10.1109/ACCESS.2020.3016255

Siddique, K., Saleem, A. R., Arslan, M., & Afzal, M. (2025). file:///C:/Users/Smart-Com/Downloads/sensors-25-01925.pdf. *Sustainability (Switzerland)*, *17*(13), 1–21. DOI: 10.3390/su17136226

Siekmann, F., Schlör, H., & Venghaus, S. (2023). Linking sustainability and the Fourth Industrial Revolution: A monitoring framework accounting for technological development. *Energy, Sustainability and Society*, *13*(1), 26. Advance online publication. DOI: 10.1186/s13705-023-00405-4

Simicevic, V. (2025). Unemployment in Croatia: Trends and Challenges in the Digital Age (2010-2024). *Croatian Regional Development Journal*, *6*(1), 1–17. DOI: 10.2478/crdj-2025-0001

Singh, S., & Goyal, M. K. (2025). A review of India's water policy and implementation toward a sustainable future. *Journal of Water and Climate Change*, *16*(2), 493–510. DOI: 10.2166/wcc.2025.560

Swarna, M. F. M., Khan, S., Ramalingam, P., & Reddy, A. (2024). Role of HR Analytics in People Management: Challenges and Opportunities in the Indian IT/ITeS Space. In *HR Analytics* (pp. 1–23). Fundamentals and Applications.

Tazhibayev, A., Utepbergenov, I., & Skliarova, I. (2025). Development of Customer-Focused Automated Systems for Transformer Design and Manufacturing: A Comprehensive Review. In *Journal of Computational and Cognitive Engineering* (Vol. 4, Number 3, pp. 251–266). Bon View Publishing Pte Ltd. DOI: 10.47852/bonviewJCCE52025158

Thomas, P., & Davis, N. (2018). The fourth industrial revolution: Shaping new era. *Journal of International Affairs*, *72*(1), 17–22. DOI: 10.2307/26588339

Tiwari, S. P. (2025). The implications of artificial intelligence in management consulting: A risk and barrier assessment. In *Multidisciplinary Reviews* (Vol. 8, Number 8). Malque Publishing. DOI: 10.31893/multirev.2025244

Tripathi, S., Bachmann, N., Brunner, M., Rizk, Z., & Jodlbauer, H. (2024). Assessing the current landscape of AI and sustainability literature: Identifying key trends, addressing gaps and challenges. *Journal of Big Data*, *11*(1), 65. Advance online publication. DOI: 10.1186/s40537-024-00912-x

Umoru, U., Ogundana, O. M., Mangena, M., & Udeozor, V. (2026). Informal Institutions and Multinationals' Drive Towards Sustainable Development Goals (SDGs): A Dark-Side Perspective. *Business Ethics, the Environment & Responsibility*, *35*(1), 75–98. DOI: 10.1111/beer.12773

Vikranth, K., & Prasad, K. K. (2019). Sustained Policies on Technical and Operational aspects of IT Industry-A Case Study of Tata Consultancy Limited. *SRINIVAS PUBLICATION International Journal of Applied Engineering and Management Letters(IJAEML) A Refereed International Journal of Srinivas University, 3*(2), 2581–7000. DOI: 10.5281/zenodo.3597751

Wasiu Dauda, B., Duru, G. O., Olagoke, M. F., & Patrick Egbon, E. (2024). Optimizing Operational Efficiency through Digital Supply Chain Transformation in U.S. Manufacturing. *International Journal of Advances in Engineering and Management*, *6*(11), 343–358. DOI: 10.35629/5252-0611343358

Weiland, S., Hickmann, T., Lederer, M., Marquardt, J., & Schwindenhammer, S. (2021). The 2030 agenda for sustainable development: Transformative change through the sustainable development goals? In *Politics and Governance* (Vol. 9, Number 1, pp. 90–95). Cogitatio Press. DOI: 10.17645/pag.v9i1.4191

Zeb, A., Shuhai, N., & Ullah, O. (2025). Socioeconomic determinants of ecological footprints: Bridging the gap between developed and developing nations. *Environment, Development and Sustainability*. Advance online publication. DOI: 10.1007/s10668-025-06081-y

Zetzsche, D. A., Buckley, R. P., Arner, D. W., & Barberis, J. N. (2017). Regulating a Revolution: From Regulatory Sandboxes to Smart Regulation. SSRN *Electronic Journal, 23*(1). DOI: 10.2139/ssrn.3018534

Zhang, L., Ling, J., & Lin, M. (2022). Artificial intelligence in renewable energy: A comprehensive bibliometric analysis. *Energy Reports*, *8*, 14072–14088. DOI: 10.1016/j.egyr.2022.10.347

Zou, S., Ju, H., & Zhang, J. (2025). Water Quality Management in the Age of AI: Applications, Challenges, and Prospects. *Water (Basel)*, *17*(11), 1641. DOI: 10.3390/w17111641

Chapter 4

# An Empirical Investigation for Assessing the Causal Relationship of Digitalization With Environmental Degradation in Selected Countries

**Ajay Kumar Singh**
http://orcid.org/0000-0003-0429-0925
*Department of Humanities and Social Sciences, Graphic Era University, Dehradun, India*

**S. Srinivasan**
http://orcid.org/0009-0002-0179-9849
*Department of Humanities and Social Sciences, Graphic Era University, Dehradun, India*

## ABSTRACT

*This chapter examines the causal implications of digitalization with environmental degradation as employing a balanced panel data of 111 countries during 2004 – 2021. Environmental degradation is measured as per capita CO2 emissions. Digital inclusion index (DII) is used as a measurement of digital inclusion. DII is the com-*

DOI: 10.4018/979-8-2600-1438-7.ch004

*bination of five variables which help to increase digitalization. Industrialization, foreign direct investment, inflation GDP deflator, per capita GDP, renewable energy consumption, education expenditure, technological diffusion and population density are also included in the empirical investigations. Instrumental variable is used to check the Robustness of the regression results. Natural logarithms of these variables are considered in regression models. Existence of causal association among these variables are estimated through Granger causality test. A bi-lateral and positive relationship is found between digitalization and environmental degradation in these nations. It claims that adoption of sustainable digitalization will enhance environmental sustainability.*

## 1. INTRODUCTION

Digital technologies (DTs) are advanced technologies that create an online platform for sharing knowledge, skills, data, product information, purchasing of products, advertisement and marketing of products. Around 50% of the population of the world are using the internet for different purposes (Cai & Hong, 2024). While 35% people are using least developed nations (WEF, 2014). DTs are helping to increase digital infrastructure, digital platform, digital transformation and digital economy and digitalization which are making innovative changes in tourism, health, environmental and ecological sectors (Bychkov & Fereferov, 2022; Singh et al., 2024; Gupta et al., 2025). While digital transformation will be improved as using more DTs in most sectors by a nation. Digitalization is a scientific process in which economic agents use different DTs for nurturing an ecosystem for exchange of knowledge, information and data at minimum costs (Singh et al., 2023). Digital economy helps to increase utilization of DTs in the economic sector for improving the environmental sector (Cai & Hong, 2024; Tao et al., 2025).

Initiation of digital economy help to integrate e-commerce, social media, telecommunication, IT services, blockchain, cloud computing, computer, internet, and software in social, economic, environmental and technological systems (Cai & Hong, 2024). Digital platforms and infrastructure are playing a mediating role to increase the accessibility, exchange and managing the data for a large number of users. Digital economy is significant to maintain environmental quality and build conducive platform to increase sustainable human development (Zhang et al., 2023; Cao & Peng, 2023), and enhances carbon efficiency. Public sector digitalization promotes technological innovation that fosters progress in sustainability aspects of the organizations (Gariba et al., 2024). DTs may be helpful to increase the appropriate educational environment (Lowan-Trudeau, 2023). Digitalization enhances transparency in the welfare program of the government (Xu et al., 2022). Effectiveness of governance is also improving due to digitalization (Xiao et al., 2024).

DTs can be an effective tool to increase economic development (ED) and maintain environmental protection (Singh & Jyoti, 2023; Kuang et al., 2024). DTs are fostering a favorable path for global countries to move towards the digital economy. Further, digital infrastructure serves a fundamental basis for DTs (He et al., 2024). Digital economy also boosts environmental sustainability (ES) and quality (Cao & Peng, 2023; An et al., 2024). ES is promotive to reduce environmental degradation, and increase economic growth, social development and human health (An et al., 2024). Further, ES deals with GHGs emissions, and extensive energy consumption. Accordingly, it reduces the extreme changes in climatic variables and environmental degradation. Environmental degradation measures the depletion of ecosystem services. Consequently, DTs are crucial drivers to develop new environmental technologies that are conducive to abate $CO_2$ emissions (Shen et al., 2023). Further, these can be efficient to attain sustainable development and SDGs (Abbas and Zaman, 2024).

Digital tools are working as efficient driver to increase transparency in SDGs progress (Hariyani et al., 2025). Sustainable development is a scientific mechanism and ecosystem in its all dimensions which ensures the need of present and future generation without reducing the quality and quantity of environmental and ecosystem services. Moreover, DTs are highly imperative to reduce energy intensity and increase sustainable energy consumption (Shen et al., 2023), enhance energy systems in an efficient way (Xu et al., 2022) and help to attain carbon neutrality goals (Shen et al., 2023). Digitalization, thus, is becoming a key pillar to reduce pollution and environmental degradation (Huang et al., 2024; Akberdina et al., 2024). Nowadays, most nations have heavy reliance on DTs to attain certain tasks in different sectors (Firoz et al., 2021; Bychkov & Fereferov, 2022; He et al., 2024). For instance, Big analytical tools is suitable to make the future prediction of climate change, $CO_2$ emissions, waste generation and other environmental challenges (Truong, 2022).

Digital devices like the internet and AI can be positive to mitigate global climate change (Young, 2020; UNDP, 2026) and reduce environmental pollution (Firoz et al., 2021; Hong & Xiao, 2024). DTs are cultivating an efficient ecosystem to preserve environment and ecosystem services. The above-mentioned technologies have the potential to make changes in economic structure, industrial revolution, social reforms and environmental protection worldwide (Singh, 2025). For instance, DTs helps to improve environmental governance and decision making capacity of the government to implement environmental law (He et al., 2024). Environmental governance is highly potential to ensure the security of natural resources. The production sector required good governance, green innovation, green and environmental technologies to increase ES. For this, digitalization is promoting green innovation and increasing the transition towards ES (Huang et al., 2024). DTs develop a digital platform for further sharing of knowledge, materials usages, energy technologies, and production techniques.

DTs can be worthy to attain the sustainable objectives of the environmental sector and these also enhance ES. Moreover, digital transformation and digital inclusion is an integration of DTs in various aspects of different sectors including business, industry, and society (Firoz et al., 2021; Goel et al., 2024). AI is helping to create new jobs and making significant transformation in the economic sector (Singh, 2025; WB, 2025). It enhances sustainability of production units in all dimensions including social and ED, and environmental quality (Xiao et al., 2024). Therefore, DTs are nurturing digital infrastructure for increasing efficiency and sustainability of organizations (Alojail & Khan, 2023). Digital transformation is presenting a new force for green development (Qing et al., 2023). The government can use DTs to increase transparency in public services and increase the benefits of government policies to all citizens (Goel et al., 2024). However, digital transformation is increasing large amounts of electronic waste and e-waste in the environment (Goel et al., 2024).

Digitalization is found crucial to increase the online marketing, while it is increasing packaging waste and contributing GHGs emissions. ES is also negatively impacted due to digitalization and digital infrastructure. ES is highly imperative to increase sustainable development. ES is adversely impacted due to over industrialization, population growth and urbanization (Singh et al., 2019). High growth of industrial and agricultural sectors is heavily accountable for environmental unsustainability worldwide. Extensive abatement of GHGs and $CO_2$ emissions are essential for ES and sustainable development (Singh et al., 2019). Increasing $CO_2$ and GHGs emissions are responsible for environmental degradation (Singh & Srinivasan, 2026). Nowadays, global countries are moving towards digitalization which has a crucial impact on all sectors which are significantly linked with ES (Firoz et al., 2021; Goel et al., 2024; Dai et al., 2025). Digitalization is found beneficial to increase the growth of industrial and agricultural sectors. Hence, digitalization has a vital impact on ES.

However, finding of previous studies could not observe a clear association between digitalization and environmental degradation. Environmental quality has a significant association with energy consumption, ED, population size, population density, urbanization, industrialization, science & technological development, green innovation, digitalization, technological innovation, human resources and digital infrastructure and DTs (Adebayo et al., 2022; Sikder et al., 2022; Cao & Peng, 2023). Population density is harmful for environmental development (Shen et al., 2023; Zhang et al., 2023; Kuang et al., 2024). Population density and its oversize are caused to increase environmental pollution (Yuan et al., 2024; Zhang, Liang et al., 2024). ES is a broad term that reduces natural resource depletion and ensures their protection (Goel et al., 2024). A group of scholars argued that digital technologies

(DTs) would nurture a favourable ecosystem to abate GHGs and $CO_2$ emissions for improving ES.

Although, existing researchers observed positive and negative impacts of DTs and digitalization on the environmental sector (Truong, 2022; Bianchini et al., 2023; Singh et al., 2024). Truong (2022) argued that DTs are helpful to address current environmental challenges. Alojail and Khan (2023) claimed that performance of all dimensions of sustainability improved as adoption of DTs. Shen et al. (2023) observed that DTs are supportive to reduce $CO_2$ emissions. Zhang et al. (2023) noted that the digital economy helps to reduce environmental pollution in China. Digital economy appears positive to reduce waste reduction and increase promotion of ES (Cai & Hong, 2024). Dai et al. (2025) also noted that digitalization could be helpful to reduce carbon emission and increasing ES in G20 nations.

Cai and Hong (2024) examined the adverse impact of the digital economy on the environment. Zhang, Liang et al. (2024) explored the contribution of the digital economy in urban pollution in China. Li et al. (2024) noted that digitalization contributes to high emissions. Qing et al. (2023) examined the impact of digitalization on pollution emission in China. Pollution emissions from firms have decreased due to adoption of digital infrastructure. Zhu et al. (2023) also found the digitalization could be helpful to reduce pollution in Chinese manufacturing firms. Yang et al. (2024) noticed that digitalization seemed significant to reduce industrial pollution.

World economies are giving crucial attention to increase their transformation towards digitalization. Accordingly, governments in most countries are adopting policies to increase the digitalization to get significant benefits from it in different sectors like agricultural, education, environmental, health infrastructure, tourism, financial and energy sectors. For instance, European nations have given more propriety towards digitalization since the last two decades. Accordingly, other developing nations like India also adopted the "digital India policy" in 2015. Previous literature identified several environmental benefits of digitalization. It is noticed that digitalization is working as a rebound effect. In general, rebound effects try to improve the efficiency of resources in multiple ways like to improve energy efficiency, resource efficiency, protection of resources, and reduce manufacturing cost and environmental risk. Digitalization may produce a positive impact on consumption and enhance ES.

Most economies are also centralizing their policies to increase digitalization for achieving sustainable development and economic benefits. Thereupon, the scientific research community is already considering extensive research to examine the positive and negative implications of digitalization in the environmental sector (Li et al., 2024). Most studies development the empirical association of digitalization, digital economy and DTs with ES (Firoz et al., 2021; Truong, 2022; Samuel et al., 2022; Istrate et al., 2024; Goel et al., 2024; Singh et al., 2024; Wong et al., 2025). However, past studies used different terms like digital economy, digital infrastructure, digital skills, digital innovation, etc. for DTs to examine their impact on environmental degradation and environmental quality (Zhang et al., 2023; Kuang et al., 2024; An et al., 2024). Few researchers examine the impact of digital inclusion on ES. Accordingly, different variables are included for environmental performance or environmental quality or environmental pollution and ES in the existing literature (Yuan et al., 2024).

Findings of previous literature have a controversial opinion about the association of DTs with the environmental sector and its sustainability. Furthermore, existing researchers could not explain which DTs help to reduce environmental degradation and enhance ES. Although, there is insignificant empirical evidence about the relationship of digital inclusion with environmental degradation across countries (Li et al., 2024). More empirical research would be worthy and valuable to understand the clear association of digitalization with environmental degradation in global countries. This chapter is primarily deals following research questions:

- What is of digitalization and DTs on the environmental sector?
- How can digitalization and DTs be imperative to reduce environmental degradation?
- What is theoretical relationship of digitalization with environmental degradation?
- Which DTs are favourable for increasing ES?
- How can global countries reduce the adverse impact of digital inclusion and digital transformation on ES?

The present research has following objectives:

- To develop theoretical relationship of digitalization with environmental degradation and ES.
- To examine the causal association of digitalization with environmental degradation.
- To suggest reliable policy proposals to minimize the negative impact of digitalization on ES and quality.

*Table 1. shows the summary diagram of the chapter.*

| **Main Objectives** |
|---|
| • To observe the impact of digitalization and environmental degradation. |
| **Number of Countries and Time Period** |
| • 111 countries are compiled in panel data during 2004 – 2021 |
| **Source of Data** |

continued on following page

*Table 1. Continued*

| **Main Objectives** |
|---|
| • World Development Indicators (The World Bank) |
| **Main indicators** |
| • Digitalization is estimated as a composition of 5 indicators which create digital platform.<br>• Environmental degradation measure in term of per capita $CO_2$ emission. |
| **Mathematically Functional Relationship among the Indicators** |
| • $(CO_2EPC) = f\{(DII), (EE), (EI), (FDINI), (GDPPC), (IGDPD), (PD), (REC), (STJAs)\}$<br>• $(DII) = f\{(CO_2EPC), (EE), (EI), (FDINI), (GDPPC), (IGDPD), (PD), (REC), (STJAs)\}$ |
| **Main regression equations** |
| • $ln(CO_2EPC)_{ct} = \beta_0 + \beta_1\, ln(DII)_{ct} + \beta_2\, ln(EE)_{ct} + \beta_3\, ln(EI)_{ct} + \beta_4\, ln(FDINI)_{ct} + \beta_5\, ln(GDPPC)_{ct} + \beta_6\, ln(IGDPD)_{ct} + \beta_7\, ln(PD)_{ct} + \beta_8\, ln(REC)_{ct} + \beta_9\, ln(STJAs)_{ct} + \lambda_{ct}$<br>• $ln(CO_2EPC)_{ct} = \xi_0 + \xi_1\, ln(DII)_{ct} + \xi_2\, ln(EE)_{ct} + \xi_3\, ln(EI)_{ct} + \xi_4\, ln(FDINI)_{ct} + \xi_5\, ln(GDPPC)_{ct} + \xi_6\, ln(IGDPD)_{ct} + \xi_7\, ln(PD)_{ct} + \xi_8\, ln(REC)_{ct} + \xi_9\, ln(STJAs)_{ct} + \mu_{ct}$<br>• $(CO2EPC)_{ct} = \Psi_0 + \sum_{j=1}^{p} \Psi_{1,j}\, (CO2EPC)_{c,t-j} + \sum_{j=0}^{p} \Psi_{2,j}\, (DTI)_{c,t-j} + \delta_{ct}$ |
| **Principles Findings** |
| • Digitalization is creating additional environmental degradation.<br>• Environmental degradation is providing motivation to global economies to increase digitalization.<br>• Environmental degradation increases as increase in demographic change, technological development, ED and FDI. |
| **Policy Implications** |
| • Use of green technologies and innovation, and creation of green jobs and develop green products and infrastructure help to increase ES.<br>• Extensive investment in energy and education sectors will enhance ES.<br>• Sustainable digital development is suggested to increase ES.<br>• Production of green energy, sustainable use of energy and innovation in energy will be helpful to increase ES.<br>• Re-use of e-wastage and e-waste management are also needed to increase ES. |
| **Innovation of the chapter** |
| • Bilateral association of digitalization and environmental degradation is identified.<br>• It increases the attention of global and national policy makers to adopt sustainable digitalization to increase ES. |

# 2. REVIEW OF LITERATURE

## 2.1. Major Causes for Environmental Degradation

Over population growth, overurbanization, and extreme industrialization are highly accountable for increasing $SO_2$, $CO_2$ and GHGs emissions in the ecosystem (Adebayo et al., 2022; Sikder et al., 2022; Cao & Peng, 2023; Zhang, Chen, et al., 2024). Environment and ecosystem are negatively impacted due to the mentioned gases. Anthropogenic activities are caused to increase energy consumption and production activities (Li et al., 2024; Singh et al., 2019). Overwhelming urbanization is reducing ecosystem services and increasing environmental degradation (Zhang, Chen, et al., 2024). Environmental quality is being degraded in highly industrialized countries like China and USA (Yang et al., 2024; Tao et al., 2025). Ecological and environmental problems are increasing due to over industrialization and urbanization in China (Wang & Ding, 2023). Foreign trade is found to increase ED, technological development and competition across countries. Extensive quantity of fossil fuels from the agricultural sector is a significant driver of climate change (Miyake, 2024; Singh et al., 2019). Increasing $CO_2$ emissions is causing greenhouse effect and global warming (Singh et al., 2019). It is highly accountable for increasing earth temperature and climate change (Zhang, Chen, et al., 2024; Li et al., 2024). Global warming has a negative impact on crops, food security, health security, income of people and overall livelihood security (Zhang, Chen, et al., 2024). As environmental protection is a core dimension of sustainable development. Thus, environmental degradation is hampering sustainable development and its promoting activities.

## 2.2. Digitalization and Economic Prosperity

Numerous studies assess the implication of digitalization and DTs in the domain of social and economic sectors (Abbas and Zaman, 2024; Singh, 2025; Tao et al., 2025). As per recent literature, digitalization is found suitable to increase the economic growth as creating new jobs in the labour market (Xu et al., 2022; Abbas and Zaman, 2024; WB, 2025). Digitalization is a significant driver to increase diffusion across sectors which further lead to increased economic growth (Abbas and Zaman, 2024). Digitalization can be considered as an engine of global ED (Zhu et al., 2023; Singh & Jyoti, 2023). Digital economy is creating a force to increase economic growth across countries (Zhang, Chen, et al., 2024). It is also helping to increase the transformation of the business sector towards e-business and online business and digital business (Abbas and Zaman, 2024).

## 2.3. Social Effects of Digitalization

Digitalization can be effective to increase social well-being of the people (Xiao et al., 2024) through increasing their social communication of people (Singh & Jyoti, 2023). Use of DTs and digitalization is evolving a conducive platform to increase social inclusion and development. DTs creates an active platform that are associated with the livelihood of people. Therefore, the process of digitization has brought significant change in the daily life of people. The active implementation of digitalization is worthy to increase the transformation of the society. For instance, digitalization is helping to increase effective and efficient communication of people

(Singh & Jyoti, 2023). Digitalization is working to increase accessibility of services, education opportunities, and social inclusion of the common public. However, extensive digitalization is creating multiple challenges for society.

Digitalization is increasing inequality in digital skills in society (Hariyani et al., 2025). It is noted for disparities in internet accessibility, digital disparities and digital divide within a country and across countries. High cost of digital devices and shortage of digital skills are creating a digital inequity in the society (Hariyani et al., 2025). It is increasing diversity in the digital landscape and technological advancement within a nation and across nations. European nations already created infrastructure for digitalization. While other nations from South Asia, Africa, Latin America are moving towards digitalization. Thus, digital diversity appears harmful for social and ED in most developing nations which are unable to create feasible digital infrastructure. Digitalization is creating problems to maintain personal identity and privacy of the people due to inefficiency of the digital landscape. Digital infrastructure and usage of digital technologies could not create an appropriate platform to provide cyber security in developing nations. Moreover, digital literacy and extensive use of DTs are creating mental health issues in many nations.

## 2.4. Digitalization and Environmental Development

Numerous studies already used diverse indicators (e.g., DTs, digital infrastructure, digitalization, digital economy, digital platform, digitalization index, etc.) related to digital inclusion to explore their implications on ES, environmental development, environmental quality, environmental performance, environmental protection, environmental regulation across countries (Liu, 2023; Zhu et al., 2023; Li et al., 2024; Xiao et al., 2024; Singh et al., 2024; Wong et al., 2025). Diverse variables are considered by the research community to analyse the association of environmental degradation with DTs and digital transformation. For instance, Li et al. (2024) detected a positive impact of digitalization on environmental degradation. While environmental degradation decreases as financial technologies increase. Previous studies applied different indicators for DTs to examine its contribution in ES and its quality. DTs are caused to increase GHGs emissions through increasing electronic wastage. DTs are accountable for resources and ecological depletion. Goel et al. (2024) examined the impact of DTs on energy consumption, e-wastage and extraction of raw materials. Firoz et al. (2021) accessed the crucial field in which DTs can be used to address environmental concerns.

Huang et al. (2024) claimed the digitalization is found favourable to increase ES and green innovation in Asian countries. Bon (2021) examined the contribution of governance and digitization in economic growth in the developing countries. Digitalization is active to increase economic sustainability and efficiency and economic growth (Gariba et al., 2024). Truong (2022) highlighted that the digital revolution has potential to solve multiple environmental issues. The findings of Truong (2022)'s suggested that DTs can be conducive to increase resource management, waste management and pollution control. DTs creates additional forces to increase environmental pollution control (He et al., 2024). Review findings of Firoz et al. (2021) proposed that DTs transform the way to control and manage pollution. DTs like AI, IoT and block chain are found effective to increase resource management (Goel et al., 2024). DTs are also contributing to increased e-waste (Goel et al., 2024).

Xu et al. (2022) noticed the DTs are applicable in multiple areas like governance, energy and agriculture which further enhance sustainable development. Hong and Xiao (2024) proved that DTs nurtures a significant path for optimizing the production system and enhancing the betterment of society and environment. However, the production sector required good governance, green innovation, green and environmental technologies for improving the environmental sector. Shen et al. (2023) reported that DTs help to reduce carbon emission and its efficiency in China. Zhang, Liang et al. (2024) found declining pollution emission due to application of DTs in China. Further, it suggested that DTs is helping to increase environmental governance. Bianchini et al. (2023) noticed that GHGs emissions decreased as application of environmental technologies in industrial production increased in the EU and United Kingdom.

## 2.5. Immediate Impact of Digitalization on Environment

Digitalization has an immediate positive and negative impact on the environment. Digitalization appears positive to reduce environmental pollution. For instance, Kuang et al. (2024) noticed that $CO_2$ emission has significantly declined due to digitalization of economy in China. Liu (2023) claimed that digital economy growth has a repressive impact on pollution in China. Yuan et al. (2024) found that the digital economy is favourable to reduce environmental pollution through increasing efficiency of resources and developing clean technologies in China. Moreover, digital transformation reduces environmental threats and resource scarcity (Akberdina et al., 2024).It is a healthier and safer solution to increase sustainable environment (UNDP, 2026). Wang et al. (2022) noticed that pollution emissions decrease as digital transformation increases. Lu et al. (2024) noted that air pollution pressure increases the intention of enterprises to develop digital transformation in China. Empirical findings of Zhu et al., (2023) also argued that digital transformation is helpful to reduce air pollution in Chinese firms. Air pollution pressure has a significant impact on digital transformation (Lu et al., 2024). Digital transformation is helping to reduce environmental challenges in G20 nations (Dai et al., 2025), and it seems positive to increase technological innovation for further improvement in environmental quality (Dai et al., 2025).

## 2.6. Negative and Adverse Implications of Digitalization in Environmental Sector

Energy and electricity consumption is significantly increased due to adoption of DTs in many nations of the world. Digitalization is helping to increase resource efficiency which is reducing GHGs emissions. Further, it is expected the ICT would contribute more than 3.2% GHGs emissions in the world by 2020. Furthermore, 4% global GHGs emissions are coming from the ICT sector as per UNEP. Application of DTs increases the demand for more materials and metals. Thus, DTs are caused to increase natural resource depletion. Goel et al. (2024) clarified that digital transformation is leading to increase in energy usage and resource depletion. The process of digitization requires extensive water and it may produce more wastage of water. Thus, digitalization may cause increased water scarcity in future. Digital transformation is contributing $CO_2$ emissions in the digital industry (Shen et al., 2023). It is a challenge that only 20% of e-waste is recycled each year due to digital transformation globally. Around 80% of global e-waste is diluted on earth. Therefore, e-waste from the digital sector is increasing exponentially and it is increasing environmental degradation (Truong, 2022; Goel et al., 2024). Wang et al. (2022) found an increasing trend in waste gas emission and wastewater due to digital transformation in China. Thus, extensive digitalization may change environmental degradation and climate change. It is projected that global temperature may rise by 1.50C by 20205 due to digital transformation (WEM, 2024). It would be very difficult for the world to minimize the-wastage due to extensive practices of DTs by the present and growing population in future.

## 2.7. Real Implications of Digitalization in Other Sectors

Existing researchers have been notified multiple real implications of digitalization in other sectors. For instance, Gariba et al. (2024) investigated the role of technology advancement and public digitization in sustainability in the European Union. It argued that technological innovation is prompting sustainability. Hence, public digitalization and technological innovation have positive correlation. Technological innovation plays a positive role to save energy (Adebayo et al., 2022). It promotes efficient use of renewable and conventional energy (Adebayo et al., 2022). The world's countries are being transformed towards a digital economy which is improving energy use efficiency (Kuang et al., 2024). Digital economy also enhances allocation of resources and their recycling for further utilization (Tao et al., 2025).

Smart grid systems are supportive to avoid the energy transmission losses by 5 – 5% (Dai et al., 2025). Application of DTs has potential to increase the growth of agricultural, industry and manufacturing sectors (Cao & Peng, 2023). Manufacturing can improve efficiency of resources more that 10% due to use of industrial IoT (Dai et al., 2025). Agricultural technologies can be effective to reduce the use of fertilizer and pesticide in cultivation by 15-25% (Dai et al., 2025).

DTs has multiple utilization in the agricultural and its allied sectors. Technological advancement is essential to reduce the challenge of climate change (Bianchini et al., 2023). DTs promote digital agriculture and reduce climate change impacts (Truong, 2022). Shen et al. (2023) noted that development of digital technology is helpful to reduce climate change effects. Use of DTs like GIS and remote sensing are improving yield and production of crops (Xu et al., 2022). Accordingly, DTs are developing best adaptation practices in the farming sector. Innovation in the energy sector is increasing due to practices of DTs and movement of digital economy (Tao et al., 2025; Wang et al., 2025). Further, energy efficiency and energy innovation are supportive to increase environmental quality. Moreover, DTs have a crucial and impactful contribution in education, health, tourism and other sectors

## 2.8. Relation between the Emerging Technologies and the SDGs

Digitalization and DTs are helping to achieve 70% of SDGs through developing various prospects and scientific mechanisms (UNDP, 2023). Most targets of SDGs are positively and negatively associated with DTs (UNDP, 2026). Further multiple goals of SDGs can be achieved through digitalization (Abbas & Zaman, 2024). Abbas and Zaman (2024) reported that digitalization is helping to increase SDGs in emerging nations. Pérez-Martínez et al. (2023) investigate the contribution of digitalization to achieve SDGs. DTs are creating more jobs for the skilled workforce. Consequently, digitalization is expected to eradicate poverty significantly in developing nations (Hariyani et al., 2025). DTs are maintaining demand and supply components of food security. DTs are increasing sustainable and responsible consumption of resources (Hariyani et al., 2025). Abbas and Zaman (2024) noted a negative implication of digitalization on poverty and inequality in emerging countries. Healthcare facilities are improving due to application of DTs (Hariyani et al., 2025). Appropriate health care facilities are helping to improve human health. DTs are creating a favorable ecosystem for international trade across nations.

Moreover, DTs is increasing the energy intensity as creating many tools to increase renewable energy (Xu et al., 2022; Cao & Peng, 2023). While consumption and production of renewable energy is environmentally favorable and reduces environmental degradation. Thus, digitalization is helping to increase green growth and development. Transfer of technologies has become easy due to the adoption of DTs. Accordingly, digitalization has appeared to improve S&T development in the world. Bychkov and Fereferov (2022) investigated the significance of DTs for predicting the environmental conditions in Siberia. Accordingly, DTs are helpful for farmers and other stakeholders to apply climate mitigation and adaptation strategies to minimize climate change impacts. Tao et al. (2025) also observed that the digital economy helps to increase innovation in the environmental sector and reduce climate change impacts. Cai and Hong (2024) investigated the implications of block chain and AI for mitigating the adverse environmental effects. Most specifically, the government can implement a climate action plan to ensure environmental quality (Hariyani et al., 2025). Consequently, digitalization and digital transformation have a crucial contribution to increase sustainable development (Alojail & Khan, 2023). Tao et al. (2025) noted that applications of AI and ICTs by the government can be effective initiatives to increase environmental performance.

## 3. RESEARCH METHODOLOGY

### 3.1. Selection of Countries

In this study, only those countries are included which have the statistical data of specified and relevant variables. Total 111 countries are considered in this study. Statistical data for selected variables for these countries are available during 2004 – 2021. Hence, balanced country-wise panel data during this time period is compiled for further statistical and empirical investigations in this research (Zhang, Chen, et al., 2024). Income-wise distribution of these countries is provided in Table 2.

*Table 2. Income-wise distribution of countries*

| Income group | Time |
|---|---|
| High Income Countries | Sweden, Latvia, Lithuania, Finland, Norway, Chile, Poland, Czech Republic, Slovak Republic, New Zealand, Ireland, Hungary, Saudi Arabia, Denmark, Barbados, Netherlands, Belgium, Italy, Slovenia, Croatia, Australia, Estonia, Greece, Cyprus, Malta, Spain, Switzerland, Israel, Canada, Germany, United Arab Emirates, Luxembourg, Austria, United Kingdom, France, Japan, Portugal, Uruguay, Korea Rep. |
| Upper middle income | Belize, Iraq, Jordan, Albania, Namibia, Indonesia, Ecuador, Fiji, Botswana, Jamaica, South Africa, Maldives, Azerbaijan, Mexico, Peru, Turkey, Brazil, Colombia, Armenia, Suriname, Romania, Moldova (Republic of), Costa Rica, Kazakhstan, Panama, Argentina, Malaysia, Georgia, China, Mauritius, Thailand, Belarus, Russian Federation |
| Lower middle income | Angola, Pakistan, Zambia, Zimbabwe, Lesotho, Cameroon, India, Timor-Leste, Kenya, Tajikistan, Nigeria, Bangladesh, Nicaragua, Cambodia, Ghana, Eswatini, Egypt, Arab Rep., Bolivia, Bhutan, Algeria, Philippines, Kyrgyz Republic, Morocco, Vietnam, Tunisia, El Salvador, Ukraine, Mongolia, Iran (Islamic Republic of) |
| Low income | Mozambique, Burundi, Liberia, Afghanistan, Uganda, Madagascar, Malawi, Sudan, Rwanda, Gambia The |

**Source:** Author's preparation.

## 3.2. Sources of Data

The statistical and empirical investigations of this research are based on secondary data. While the required data is derived from World Development Indicators (WDI) (the World Bank), FAO and OECD. The necessary data is also used from the published research articles and government reports.

## 3.3. Theoretical Interlinkages Digitalization with Environmental Degradation

Theoretically, digitalization has a multifaceted relationship with environmental degradation. It appears that digitalization has a negative, positive and rebound impact on the environmental sector. Digitalization contributes environmental degradation due to massive increase in electronic and energy wastage (WEM, 2024). It may also increase energy demand and consumption which have a negative impact on the environment and ecosystem. High consumption of energy and electricity in digitalization enhance overwhelming pressure on ecosystems. Extensive digitalization also contributes to digital gadgets, e-wastage in the ecosystem (WEM, 2024). Moreover, production of digital devices and digital infrastructure may increase the demand of heavy metals like physical elements and metals in the ecosystem. Consequently, use of heavy metal in digitalization may increase biodiversity loss. Extensive digitalization would also increase water demand and its wastages. Digitalization may bring negative implications for human health.

*Figure 1. Theoretical interlinkagse of digitlization with environmental degrdadation*

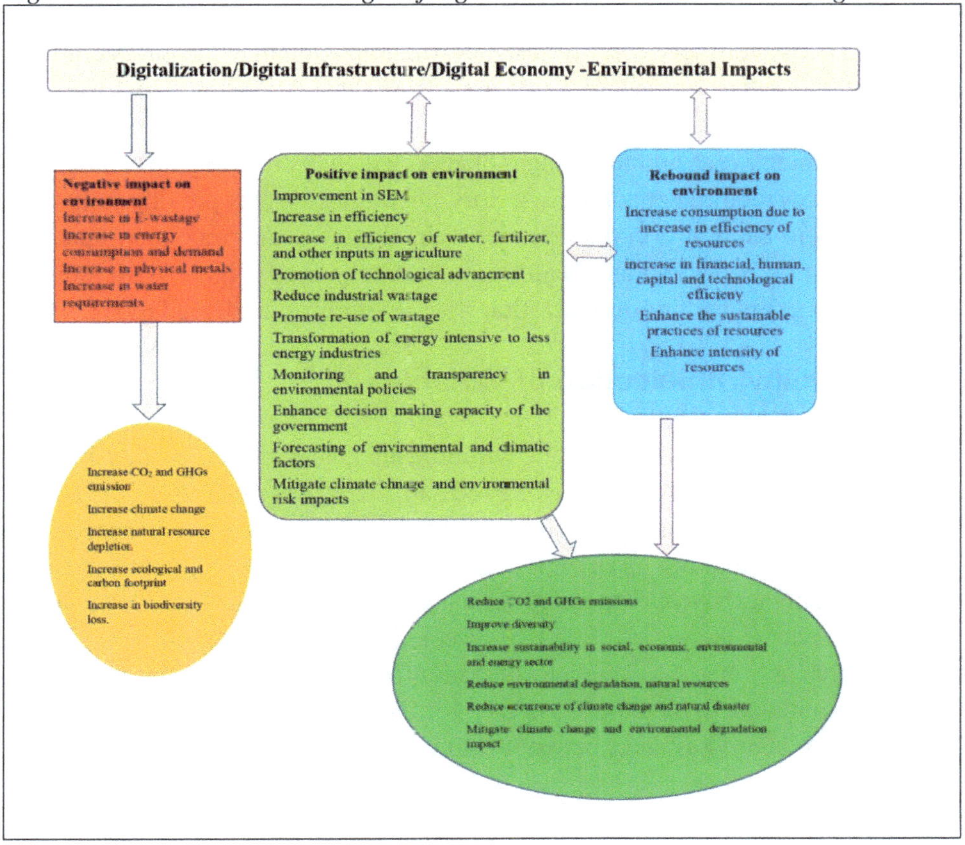


On the other hand, digitalization and DTs play a positive role to increase sustainability in most sectors (Xu et al., 2022; Gariba et al., 2024). For instance, IoT sensors may be conducive to increase smart energy management (SEM). SEM would reduce environmental risk. DTs may be imperative to increase water and energy efficiency, and reduce wastage of water and energy especially (Yuan et al., 2024). AI may be important to maintain a waste management system, increase recycling of waste materials and efficiency of resources. Thus, digitalization may be creative to increase agricultural sustainability. Use of digital devices may save time and requirements of physical resources. Advanced DTs improve resource use efficiency (Goel et al., 2024). Accordingly, digitalization and DTs can be fruitful to reduce climate change impact. DTs are supportive to make future predictions about climate change and environmental issues (Truong, 2022). Thus, governmental and concerned stakeholders make the future plan to improve ES.

Digitalization and DTs also have a rebound effect on the environment. Rebound effect may bring negative and positive externalities for the environmental sector and ecosystem services. For instance, digitalization may increase additional consumption and use of resources due increasing their efficiency. Moreover, digitalization may increase the transformation of industries from energy-intensive to less energy-intensive. Minimum usages of energy in industries may be beneficial to meet the energy requirement of other sectors. Digitalization may provide motivation to industries to adopt less carbon emitter technologies. Other rebound impacts of digitalization on education and health sectors are reported. Figure 1 explores the theoretical interlinkages of digitalization with environmental degradation.

### 3.4. Reliability of Selection of Variables

Previous researchers argued that environmental degradation is being hampered due to increasing $CO_2$ emissions (Hong & Xiao, 2024; Dai et al., 2025). However, $SO_2$, $NH_4$, CO, etc. also enhance environmental degradation. However, per capita $CO_2$ emissions can be included as an important indicator of environmental degradation. Numerous scholars have incorporated similar variables to assess the performance of the environment (Sikder et al., 2022; Shen et al., 2023; Zhang, Chen, et al., 2024). This research assumes that practices of minimizing per capita $CO_2$ emissions is a significant initiative to increase ES in the global countries. Accordingly, per capita $CO_2$ emission is used as an effective measurement for environmental degradation in this chapter.

Thereupon, there are many DTs like big data analytical tools, automation process and internet of things (IoT) are being used by different sectors for various purposes (Hong & Xiao, 2024; Goel et al., 2024). For instance, AI helps to reduce energy consumption, and increase sustainable practices of resources (Hong & Xiao, 2024). Big data is being used by China for improving green development patterns (Zhang, Liang et al., 2024). The mentioned DTs have the potential to address environmental issues (Truong, 2022). AI and DTs have significant environmental impacts (Samuel et al., 2022). OECD (2026) also provided a specific set of variables to examine the performance of digital transformation. As statistical data of the above-mentioned variables is not available for the selected countries. Thus, this study includes internet users, fixed telephone subscriptions, fixed broadband subscribers, ATMs, and mobile cellular subscriptions to integrate as an index i.e., digital inclusion index (*DII*). These indicators help to develop appropriate digital transformation in a nation (Singh et al., 2024). Abbas and Zaman (2024) used internet users as a representative variable for digitalization. Thus, the integration of these variables is considered as a *DII* for the selected countries. In this chapter, *DII* determines the relative performance of global countries in digital transformation. These are effective variables that promote digital infrastructure and digital transformation (An et al., 2024). Simple descriptive analysis is used to develop the *DII* in this research and technique for its estimation is adopted from studies of Singh and Jyoti (2023); Singh et al. (2024).

*Table 3. Description of the variables*

| Variables | Symbol | Unit | Proxy variables for | Variable's Category |
|---|---|---|---|---|
| Per capita $CO_2$ emissions | *$CO_2EPC$* | Metric tons | Environmental degradation | DVs/IVs |
| Digital inclusion index | *DII* | Number | Digitalization | |
| Education expenditure (% of GNI) | *EE* | % | Public Investment in Education sector | Control variables (*CVs*) |
| Employment in industry (% of total employment) | *EI* | % | Industrialization | |
| Foreign direct investment, net inflows (% of GDP) | *FDINI* | % | Foreign investment | |
| GDP per capita (constant 2015 US$) | *GDPPC* | US$ | ED | |
| Inflation, GDP deflator (annual %) | *IGDPD* | % | | |
| Population density (people per sq. km of land area) | *PD* | Number | Demographic change | |
| Renewable energy consumption (% of total final energy consumption) | *REC* | % | Development and innovation in energy sector | |
| Scientific and technical journal articles | *STJAs* | Number | Technological diffusion | |
| GDP per person employed (constant 2017 PPP $) | *GDPPE* | PPP US$ | ED | Instrumental variable |

**Source:** Variables are selected as per the previous literature and availability of statistical data.

Moreover, education is creative to increase ED. Human skilled development is highly potential to apply DTs in the production sector effectively. Education has appeared as a crucial driver to increase social and human development. Education expenditure, thus, is used as a proxy variable to capture the impact of skilled development and public investment in the education sector on environmental degradation and digitalization. However, environmental degradation may increase as employment opportunities in the industrial sector increase. Sikder et al. (2022) noted that $CO_2$ emissions increase as industrialization increases. Conversely, industrial development may be positive to promote digitalization.

*FDINI* are helpful to increase technological, infrastructure and business development (Yuan et al., 2024). *FDINI* works as an effective driver to increase technology transfer and capital investment. GDP per capita measures the level of ED (Adebayo et al., 2022; Shen et al., 2023; Zhang et al., 2023; Yuan et al., 2024), and its effective measures of ED (Zhang, Chen, et al., 2024). However, extensive ED brings more environmental pollution and destruction in ecosystem services (Yuan et al., 2024; Singh & Srinivasan, 2026). Environmental degradation and digitalization have a crucial relationship with inflation GDP deflator. Increases in the price of raw materials may reduce production and utilization of natural resources. Therefore, somehow inflation may be positive to increase ES.

*Figure 2. Nexus of digital inclusion with environmental degradation and other variables*

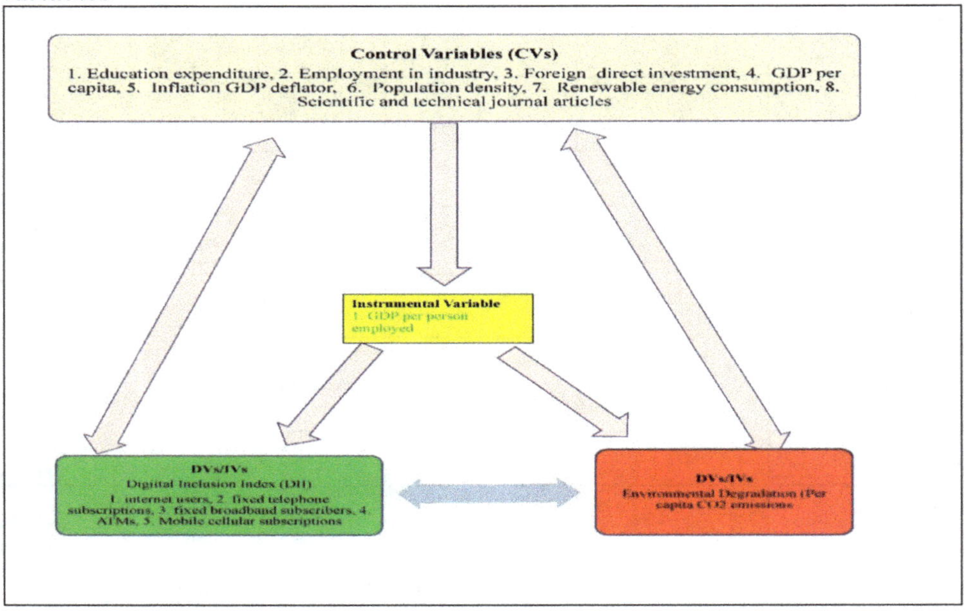


**Source:** *Author's creation.*

Production of energy from various sources like sun, water and air is known as renewable energy. Accordingly, energy can be used for multiple purposes in a nation. Renewable energy consumption (*REC*) helps to improve environmental quality (Istrate et al., 2024). Digitalization is effective to increase energy intensity and its saving (Xu et al., 2022; Shen et al., 2023; Cao & Peng, 2023). While digitalization may cause increased energy consumption (WEM, 2024). Increasing *REC* also signifies the development and innovation in the energy sector. Consequently, *REC* may also provide incentive to energy producers to adopt digital practices. Henceforth, *REC* is helpful to increase digitalization. Scientific research articles are an effective medium to increase technological diffusion across scientific sectors. It creates a conducive ecosystem to develop and discover advanced technologies for all sectors. Thus, these are originators of technological innovation and development which further promote DTs, digitalization, digital infrastructure and digital platform (Dai et al., 2025). Technological innovation is also the originator of environmental and green technologies which are beneficial for the environmental sector. However, technological diffusion may be positive to increase industrial growth. Consequently, overwhelming industrialization may enhance environmental degradation (Zhang, Chen, et al., 2024; Singh & Srinivasan, 2026). Population has negative implications on the environmental sector. Thereupon, GDP per person employed is used as an instrumental variable (*IV*) to check the robustness of empirical findings. Concise summary of all variables is highlighted in Table 3. Figure 2 infer the segregation of these variables. Figure 2 also shows the inter-causal relationship of digital inclusion with environmental degradation.

### 3.5. Statistical and Empirical Analysis

The simple descriptive analysis (i.e., mean, percentage, and correlation coefficients analysis) is applied in this research. Thereupon, past researchers developed different empirical models to assess the influence of DTs and digital economy and other variables on environmental degradation, and pollution (Zhang et al., 2023; Shen et al., 2023; Liu, 2023; Zhang, Chen, et al., 2024; Xiao et al., 2024). Gariba et al. (2024) investigated the role of public digitalization in ES using structural equation modelling. However, the Environmental Kuznets curve (EKC) theory is the oldest theory which explores the association of environmental degradation with economic growth. Since, economic growth and development has a significant reliance on digitalization and DTs. EKC theory is not applied to observe the association of digitalization and environmental degradation in this research. Furthermore, the ARDL model is applied by Sikder et al. (2022) to examine the impact of economic growth, industrialisation and energy use hon $CO_2$ emissions. Accordingly, log-linear forms of regression equations are formulated in this research. The relationship of $CO_2EPC$ and $DII$ with explanatory variables are specified as:

$$(CO_2EPC) = f\{(DII), (EE), (EI), (FDINI), (GDPPC), (IGDPD), (PD), (REC), (STJAs)\} \tag{1}$$

$$(DII) = f\{(CO_2EPC), (EE), (EI), (FDINI), (GDPPC), (IGDPD), (PD), (REC), (STJAs)\} \tag{2}$$

The above-mentioned equations are transformed in following equations:

$$ln(CO_2EPC)_{ct} = \beta_0 + \beta_1\, ln(DII)_{ct} + \beta_2\, ln(EE)_{ct} + \beta_3\, ln(EI)_{ct} + \beta_4\, ln(FDINI)_{ct} + \beta_5\, ln(GDPPC)_{ct} + \beta_6\, ln(IGDPD)_{ct} + \beta_7\, ln(PD)_{ct} + \beta_8\, ln(REC)_{ct} + \beta_9\, ln(STJAs)_{ct} + \lambda_{ct} \quad (3)$$

$$ln(CO_2EPC)_{ct} = \xi_0 + \xi_1\, ln(DII)_{ct} + \xi_2\, ln(EE)_{ct} + \xi_3\, ln(EI)_{ct} + \xi_4\, ln(FDINI)_{ct} + \xi_5\, ln(GDPPC)_{ct} + \xi_6\, ln(IGDPD)_{ct} + \xi_7\, ln(PD)_{ct} + \xi_8\, ln(REC)_{ct} + \xi_9\, ln(STJAs)_{ct} + \mu_{ct} \quad (4)$$

Here, $\beta_0$ and $\xi_0$ is constant coefficient; $\beta_1$, ..., $\beta_9$ and $\xi_1$, $\xi_2$, ...., $\xi_9$ are coefficient of corresponding *EV*s; $\lambda_{ct}$ and $\mu_{ct}$ are error-term; *c* is cross-sectional country; and *t* is time period; and *ln* is the log of respective variables in equation (3) and equation (4). The specification of the variables is given in Table 3.

## 3.6. Robustness Test and Validity of Empirical Results

Robustness of empirical findings are estimated through inclusion of instrument variable in equation (3) and equation (4). GDP per person employed (*GDPPE*) is included as instrumental variables. For this, following regression equations are formulated:

$$ln(CO_2EPC)_{ct} = \alpha_0 + \alpha_1\, ln(GDPPE)_{ct} + \phi_{ct} \quad (5)$$

$$ln(DII)_{ct} = \gamma_0 + \gamma_1\, ln(GDPPE)_{ct} + \gamma_{ct} \quad (6)$$

Here, $\alpha_0$ and $\gamma_0$ are constant coefficients; $\alpha_1$ and $\gamma_1$ are coefficient of respective variables in equation (5) and (6). *GDPPE* produce a significant impact on $CO_2EPC$ and *DII.* We also estimate the influence of *ED* and *DII* on *GDPEE* for inclusion of *GDPEE* as an instrumental variable. Thereupon, *GDPPE* can be used as an instrumental variable for robustness check of regression results of equation (3) and equation (4). The validity of regression coefficients is observed as estimating the correlation coefficients of various lags of error-terms of equation (3) and equation (4) (Singh & Srinivasan, 2026). Finally, Granger causality test is applied to examine the causal association of *DII* and $CO_2EPC$ with explanatory variables (Singh et al.,

2024). Following model is applied to identify the causal association of $CO_2EPC$ with digitalization:

$$(CO2EPC)_{ct} = \Psi_0 + \sum_{j=1}^{p} \Psi_{1,j} (CO2EPC)_{c,t-j} + \sum_{j=0}^{p} \Psi_{2,j} (DTI)_{c,t-j} + \delta_{ct} \quad (7)$$

Here, $j$ is various lags of dependent and independent various up to $p$; $t$ is time up to $T$; is fixed effect; $\Psi_1$ and $\Psi_2$ are coefficients of respective lags of related variables; $\delta_{ct}$ is error term in the mentioned equation. The causal association of other variables with environmental degradation and digitalization are also estimated as using the above-mentioned equation.

### 3.7. Final Estimation and Application of Statistical Software

The coefficient of *EV*s with *DII* and environmental degradation are estimated through *PCSE*s estimation as assuming that country-wise panel data have serial correlation, autocorrelation and heteroskedasticity (Singh et al., 2019; Li et al., 2024; Singh & Srinivasan, 2026). The existence of multi-correlation is detected through variance of inflation factors (*VIF*). MS excel is used to clean the statistical data and compile country-wise panel data. Correlation coefficients among the variables are estimated through SPSS software. The regression coefficients of the *EV*s with outputs are estimated through STATA software.

## 4. RESULTS AND DISCUSSION

### 4.1. Statistical Measurement of the Variables

Table 4 explore the statistical properties of the dependent and independent variables.

### 4.2. Correlation among the Variables

The correlation coefficients of all variables (except *IGDPD*, *REC* and *PD*) with $CO_2EPC$ are observed to be positive (Table 5). Thus, estimates suggest that environmental degradation is positively associated with digitalization ($r$ = 0.712**), education expenditure ($r$ = 0.183**), employment in industry ($r$ = 0.429**), *FDINI* ($r$ = 0.098**), per capita GDP ($r$ = 0.689**), technological diffusion ($r$ = 0.226**) and GDP per person employed ($r$ = 0.769**). Population density ($r$ = - 0.024), *REC* ($r$= - 0.565**) and *IGDP* ($r$= - 0.096**) are negatively correlated with environmental degradation. Moreover, environmental degradation ($r = 0.712^{**}$), education expenditure ($r = 0.268^{**}$), employment in industries ($r = 0.469^{**}$), *FDINI* ($r = 0.107^{**}$), GDP per capita ($r = 0.734^{**}$), GDP per person employed ($r = 0.781^{**}$), *PD* ($r = 0.097^{**}$) and technological diffusion ($r = 0.271^{**}$) are positively correlated with digitalization. Education expenditure has a positively correlation with employment in industries, *FDINI*, *GDPPC* and *GDPPE*.

Digitalization, education expenditure, *GDPPC*, *GDPPE* and technological diffusion are positively correlated with employment in industries. Most variables (excluding *IGDPD* and *REC*) are positively correlated with *GDPPC* and *GDPPE*. Furthermore, it is noted a statistically significant association of *IGDPD*, *REC* and technological diffusion with other variables. It is, thus, found a complex association among the explanatory variables.

*Table 4. Statistical properties of the variables*

| Variable | | Mean | Std. Dev. | Min | Max | Observations | Skewness |
|---|---|---|---|---|---|---|---|
| *ln(DII)* | overall | -1.4533 | 1.0937 | -7.7083 | -0.1366 | N=1998 | -1.7454 |
| | between | | 0.9768 | -5.4516 | -0.1771 | n=111 | |
| | within | | 0.5001 | -4.5344 | 0.9449 | T=18 | |
| *ln($CO_2$EPC)* | overall | 0.8484 | 1.3731 | -3.8263 | 3.3159 | N=1998 | -0.8776 |
| | between | | 1.3656 | -3.3403 | 3.0869 | n=111 | |
| | within | | 0.1907 | -0.4296 | 1.8657 | T=18 | |
| *ln(EI)* | overall | 2.9427 | 0.4499 | 0.8839 | 3.7024 | N=1998 | -1.4354 |
| | between | | 0.4357 | 1.1109 | 3.6517 | n=111 | |
| | within | | 0.1194 | 2.1099 | 3.7665 | T=18 | |
| *ln(FDINI)* | overall | 1.0593 | 1.2728 | -6.3935 | 6.1072 | N=1998 | -0.5027 |
| | between | | 0.9898 | -2.6601 | 3.9187 | n=111 | |
| | within | | 0.8054 | -5.0811 | 5.2799 | T=18 | |
| *ln(GDPPC)* | overall | 8.7594 | 1.3909 | 5.5735 | 11.6300 | N=1998 | -0.0829 |
| | between | | 1.3896 | 5.6702 | 11.5725 | n=111 | |
| | within | | 0.1417 | 7.9589 | 9.3166 | T=18 | |
| *ln(GDPPE)* | overall | 10.3708 | 1.0138 | 7.4423 | 12.5259 | N=1998 | -0.6400 |
| | between | | 1.0097 | 7.5385 | 12.4248 | n=111 | |
| | within | | 0.1303 | 9.5689 | 10.9609 | T=18 | |
| *ln(IGDPD)* | overall | 1.2935 | 1.2541 | -8.3453 | 6.4051 | N=1998 | -0.8428 |
| | between | | 0.8488 | -0.8179 | 3.2330 | n=111 | |
| | within | | 0.9265 | -6.2864 | 5.6593 | T=18 | |

continued on following page

*Table 4. Continued*

| Variable | | Mean | Std. Dev. | Min | Max | Observations | Skewness |
|---|---|---|---|---|---|---|---|
| *ln(REC)* | overall | 2.7501 | 1.4891 | -4.6052 | 4.5648 | N=1998 | -1.8120 |
| | between | | 1.4490 | -4.4446 | 4.5297 | n=111 | |
| | within | | 0.3685 | -4.7426 | 4.7437 | T=18 | |
| *ln(STJAS)* | overall | 7.0241 | 2.7603 | -3.0931 | 13.4147 | N=1998 | -0.2048 |
| | between | | 2.7083 | 1.5525 | 12.6421 | n=111 | |
| | within | | 0.5888 | -4.6162 | 9.6663 | T=18 | |
| *ln(ED)* | overall | 1.3917 | 0.4061 | -0.1625 | 2.2752 | N=1998 | -0.8243 |
| | between | | 0.3882 | -0.1625 | 2.2140 | n=111 | |
| | within | | 0.1246 | 0.4994 | 2.0433 | T=18 | |
| *ln(PD)* | overall | 4.2530 | 1.3278 | 0.4902 | 7.4606 | N=1998 | -0.3705 |
| | between | | 1.3303 | 0.6083 | 7.2251 | n=111 | |
| | within | | 0.0915 | 3.6097 | 4.5969 | T=18 | |

**Source:** Author's estimation.

*Table 5. Correlation matrix*

| Variables | $CO_2EPC$ | *DII* | *EE* | *EI* | *FDINI* | *GDPPC* |
|---|---|---|---|---|---|---|
| $CO_2EPC$ | 1 | 0.712** | 0.183** | 0.429** | 0.098** | 0.689** |
| *DII* | 0.712** | 1 | 0.268** | 0.469** | 0.107** | 0.734** |
| *EE* | 0.183** | 0.268** | 1 | 0.179** | 0.082** | 0.258** |
| *EI* | 0.429** | 0.469** | 0.179** | 1 | -0.02 | 0.161** |
| *FDINI* | 0.098** | 0.107** | 0.082** | -0.020 | 1 | 0.147** |
| *GDPPC* | 0.689** | 0.734** | 0.258** | 0.161** | 0.147** | 1 |
| *GDPPE* | 0.769** | 0.781** | 0.278** | 0.340** | 0.153** | 0.913** |
| *IGDPD* | -0.096** | -0.178** | -0.099** | -0.091** | -0.039* | -0.145** |
| *PD* | -0.024 | 0.097** | -0.105** | -0.002 | 0.205** | 0.054** |
| *REC* | -0.565** | -0.578** | -0.183** | -0.620** | -0.092** | -0.301** |
| *STJAs* | 0.226** | 0.271** | -0.114** | 0.221** | -0.058** | 0.170** |

*Table 6. Correlation matrix Conti...*

| Variables | *GDPPE* | *IGDPD* | *PD* | *REC* | *STJAs* |
|---|---|---|---|---|---|
| $CO_2EPC$ | 0.769** | -0.096** | -0.024 | -0.565** | 0.226** |
| *DII* | 0.781** | -0.178** | 0.097** | -0.578** | 0.271** |
| *EE* | 0.278** | -0.099** | -0.105** | -0.183** | -0.114** |
| *EI* | 0.340** | -0.091** | -0.002 | -0.620** | 0.221** |
| *FDINI* | 0.153** | -0.039* | 0.205** | -0.092** | -0.058** |
| *GDPPC* | 0.913** | -0.145** | 0.054** | -0.301** | 0.170** |
| *GDPPE* | 1 | -0.147** | 0.042* | -0.476** | 0.149** |
| *IGDPD* | -0.147** | 1 | -0.077** | 0.112** | -0.066** |
| *PD* | 0.042* | -0.077** | 1 | -0.139** | 0.042* |
| *REC* | -0.476** | 0.112** | -0.139** | 1 | -0.186** |
| *STJAs* | 0.149** | -0.066** | 0.042* | -0.186** | 1 |

**Source:** Author's estimation. **Note:** ** shows that correlation coefficient is significant at the 0.01 level and * shows that correlation coefficient is significant at the 0.05 level.

## 4.3. Statistical Interpretation of Regression Results

The *VIF* values signify that explanatory variables do not have multicollinearity (Table 6 and Table 7). All *EV*s have independent impact on environmental degradation and digitalization. Also, these models have reliability and consistency. Around 91.89% variation in environmental degradation can be captured by the undertaken variables according to $R^2$ value (Table 6). While 78.24% variation in digitalization can be captured by undertaken variables as per estimated to $R^2$ value (Table 7).

The coefficients of *DII* with $CO_2EPC$ are reported positive and vice-versa. The result infer that digital inclusion is caused to increase environmental degradation. Multiple studies have already detected that digitalization is causing a large quantity of electronic and ICT wastage (WEM, 2024). Few studies like Kuang et al. (2024) argued that the digital economy helps to reduce $CO_2$ emissions. Firoz et al. (2021); Hong and Xiao (2024) also noted that AI can be applied to reduce environmental pollution. An et al. (2024) also noted a positive contribution of the digital economy in green innovation. However, our result specified that environmental degradation is expected to increase as digitalization increases. The global countries, therefore, should develop environmentally friendly DTs and sustainable digitalization to reduce environmental degradation (UNDP, 2026). Environmental degradation is found positive to increase digital inclusion. It means that environmental degradation may provide a motivation to industrial and other sectors to take precautionary actions in terms of DTs and digitalization to increase ES. Moreover, the government may also take obligatory actions and make it mandatory for industries to reduce environmental pollution.

Education helps to increase understanding of the people to apply DTs for different purposes. Furthermore, educated people are more conscious towards environmental issues. Further, a positive coefficient of education expenditure with *DII* is detected. The result indicates that education expenditure helps to increase digital inclusion. Industrial development is caused to increase $CO_2$ emissions in the environment (Sikder et al., 2022). It is, thus, noted as a positive coefficient of *EI* with $CO_2EPC$. Shen et al. (2023) argued that digital industrialization is causing increased environmental degradation. Hong and Xiao (2024) also noticed that industrialization is responsible for increasing environmental degradation. While industrialization is found to be a promotive indicator of digitalization. However, Tao et al. (2025) noted the industrial structure may cause a reduction in environmental quality.

*Table 7. Impact of digitalization and CVs on environmental degradation*

| **Number of obs.** | | **1998** | | $R^2$ | | **0.9189** |
|---|---|---|---|---|---|---|
| **Number of groups** | | **111** | | *Wald Chi²* | | **48244.86*** |
| **Obs. per group** | | **18** | | *Mean VIF* | | **2.04** |
| *ln($CO_2EPC$)=[DV]* | *Reg. Coef.* | *Std. Err.* | *z* | *P>\|z\|* | **[95% Conf. Interval]** | |
| ln(DII) | 0.2366* | 0.0437 | 5.41 | 0.000 | 0.1509 | 0.3224 |
| *ln(EI)* | 0.6300* | 0.0237 | 26.63 | 0.000 | 0.5837 | 0.6764 |
| *ln(FDINI)* | 0.0265* | 0.0054 | 4.9 | 0.000 | 0.0159 | 0.0370 |
| *ln(GDPPC)* | 0.4551* | 0.0241 | 18.86 | 0.000 | 0.4078 | 0.5024 |
| *ln(IGDPD)* | 0.0197** | 0.0090 | 2.19 | 0.028 | 0.0021 | 0.0373 |
| *ln(REC)* | -0.2231* | 0.0032 | -69.32 | 0.000 | -0.2294 | -0.2168 |
| *ln(STJAS)* | 0.0388* | 0.0015 | 25.3 | 0.000 | 0.0358 | 0.0418 |
| *ln(EE)* | -0.0122 | 0.0128 | -0.95 | 0.341 | -0.0374 | 0.0129 |
| *ln(PD)* | -0.1192* | 0.0037 | -31.8 | 0.000 | -0.1265 | -0.1118 |
| *Cons. Coef.* | -3.8364* | 0.3325 | -11.54 | 0.000 | -4.4881 | -3.1847 |

**Source:** Author's estimation.

*Table 8. Impact of environmental degradation and CVs on digitalization*

| **Number of obs.** | | **1998** | | $R^2$ | | **0.7824** |
|---|---|---|---|---|---|---|
| **Number of groups** | | **111** | | *Wald* $Chi^2$ | | **3091.06*** |
| **Obs. per group** | | **18** | | *Mean VIF* | | **3.21** |
| *ln(DII)=[DV]* | *Reg. Coef.* | *Std. Err.* | *z* | P>\|z\| | **[95%Conf.** | **Interval]** |
| *ln($CO_2$EPC)* | 0.4026* | 0.0229 | 17.560 | 0.000 | 0.3576 | 0.4475 |
| *ln(EI)* | 0.4000* | 0.0355 | 11.280 | 0.000 | 0.3305 | 0.4695 |
| *ln(FDINI)* | 0.0574* | 0.0145 | 3.960 | 0.000 | 0.0290 | 0.0858 |
| *ln(GDPPC)* | 0.2137* | 0.0246 | 8.690 | 0.000 | 0.1655 | 0.2619 |
| *ln(IGDPD)* | -0.0619* | 0.0179 | -3.470 | 0.001 | -0.0969 | -0.0269 |
| *ln(REC)* | 0.0770* | 0.0080 | 9.590 | 0.000 | 0.0612 | 0.0927 |
| *ln(STJAS)* | 0.0131*** | 0.0077 | 1.690 | 0.091 | -0.0021 | 0.0282 |
| *ln(EE)* | 0.0548 | 0.0367 | 1.490 | 0.135 | -0.0171 | 0.1268 |
| *ln(PD)* | 0.0419* | 0.0074 | 5.650 | 0.000 | 0.0274 | 0.0564 |
| *Cons. Coef.* | -5.3822* | 0.3735 | -14.410 | 0.000 | -6.1142 | -4.6502 |

**Source:** Author's estimation.

*FDINI* is highly effective to increase ED through creating more business and job opportunities, and infrastructure and technological development (Kuang et al., 2024; Yuan et al., 2024). Furthermore, *FDINI* also generates physical assets and technological innovation. Therefore, the impact of *FDINI* on *DII* is found positive. Conversely, industrial development causes more environmental degradation. The coefficient of *FDINI* with *$CO_2$EPC* is detected positive. The estimate implies that *FDINI* is primarily leading to increased environmental degradation. Empirical research of Tao et al. (2025) also noted that inward FDI may reduce the positive impact of the digital economy on the environment. Findings of Tao et al. (2025)'study were based on panel data of 70 nations during 2003 – 2023. The production sector requires more natural resources and ecosystem service. ED is caused to increase environmental degradation. Recent findings of Singh & Srinivasan, 2026) also stated a positive contribution of ED in environmental degradation. Environmental degradation is expected to increase as inflation increases. *REC* is useful to reduce burden on ecosystem services and it increases environmental development. Thereupon, *REC* is found positive and significant to increase digitalization. The discovery and dissemination of new technologies and innovation depend on scientific research articles. It helps to increase the knowledge transfer across scientists and researchers. Thereupon, it may be an effective determinant to increase industrial development. While technological dissemination is found valuable to increase digitalization.

## 4.4. Results of Robustness Test and Validity of Coefficients

*Table 9. Coefficients of CVs and IVs with digitization and environmental degradation*

| *DVs* | *ln($CO_2$EPC)=[DV]* | *ln($CO_2$EPC)=[DV]* | *ln(DII)=[DV]* | *ln(DII)=[DV]* |
|---|---|---|---|---|
| *CVs/IV* | *Reg. Coef.* | *Reg. Coef.* | *Reg. Coef.* | *Reg. Coef.* |
| *ln(DII)* | 0.2351*<br>(0.0441) | 0.2366*<br>(0.0437) | - | - |
| *ln($CO_2$EPC)* | - | - | 0.3962*<br>(0.0238) | 0.4026*<br>(0.0229) |
| *ln(EI)* | 0.6212*<br>(0.0255) | 0.6300*<br>(0.0237) | 0.3357*<br>(0.0315) | 0.4000*<br>(0.0355) |
| *ln(FDINI)* | 0.0269*<br>(0.0054) | 0.0265*<br>(0.0054) | 0.0602*<br>(0.0145) | 0.0574*<br>(0.0145) |
| *ln(GDPPC)* | 0.4376*<br>(0.0218) | 0.4551*<br>(0.0241) | 0.0904*<br>(0.0366) | 0.2137*<br>(0.0246) |
| *ln(IGDPD)* | 0.0189**<br>(0.0093) | 0.0197**<br>(0.009) | -0.0667*<br>(0.0178) | -0.0619*<br>(0.0179) |
| *ln(REC)* | -0.2212*<br>(0.0036) | -0.2231*<br>(0.0032) | 0.0892*<br>(0.0073) | 0.0770*<br>(0.008) |
| *ln(STJAS)* | 0.0388*<br>(0.0015) | 0.0388*<br>(0.0015) | 0.0134***<br>(0.0077) | 0.0131***<br>(0.0077) |
| *ln(EE)* | -0.0113<br>(0.0128) | -0.0122<br>(0.0128) | 0.0611***<br>(0.0364) | 0.0548<br>(0.0367) |
| *ln(PD)* | -0.1183*<br>(0.0034) | -0.1192*<br>(0.0037) | 0.0472*<br>(0.0072) | 0.0419*<br>(0.0074) |
| *ln(GDPPE)* | 0.0295<br>(0.0256) | - | 0.2054*<br>(0.0301) | - |
| *Cons. Coef.* | -3.9749*<br>(0.3877) | -3.8364*<br>(0.3325) | -6.3022*<br>(0.3523) | -5.3822*<br>(0.3735) |

**Source:** Author's estimation. **Note:** *, ** and *** infer that coefficients are statistically significant at 1%, 5% and 10%, significance level, respectively.

GDP per person employed is used as an instrumental variable (*IV*) as an independent variable in equation (3) and equation (4). The coefficients of explanatory variables and *CV*s with environmental degradation and *DII* are found similar to considering *IV* as independent variable (Table 8). It signifies that the coefficients have validity. Moreover, the first 8 lags of error-term in both models have a significant correlation with their preceding lags (Table 9). Hence, the results imply that regression coefficients have internal consistency and validity.

*Table 10. Correlation matrix among the various lags of error terms*

| **Validity of coefficients of digitalization and *CVs* with environmental degradation** | | | | | | | | |
|---|---|---|---|---|---|---|---|---|
| **No. of lags (s)** | ***L1*** | ***L2*** | ***L3*** | ***L4*** | ***L5*** | ***L6*** | ***L7*** | ***L8*** |
| *L*1 | 1.000 | | | | | | | |
| *L*2 | 0.9627* | 1.000 | | | | | | |
| *L*3 | 0.9340* | 0.9628* | 1.000 | | | | | |
| *L*4 | 0.9009* | 0.9342* | 0.9618* | 1.000 | | | | |
| *L*5 | 0.8713* | 0.8990* | 0.9327* | 0.9608* | 1.000 | | | |
| *L*6 | 0.8423* | 0.8679* | 0.8958* | 0.9313* | 0.9595* | 1.000 | | |
| *L*7 | 0.8199* | 0.8380* | 0.8633* | 0.8928* | 0.9294* | 0.9579* | 1.000 | |
| *L*8 | 0.8058* | 0.8165* | 0.8324* | 0.8601* | 0.8903* | 0.9283* | 0.9579* | 1.0000 |
| Validity of coefficients of environmental degradation and *CVs* with digitalization | | | | | | | | |
| No. of lags (s) | *L*1 | *L*2 | *L*3 | *L*4 | *L*5 | *L*6 | *L*7 | *L*8 |
| *L*1 | 1.000 | | | | | | | |
| *L*2 | 0.9303* | 1.000 | | | | | | |
| *L*3 | 0.8215* | 0.9295* | 1.000 | | | | | |
| *L*4 | 0.6952* | 0.8199* | 0.9293* | 1.000 | | | | |
| *L*5 | 0.5747* | 0.6833* | 0.8150* | 0.9289* | 1.000 | | | |
| *L*6 | 0.4790* | 0.5527* | 0.6698* | 0.8093* | 0.9261* | 1.000 | | |
| *L*7 | 0.3999* | 0.4544* | 0.5343* | 0.6570* | 0.8061* | 0.9283* | 1.000 | |
| *L*8 | 0.3221* | 0.3739* | 0.4377* | 0.5271* | 0.6625* | 0.8211* | 0.9386* | 1.000 |

**Source:** Author's estimation. **Note:** * shows that correlation coefficient is significant at the 0.05 level.

## 4.5. Results of Granger Causality Test

*Table 11. Causal relationship of environmental degradation and digital inclusion with CVs*

| *DV* | **Environmental degradation** | | | |
|---|---|---|---|---|
| *Indicators* | *W*-**bar** | *Z*-**bar** | *Z*-**bar tilde** | *Conclusion* |
| *ln*(*DII*) | 2.1797 | 8.7886* | 5.6736* | $H_0$ rejected |
| *ln*(*EI*) | 2.9537 | 14.5546* | 10.0082* | $H_0$ rejected |
| *ln*(*FDINI*) | 1.9036 | 6.7319* | 4.1274* | $H_0$ rejected |
| *ln*(*GDPPC*) | 4.8948 | 29.0155* | 20.8794* | $H_0$ rejected |
| *ln*(*IGDPD*) | 1.6869 | 5.1176* | 2.9138* | $H_0$ rejected |

continued on following page

*Table 11. Continued*

| *DV* | Environmental degradation | | | |
|---|---|---|---|---|
| *Indicators* | *W*-bar | *Z*-bar | *Z*-bar tilde | *Conclusion* |
| *ln(REC)* | 3.8114 | 20.9444* | 14.8118* | $H_0$ rejected |
| *ln(STJAS)* | 2.5854 | 11.8108* | 7.9455* | $H_0$ rejected |
| *ln(PD)* | 3.8039 | 20.8888* | 14.7700* | $H_0$ rejected |
| *ln(GDPPE)* | 3.1700 | 16.1659* | 11.2195* | $H_0$ rejected |
| *DV* | Digital inclusion | | | |
| *ln($CO_2$EPC)* | 2.4900 | 11.1004* | 7.4115* | $H_0$ rejected |
| *ln(EI)* | 3.1617 | 16.1046* | 11.1734* | $H_0$ rejected |
| *ln(FDINI)* | 1.7307 | 5.4437* | 3.1589* | $H_0$ rejected |
| *ln(GDPPC)* | 2.6949 | 12.6264* | 8.5586* | $H_0$ rejected |
| *ln(IGDPD)* | 1.5105 | 3.8028* | 1.9254* | $H_0$ rejected |
| *ln(REC)* | 3.1581 | 16.0777* | 11.1532* | $H_0$ rejected |
| *ln(STJAS)* | 3.4341 | 18.1338* | 12.6989* | $H_0$ rejected |
| *ln(PD)* | 3.6800 | 19.9653* | 14.0758* | $H_0$ rejected |
| *ln(GDPPE)* | 2.9877 | 14.8081* | 10.1987* | $H_0$ rejected |

**Source:** Author's estimation. **Note:** * indicate that coefficients are statistically significant at 1% significance level.

Most variables have a causal relationship with *DV*s (Table 10). Thus, future prediction of environmental degradation and digitalization can be estimated using these variables. Thereupon, it also appeared a positive and bi-lateral relationship between environmental degradation and digital inclusion (Table 10). Hence, undertaken variables can be applied significantly to make the future prediction about environmental degradation and digitalization.

## 5. CONCLUSION

The existing review implies that digitalization is helpful to reduce environmental degradation. However, digitalization and digital infrastructure are causing increased wastage of raw materials, e-wastage, and packaging in online marketing. Wastage from the electricity sector is also increasing due to adoption of digitalization. Moreover, digitalization is also increasing an additional burden on the energy sector. Most scholars also argued that extensive development of digitalization in different sectors are contributing $CO_2$ and GHGs emissions. Thus, digitalization also brings new challenges for the environmental sector. Extensive digitalization may be more dangerous in developing nations which are moving towards digitalization. Moreover, previous scholars have adopted different variables for digitalization and environmental degradation for assessing their inter-causal relationship across countries. Therefore, findings of previous literature do not provide clear association among the mentioned variables. The empirical findings of this research imply that environmental degradation is increasing due to demographic change, ED and FDI. Employment in the industrial sector, *FDINI*, ED, inflation and scientific development are diminishing environmental quality. Thus, practices of sustainable ED are required to increase environmental quality. Industrial sector should apply green technologies and innovation to ES. Moreover, generation of green employment in all sectors would be greatly beneficial to increase ES. Furthermore, industries should create green jobs and develop green products to increase environmental quality. Education expenditure and *REC* help to reduce environmental degradation. Hence, extensive investment in energy and education sectors are required to increase ES in the global countries. The global nations should also apply scientific mechanisms to produce extensive energy from renewable sources. Most specifically, global nations should also pursue sustainable use of energy for improving ES. Our results reveal that digitization and digital infrastructure are caused to increase environmental degradation. Therefore, the global countries should think about increasing sustainable digital development to increase the protection of ecosystem services and reduce environmental degradation. Sustainable digitalization will ensure the ES effectively (UNDP, 2026). Thus, use of green digital technologies and green innovation in digital sector is required to increase ES. Moreover, industrialization, *FDINI*, *ED*, *REC*, technological diffusion and education expenditure showed a positive impact on digitalization. Thereupon, inflation is found harmful for the environmental sector and digitalization. Moreover, green industrialization and green *ED* would be imperative to increase ES.

## 6. POLICY SUGGESTIONS

It is essential to increase innovation in digitalization for improving ES in the global countries. Adoption of green innovation for developing digital platform would be beneficial to ensure a sustainable future of present and coming generation worldwide. Environmental degradation to be increased as industrialization, ED and technological diffusion increase. Digitalization improves as FDI, education expenditure, per capita GDP, industrialization and REC increase. REC and education expenditure are found positive to reduce environmental degradation. Further, extensive use of REC in industrial and agricultural sectors would be positive to sustain the common properties of ecosystem services which help to increase sustainable development in global countries. Further, extensive investment in education and green sectors helps are also required. Technological advancement and digitalization are positively associated with ES (Samuel et al., 2022). Therefore, balanced application of DTs may be favorable for reducing their negative impact on the environmental sector. For instance, reducing digital wastages may be a fruitful initiative to minimize the negative impact of digitalization on ES.

Responsible e-waste management practices through increasing sustainable digital transformation is required in developing nations (WEM, 2024). Re-use of industrial and digital wastages would be beneficial for production and environmental sectors. The global countries should be keen to enhance technology innovation and public digitalization to attain sustainable development goals (SDGs). Public digitalization is also abating GHGs emissions. Huge investment is essential in the IT sector to increase digital infrastructure. Development of green infrastructure is essential to increase ES in the long-term. Digital literacy of people would be improved as application of DTs in increase their life (Alojail & Khan, 2023). The global communities should improve their digital literacy to attain greater benefits from digitalization and DTs. Human survival is not possible without DTs. Thus, sustainable practices of digitalization and DTs by all people would help to increase sustainable development. For instance, the necessary application of DTs by the public will enhance their mental and physical health. Sustainable digital development would be creative to meet sustainable need of people in diverse fields. Sustainable development and SDGs are also critically linked with DTs.

It is a crucial challenge for global communities to reduce environmental degradation in the current digital era. Therefore, global countries should create green digital infrastructure to protect the environmental sector and ecological services. Environmental degradation is continuously degraded due to technological change and DTs. The global countries, therefore, should increase their dependence on green DTs to abate $CO_2$ and GHGs emissions. Green urbanization may be a significant initiative towards ES and sustainable development. Green urbanization may be improved as protection of tree, river, and other ecosystem services in urban area. The government should promote green business opportunities for people in rural and urban areas. Financial organizations should increase their investment in green projects. Agricultural intensification must be improved by applying green DTs, appropriate technology and environmental technologies. Green management practices in all sectors must be initiated to increase ES (Cai & Hong, 2024). Moreover, FDI must be initiated for developing Green Park, green business, green jobs, and green infrastructure to increase ES in the world.

## 7. INNOVATION OF THIS STUDY AND FURTHER RESEARCH DIRECTIONS

The theoretical literature with regards to DTs, digitalization, digital economy and digital infrastructure and environmental degradation are given in a holistic perspective in this research. The validity of empirical results is tested with some other statistical and empirical models. Finally, scope and area of further research are also finalized in this study. This study includes 111 countries which have diversity in undertaken explanatory variables. The empirical findings cannot be generalized across countries due to the existence of high diversity in DTs, and other variables. This research provides comprehensive and robust policy suggestions for abatement of $CO_2$ emissions. Some proxy variables for digitalization and environmental degradation are included in the empirical models. Hence, this research could not capture the actual and overall impact of digitalization on environmental degradation and vice-versa due to unavailability of recent data on advanced DTs for these countries. Furthermore, per capita $CO_2$ emission is only one indicator that measures environmental degradation. This research also could use some certain *CVs* in the empirical investigations. For example, this research could not examine the implications of advanced DTs like AI, cloud computing, 3D printing, IoT, big data etc. on environmental degradation. Moreover, primary data-based study can be conducted to examine the contribution of DTs and digitalization for improving ES in agricultural, tourism, transport, industrial and infrastructure. Existing scientists can also assess the consequences of the environmental sector on digital infrastructure and digitalization. Scientific research community should examine how advanced innovation and DTs in the digital sector would help to increase ES.

## REFERENCES


Abbas, S. A., & Zaman, A. (2024). Does digitalisation help achieve (selected) socio-economic SDGs: Evidence from emerging economies? *Sustainable Development (Bradford)*, *32*(6), 6088–6103. DOI: 10.1002/sd.3014

Adebayo, T. S., Oladipupo, S. D., Kirikkaleli, D., & Adeshola, I. (2022). Asymmetric nexus between technological innovation and environmental degradation in Sweden: An aggregated and disaggregated analysis. *Environmental Science and Pollution Research International*, *29*(24), 36547–36564. DOI: 10.1007/s11356-021-17982-6

Akberdina, V., Kuzmin, E., Kyriakopoulos, G. L., & Kumar, V. (2024). Editorial: Sustainability of digital transformation for the environment. *Frontiers in Environmental Science*, *12*(1), 1–4. DOI: 10.3389/fenvs.2024.1371047

Alojail, M., & Khan, S. B. (2023). Impact of digital transformation toward sustainable development. *Sustainability (Basel)*, *15*(1), 1–20. DOI: 10.3390/su152014697

An, Q., Wang, R., Wang, Y., & Pavel, K. (2024). The impact of the digital economy on sustainable development: Evidence from China. *Frontiers in Environmental Science*, *12*(1), 1–13. DOI: 10.3389/fenvs.2024.1341471

Bianchini, S., Damioli, G., & Ghisetti, C. (2023). The environmental effects of the "twin" green and digital transition in European regions. *Environmental and Resource Economics*, *84*(1), 877–918. DOI: 10.1007/s10640-022-00741-7

Bon, V. (2021). *The digitalization & economic growth relationship in developing countries and the role of governance*. Scientific Annals of Economics and Business, Alexandru Ioan Cuza University. *Faculty of Economics and Business Administration*, *68*(4), 481–493.

Bychkov, I. V., & Fereferov, E. S. (2022). Digital technologies for monitoring and forecasting the environmental situation in Siberia. *Herald of the Russian Academy of Sciences*, *92*(1), 133–140. DOI: 10.1134/S101933162202006X

Cai, T., & Hong, Z. (2024). Exploring the structure of the digital economy through blockchain technology and mitigating adverse environmental effects with the aid of artificial neural networks. *Frontiers in Environmental Science*, *12*(1), 1–14. DOI: 10.3389/fenvs.2024.1315812

Cao, Z., & Peng, L. (2023). The impact of digital economics on environmental quality: A system dynamics approach. *SAGE Open*, *13*(4), 1–10. DOI: 10.1177/21582440231219350

Dai, J., Zhou, B., & Meng, W. (2025). The impact of digitalization on environmental sustainability: New insights from G20 nations. *Journal of Environmental Management, 394*, 127225. DOI: 10.1016/j.jenvman.2025.127225

Firoz, A. K., Zo, H., & Chiravuri, A. (2021). Digital transformation and environmental sustainability: A review and research agenda. *Sustainability (Basel), 13*(3), 1530. Advance online publication. DOI: 10.3390/su13031530

Gariba, M. I., Arthur, E. E., & Odei, S. A. (2024). Assessing the impact of public digitalization on sustainability: The mediating role of technological innovation in the context of the EU. *Discover Sustainability*, *5*(1), 1–10. DOI: 10.1007/s43621-024-00397-x

Goel, A., Masurkar, S., & Pathade, G. R. (2024). An overview of digital transformation and environmental sustainability: Threats, opportunities, and solutions. *Sustainability (Basel), 16*(24), 1–13. DOI: 10.3390/su162411079

Gupta, M., Sharma, B., & Singh, A. K. (2025). Impact of digital technologies on tourist arrival in selected economies. In Lytras, M., Alkhaldi, A., & Ordóñez de Pablos, P. (Eds.), *Harnessing AI, Blockchain, and Cloud Computing for Enhanced e-Government Services* (pp. 441–474). IGI Global Scientific Publishing., DOI: 10.4018/979-8-3693-7678-2.ch014

Hariyani, D., Hariyani, P., & Mishra, S. (2025). Digital technologies for the sustainable development Goals. *Green Technologies and Sustainability*, *3*(3), 100202. DOI: 10.1016/j.grets.2025.100202

He, G., Jiang, H., & Zhu, Y. (2024). The effect of digital technology development on the improvement on environmental governance capacity: A case study of China. *Ecological Indicators*, *165*(1), 1–12. DOI: 10.1016/j.ecolind.2024.112162

Hong, Z., & Xiao, K. (2024). Digital economy structuring for sustainable development: The role of blockchain and artificial intelligence in improving supply chain and reducing negative environmental impacts. *Scientific Reports*, *14*(1), 1–10. DOI: 10.1038/s41598-024-53760-3

Huang, C., Wang, C., Rani, T., & Rehman, S. A. U. (2024). Digitalization's role in shaping climate change, renewable energy, and technological innovation for achieving sustainable development in top Asian countries. *Energy & Environment*, *0*(0), 0958305X241258799. Advance online publication. DOI: 10.1177/0958305X241258799

Istrate, R., Tulus, V., Grass, R. N., Vanbever, L., Stark, W. J., & Guillén-Gosálbez, G. (2024). The environmental sustainability of digital content consumption. *Nature Communications*, *15*(1), 24–37. DOI: 10.1038/s41467-024-47621-w

Kuang, Y., Fan, Y., Bin, J., & Fan, M. (2024). Impact of the digital economy on carbon dioxide emissions in resource-based cities. *Scientific Reports*, *14*(1), 1–16. DOI: 10.1038/s41598-024-66005-0

Li, S., Hu, K., & Kang, X. (2024). Impact of financial technologies, digitalization, and natural resources on environmental degradation in G-20 countries: Does human resources matter? *Resources Policy*, *93*, 105041. DOI: 10.1016/j.resourpol.2024.105041

Liu, W. (2023). The digital economy and environmental pollution: New evidence based on the support of logistics development. *Journal of Cleaner Production*, *427*, 139210. DOI: 10.1016/j.jclepro.2023.139210

Lowan-Trudeau, G. (2023). Digital technologies and environmental education. *The Journal of Environmental Education*, *54*(1), 1–7. DOI: 10.1080/00958964.2022.2152413

Lu, Q., Shen, Y., & Yu, K. (2024). Digital transformation of enterprises under the pressure of air pollution. *Applied Economics*, *1*(1), 1–12. DOI: 10.1080/00036846.2024.2385755

Miyake, K. K. (2024). Abolition-democracy and the future of climate change. *Environment and Planning. E, Nature and Space*, *7*(6), 2365–2385. DOI: 10.1177/25148486241287028

OECD. (2026). The OECD Going Digital Measurement Roadmap 2026. OECD Digital Economy Paper, 382. [Online]. https://www.oecd.org/content/dam/oecd/en/publications/reports/2026/03/the-oecd-going-digital-measurement-roadmap-2026_590c5900/b455e132-en.pdf

Pérez-Martínez, J., Hernandez-Gil, F., Miguel, G. S., Ruiz, D., & Arredondo, M. T. (2023). Analysing associations between digitalization and the accomplishment of the sustainable development goals. *The Science of the Total Environment*, *857*(3), 1–12. DOI: 10.1016/j.scitotenv.2022.159700

Qing, Z., Dan, M., & Xin, H. (2023). Digital transformation and firms' pollution emissions. *Technological Forecasting and Social Change*, *197*(1), 1–12. DOI: 10.1016/j.techfore.2023.122910

Samuel, G., Lucivero, F., & Somavilla, L. (2022). The environmental sustainability of digital technologies: Stakeholder practices and perspectives. *Sustainability (Basel)*, *14*(7), 1–14. DOI: 10.3390/su14073791

Shen, Y., Yang, Z., & Zhang, X. (2023). Impact of digital technology on carbon emissions: Evidence from Chinese cities. *Frontiers in Ecology and Evolution, 11*(1), 1–17. DOI: 10.3389/fevo.2023.1166376

Sikder, M., Wang, C., Yao, X., Huai, X., Wu, L., Yeboah, F. K., Wood, J., Zhao, Y., & Dou, X. (2022). The integrated impact of GDP growth, industrialization, energy use, and urbanization on $CO_2$ emissions in developing countries: Evidence from the panel ARDL approach. *The Science of the Total Environment, 837*, 155795. DOI: 10.1016/j.scitotenv.2022.155795

Singh, A. K. (2025). Importance of digital technologies in economic sector of selected countries. In Ahmadi, A., Mna, A., & Slimani, A. (Eds.), *Renewable Energy and the Economic Welfare of Society* (pp. 335–370). IGI Global Scientific Publishing., DOI: 10.4018/979-8-3693-7580-8.ch015

Singh, A. K., Issac, J., & Narayanan, K. G. S. (2019). Measurement of environmental sustainability index and its association with socio-economic indicators in selected Asian economies: An empirical investigation. *International Journal of Environment and Sustainable Development, 18*(1), 57–100. DOI: 10.1504/IJESD.2019.098641

Singh, A. K., & Jyoti, B. (2023). Empirical evidence from different income group countries on the interdependency between digitalization and economic development. In Patricia Ordóñez de Pablos and Xi Zhang (Eds.), 5G, Artificial Intelligence, and Next Generation Internet of Things: Digital Innovation for Green and Sustainable Economies, (pp. 44-85). IGI Global. DOI: DOI: 10.4018/978-1-6684-8634-4.ch003

Singh, A. K., Kumar, S., & Gupta, M. (2024). Relationship between digitalization and environmental sustainability in selected countries. In Yıldırım, S., Yıldırım, D., Demirtaş, I., & Kandpal, V. (Eds.), *Green Transition Impacts on the Economy, Society, and Environment* (pp. 83–107). IGI Global., DOI: 10.4018/979-8-3693-3985-5.ch006

Singh, A. K., Sharma, A. K., & Jyoti, B. (2023). Does economic development have a causal relationship with environmental degradation? Experience from different income group countries. In Sart, G. (Ed.), *Considerations on Education for Economic, Social, and Environmental Sustainability* (pp. 300–333). IGI Global., DOI: 10.4018/978-1-6684-8356-5.ch015

Singh, A. K., & Srinivasan, S. (2026). Environmental degradation influencing factors in different income groups countries. In Köktaş, A., & Gölçek, A. (Eds.), *Inequality and Environmental Degradation in a Prosperity-Driven World* (pp. 149–186). IGI Global Scientific Publishing., DOI: 10.4018/979-8-3373-1862-2.ch006

Tao, J., Cai, M. M., & Wang, Q. J. (2025). Impact of digital economy on environmental performance among worldwide countries: Role of emerging technologies and energy consumption. *Journal of Environmental Management*, *395*, 127860. DOI: 10.1016/j.jenvman.2025.127860

Truong, T. C. (2022). The impact of digital transformation on environmental sustainability. *Advances in Multimedia*, *2022*(1), 1–12. DOI: 10.1155/2022/6324325

United Nations Development Programme (UNDP). (2023). [Online]. https://www.undp.org/press-releases/digital-technologies-directly-benefit-70-percent-sdg-targets-say-itu-undp-and-partners

United Nations Development Programme (UNDP). (2026). Digitalization for sustainability. [Online]. https://www.unep.org/topics/digital-transformations/digitalization-sustainability

Wang, L., Liu, S., & Xiong, W. (2022). The impact of digital transformation on corporate environment performance: Evidence from China. *International Journal of Environmental Research and Public Health*, *9*(19), 12–24. DOI: 10.3390/ijerph191912846

Wang, Q. J., Zhu, Y. J., Zhang, Y., & Chang, C. P. (2025). Impact of digital economy on energy efficiency: Role of emerging technologies such as AI. *Energy Economics*, *150*, 108840. DOI: 10.1016/j.eneco.2025.108840

Wang, R., & Ding, C. (2023). Bilateral impact of digital economy on air pollution: Emissions increase and reduction effects. *Frontiers in Environmental Science*, *11*(1), 1–18. DOI: 10.3389/fenvs.2023.1134334

Wong, X., Kang, W., Kim, J., Xu, Y., & Wang, A. (2025). The criticality of the digital economy in environmental sustainability: Fresh insights from a wavelet-based quantile-on-quantile approach. *Sustainability (Basel)*, *17*(2), 1–17. DOI: 10.3390/su17020622

World Bank (WB). (2025). “Digital Progress and Trends Report 2025: Strengthening AI Foundations.” Overview booklet. World Bank, Washington, DC. [Online]. https://openknowledge.worldbank.org/server/api/core/bitstreams/d2ac1ea9-b70e-4080-b5de-8b31098e992f/content

World Economic Forum (WEM). (2024). Least-developed countries can aid sustainable digital transformation through e-wastage management. [Online]. https://www.weforum.org/stories/2024/11/least-developed-countries-sustainable-ewaste-management/

Xiao, D., Xu, J., & Li, Q. (2024). The “double-edged sword” effect of air quality information disclosure policy–empirical evidence based on the digital transformation of Chinese listed companies. *Energy Economics*, *133*(1), 10–21. DOI: 10.1016/j.eneco.2024.107513

Xu, J., She, S., & Liu, W. (2022). Role of digitalization in environment, social and governance, and sustainability: Review-based study for implications. *Frontiers in Psychology*, *13*(1), 1–15. DOI: 10.3389/fpsyg.2022.961057

Yang, J., Wang, Y., Tang, C., & Zhang, Z. (2024). Can digitalization reduce industrial pollution? roles of environmental investment and green innovation. *Environmental Research*, *240*(1), 117442. DOI: 10.1016/j.envres.2023.117442

Young, J. C. (2020). Environmental colonialism, digital indigeneity, and the politicization of resilience. *Environment and Planning. E, Nature and Space*, *4*(2), 230–251. DOI: 10.1177/2514848619898098

Yuan, H., Li, X., & Zhong, S. (2024). The impact of digital economy on environmental pollution: Evidence from 267 cities in China. *PLoS One*, *19*(1), 1–10. DOI: 10.1371/journal.pone.0297009

Zhang, J., Liang, F., & Gao, P. (2024). Can big data reduce urban environmental pollution? Evidence from China’s digital technology experimental zone. *PLoS One*, *20*(1), 1–11. DOI: 10.1371/journal.pone.0288429

Zhang, Z., Chen, L., Li, J., & Ding, S. (2024). Digital economy development and carbon emissions intensity – mechanisms and evidence from 72 countries. *Scientific Reports*, *18*(14), 1–19. DOI: 10.1038/s41598-024-78831-3

Zhang, Z., Ding, Z., Geng, Y., Pan, L., & Wang, C. (2023). The impact of digital economy on environmental quality: Evidence from China. *Frontiers in Environmental Science*, *11*(1), 1–17. DOI: 10.3389/fenvs.2023.1120953

Zhu, Q., Ma, D., & He, X. (2023). Digital transformation and firms’ pollution emissions. *Technological Forecasting and Social Change*, *197*, 122910. DOI: 10.1016/j.techfore.2023.122910

# Chapter 5
# Rethinking Virtual Water Trade in the Circular Economy for Sustainable Production and Consumption

**Mounsif Ridaoui**
http://orcid.org/0009-0007-9482-6215
*Research in Economics and Management of Organisations Laboratory, National School of Business and Management, Sultan Moulay Slimane University, Morocco*

**Aziz Razzouki**
*Research in Economics and Management of Organisations Laboratory, National School of Business and Management, Sultan Moulay Slimane University, Morocco*

**Mohamed Oudgou**
*Research in Economics and Management of Organisations Laboratory, National School of Business and Management, Sultan Moulay Slimane University, Morocco*

**Abdeslam Boudhar**
*Research in Economics and Management of Organisations Laboratory, National School of Business and Management, Sultan Moulay Slimane University, Morocco*

DOI: 10.4018/979-8-2600-1438-7.ch005

## ABSTRACT

*This chapter rethinks virtual water trade, the water embedded in traded goods, through the lens of the circular economy to clarify when trade supports, or undermines, sustainability in water-scarce contexts. The chapter develops a conceptual framework for circular virtual water governance that aligns trade-driven virtual water flows with resource-efficient and equitable production and consumption. The framework integrates blue, green, and grey water footprint accounting; supply-chain and life-cycle perspectives to identify hotspots and prevent problem shifting; and a feedback-oriented governance logic linking producers, consumers, policymakers, and sustainability indicators. Circular interventions are mapped to CE principles (reduce, reuse/reallocate, recycle) via examples including irrigation efficiency, treated wastewater reuse, pollution prevention, eco-design, and traceability. The chapter concludes with policy and research priorities to operationalize circular VWT strategies that strengthen water security, food security, economic resilience, and environmental integrity.*

## I. INTRODUCTION

Water is increasingly recognized as a critical resource for the sustainability of global production and consumption systems. Driven by population growth, climate change, and rising agricultural and industrial demand, water scarcity has emerged as a central concern for policymakers and researchers. At the same time, the world faces multiple environmental challenges, including biodiversity loss, rising levels of pollution, soil and water degradation, and the overexploitation of natural resources (Jackson, 2016), all of which require urgent intervention to safeguard remaining resources and support the transition toward more sustainable production systems (Markard et al., 2012; WBCSD, 2010). Within this context, the concept of the circular economy has gained prominence as a promising alternative capable of promoting sustainable resource management while addressing economic constraints, market uncertainties, and supply-related risks that increasingly threaten the financial stability of firms and national economies (Sachs, 2015).

Owing to this strategic relevance, the circular economy now occupies a central place in international policy frameworks, such as the European Circular Economy Package (European Commission, 2015), and has become a growing priority for decision-makers (Brennan et al., 2015) as well as a dynamic field of research (Geissdoerfer et al., 2017). Despite these efforts, water, an essential and irreplaceable resource, has been in continuous decline due to several interrelated factors, most notably the adverse effects of climate change, the rapid increase in human consumption driven by population expansion, and the persistent overexploitation of freshwater reserves. Water insecurity increasingly translates into broader food and energy insecurity, reinforcing the systemic nature of global water challenges. In 2015, the United Nations projected that by 2050 nearly half of the world's population would be living in water-stressed regions (UN, 2015), while the World Economic Forum identified water stress as a major global risk with the potential to destabilize international security (World Economic Forum, 2015). These warnings underscore the urgent need for integrated and coordinated management of this scarce resource. Given its growing scarcity, water is now widely recognized as an economic good with distinctive characteristics.

The OECD has classified water as an "economic good" based on the premise that scarce economic resources must be mobilized to provide it in the quality, form, location, and timing required by different user. This perspective is reinforced by the fourth principle of the Forum's 2015 framework, which states that water has "economic value in all its competing uses and should be recognized as an economic good" (World Economic Forum, 2015). Several scholars, including Zisopoulou et al., (2022), have further demonstrated that water meets the criteria of an economic good according to Robbins' definition (Robbins, 1984), largely due to its non-producible nature and its fundamental role in sustaining human life. The severity of the global water crisis is further illustrated by recent statistics. In 2022, approximately 2.2 billion people, representing nearly 27% of the global population, lacked access to safely managed drinking water, defined as water available on premises, free from contamination, and accessible when required (WHO & UNICEF, 2024). By 2025, estimates show that this situation persists, with around 2.1 billion individuals, or one in four people worldwide, still deprived of safely managed drinking water services (WHO & UNICEF, 2024). These alarming figures highlight the continued disparities in water access and confirm that water scarcity remains one of the most pressing challenges to global sustainability, economic stability, and human well-being. One important concept that has gained prominence over the past two decades is virtual water trade (VWT), referring to the hidden flows of water embodied in goods and services exchanged across borders (Allan, 2005; Allan, 1997; Hoekstra & Mekonnen, 2012).

By allowing water-scarce countries to import water-intensive products, VWT represents a strategic mechanism for addressing resource inequalities and food security challenges, but it also creates risks of environmental externalization and dependency (Mekonnen et al., 2024). In parallel, the notion of the circular economy (CE) has emerged as a paradigm to foster sustainability by moving beyond the linear "take, make, dispose" model of resource use (Geissdoerfer et al., 2017; Kirchherr et al., 2017). CE promotes systemic efficiency, resilience, and regeneration, but water has often been underexplored within this framework, particularly in relation to global trade. This chapter proposes to rethink virtual water trade through the lens of the circular economy and to build a conceptual framework that aligns VWT with strategies for sustainable production and consumption.

Given current environmental and economic constraints, the linear "take–make–dispose" production–consumption model has revealed significant structural weaknesses. This model, long based on the assumption of unlimited natural resource availability and the capacity of ecosystems to absorb waste, relies on the continuous extraction of raw materials, leading to the overexploitation of natural resources and the depletion of non-renewable stocks (Korhonen, Nuur, et al., 2018; Pearce & Turner, 1989). It is further characterized by production systems that consume large amounts of energy and contribute substantially to atmospheric pollution through greenhouse gas emissions. The waste generated throughout linear production cycles is often non-recoverable and cannot be reintegrated into natural systems, thereby exacerbating biodiversity loss and disregarding the biophysical reality that natural resources are finite and that ecological imbalances can threaten the survival of all living beings.

Economically, the linear model exposes firms and economies to heightened volatility in raw material prices, recurrent disruptions in supply chains, and increased vulnerability to global shocks (Bocken et al., 2016). From a social perspective, it reinforces inequalities in access to natural resources while encouraging unsustainable patterns of consumption. Overall, this model is fundamentally incompatible with long-term sustainability objectives, which require a reduction in waste generation and a transition toward circular approaches that prioritize resource efficiency, closed-loop processes, and the preservation of natural capital.

Water is an essential resource for life and plays a fundamental role in the production of goods and services, particularly in agriculture, agri-food value chains, and the industrial sector. By its very nature, water follows a circular biogeochemical cycle. In order to address the multiple challenges associated with this resource, the principles of the circular economy can be applied to improve water management, notably in response to water scarcity (IWA, 2016; Lasseur et al., 2025.; Voulvoulis, 2018). The concept of the circular economy has been increasingly applied across a wide range of sectors. Prieto-Sandoval et al. (2018) highlighted the diversity of these applications, particularly in relation to eco-innovation. However, the practical implementation of circular economy strategies remains insufficiently defined and conceptually unclear (Pauliuk, 2018). Although the circular economy aims to optimize resource use and reduce waste, current analytical frameworks primarily focus on solid material flows, energy use, and carbon emissions, while largely neglecting water flows (Beckett & Terziovski, 2025; Nika et al., 2020).

Within the water sector, several studies have addressed the application of the "6R" principles to wastewater management. Nevertheless, the existing circular economy literature reveals a significant gap in examining the water sector from a circular economy perspective, particularly with regard to water resource management in agriculture, agricultural product trade, and, consequently, the international trade of virtual water, as well as the opportunities offered by the implementation of circular economy principles in this sector.

Rethinking Virtual Water Trade (VWT) through the lens of the circular economy provides a relevant analytical framework for capturing water efficiency, resource regeneration, and systemic interlinkages, integrating circular economy principles into VWT analysis allows for a more comprehensive assessment of how international trade redistributes water resources, not only in quantitative terms but also in relation to sustainability, resilience, and territorial water stress. This perspective supports the design of trade and agricultural policies that better align economic performance with sustainable water resource management.

This chapter aims to rethink Virtual Water Trade (VWT) through the lens of the circular economy and to develop a conceptual framework that aligns VWT with strategies for sustainable production and consumption. To this end, the chapter is structured as follows: The first section presents the theoretical background, focusing on the concepts of virtual water trade and the circular economy, while also addressing the integration of Life Cycle Assessment (LCA) and Circularity Economy (CE) in water resource management. The second section examines the Virtual Water Trade–Circular Economy nexus, highlighting their interconnections and complementarities. The third section proposes a conceptual framework for integrating circular economy principles into virtual water trade analysis. The final section discusses the implications and future research directions, before concluding with a synthesis of the main findings and contributions.

## II. THEORETICAL BACKGROUND

### 1. Virtual Water Trade: Definition, root and historical evolution of the concept

The concept of virtual water was first introduced in the early 1990s by the British geographer J.A. Allan as an alternative approach to mitigating potential conflicts over water resources, particularly in the Middle East. The core idea was that water-abundant countries could specialize in the production of water-intensive agricultural commodities, while water-scarce countries could rely on imports of these products rather than producing them domestically at a high-water cost. Allan's work was strongly inspired by classical theories of international trade, especially those related to comparative advantage and resource endowment. Several scholars, including Merrett (1997), Brill, (2002), and Lant (2003), have demonstrated that the concept of virtual water trade is closely aligned with Ricardo's theory of comparative advantage. In this perspective, the relative abundance of water can be regarded as a factor of production capable of generating regional comparative advantages, thereby influencing patterns of specialization and international trade (Duchin & López-Morales, 2012). As formalized by Allan (1997), virtual water trade enables countries to gain indirect and often low-cost access to global water resources through international trade, thereby reducing pressure on domestic water supplies. Virtual water refers to the total volume of water consumed throughout the production process of a good that is exported to another region where it is ultimately consumed (Allan, 1997). Beyond its role in water conflict mitigation, virtual water trade can also be considered a strategic tool for reducing domestic agricultural production pressures in water-scarce countries, thus contributing to food security and economic stability (Sandström et al., 2018; Wang et al., 2024).

The magnitude and direction of virtual water flows are shaped by a wide range of factors, including production systems, distance between countries, GDP, population, climatic conditions, and the availability of arable land (Duarte & Yang, 2011; Egan, 2011; Fracasso, 2014; Odey et al., 2021). In addition, geopolitical considerations play an increasingly important role in influencing virtual water trade patterns at the regional and global levels (Meng et al., 2017; Tian et al., 2018). Moreover, it can be considered an alternative strategy to reduce agricultural imports in certain countries, thereby contributing to food security and economic stability (Sandström et al., 2018). Building on the concept of the ecological footprint, Hoekstra introduced the concept of the water footprint in 2002 as a complementary approach to the notion of virtual water. The water footprint provides a consumption-based perspective on water use and is defined as "the volume of water necessary for the production of goods and services consumed by the inhabitants of a country" (Hoekstra & Chapagain, 2007). Unlike traditional water use indicators, the water footprint captures both direct and indirect water consumption embedded in production and trade. Hoekstra distinguished three main components of the water footprint. Green water refers to effective precipitation and soil moisture that are stored in the soil and directly used by plants. Blue water represents the volume of surface and groundwater withdrawn and either incorporated into a product or returned to another watershed or the sea. Grey water denotes the volume of freshwater required to assimilate pollutant loads generated by production processes, based on prevailing ambient water quality standards (Hoekstra, 2017). The joint consideration of the concepts of virtual water and water footprint can provide effective solutions for enhancing both water security and food security, while supporting the sustainable management of water supply and demand. These approaches offer valuable insights into the allocation of water resources embedded in production and trade, thereby contributing to more informed and sustainable decision-making. Empirical studies (Antonelli et al., 2017; Antonelli & Tamea, 2015; Vallino et al., 2021) have shown that virtual water trade can play a crucial role in ensuring food security, particularly in the MENA region, which is among the most vulnerable regions to climate change and its impacts on economic sectors, especially agriculture (Razzouki et al., 2025). These findings highlight the importance of integrating virtual water trade considerations into agricultural planning and policy strategies in water-scarce and climate-vulnerable regions (Ridaoui, et al., 2025). However, by enabling the importation of water-intensive agricultural products instead of relying on the exploitation of scarce domestic water resources, the virtual water trade plays a crucial role in reducing pressure on both surface and groundwater resources, particularly in arid and semi-arid countries. Virtual water trade also contributes to a more efficient global distribution of water resources by reallocating water use across regions in accordance with comparative advantages. At the same time, it supports food security by ensuring stable access to agricultural commodities through international markets, thereby enhancing the resilience of food systems (Dalin et al., 2012; Debaere and Konar, 2022).

To support effective agricultural planning and international trade strategies, it is essential to quantify the water footprint of products, regions, or countries. A variety of methodological approaches have been developed to measure and assess water footprints, and the choice of method depends on several factors, including the complexity of the production system, data availability (Yang et al., 2013), production technologies, geographical context, climatic conditions, and the nature of the products considered (Aldaya et al., 2020). These methods can be broadly classified into two main approaches: bottom-up and top-down, with a third hybrid approach combining elements of both (figure1).

The bottom-up approach is based on process-level assessments and typically relies on the Water Footprint Assessment (WFA) framework as proposed by Hoekstra (2017), as well as on Life Cycle Assessment (LCA) methodologies. This approach employs biophysical and crop models such as CROPWAT (Hoekstra & Hung, 2002), EPIC (Liu et al., 2007), AquaCrop (Chukalla et al., 2015; Zhuo et al., 2016), and LPJmL (Fader et al., 2011) to estimate the water footprint of agricultural products. While bottom-up methods offer high spatial and process-level resolution, they generally do not distinguish between intermediate and final users of water embedded in production chains (Feng et al., 2011). In contrast, the top-down approach uses more aggregated and system-wide methods to quantify both direct and indirect water footprints. It commonly relies on input–output (IO) tables, which provide a comprehensive representation of production and consumption relationships across regions and economic sectors. This framework enables the identification of water-intensive sectors and the assessment of their impacts along supply chains, and it has been widely applied in environmental, ecological, energy, and economic analyses

(Wiedmann, 2009). To overcome the limitations of both approaches, a hybrid method combining bottom-up and top-down perspectives has been increasingly adopted, allowing for a more consistent and comprehensive assessment of water footprints across scales.

*Figure 1. Water footprint assessment approaches*

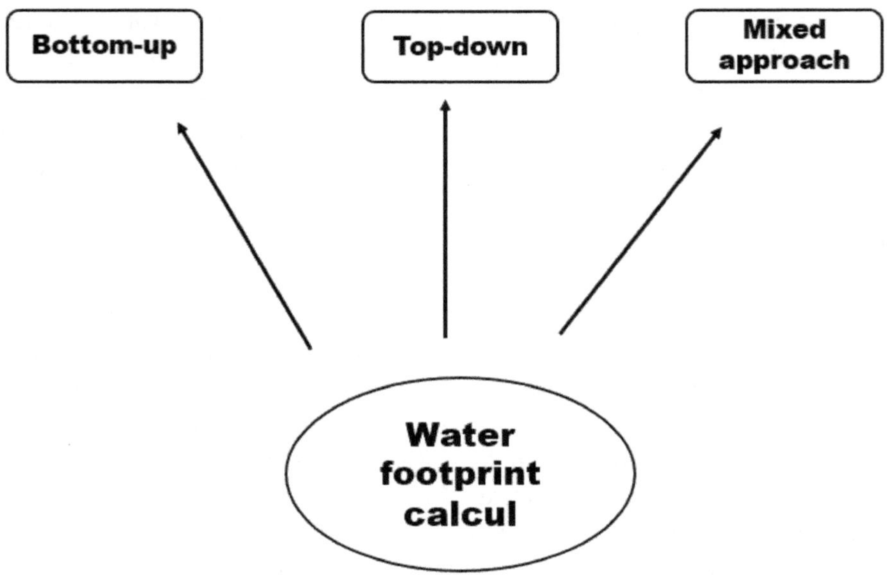


*Source: Author's own elaboration based on the reviewed literature. Designed using Microsoft PowerPoint*

Despite the widely acknowledged benefits of virtual water trade, this concept has been subject to substantial criticism, particularly regarding the risk of dependency on external water resources. Several studies have shown that some countries may become increasingly dependent on food imports, exposing them to volatility in global markets and heightened vulnerability to climate change impacts (Dalin et al., 2012; Seekell et al., 2011; Tamea et al., 2016). Beyond dependency risks, virtual water trade also generates significant ecological externalities in exporting countries. D'Odorico et al. (2014) highlighted that water-exporting regions often bear the environmental costs associated with intensified agricultural production, including the overexploitation of surface and groundwater resources, particularly in a context of accelerating climate change. Similarly, Zhong et al. (2023) demonstrated that the global virtual water trade system tends to displace water stress from importing, water-scarce countries to exporting regions, where agricultural exports are closely linked to increasing water pressure and environmental degradation (Lenzen et al., 2012). These dynamics contribute to pronounced North–South asymmetries in virtual water flows and to structural imbalances in global trade, reinforcing economic water scarcity and unequal distribution of environmental burdens across regions (Vallino et al., 2020).

## 2. Circular Economy and Sustainable Production/Consumption

Reflection on the concept of the circular economy dates back to the 1970s (Ellen MacArthur Foundation, 2013). Pearce and Turner (1989) are widely recognized as among the first scholars to formally introduce the concept in their seminal work Economics of Natural Resources and the Environment. Their contribution was strongly inspired by the earlier work of Boulding (1966), who conceptualized the Earth as a closed and finite system with a limited assimilative capacity. This perspective highlighted the necessity of effectively managing economic activities in order to preserve the environment and maintain a balance between natural resources and economic development. Pearce and Turner (1989) emphasized the critical role of natural resources as essential inputs to production and consumption processes, thereby shaping economic performance. They also drew attention to the linear and open-ended nature of contemporary economic systems, which rely heavily on resource extraction and waste disposal. In contrast, the core idea of the circular economy is to recover and recycle valuable materials from end-of-life products and reintegrate them into new production processes, thereby enhancing the value of waste while minimizing environmental degradation (Kakwani & Kalbar, 2020). In this sense, goods at the end of their life cycle can be transformed into secondary raw materials and reused as production inputs for future goods (Stahel, 1982). The Ellen MacArthur Foundation (EMF) has played a pivotal role in advancing and disseminating the concept of the circular economy, particularly in areas such as waste management, food systems, and the development of indicators and measurement frameworks (EMF, 2017). The EMF defines the circular economy as "an industrial economy that is restorative or regenerative by intention and design" (Ellen MacArthur Foundation, 2013). Building on this definition, Bocken et al. (2016) further characterized the circular economy as encompassing "design and business model strategies that slow, close, and narrow resource loops.". In the context of waste management, circular economy principles are commonly operationalized through the strategies of reducing, reusing, recycling, and recovering materials. Reducing refers to minimizing resource use and waste generation at the source through efficiency improvements, reusing involves extending the lifespan of products and components via repeated use, repair, or refurbishment, recycling consists of reprocessing waste materials into secondary raw materials, while recovery encompasses the extraction of residual value from waste streams, particularly through energy or material recovery processes (Winans et al., 2017).

Beyond the academic and scientific literature, the concept of the circular economy has attracted significant attention from governments and intergovernmental organizations. Notably, Germany integrated circular economy principles into its national legislation as early as 1996 through the enactment of the ''Closed Substance Cycle and Waste Management Act'' (Su et al., 2013). This was followed by Japan's circular economy initiatives in 2002 (METI, 2004), China's Circular Economy Promotion Law in 2009 (Lieder & Rashid, 2015), and the adoption of the European Union's Circular Economy Strategy in 2012 (European Commission, 2015).

*Figure 2. Circular economy core*

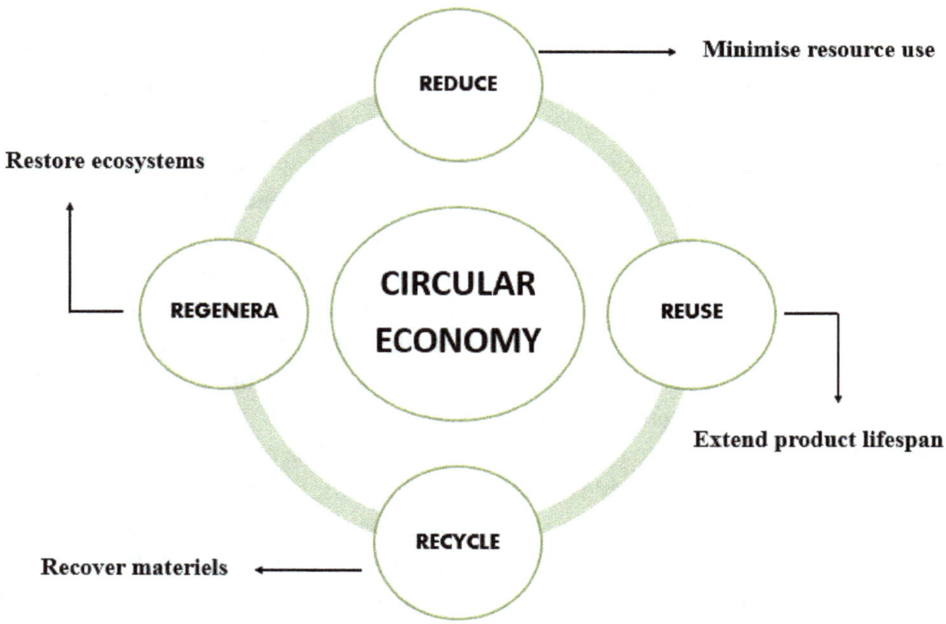


*Source: Author's own elaboration based on the circular economy literature. Designed using Microsoft PowerPoint.*

Although the circular economy (CE) has attracted growing attention over time, particularly as a policy and analytical framework aimed at preserving natural resources and reducing environmental impacts, its practical applications have largely focused on material and energy flows, such as waste reduction, recycling, and industrial symbiosis. Water resources, despite being indispensable inputs to production systems, have received relatively limited attention within CE frameworks. Existing CE studies predominantly emphasize solid waste management and material circularity, while water is often treated as an auxiliary or supporting resource rather than a core component of circular strategies (Geissdoerfer et al., 2017; Korhonen et al., 2018). Moreover, prevailing CE assessment indicators and evaluation frameworks tend to prioritize material cycles and carbon-related impacts, frequently neglecting water or addressing it only through secondary dimensions, such as water-use efficiency or virtual water flows (Morseletto, 2020; Smol et al., 2015). This marginalization of water constrains the potential of the circular economy to effectively address water-related challenges, particularly water scarcity and stress in arid and semi-arid regions, where water availability constitutes a key determinant of both economic and environmental sustainability. Consequently, there is a growing need to integrate water redistribution and circular water management into CE models, thereby enhancing opportunities for water circularity across global value chains.

## 3. Integrating LCA and CE in Water Management

Life Cycle Assessment (LCA) is a standardized and widely recognized methodology for environmental life cycle evaluation, extensively applied in both industrial practice and scientific research. It enables the comprehensive assessment of environmental footprints by providing a systematic and holistic framework to quantify the environmental impacts of a product, service, or process throughout its entire life cycle, from raw material extraction to end-of-life management (ISO 14040, 2006; Suh & Huppes, 2005). In footprint analysis, LCA-based approaches underpin the calculation of key indicators such as carbon, water, and material footprints. The significance of LCA lies in its ability to compare products originating from different regions that rely on heterogeneous inputs and operate under diverse environmental conditions, while simultaneously evaluating total resource consumption in relation to associated environmental impacts, thereby supporting sustainability assurance (Yang et al., 2013). Furthermore, LCA serves as a robust analytical tool for quantifying environmental impacts and resource use across product life cycles, contributing to the design, evaluation, and monitoring of circular economy strategies (Batlles de la Fuente et al., 2023). It also facilitates the identification of environmental hotspots along value chains, thereby supporting informed decision-making for sustainable production and consumption (Boulay et al., 2013).

LCA is widely applied to measure environmental footprints across industrial sectors and manufactured products by adopting cradle-to-grave or cradle-to-cradle perspectives. Through this life-cycle-based approach, LCA systematically evaluates environmental pressures, resource use, and emissions, while preventing problem shifting between different life cycle stages and impact categories. LCA is also employed to assess water-related impacts, however, in contrast to the Water Footprint

Assessment framework proposed by Hoekstra, which distinguishes between blue, green, and grey water, LCA primarily accounts for blue and grey water using quantitative and impact-based indicators within the life cycle impact assessment phase (Boulay et al., 2013; Pfister et al., 2017). For instance, indicators such as eutrophication potential, acidification potential, and toxicity-related metrics are commonly used in LCA to evaluate water pollution, relying on established life cycle inventory databases such as GaBi and Ecoinvent (Feng et al., 2014; Gerbens-Leenes et al., 2018). Moreover, LCA enables the integration of environmental footprint indicators into circular economy strategies, thereby linking resource efficiency improvements with quantified environmental outcomes (Finkbeiner et al., 2006; A. Hoekstra et al., 2011; ISO 14044, 2006).

Recent studies demonstrate that integrating Life Cycle Assessment (LCA) with Circular Economy (CE) principles can significantly enhance water management strategies. For instance, Mirabi et al. (2025) examined household consumption patterns in Iran through a combined LCA–CE framework and found that lower-income groups exhibited higher water use per unit of expenditure, whereas higher-income groups tended to consume more water-intensive products, particularly meat. These findings reveal pronounced socio-economic disparities in water use efficiency and underscore the necessity of systemic analytical approaches capable of capturing both environmental and social dimensions. In this regard, the integration of LCA and CE offers a robust methodological pathway for embedding Virtual Water Trade (VWT) within circular and sustainable production–consumption systems.

Life Cycle Assessment (LCA) and Circular Economy (CE) principles can play a pivotal role in sustainable water resource management. Integrating LCA with CE principles provides a robust methodological framework for the development of circular Virtual Water Trade (VWT) strategies. On the one hand, LCA enables the systematic quantification and assessment of environmental impacts along agri-food value chains, from agricultural production to final consumption. On the other hand, CE principles aim to improve resource-use efficiency, reduce environmental externalities, and promote closed-loop systems (Geissdoerfer et al., 2017; ISO 14040, 2006).

The combined LCA–CE approach enhances water management by facilitating the identification of water-intensive stages within agri-food supply chains, the evaluation of circular interventions such as dietary shifts, the assessment of trade-offs between domestic production and the importation of virtual water, the reduction of food losses and waste, the valorization of agricultural by-products, and the reuse of treated wastewater (Castellani et al., 2019; A. Hoekstra et al., 2011; Morseletto, 2020). Moreover, the integration of LCA and CE aligns water conservation objectives with economic efficiency and social equity, thereby enabling the design of

VWT strategies that strengthen long-term water security, particularly in regions facing chronic water scarcity (Allan, 1998; Dalin et al., 2012; Vanham et al., 2013).

## III. THE VIRTUAL WATER TRADE–CIRCULAR ECONOMY NEXUS

### 1. Resource Optimization

Virtual Water Trade (VWT) has emerged as a pivotal mechanism for optimizing the global allocation of freshwater resources, particularly in a context marked by increasing water scarcity, climate variability, and rising food demand. By enabling water-intensive commodities to be produced in water-abundant regions and consumed in water-scarce ones, VWT facilitates a reallocation of water resources that transcends physical hydrological boundaries. From both economic and environmental perspectives, VWT enhances allocative efficiency by alleviating pressure on local water resources in arid and semi-arid regions. Countries facing structural water scarcity can thus satisfy domestic food demand through imports rather than relying on water-intensive domestic production, thereby preserving limited freshwater stocks for higher-value uses such as domestic supply and industrial activities.

Empirical evidence supports the role of VWT in generating global water savings. Yang et al. (2006) demonstrated that the flow of virtual water from countries with high crop water productivity to those with lower productivity results in net water savings at the global scale. These savings are particularly pronounced when production relies predominantly on green water, which typically entails a lower opportunity cost compared to blue water used for irrigation. Consequently, the dominance of green water in exporting regions contributes to a more efficient and sustainable use of global water resources.

Recent studies have further highlighted the role of optimization models in guiding water-efficient production and trade patterns. Delpasand et al. (2023), for instance, developed an optimization framework to identify an optimal agricultural production portfolio in Iran. Their findings indicate that cereals, particularly wheat, are the most water-intensive crops in terms of both direct and indirect water use, whereas potatoes and tomatoes emerge as relatively water-efficient crops with higher economic returns. The authors also show that increases in water prices tend to reduce industrial imports, as domestic industrial production becomes more profitable and offsets declining net revenues from agricultural activities. These results underscore the importance of incorporating water pricing and virtual water considerations into integrated resource allocation strategies.

At the global level, VWT reinforces patterns of comparative advantage in agricultural production not only based on traditional factors such as land and labor (Duarte et al., 2019; Qian et al., 2019), but also on water endowments and water-use efficiency (Fracasso, 2014; Fracasso et al., 2016). Regions endowed with abundant water resources and higher levels of water productivity tend to specialize in and export water-intensive crops, while water-scarce regions increasingly become net importers of virtual water. Several empirical studies confirm that international agricultural trade generates substantial global water savings by shifting production toward regions with lower water footprints per unit of output (Dalin et al., 2012). These efficiency gains stem from heterogeneity in climatic conditions, irrigation technologies, and agronomic practices, all of which critically influence crop water productivity (Wichelns, 2004).

Moreover, VWT contributes to risk mitigation and system resilience by diversifying sources of food supply. In the face of droughts, climate shocks, or hydrological variability, reliance on international trade allows countries to buffer domestic production shortfalls. In this sense, VWT functions as an indirect adaptation strategy to water scarcity and climate change, reinforcing the stability of food systems while optimizing water use across interconnected production–consumption networks.

## 2. Global Application of Circular Principles

### 2.1. Reduce: lowering water pressure in water-scarce regions

By substituting local production with imports of water-intensive goods, Virtual Water Trade (VWT) operationalizes the "reduce" principle by lowering freshwater withdrawals in water-scarce regions. However, the concept of reduction can be interpreted in multiple ways. In the water literature, reduction may refer to using less water per unit of output (Smol et al., 2020), extracting smaller volumes from water sources (Demartini et al., 2018), or improving water-use efficiency through technological and managerial advances (Brears, 2019). Within the circular economy paradigm, the reduction principle lies at its core and aims to minimize the extraction and consumption of natural resources at the source.

In the context of water resources, this principle translates into limiting freshwater withdrawals, particularly in regions experiencing chronic water stress, where agriculture accounts for nearly 70% of global freshwater abstractions and constitutes a major driver of water scarcity in arid and semi-arid areas. In this respect, VWT plays a pivotal role by enabling water-scarce countries to satisfy domestic demand through the importation of water-intensive products rather than relying on inefficient and environmentally unsustainable local production systems. In countries characterized by limited water availability, the continued domestic production of highly water-consuming crops, such as cereals, often exacerbates groundwater depletion, ecosystem degradation, and competition among water users. Conversely, importing these commodities from regions with greater water availability and higher water productivity can substantially reduce national water withdrawals. A growing body of empirical evidence supports the water-saving potential of this mechanism. For instance, Ridaoui et al. (2025) found that Morocco, a semi-arid country, saved approximately 50 $Mm^3$ of water through cereal imports from the European Union. Similarly, Korea achieved significant water savings by importing soybeans and maize (Yoo et al., 2012). At the global scale, Yang et al. (2006) demonstrated that international agricultural trade generates net water savings by reallocating production from regions with low crop water productivity to those with higher productivity.

These findings indicate that VWT functions as an indirect demand-side water management instrument, alleviating pressure on domestic water resources. From a circular economy perspective, this implies that VWT contributes to resource reduction not only in quantitative terms but also qualitatively, by avoiding the use of scarce and high-value water resources in environmentally vulnerable regions. In water-scarce areas such as the Middle East and North Africa (MENA), climate change has already exerted substantial pressure on agricultural systems (Razzouki et al., 2025), rendering food imports a structural strategy for mitigating water stress. Moreover, VWT supports the preservation of limited freshwater reserves, allowing their reallocation to essential uses such as drinking water supply, sanitation, and high value-added industrial activities. In this sense, virtual water trade embodies the reduction principle of the circular economy by minimizing unsustainable water extraction while enhancing long-term water security.

## 2.2. Reuse / Reallocate: Virtual Water Trade as Cross-Border Water Reallocation.

At the outset, it is essential to distinguish between water reuse and water recycling, as these two concepts are often conflated in the literature. Water reuse differs fundamentally from recycling. According to Morseletto et al. (2022), water reuse refers to the use of water for the same or a different purpose without undergoing additional treatment, whereas recycling explicitly involves treatment processes that enable water to be reintroduced into the production or consumption cycle. Thus, the presence or absence of treatment constitutes the key criterion distinguishing reuse from recycling. In line with the "reuse" principle of the circular economy, Virtual Water Trade (VWT) can be conceptualized as a transboundary mechanism for water reallocation, allowing a single unit of water to satisfy multiple regional demands. Beyond its role in reducing local water withdrawals, VWT may therefore be interpreted as a form of functional and spatial reuse within a global circular economy framework. Through international trade, water embedded in exported goods effectively flows from relatively water-abundant regions to water-scarce ones, thereby transcending national hydrological boundaries and creating a globally interconnected water system.

While reuse in conventional circular economy applications typically refers to the physical reuse of materials, in the case of water resources, reuse can also be understood in a functional and geographical sense. The reallocation of water through virtual water trade enhances allocative efficiency by directing water use toward regions where it can be employed more productively, both economically and environmentally. As a result, the same unit of water utilized in a producing country can effectively meet consumption needs in another country, thereby avoiding additional water mobilization elsewhere. A growing body of literature highlights the importance of VWT in shaping global water allocation patterns. Allan (1998); Dalin et al. (2012); Duarte et al. (2016) and Tamea et al. (2014) demonstrated that international trade networks play a central role in the redistribution of water resources at the global scale, contributing to substantial global water savings. From this perspective, VWT reinforces circularity by reallocating water to its most efficient uses across regions.

Importantly, this transboundary reallocation also contributes to reducing regional inequalities in water availability. Water-scarce countries can externalize part of their water demand through imports, while water-abundant countries may specialize in water-intensive production without exacerbating local water scarcity. Such an arrangement reflects a systemic approach to water nance, in which water resources are effectively "reused" across multiple regions through trade, in accordance with the reuse principle of the circular economy.

## 2.3. Recycle: Adoption of Water-Saving Technologies and Sustainable Farming

As discussed earlier, recycling refers to the use of water after it has undergone treatment. Within the circular economy framework, however, the recycling principle extends beyond physical treatment processes and emphasizes the recovery, regeneration, and efficient use of resources through technological and organizational innovation. In the context of Virtual Water Trade (VWT), this principle is manifested indirectly through the incentives it creates for exporting countries to adopt water-saving technologies and more sustainable agricultural practices. As international markets increasingly incorporate environmental standards and sustainability requirements, producers are encouraged to improve water-use efficiency and reduce the water footprint of exported commodities. Water-exporting regions therefore face growing pressure to maintain competitiveness while complying with environmental constraints (Wang et al., 2017). This has stimulated the adoption of advanced irrigation systems, such as drip irrigation and precision irrigation, as well as the integration of climate-smart and environmentally sound agricultural practices. In addition, the reuse of non-conventional water sources in agriculture and the implementation of soil-moisture management techniques contribute to reducing overall water consumption while maintaining or even enhancing agricultural productivity (Chen et al., 2021). These technological and managerial innovations enable the effective "recycling" of water within production systems by maximizing the value derived from each unit of water used. Optimization studies further illustrate this dynamic. For example, Delpasand et al. (2023) demonstrated that integrating water pricing and virtual water considerations into agricultural planning encourages a shift toward less water-intensive and more economically profitable crops. Such adjustments not only reduce water consumption but also enhance the economic resilience of agricultural systems.

By linking trade dynamics, pricing mechanisms, and technological adoption, virtual water trade supports a virtuous cycle of efficiency gains and resource conservation. From a circular economy perspective, the promotion of water-saving technologies and sustainable agricultural practices strengthens the regenerative capacity of agricultural systems. By reducing losses, enhancing reuse within production processes, and decreasing reliance on scarce blue water resources, VWT contributes to closing the loop between water use, productivity, and environmental sustainability. In this sense, virtual water trade reinforces the recycling pillar of the circular economy, even in the absence of direct physical recycling of water across national borders.

## 3. Risks and Trade-Offs

### 3.1. Import Dependency and Food Security Concerns

While virtual water trade (VWT) can deliver substantial gains in water-use efficiency and facilitate the reallocation of scarce resources, it also entails a set of risks affecting food security, environmental integrity, economic resilience, and governance. These risks call for a balanced and integrated policy approach and must be carefully addressed to ensure long-term sustainability and equity. However, dependence on food imports is the most frequently cited risk associated with VWT, particularly for water-scarce countries that externalize a substantial share of their agricultural production (D'Odorico et al., 2019; Antonelli and Francesco, 2017; Wichelns, 2015). Although import reliance can ease domestic water stress, it may also increase exposure to external shocks, including global price volatility, trade restrictions, geopolitical tensions, and supply-chain disruptions (Wichelns, 2015).

Recent global crises, including climate-induced production shocks and disruptions in international trade, have demonstrated that excessive dependence on food imports can undermine national food security and reduce policy autonomy. From a resilience perspective, virtual water trade may therefore create a trade-off between water security and food sovereignty, especially in developing and semi-arid countries. As several studies argue, VWT should complement rather than fully substitute domestic food production, particularly for strategic staples. This vulnerability was starkly illustrated by the Russia–Ukraine war, which severely disrupted global wheat supply chains. As documented by Luwedde and Nakazi (2024), the conflict led to sharp declines in wheat availability and rising prices in import-dependent African countries such as Uganda, largely due to supply shortages, export restrictions, and increased fertilizer costs. This case highlights how reliance on a limited number of major exporting countries can amplify exposure to geopolitical shocks, thereby reinforcing the risks associated with excessive dependence on virtual water imports embedded in staple food commodities.

## 3.2. Ecosystem Degradation in Exporting Regions

Another major concern relates to the environmental burden transferred to exporting regions, particularly those specializing in water-intensive crops for international markets. In some cases, export-oriented agricultural production has led to overexploitation of surface and groundwater resources (Mekonnen et al., 2024), carbon emission (Yin et al., 2021), soil salinization, biodiversity loss, and degradation of aquatic ecosystems.

Although VWT may generate global water savings, these gains are not always spatially or ecologically neutral. Exporting regions with weak environmental regulation or limited enforcement capacity may bear disproportionate ecological costs, effectively becoming "virtual water sacrifice zones." This raises concerns about environmental justice and the uneven distribution of environmental externalities across countries.

## 3.3. Fragmentation of Global Value Chains

Virtual water trade is embedded within increasingly complex and fragmented global value chains. While such fragmentation enhances efficiency and specialization, it can also reduce transparency regarding the environmental footprint of traded goods, including water use. The spatial separation between production and consumption complicates accountability, as consumers and policymakers in importing countries are often disconnected from the environmental impacts occurring in exporting regions. This fragmentation may weaken incentives for sustainable water management, particularly when water costs are not adequately reflected in market prices. Moreover, disruptions in GVCs, caused by climate extremes, pandemics, or geopolitical conflicts, can amplify vulnerabilities for both exporters and importers.

The risks associated with virtual water trade highlight the urgent need for integrated and multi-level governance frameworks that align trade policies, water management, agricultural strategies, and environmental regulations (Kim et al., 2025). Current governance structures often operate in silos, failing to account for the cross-border and cross-sectoral nature of virtual water flows. Effective governance of VWT requires the incorporation of water footprint indicators, environmental standards, and sustainability criteria into trade agreements and national policies. It also calls for stronger international cooperation to ensure that water savings at the global level do not come at the expense of local ecosystems or social equity. Without such coordination, virtual water trade risks reinforcing existing inequalities and environmental degradation rather than contributing to a circular and sustainable water economy.

## IV. PROPOSED CONCEPTUAL FRAMEWORK

### 1. Conceptual Model

The proposed conceptual model (Figure 3) is grounded in a systemic and circular representation of the interactions among actors, virtual water flows, assessment mechanisms, and governance structures. It seeks to move beyond a linear interpretation of virtual water trade by explicitly integrating principles of the circular economy and adaptive governance into the analysis.

At the core of the framework are virtual water flows embodied in agricultural products, disaggregated into blue, green, and grey water components and materialized through international agricultural trade. These flows emerge directly from the decisions of economic actors, particularly producers and consumers. On the supply side, agricultural producers shape the intensity and composition of embodied virtual water through their choices of cropping patterns, irrigation technologies, and production practices. On the demand side, consumers influence the direction and magnitude of trade flows, and, consequently, associated virtual water transfers, through consumption levels, dietary patterns, and sustainability preferences. Sustainability indicators play a central role in assessing the virtual water flows generated by these interactions. These indicators quantify pressures on water resources and evaluate the overall performance of the system. They include, in particular, water footprint metrics (blue, green, and grey water), the economic productivity of water, environmental impacts derived from Life Cycle Assessment (LCA), as well as dimensions related to resilience and equity. This evaluation stage constitutes a critical component of the model, as it translates physical and economic flows into decision-relevant information.

*Figure 3. Proposed conceptual framework for rethinking virtual water trade through the circular economy.*

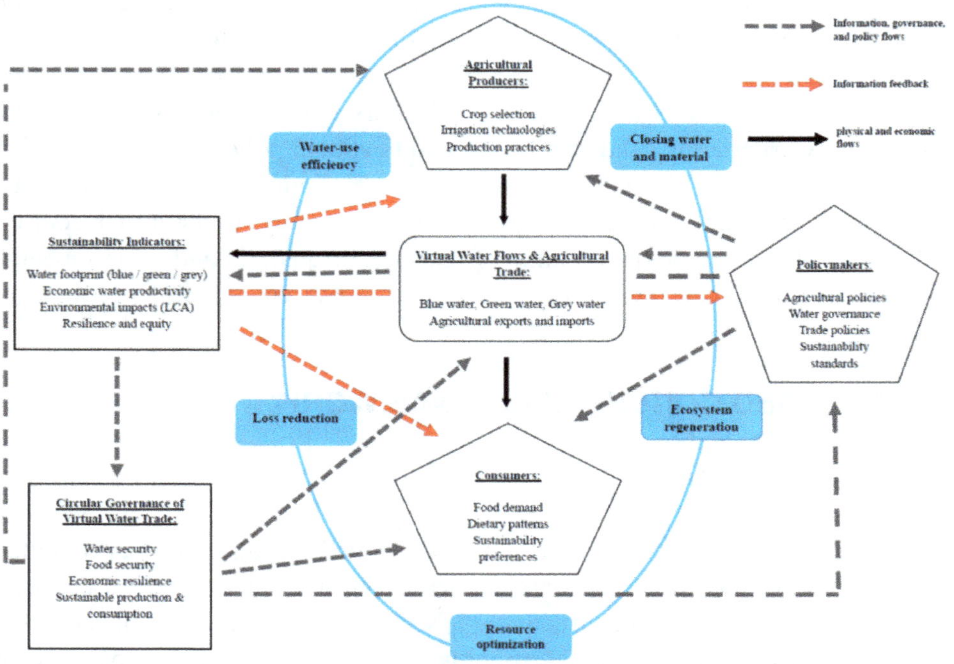


*Source: Author's elaboration based on a synthesis of the literature on virtual water trade, circular economy, water footprint accounting, and sustainable production and consumption. Designed using Microsoft PowerPoint.*

The outputs of the sustainability assessment subsequently inform the circular governance of virtual water trade. This governance function provides strategic guidance and coordination by integrating evaluation results to shape actors' behavior and policy orientations. It operates through public policy instruments, regulatory mechanisms, economic incentives, and sustainability standards, implemented by policymakers and institutions. While circular governance does not directly generate physical flows, it acts as a key leverage point for adjusting and optimizing the system.

In turn, circular governance influences producers, consumers, and decision-makers through informational and policy feedback loops. These feedback mechanisms enable the continuous adjustment of production practices, consumption patterns, and regulatory frameworks in response to observed system performance. Through this adaptive feedback process, virtual water trade is transformed into an evolving and learning-oriented system consistent with circular economy principles.

Overall, the model highlights a dynamic loop in which actors' decisions generate virtual water flows that are evaluated using sustainability indicators and subsequently feed into a circular governance framework capable of reorienting the system toward water security, food security, economic resilience, and sustainable production and consumption. This conceptual framework thus provides an integrated analytical basis for assessing and steering virtual water trade from a long-term sustainability perspective.

## V. IMPLICATIONS AND FUTURE RESEARCH DIRECTIONS

### 1. Policy Implications

*Incorporating water footprint standards into trade agreement*

The integration of water footprint–related criteria into trade agreements would enhance transparency regarding the water implications of traded agricultural products and promote more informed decision-making by both exporting and importing countries. Such standards could take the form of mandatory reporting requirements, benchmarking systems, or differentiated tariff and non-tariff measures based on water-use efficiency and environmental performance. For instance, preferential market access could be granted to products that comply with defined water sustainability thresholds, while water-intensive products originating from regions experiencing high levels of water stress could be subject to more stringent conditions.

*Using VWT as a tool to reduce global water stress*

The framework highlights that the benefits of virtual water trade are not automatic but are highly contingent on the prevailing governance context. In the absence of adequate coordination, virtual water trade may merely shift water stress from importing to exporting regions, particularly when agricultural exports rely on unsustainable groundwater extraction or environmentally harmful production practices. Policymakers should therefore move beyond a purely volumetric understanding of virtual water flows and incorporate indicators of water scarcity, ecosystem impacts, and economic water productivity into trade-related decision-making. In this regard, the proposed model supports the design of differentiated trade strategies that account for regional water endowments and sustainability performance. For example, strategic staple commodities may be partially imported to conserve scarce domestic water resources, while less water-intensive or higher value-added crops are prioritized for local production and export. At the global level, enhanced cooperation and improved information sharing on virtual water flows can help align national trade strategies with broader objectives of reducing water stress and strengthening system-wide resilience.

*Aligning trade policies with CE strategies*

Aligning trade policies with circular economy strategies requires the promotion of practices that enhance water productivity, reduce pollution, and close resource loops along agricultural value chains. Policy instruments may include incentives for water-efficient technologies, support for wastewater reuse in agriculture, eco-design standards for agri-food products, and the internalization of environmental externalities through pricing and taxation mechanisms. Trade policy can also foster circular business models, such as the valorization of agricultural by-products and the reduction of post-harvest losses, which indirectly lower virtual water demand.

## 2. Implications for Businesses and Supply Chains

*Reducing embodied water in production processes*

A primary implication for businesses concerns the need to reduce the volume of water embedded in production processes. Firms can achieve this by improving water-use efficiency at both the farm and processing stages through the adoption of water-saving technologies, precision irrigation, and enhanced crop and input management practices. In agricultural and agro-industrial systems, the optimization of production techniques not only lowers blue and green water consumption but also reduces grey water footprints associated with pollution and nutrient runoff. From a supply chain perspective, sourcing strategies that prioritize inputs from regions or producers characterized by higher water productivity and lower levels of water stress can substantially reduce overall water use. Companies can integrate water footprint metrics into supplier selection and performance assessment, thereby incentivizing upstream actors to adopt more efficient and environmentally sustainable practices. Such measures help mitigate water-related risks, including supply disruptions and regulatory constraints, while strengthening firms' long-term resilience.Haut du formulaire

*Developing circular business models*

The framework also highlights the importance of developing circular business models as a means of reducing virtual water demand and improving resource efficiency across value chains. Circular approaches emphasize the reuse, recycling, and valorization of resources, which can substantially lower water requirements per unit of output. In the agri-food sector, this includes the reuse of treated wastewater, the recovery of nutrients from agricultural residues, and the valorization of by-products for animal feed, bioenergy, or bio-based materials.

Enhancing traceability and reporting on water use

Improved reporting on water use and water-related impacts also facilitates compliance with sustainability certification schemes, environmental disclosure requirements, and due diligence regulations increasingly adopted in global markets. By systematically measuring and disclosing water footprint indicators, firms can identify hotspots of water inefficiency, prioritize targeted interventions, and demonstrate accountability to stakeholders. In this context, enhanced traceability and reporting serve not only as risk management tools but also as strategic instruments for aligning business practices with circular economy principles and long-term sustainability objectives

## 3. Implications for Academic Research

*Integrating MRIO models and CE frameworks*

A key research implication lies in the integration of multi-regional input–output (MRIO) models with circular economy frameworks to better capture the systemic nature of virtual water flows. While MRIO models have been widely used to quantify embodied water in international trade, they often remain embedded in linear production–consumption paradigms. Future research should extend these models by incorporating circularity dimensions, such as resource reuse, waste recovery, and efficiency improvements along value chains. Linking MRIO-based virtual water accounts with CE indicators would enable researchers to assess not only the magnitude of water flows but also the effectiveness of circular strategies in reducing water intensity and environmental impacts. Such integration would also facilitate the evaluation of trade-offs between economic performance, water savings, and environmental outcomes, thereby providing a more comprehensive analytical foundation for sustainable trade policy design.

*Conducting case studies in water-scarce contexts*

Empirical case studies in water-scarce and climate-vulnerable regions represent another important research direction. Regions such as the Middle East and North Africa (MENA) and Sub-Saharan Africa (SSA) are particularly relevant due to their high levels of water stress, dependence on food imports, and exposure to climate variability. Applying the proposed framework in these contexts would allow researchers to examine how virtual water trade interacts with domestic water constraints, food security objectives, and development priorities.

*Designing scenarios for future circular water trade systems*

Future research should focus on the development of scenario-based analyses to explore alternative pathways for circular and sustainable water trade systems. Scenario design can help assess how changes in trade patterns, technological innovation, climate conditions, and policy interventions may affect virtual water flows over time. Integrating MRIO models with scenario analysis allows researchers to simulate the impacts of circular economy strategies—such as increased water reuse, reduced food loss, or shifts toward less water-intensive consumption patterns—on global and regional water use. These forward-looking approaches are particularly valuable for identifying potential risks, synergies, and unintended consequences associated with different transition pathways. By providing insights into long-term dynamics and uncertainty, scenario-based research can support the design of adaptive governance frameworks capable of steering virtual water trade toward enhanced water security, economic resilience, and sustainability.

## VI. CONCLUSION

This chapter rethinks virtual water trade (VWT) through the lens of the circular economy (CE) and proposes a conceptual framework to align trade-driven virtual water flows with sustainable production and consumption. The key message is that VWT can contribute to water-use efficiency and relieve local water stress, but its benefits are conditional and may be offset by major trade-offs, including environmental degradation in exporting regions, increased import dependence, and governance and equity challenges across global value chains.

To address these issues, the framework combines (i) disaggregated water footprint accounting (blue, green, and grey), (ii) supply-chain and life-cycle perspectives to avoid problem shifting and identify hotspots, and (iii) a circular governance logic that links indicators to decision-making by producers, consumers, and policymakers. Overall, the chapter highlights that governing VWT for sustainability requires coordinated water, agricultural, and trade policies, alongside circular interventions that improve water productivity, reduce pollution, enhance traceability, and strengthen resilience. This integrated approach provides a basis for designing more resource-efficient and equitable trade pathways, especially in water-scarce regions. From a policy perspective, this chapter suggests that policymakers should consider more than just the volume of water involved in trade and promote indicators that reflect resource efficiency, ecological pressures, and the distribution of environmental costs throughout supply chains, through closer coordination between trade policy, water policy, agricultural planning, and sustainability regulations.

## REFERENCES


Aldaya, M. M., Garrido, A., & Llamas, R. (2020). Water footprint and virtual water trade: The birth and growth of a new research field in Spain. *Water (Basel), 12*(9), 2641. Advance online publication. DOI: 10.3390/w12092641

Allan, J. a. (1997). *"Virtual water": a long term solution for water short Middle Eastern economies?* School of Oriental and African Studies, University of London., September., http://www.ciaonet.org/wps/aln02/

Allan, J. (2005). Virtual Water: A Strategic Resource Global Solutions to Regional Deficits. *Groundwater, 36*(4), 545–546. DOI: 10.1111/j.1745-6584.1998.tb02825.x

Allan, J. A. (1998). Virtual water: A strategic resource. *Groundwater, 36*(4), 545–547. DOI: 10.1111/j.1745-6584.1998.tb02825.x

Antonelli, M., Laio, F., & Tamea, S. (2017). Water Resources, Food Security and the Role of Virtual Water Trade in the MENA Region. In *Environmental Change and Human Security in Africa and the Middle East* (pp. 199–217). DOI: 10.1007/978-3-319-45648-5_11

Antonelli, M., & Tamea, S. (2015). Food-water security and virtual water trade in the Middle East and North Africa. *International Journal of Water Resources Development, 31:3*(July), 326–342. DOI: 10.1080/07900627.2015.1030496

Batlles de la Fuente, A., Franco-Garcia, L., Belmonte, L., & Plaza-Úbeda, J. (2023). *Technological Innovations Promoting Circular Economy: A Profitable Tool to Close Resource Loops.*, DOI: 10.1007/978-3-031-33982-0_1

Beckett, R. C., & Terziovski, M. (2025). Integrating Circular Economy Principles in Water Resilience: Implications for Corporate Governance and Sustainability Reporting. In *Journal of Risk and Financial Management* (Vol. 18, Issue 5, p. 261). DOI: 10.3390/jrfm18050261

Bocken, N., Pauw, I., Bakker, C. A., & van der Grinten, B. (2016). Product design and business model strategies for a circular economy. *J. Ind. Prod. Eng., 1015.*

Boulay, A., Hoekstra, A. Y., & Vionnet, S. (2013). Complementarities of Water-Focused Life Cycle Assessment and Water Footprint Assessment. *Environmental Science & Technology, 47*(21), 11926–11927. DOI: 10.1021/es403928f PMID: 24147821

Boulding, K. E. (1966). The Economics of Knowledge and the Knowledge of Economics. *The American Economic Review, 56*(1), 1–13.

Brears, R. (2019). *Developing the Circular Water Economy*. DOI: 10.1007/978-3-030-32575-6

Brennan, G., Tennant, M., & Blomsma, F. (2015). Business and production solutions: Closing the Loop in Kopnina, H. and Shoreman-Ouimet, E. (Eds). Sustainability: Key Issues. EarthScan. In Routledge (Ed.), *Sustainability: Key Issues* (pp. 219–239). DOI: 10.4324/9780203109496-11

Castellani, V., Beylot, A., & Sala, S. (2019). Environmental impacts of household consumption in Europe: Comparing process-based LCA and environmentally extended input-output analysis. *Journal of Cleaner Production*, *240*, 117966. DOI: 10.1016/j.jclepro.2019.117966 PMID: 31839696

Chen, C.-Y., Wang, S.-W., Kim, H., Pan, S.-Y., Fan, C., & Lin, Y. J. (2021). Non-conventional water reuse in agriculture: A circular water economy. *Water Research*, *199*, 117193. DOI: 10.1016/j.watres.2021.117193 PMID: 33971532

Chukalla, A. D., Krol, M. S., & Hoekstra, A. Y. (2015). Green and blue water footprint reduction in irrigated agriculture: Effect of irrigation techniques, irrigation strategies and mulching. *Hydrology and Earth System Sciences*, *19*(12), 4877–4891. DOI: 10.5194/hess-19-4877-2015

D'Odorico, P., Carr, J., Dalin, C., Dell'Angelo, J., Konar, M., Laio, F., Ridolfi, L., Rosa, L., Suweis, S., Tamea, S., & Tuninetti, M. (2019). Global virtual water trade and the hydrological cycle: Patterns, drivers, and socio-environmental impacts. *Environmental Research Letters*, *14*(5), 053001. Advance online publication. DOI: 10.1088/1748-9326/ab05f4

D'Odorico, P., Carr, J., Laio, F., Ridolfi, L., & Vandoni, S. (2014). Feeding humanity through global food trade. *Earth's Future*, *2*(9), 458–469. Advance online publication. DOI: 10.1002/2014EF000250

Dalin, C., Konar, M., Hanasaki, N., Rinaldo, A., & Rodriguez-iturbe, I. (2012). *Evolution of the Global Virtual Water Trade Network* (Issue June 2014). DOI: 10.1073/pnas.1203176109

Dalin, C., Konar, M., Hanasaki, N., Rinaldo, A., & Rodriguez-Iturbe, I. (2012). Evolution of the Global Virtual Water Trade Network. *Proceedings of the National Academy of Sciences of the United States of America*, *109*(16), 5989–5994. DOI: 10.1073/pnas.1203176109 PMID: 22474363

Debaere, P., & Konar, M. (2022). Water resources and trade: A research vision. *PLOS Water*, *1*(2), e0000010. DOI: 10.1371/journal.pwat.0000010

Delpasand, M., Bozorg-Haddad, O., Goharian, E., & Loáiciga, H. A. (2023). Virtual water trade: Economic development and independence through optimal allocation. *Agricultural Water Management*, *275*, 108022. DOI: 10.1016/j.agwat.2022.108022

Demartini, M., Pinna, C., Aliakbarian, B., Tonelli, F., & Terzi, S. (2018). Soft Drink Supply Chain Sustainability: A Case Based Approach to Identify and Explain Best Practices and Key Performance Indicators. In *Sustainability* (Vol. 10, Issue 10, p. 3540). DOI: 10.3390/su10103540

Duarte, R., Pinilla, V., & Serrano, A. (2016). Understanding agricultural virtual water flows in the world from an economic perspective: A long term study. *Ecological Indicators*, *61*, 980–990. DOI: 10.1016/j.ecolind.2015.10.056

Duarte, R., Pinilla, V., & Serrano, A. (2019). Long Term Drivers of Global Virtual Water Trade: A Trade Gravity Approach for 1965–2010. *Ecological Economics*, *156*(June 2017), 318–326. DOI: 10.1016/j.ecolecon.2018.10.012

Duarte, R., & Yang, H. (2011). INPUT–OUTPUT AND WATER: INTRODUCTION TO THE SPECIAL ISSUE ROSA. *Economic Systems Research, 23(4)*(March 2014), 341–351. DOI: 10.1080/09535314.2011.638277

Duchin, F., & López-Morales, C. (2012). Do Water-Rich Regions Have a Comparative Advantage in Food Production? Improving the Representation of Water for Agriculture in Economic Models. *Economic Systems Research*, *24*(4), 371–389. DOI: 10.1080/09535314.2012.714746

Egan, M. (2011). The Water Footprint Assessment Manual. Setting the Global Standard. In *Social and Environmental Accountability Journal* (Vol. 31, Issue 2). DOI: 10.1080/0969160X.2011.593864

Ellen MacArthur Foundation. (2013). *Towards the Circular Economy*.

EMF (Ellen MacArthur Foundation). (2017). *Our Mission Is to Accelerate the Transition to a Circular Economy*. Ellen MacArthur Foundation. https://www.ellenmacarthurfoundation.org/

European Commission. (2015). *Closing the Loop - an EU Action Plan for the Circular Economy, Com(2015) 614 Communication from the Commission to the European Parliament, the Council, the European Economic and Social Committee and the Committee of the Regions*.

Fader, M., Gerten, D., Thammer, M., Heinke, J., Lotze-Campen, H., Lucht, W., & Cramer, W. (2011). Internal and external green-blue agricultural water footprints of nations, and related water and land savings through trade. *Hydrology and Earth System Sciences*, *15*(5), 1641–1660. DOI: 10.5194/hess-15-1641-2011

Feng, K., Chapagain, A., Suh, S., Pfister, S., & Hubacek, K. (2011). Comparison of bottom-up and top-down approaches to calculating the water footprints of nations. *Economic Systems Research*, *23*(4), 371–385. DOI: 10.1080/09535314.2011.638276

Feng, K., Hubacek, K., Siu, Y. L., & Li, X. (2014). The energy and water nexus in Chinese electricity production: A hybrid life cycle analysis. *Renewable & Sustainable Energy Reviews*, *39*, 342–355. DOI: 10.1016/j.rser.2014.07.080

Finkbeiner, M., Inaba, A., Tan, R., Christiansen, K., & Klüppel, H.-J. (2006). The New International Standards for Life Cycle Assessment: ISO 14040 and ISO 14044. *The International Journal of Life Cycle Assessment*, *11*(2), 80–85. DOI: 10.1065/lca2006.02.002

Fracasso, A. (2014). A gravity model of virtual water trade. *Ecological Economics*, *108*, 215–228. DOI: 10.1016/j.ecolecon.2014.10.010

Fracasso, A., Sartori, M., & Schiavo, S. (2016). Determinants of virtual water flows in the Mediterranean. *The Science of the Total Environment*, *543*, 1054–1062. https://doi.org/https://doi.org/10.1016/j.scitotenv.2015.02.059. DOI: 10.1016/j.scitotenv.2015.02.059 PMID: 25708715

Geissdoerfer, M., Savaget, P., Bocken, N. M. P., & Hultink, E. J. (2017). The Circular Economy – A new sustainability paradigm? *Journal of Cleaner Production*, *143*, 757–768. https://doi.org/https://doi.org/10.1016/j.jclepro.2016.12.048. DOI: 10.1016/j.jclepro.2016.12.048

Gerbens-Leenes, P. W., Hoekstra, A. Y., & Bosman, R. (2018). The blue and grey water footprint of construction materials: Steel, cement and glass. *Water Resources and Industry*, *19*(April 2017), 1–12. DOI: 10.1016/j.wri.2017.11.002

Hoekstra, A., Chapagain, A., Aldaya, M., & Mekonnen, M. (2011). *The Water Footprint Assessment Manual*. DOI: 10.4324/9781849775526

Hoekstra, A., & Hung, P. Q. (2002). Virtual water trade: A quantification of virtual water flows between nations in relation to international crop trade. *Water Science and Technology*, *49*, 203–209.

Hoekstra, A., & Mekonnen, M. (2012). The Water Footprint of Humanity. *Proceedings of the National Academy of Sciences of the United States of America*, *109*(9), 3232–3237. DOI: 10.1073/pnas.1109936109 PMID: 22331890

Hoekstra, A. Y. (2017). Water Footprint Assessment in Supply Chains. *Springer Series in Supply Chain Management*, *4*, 65–85. DOI: 10.1007/978-3-319-29791-0_4

Hoekstra, A. Y., & Chapagain, A. K. (2007). Water footprints of nations: Water use by people as a function of their consumption pattern. *Water Resources Management, 21*(1), 35–48. DOI: 10.1007/s11269-006-9039-x

ISO 14040. (2006). *Environmental Management - Life Cycle Assessment - Principles and Framework (ISO 14040:2006), Geneva, Switzerland.*

ISO 14044. (2006). *Environmental Management—Life Cycle Assessment—Requirements and Guidelines* (Vol. 2006).

IWA. (2016). *Water Utility Pathways in a Circular Economy*. https://nextgenwater.eu/wp-content/uploads/2018/10/IWA_Circular_Economy_screen-1.pdf

Jackson, T. T. A.-T. T. -. (2016). *Prosperity without growth : foundations for the economy of tomorrow* (Second edition NV-1 online resource : illustrations (black and white)). Routledge. https://doi.org/ LK - https://worldcat.org/title/969665612

Kakwani, N. S., & Kalbar, P. P. (2020). Review of Circular Economy in urban water sector : Challenges and opportunities in India. *Journal of Environmental Management, 271*(August 2019). DOI: 10.1016/j.jenvman.2020.111010

Kim, D., Steinbach, S., & Zurita, C. (2025). Virtual Water Trade and Economic Integration: The Role of Trade Agreements in Global Water Redistribution. *Applied Economic Perspectives and Policy, 47*(5), 1998–2018. https://doi.org/https://doi.org/10.1002/aepp.70021. DOI: 10.1002/aepp.70021

Kirchherr, J., Reike, D., & Hekkert, M. (2017). Conceptualizing the circular economy: An analysis of 114 definitions. *Resources, Conservation and Recycling, 127*, 221–232. https://doi.org/https://doi.org/10.1016/j.resconrec.2017.09.005. DOI: 10.1016/j.resconrec.2017.09.005

Korhonen, J., Honkasalo, A., & Seppälä, J. (2018). Circular Economy: The Concept and its Limitations. *Ecological Economics, 143*, 37–46. https://doi.org/https://doi.org/10.1016/j.ecolecon.2017.06.041. DOI: 10.1016/j.ecolecon.2017.06.041

Korhonen, J., Nuur, C., Feldmann, A., & Birkie, S. E. (2018). Circular economy as an essentially contested concept. *Journal of Cleaner Production, 175*, 544–552. https://doi.org/https://doi.org/10.1016/j.jclepro.2017.12.111. DOI: 10.1016/j.jclepro.2017.12.111

Lant, C. (2003). Commentary. *Water International, 28*(1), 113–115. DOI: 10.1080/02508060.2003.9724813

Lasseur, N. M. C. G., Holstead, K., & Huitema, D. (2025). How is the governance of circular economy of water organized? A systematic review of the literature. *Ecology and Society*, *30*(3), art36. Advance online publication. DOI: 10.5751/ES-16390-300336

Lenzen, M., Moran, D., Kanemoto, K., Foran, B., Lobefaro, L., & Geschke, A. (2012). International trade drives biodiversity threats in developing nations. *Nature*, *486*(7401), 109–112. DOI: 10.1038/nature11145 PMID: 22678290

Lieder, M., & Rashid, A. (2015). Towards Circular Economy implementation: A comprehensive review in context of manufacturing industry. *Journal of Cleaner Production*, *115*, 36–51. Advance online publication. DOI: 10.1016/j.jclepro.2015.12.042

Liu, J., Williams, J. R., Zehnder, A. J. B., & Yang, H. (2007). GEPIC - modelling wheat yield and crop water productivity with high resolution on a global scale. *Agricultural Systems*, *94*(2), 478–493. DOI: 10.1016/j.agsy.2006.11.019

Luwedde, J., & Nakazi, F. (2024). In Mhlanga, D., & Ndhlovu, E. (Eds.), *Implications of Russia-Ukraine War on Uganda's Fertilizer and Wheat Supply BT - The Russia-Ukraine Conflict and Development in Africa: Implications for Sustainable Development* (pp. 315–323). Springer Nature Switzerland., DOI: 10.1007/978-3-031-63333-1_19

Markard, J., Raven, R., & Truffer, B. (2012). Sustainability transitions: An emerging field of research and its prospects. *Research Policy*, *41*(6), 955–967. DOI: 10.1016/j.respol.2012.02.013

Mekonnen, M. M., Kebede, M. M., Demeke, B. W., Carr, J. A., Chapagain, A., Dalin, C., Debaere, P., D'Odorico, P., Marston, L., Ray, C., Rosa, L., & Zhuo, L. (2024). Trends and environmental impacts of virtual water trade. *Nature Reviews. Earth & Environment*, *5*(12), 890–905. DOI: 10.1038/s43017-024-00605-2

Meng, B., Fang, Y., Guo, J., & Yaxiong, Z. (2017). Measuring China ' s domestic production networks through Trade in Value-added perspectives. *Economic Systems Research*, *29*(January), 48–65. DOI: 10.1080/09535314.2017.1282435

Merrett, S. (1997). *Introduction To The Economics Of Water Resources: An International Perspective* (Routledge (ed.); 1st Editio). 10.4324/9780203645390

METI. (2004). *Handbook on Resource Recycling Legislation and 3R Initiatives*.

Mirabi, M., Javan, K., Darestani, M., & Karrabi, M. (2025). Integrating Circular Economy and Life Cycle Assessment in Virtual Water Management: A Case Study of Food Consumption Across Economic Classes in Iran. *Sustainability (Basel)*, *17*(6), 1–16. DOI: 10.3390/su17062743

Morseletto, P. (2020). Targets for a circular economy. *Resources, Conservation and Recycling, 153*, 104553. DOI: 10.1016/j.resconrec.2019.104553

Morseletto, P., Mooren, C. E., & Munaretto, S. (2022). Circular Economy of Water: Definition, Strategies and Challenges. *Circular Economy and Sustainability*, *2*(4), 1463–1477. DOI: 10.1007/s43615-022-00165-x

Nika, C. E., Vasilaki, V., Expósito, A., & Katsou, E. (2020). Water Cycle and Circular Economy: Developing a Circularity Assessment Framework for Complex Water Systems. *Water Research, 187*, 116423. DOI: 10.1016/j.watres.2020.116423 PMID: 32979579

Odey, G., Adelodun, B., Kim, S. H., & Choi, K. S. (2021). Conflicting Drivers of Virtual Water Trade: A Review Based on the "virtual Water Concept.". *Water Economics and Policy*, *7*(3), 2150011. Advance online publication. DOI: 10.1142/S2382624X21500119

Pauliuk, S. (2018). Critical appraisal of the circular economy standard BS 8001:2017 and a dashboard of quantitative system indicators for its implementation in organizations. *Resources, Conservation and Recycling, 129*, 81–92. DOI: 10.1016/j.resconrec.2017.10.019

Pearce, D., & Turner, R. (1989). Economics of natural resources and the environment. In *Johns Hopkins University Press*. DOI: 10.56021/9780801839863

Pfister, S., Boulay, A. M., Berger, M., Hadjikakou, M., Motoshita, M., Hess, T., Ridoutt, B., Weinzettel, J., Scherer, L., Döll, P., Manzardo, A., Núñez, M., Verones, F., Humbert, S., Buxmann, K., Harding, K., Benini, L., Oki, T., Finkbeiner, M., & Henderson, A. (2017). Understanding the LCA and ISO water footprint: A response to Hoekstra (2016) "A critique on the water-scarcity weighted water footprint in LCA. *Ecological Indicators, 72*, 352–359. DOI: 10.1016/j.ecolind.2016.07.051 PMID: 30344449

Prieto-Sandoval, V., Jaca, C., & Ormazabal, M. (2018). Towards a consensus on the circular economy. *Journal of Cleaner Production, 179*, 605–615. DOI: 10.1016/j.jclepro.2017.12.224

Qian, Y., Tian, X., Geng, Y., Zhong, S., Cui, X., Zhang, X., Moss, D. A., & Bleischwitz, R. (2019). Driving Factors of Agricultural Virtual Water Trade between China and the Belt and Road Countries. *Environmental Science & Technology*, *53*(10), 5877–5886. DOI: 10.1021/acs.est.9b00093 PMID: 31013057

Razzouki, A., Ridaoui, M., Oudgou, M., & Boudhar, A. (2025). Econometric Analysis of Climate Change Impacts on Agricultural Output in the MENA Region. In *Economies* (Vol. 13, Issue 12, p. 340). DOI: 10.3390/economies13120340

Ridaoui, M., Razzouki, A., Oudgou, M., & Boudhar, A. (2025). Revisiting agricultural policies in Morocco through the lens of virtual water trade: a literature review. *Frontiers in Water, Volume 7-2025*. https://doi.org/10.3389/frwa.2025.1717928

Ridaoui, M., Razzouki, A., Ouhbi, H., Oudgou, M., & Boudhar, A. (2025). Exploring the Dynamics of Virtual Water Trade in Crop Products Between Morocco and the European Union. *Water (Basel)*, *17*(18), 2664. DOI: 10.3390/w17182664

Robbins, Lord. (1984). An Essay on the Nature and Significance of Economic Science. *An Essay on the Nature and Significance of Economic Science*. DOI: 10.1007/978-1-349-17510-9

Sachs, J. D. (2015). *The age of sustainable development*. Columbia University Press. DOI: 10.7312/sach17314

Sandström, V., Lehikoinen, E., & Peltonen-Sainio, P. (2018). Replacing Imports of Crop Based Commodities by Domestic Production in Finland: Potential to Reduce Virtual Water Imports. *Frontiers in Sustainable Food Systems*, *2*(October), 1–13. DOI: 10.3389/fsufs.2018.00067

Seekell, D. A., D'Odorico, P., & Pace, M. L. (2011). Virtual water transfers unlikely to redress inequality in global water use. *Environmental Research Letters*, *6*(2), 024017. Advance online publication. DOI: 10.1088/1748-9326/6/2/024017

Smol, M., Adam, C., & Preisner, M. (2020). Circular economy model framework in the European water and wastewater sector. *Journal of Material Cycles and Waste Management*, *22*(3), 682–697. DOI: 10.1007/s10163-019-00960-z

Smol, M., Kulczycka, J., Henclik, A., Gorazda, K., & Wzorek, Z. (2015). The possible use of sewage sludge ash (SSA) in the construction industry as a way towards a circular economy. *Journal of Cleaner Production*, *95*, 45–54. DOI: 10.1016/j.jclepro.2015.02.051

Stahel, W. R. (1982). *The product life factor. An Inquiry into the Nature of Sustainable Societies. The Role of the Private Sector*. Houston Area Research Centre.

Su, B., Heshmati, A., Geng, Y., & Yu, X. (2013). A review of the circular economy in China: Moving from rhetoric to implementation. *Journal of Cleaner Production*, *42*, 215–227. DOI: 10.1016/j.jclepro.2012.11.020

Suh, S., & Huppes, G. (2005). Methods for life cycle inventory of a product. *Journal of Cleaner Production, 13*(7), 687–697. DOI: 10.1016/j.jclepro.2003.04.001

Tamea, S., Carr, J. A., Laio, F., & Ridolfi, L. (2014). Drivers of the virtual water trade. *Water Resources Research, 50*(1), 17–28. DOI: 10.1002/2013WR014707

Tamea, S., Laio, F., & Ridolfi, L. (2016). Global effects of local food-production crises: A virtual water perspective. *Scientific Reports, 6*(May 2015), 1–14. DOI: 10.1038/srep18803

Tian, X., Geng, Y., Sarkis, J., & Zhong, S. (2018). Trends and features of embodied flows associated with international trade based on bibliometric analysis. *Resources, Conservation and Recycling, 131*(September 2017), 148–157. DOI: 10.1016/j.resconrec.2018.01.002

UN. (2015). *Transforming Our World: The 2030 Agenda for SustainableDevelopment*. Springer., DOI: 10.1007/978-3-031-07461-5_1

Vallino, E., Ridolfi, L., & Laio, F. (2020). Measuring economic water scarcity in agriculture: A cross-country empirical investigation. *Environmental Science & Policy, 114*, 73–85. DOI: 10.1016/j.envsci.2020.07.017

Vallino, E., Ridolfi, L., & Laio, F. (2021). Trade of economically and physically scarce virtual water in the global food network. *Scientific Reports, 11*(1), 1–19. DOI: 10.1038/s41598-021-01514-w PMID: 34815433

Vanham, D., Hoekstra, A. Y., & Bidoglio, G. (2013). Potential water saving through changes in European diets. *Environment International, 61*, 45–56. DOI: 10.1016/j.envint.2013.09.011 PMID: 24096041

Voulvoulis, N. (2018). Water reuse from a circular economy perspective and potential risks from an unregulated approach. *Current Opinion in Environmental Science & Health, 2*, 32–45. DOI: 10.1016/j.coesh.2018.01.005

Wang, Y. B., Liu, D., Cao, X. C., Yang, Z. Y., Song, J. F., Chen, D. Y., & Sun, S. K. (2017). Agricultural water rights trading and virtual water export compensation coupling model: A case study of an irrigation district in China. *Agricultural Water Management, 180*, 99–106. DOI: 10.1016/j.agwat.2016.11.006

Wang, Z., Li, T., Liang, W., Fu, B., Li, J., & Yan, J. (2024). Uncovering the structure and evolution of global virtual water and agricultural land network. *Sustainable Production and Consumption, 51*, 599–611. DOI: 10.1016/j.spc.2024.08.017

WBCSD. (2010). Vision 2050. In *The New Agenda for Business*.

WHO & UNICEF. (2024). Progress on Household Drinking Water, Sanitation and Hygiene 2000-2024. In *UNICEF journal*. https://www.eea.europa.eu/publications/industrial-waste-water-treatment-pressures%0Ahttp://files/558/Rapport EEA Industrial waste water treatment – pressures on Europe's environment.pdf

Wichelns, D. (2004). The policy relevance of virtual water can be enhanced by considering comparative advantages. *Agricultural Water Management*, *66*(1), 49–63. DOI: 10.1016/j.agwat.2003.09.006

Wichelns, D. (2015). Virtual Water and Water Footprints: Overreaching Into the Discourse on Sustainability, Efficiency, and Equity. *Water Alternatives*, *8*, 396–414.

Wiedmann, T. (2009). A first empirical comparison of energy Footprints embodied in trade - MRIO versus PLUM. *Ecological Economics*, *68*(7), 1975–1990. DOI: 10.1016/j.ecolecon.2008.06.023

Winans, K., Kendall, A., & Deng, H. (2017). The history and current applications of the circular economy concept. *Renewable & Sustainable Energy Reviews*, *68*, 825–833. DOI: 10.1016/j.rser.2016.09.123

World Economic Forum. (2015). *Global Risks 2015; World Economic Forum: Geneva, Switzerland.* http://www3.weforum.org/docs/WEF_Global_Risks_2015_Report15.pdf

Yang, H., Pfister, S., & Bhaduri, A. (2013). Accounting for a scarce resource: Virtual water and water footprint in the global water system. *Current Opinion in Environmental Sustainability*, *5*(6), 599–606. DOI: 10.1016/j.cosust.2013.10.003

Yang, H., Wang, L., Mikayilov, F., & Zehnder, A. (2006). Virtual water trade: An assessment of water use efficiency in the international food trade. *Hydrology and Earth System Sciences*, *10*(3), 443–454. Advance online publication. DOI: 10.5194/hess-10-443-2006

Yin, Y., Luan, X., Sun, S., Wang, Y., Wu, P., & Wang, X. (2021). Environmental impact of grain virtual water flows in China: From 1997 to 2014. *Agricultural Water Management*, *256*, 107127. DOI: 10.1016/j.agwat.2021.107127

Yoo, S.-H., Kim, T., Im, J.-B., & Choi, J.-Y. (2012). Estimation of the international virtual water flow of grain crop products in Korea. *Paddy and Water Environment -. Paddy and Water Environment*, *10*(2), 83–93. Advance online publication. DOI: 10.1007/s10333-011-0267-1

Zhong, R., Chen, A., Zhao, D., Mao, G., Zhao, X., Huang, H., & Liu, J. (2023). Impact of international trade on water scarcity: An assessment by improving the Falkenmark indicator. *Journal of Cleaner Production, 385*, 135740. DOI: 10.1016/j.jclepro.2022.135740

Zhuo, L., Mekonnen, M. M., & Hoekstra, A. Y. (2016). The effect of inter-annual variability of consumption, production, trade and climate on crop-related green and blue water footprints and inter-regional virtual water trade: A study for China (1978-2008). *Water Research, 94*, 73–85. DOI: 10.1016/j.watres.2016.02.037 PMID: 26938494

Zisopoulou, K., Zisopoulos, D., & Panagoulia, D. (2022). Water Economics: An In-Depth Analysis of the Connection of Blue Water with Some Primary Level Aspects of Economic Theory I. *Water (Basel), 14*(1), 103. Advance online publication. DOI: 10.3390/w14010103

# Chapter 6
# Digital Twin-Enabled Systems for Optimizing Bio-Waste-Based Farming Models

**Leena Arya**
http://orcid.org/0000-0002-9249-732X
*Koneru Lakshmiah Education Foundation, India*

**Nagarjuna Karyemsetty**
http://orcid.org/0000-0002-7640-7099
*Koneru Lakshmiah Education Foundation, India*

**Kamal Kant Verma**
http://orcid.org/0000-0003-0030-3688
*School of Computer Science and Engineering, IILM University, India*

**Avadhesh Kumar Gupta**
http://orcid.org/0000-0001-6280-1864
*School of Computer Science and Engineering, IILM University, India*

**Ravi Rastogi**
http://orcid.org/0000-0002-1118-3020
*JIMS Engineering Management Technical Campus, India*

## ABSTRACT

*Digital Twin (DT) technology enables system-level integration of bio-waste valorization with precision agriculture to advance circularity, sustainability, and resilience. This chapter presents a unified DT framework as sensing, data infrastructure, virtual*

DOI: 10.4018/979-8-2600-1438-7.ch006

*models, and service interfaces and outlines enabling technologies (IoT, remote sensing, edge/cloud, AI/ML, blockchain). It maps the bio-waste-to-farm value chain (collection, conversion, refinement, logistics, soil-adaptive application) and demonstrates closed-loop capabilities: real-time monitoring, predictive analytics, and prescriptive optimization. Field and pilot evidence show measurable gains in nutrient-use efficiency, yield, emissions reduction, and operational resilience. Persistent barriers i.e., data fragmentation, interoperability, model validation, cost, and privacy are discussed, with recommended pathways (stakeholder co-creation, standards, federated learning, XAI, dynamic LCA) to scale equitable DT adoption for a circular bioeconomy.*

## 1. INTRODUCTION

The most pressing issues of our time, such as sustainability and global food security, are transforming agriculture as an economic sector. Worldwide, over 1.3 billion tons of bio-waste are generated every year, a lot of it is either thrown away or improperly discarded, which creates and intensifies greenhouse gas emissions and environmental damage. Concurrently, more resilient, sustainable, and efficient agricultural systems are needed to meet the demands of a growing global population, which is projected to reach 9.7 billion by 2050 (Aboueata et al., 2021).

Global agriculture is at a turning point. The escalating demand for food brought about by climate change's devastating impacts on agricultural yields (Rahman et al., 2022; Suryani et al., 2022) as well as the burning fossil fuels and synthetic fertilizers, has created an urgent need for innovative, game-changing solutions to food security (Aboueata et al., 2021) (Aboueata et al., 2021; Lakhiar et al., 2024). Concurrently, the linear "take-make-dispose" model produces enormous amounts of organic waste, which is a huge, underutilized source of energy and nutrients as well as a burden on the environment. A strong route to circularity and less environmental impact that supports net-zero goals is to incorporate bio-waste valorization, the process of turning waste into useful resources like compost, biofertilizers, or bioenergy into farming practices (Manta, 2026).

However, there are many obstacles in the way of optimizing intricate bio-waste-based farming systems. It will take unprecedented levels of coordination, data integration, and predictive capability to manage multiple waste streams, guarantee effective conversion processes, apply bio-products precisely to match crop needs, track environmental impacts in real-time, and navigate complex supply chains (Melesse et al., 2023; Busse et al., 2021; Singh et al., 2023). The granularity, responsiveness, and holistic viewpoint required for true optimization and resilience are frequently absent from traditional approaches.

Enter the world of the Digital Twin (DT). It is becoming a key part of Industry 4.0 and smart systems. A Digital Twin is a virtual, dynamic copy of a physical object, process, or system. It receives real-time updates through sensors and connected devices (IoT) (Sushanth & Sujatha, 2018; Alam & El Saddik, 2017; Jones et al., 2020; Tao et al., 2019). It can simulate, predict, analyze, and improve the performance of its physical counterpart using technologies like cloud computing, big data analysis, artificial intelligence (AI), machine learning (ML), and the Internet of Things (IoT) (Qi et al., 2021; Botín-Sanabria et al., 2022; Mihai et al., 2022). While it started mainly in manufacturing, DTs are quickly changing agriculture. They can predict crop conditions (Melesse et al., 2024; Jiang et al., 2022), improve resource use (Pylianidis et al., 2021; Purcell & Neubauer, 2023), enhance greenhouse management (Ariesen-Verschuur et al., 2022; Slob et al., 2023), secure supply chains (Melesse et al., 2023; Singh et al., 2023; Ding et al., 2023), and even model entire forestry ecosystems(Qiu et al., 2023; Nie et al., 2022) and livestock farms (Neethirajan & Kemp, 2021; Symeonaki et al., 2024).

In particular, DTs have a great deal of untapped potential for bio-waste-integrated agriculture. DTs can help close the gap between the digital tools required for sustainable intensification and the physical complexity of farming systems (Verdouw et al. (2021). They provide the structure for:

1. Model Complexity: Build lifelike virtual depictions of the whole bio-waste-to-farm value chain, including crop growth, environmental interactions, waste collection, processing of bioproducts, and application (Verdouw & Kruize, 2017; Koulouris et al., 2021).

2. Facilitate Real-Time Control and Monitoring: Combine sensor data from fields, logistics, and processing facilities to continuously monitor resource flows, crop health, process efficiency, and environmental conditions (Nasirahmadi & Hensel, 2022; Wang, 2024).

3. Predict & Simulate: Make use of AI/ML algorithms in the DT to prepare for potential nutrient imbalances or process failures, forecast crop yields under different bio-product application scenarios, model the effects of climate change, and optimize logistics (Min et al., 2019; Zhang et al., 2025; Escribà-Gelonch et al., 2024).

4. Optimize Decision-Making: Give farmers, processors, and legislators practical advice on how to increase resource recovery, reduce waste and emissions, increase crop productivity in a sustainable manner, and boost system resilience and economic viability in general (Verdouw et al., 2021; Purcell & Neubauer, 2023; Saha et al., 2025).

## 2. DIGITAL TWINS IN AGRICULTURE

The agricultural sector is undergoing a rapid revolution thanks to digital twin (DT) systems, which provide intelligent, real-time digital representations of physical farm entities. These systems integrate data from sensors, machinery, environmental sources, and biological processes to model, monitor, and enhance agricultural workflows (Pylianidis et al., 2021; Purcell & Neubauer, 2023; Wang, 2024). DTs provide data-driven solutions for precision farming, supply chain resilience, and sustainable land use in response to global challenges like climate change, resource constraints, and rising food demand (Saha et al., 2024; Monteiro et al., 2018; El Saddik, 2018). This section thoroughly examines the fundamental architecture, enabling technologies, existing applications, and gaps in integrating bio-waste into agricultural DT systems.

### 2.1. Core Architecture

Four interconnected layers make up the architecture of agricultural digital twins: data infrastructure, virtual, physical, and service components (Spyrou et al., 2023). The physical layer is comprised of crops, livestock, soil, and agricultural equipment that has sensors enabled by the Internet of Things, such as GPS-based tractors, multispectral cameras mounted on UAVs, or soil moisture probes (Saha et al., 2024; Sushanth & Sujatha, 2018; Botín-Sanabria et al., 2022).

The virtual layer replicates physical assets using computational models. These models include physics-based simulations, like crop growth models, data-driven algorithms, such as machine learning-based yield predictors, and 3D visualizations, including field topographies and digital maps (Melesse et al., 2024; Pylianidis et al., 2021).

The data infrastructure layer enables a two-way data flow. It connects the perception layer, which includes sensors, the network layer, which features technologies like LoRaWAN and 5G, and the processing layer. This processing layer uses edge and cloud computing platforms, such as AWS and Azure IoT (Alam & El Saddik, 2017; Mihai et al., 2022). The service layer sits at the top and provides useful outputs such as crop health forecasts, automated machinery adjustments, and irrigation dashboards. Innovative farming environments are increasingly adopting scalable and modular architectural blueprints provided by frameworks such as FIWARE (Saha et al., 2024; Verdouw & Kruize, 2017) and C2PS (Alam & El Saddik, 2017). environments.

## 2.2. Key Enabling Technologies

A number of convergent technologies are essential to the basic operation of DTs in agriculture:

- IoT & Remote Sensing: To provide multi-scale environmental insights, sensors that measure soil nutrients, pH, and moisture are paired with satellite data (e.g., Sentinel-2, PlanetScope) (Lakhiar et al., 2024; Vijayalakshmi et al., 2023). These technologies support data collection and real-time monitoring.
- AI and Machine Learning: Techniques such as convolutional neural networks (CNNs) help detect plant diseases. Ensemble models such as random forests can predict yields and detect pest outbreaks (Min et al., 2019; Nie et al., 2022). Simulation tools allow for "what-if" analysis to evaluate the effects of drought, irrigation methods, or nutrient planning (Qi et al., 2021; Mihai et al., 2022).
- Cloud and Edge Computing: Platforms like Google Earth Engine allow for large-scale data collection and historical trend analysis. Edge computing supports localized, quick tasks such as on-field pest alerts (Botín-Sanabria et al., 2022; Wang, 2024).
- Blockchain and Digital Threads: Blockchain keeps data trustworthy in digital thread-enabled supply chains (Ding et al., 2023). Digital threads support the flow of agricultural data throughout different stages of the crop lifecycle (Qi et al., 2021).

## 2.3. Current Applications

### 2.3.1 Crop Monitoring and Management

DTs are frequently employed in yield prediction and crop health evaluation. Variable rate application (VRA) maps are produced by platforms such as EOSDA Crop Monitoring, using NDVI and NDMI indices derived from satellite imagery, in conjunction with real-time sensor data (Zhang et al., 2025). Over 90% accuracy in yield estimation can be attained by predictive models that integrate weather analytics, soil composition, and phenological stages (Arya et al., 2025; Melesse et al., 2024).

### 2.3.2 Livestock Production

Wearable sensors are used by digital twins on livestock farms to track various health indicators, such as feeding, mobility, and temperature. Artificial intelligence (AI) models identify anomalous behaviour, forecast disease outbreaks, and recommend the best feeding schedules (Kumar et al., 2024; Neethirajan & Kemp, 2021; Symeonaki et al., 2024). Animal welfare has been improved, and mortality rates have decreased in real-world applications.

### 2.3.3 Supply Chain Optimization

Multimodal DTs that model logistics, resource scheduling, and warehouse operations are helping agricultural supply chains. Input delivery and harvesting operations are being optimized with the use of blockchain-based scheduling systems for machinery and logistics (Busse et al., 2021; Ding et al., 2023). These types of systems improve traceability from "farm to fork," increase transparency, and lower operating costs (Singh et al., 2023).

### 2.3.4 Forestry and Greenhouse Systems

To model growth, carbon sequestration, and biomass productivity, forestry DTs employ programs such as Landsat and 3D engines (Jiang et al., 2022; Qiu et al., 2023). To control humidity, temperature, and lighting for the best plant growth in greenhouse farming, DTs integrate crop physiology models with microclimate data (Abbas et al., 2023; Ariesen-Verschuur et al., 2022; Slob et al., 2023).

## 2.4. Gaps in Bio-Waste Integration

Even though DT is widely used, they still make a very small contribution to bio-waste-based farming. In favor of crop productivity or logistics management, most current DTs overlook circular pathways such as anaerobic digestion, composting, and nutrient recycling (Purcell & Neubauer, 2023; Arsic et al., 2023).

Data fragmentation is a major problem because important parameters such as substrate composition, microbial activity, and nutrient release from organic waste are rarely included in DT models (Zhang et al., 2025). Furthermore, current digital models are unable to simulate soil enrichment dynamics, digestate emissions, and temporal nutrient cycling, all of which are essential for evaluating the impacts of bio-waste (Verdouw et al., 2021).

Furthermore, the lack of standardised validation processes, due to the wide variation in waste streams, limits the model's broader applicability. Social and technical challenges like high IoT deployment costs and cybersecurity flaws (Arya et al., 2023; Nagaraj et al., 2023), and issues with system interoperability between farm DTs and waste management SCADA platforms (Almaiah et al., 2023; Botín-Sanabria et al., 2022; Mihai et al., 2022) further stop adoption.

Future work must create unified DT frameworks for closed-loop agricultural systems that include hybrid AI-mechanistic models for dynamic simulation of bio-waste behavior, real-time waste sensors, and modular architectures like FIWARE NGSI in order to close these gaps.

## 2.5 Transition to Proposed Framework

Based on the literature reviewed, it's clear that Digital Twin applications for precision agriculture have come a long way, but there is still a big gap in how these technologies can be combined with bio-waste valorization systems in a way that is both unified and systematic. Most of the research that has been done so far has looked at individual parts, like crop monitoring, supply chain optimization, or waste processing. There hasn't been much focus on how these parts work together in a circular bioeconomy framework. To fill this gap, this chapter suggests a complete Digital Twin-enabled framework that brings together bio-waste management, resource optimization, and precision farming into a single, closed-loop system (Vargas et al., 2025). This shift from theoretical ideas to a structured model lays the groundwork for both understanding the concept and applying it in sustainable, data-driven agricultural ecosystems.

# 3. THE SPECIFIC CASE FOR DIGITAL TWINS IN BIO-WASTE-BASED FARMING

Digital twin (DT) technology offers an all-inclusive, system-level approach to integrating waste valorization into sustainable agriculture. By utilizing DTs to optimize waste handling, nutrient recycling, and environmental monitoring through the real-time virtualization of physical processes, heterogeneous organic waste can be transformed into a reliable resource stream for precision farming (Howard et al., 2022; Escribà-Gelonch et al., 2024).

## 3.1. Mapping the Bio-Waste-to-Farm Value Chain

The bio-waste-to-farm system operates through an integrated value chain spanning waste sourcing, conversion, logistics, and precision agriculture, transforming heterogeneous organic waste (crop residues, food waste, biosolids) into valorised bio-products (compost, digestate, biofertilizers) for agricultural use. Key processes include:

- Waste Collection & Preprocessing: Removal of Segregation, shredding, and contamination.
- Conversion Technologies: composting, anaerobic digestion, or pyrolysis.
- Product Improvement: Enhancement of nutrients and reduction of pathogens.
- Distribution: Farm routing has been optimized.
- Soil-Adaptive Application: Precise implementation according to crop needs.

Every stakeholder in this chain has unique difficulties. Contamination is a problem for waste producers (food processors, municipalities); conversion facilities handle variable feedstocks (Arsic et al., 2023); logistics companies face inefficient routing (Ding et al., 2023); and farmers need precise timing of nutrient release (Melesse et al., 2023).

By combining blockchain-backed traceability and AI-powered simulation engines with IoT sensors—such as real-time compost thermometers, GPS vehicle trackers, and soil nutrient probes—DTs help coordinate this system. For instance, by dynamically modifying aeration and moisture levels, the use of a composting digital twin increased process efficiency by 22% in Colombia (Melesse et al., 2023). Additionally, the Agri-Food Supply Chain Digital Twin (AFSC-DT) serves as a control tower for modelling biomass flows and improving bioproduct quality throughout their lifecycle.

*Figure 1. Framework of Digital Twin Systems in Bio-Waste-Based Farming*

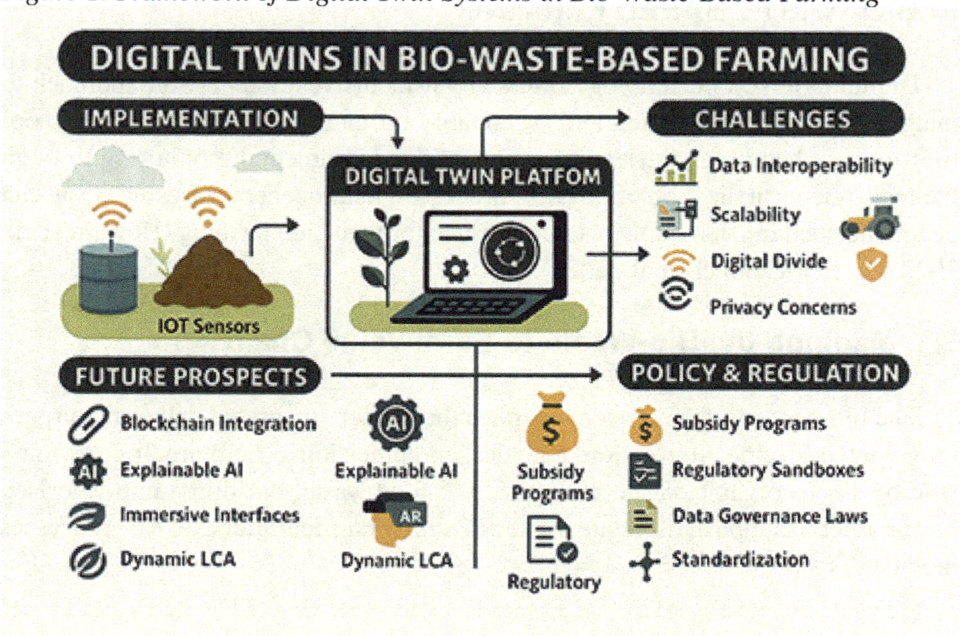

The essential elements for integrating digital twins into bio-waste farming systems are depicted in Figure 1. It highlights how IoT sensors can be integrated into a centralized DT platform, lists the main deployment issues (like privacy, scalability, and data interoperability), and forecasts upcoming innovations like blockchain, augmented reality interfaces, and explainable AI. It also emphasizes how crucial regulatory compliance and supportive policy frameworks are to the expansion of such systems.

## 3.2 Unique Challenges Addressed by DTs

### 3.2.1 Heterogeneity of Bio-Waste Streams & Conversion Processes

The high variability in waste composition (moisture, carbon-to-nitrogen ratios, contaminants) makes process consistency difficult to achieve. DTs overcome this by using spectral analysis for AI-powered waste classification (Botín-Sanabria et al., 2022) and by simulating fermentation conditions to adjust digester parameters like pH and temperature in real time (Koulouris et al., 2021).

### 3.2.2 Dynamic Nutrient Cycling and Soil-Bio-Product Interactions

Traditional models cannot dynamically simulate nutrient release from organic amendments. DTs integrate mechanistic decomposition models with ML-algorithms trained on soil sensor data (Min et al., 2019), producing predictive nitrogen mineralization maps aligned with crop uptake curves (Verdouw et al., 2021).

### 3.2.3 Precision Application of Bio-Products

Applying compost or digestate uniformly increases the risk of leaching and leads to inefficient nutrient use. DTs combine soil conductivity, bio-product viscosity, and UAV multispectral data to create 3D Variable Rate Application (VRA) maps (Vijayalakshmi et al., 2023). To ensure safe use on high-risk crops, DTs also replicate pathogen decay timelines (Koulouris et al., 2021).

### 3.2.4 Monitoring of Environmental Impacts in Real-Time

Data from legacy systems is frequently low-resolution and delayed. To enable proactive environmental management, DTs use IoT-based GHG ($CH_4$/$N_2O$) sensors connected to microclimate forecasts (Mihai et al., 2022) and model nitrate leaching in response to irrigation or rainfall (Zhang et al., 2025; Arya et al., 2023).

### 3.2.5 Integration of Waste Logistics with Farm Operations

Transport delays and mismatches between waste supply and field demand stem from disconnected systems. DTs address this by using edge computing to dynamically reroute vehicles during disruptions (Mihai et al., 2022) and blockchain-secured logistics planning (Ding et al., 2023).

## 3.3 Potential Benefits: Bridging Circularity and Resilience

### 3.3.1 Improved Resource Efficiency and Circularity

By dynamically tracking material flows, DTs allow greenhouse systems to reuse $CO_2$ derived from waste. The use of chemical fertilizer is decreased when nutrient recycling efficiency rises by 30 to 50% (Singh et al., 2023).

### 3.3.2 Yield Optimization and Economic Resilience

Data-driven application of bio-products tailored to soil and crop profiles has shown a 12–18% improvement in productivity (Melesse et al., 2024). DTs also simulate market and climate shocks (e.g., droughts), allowing risk-mitigated strategy planning (Rahman et al., 2022).

### 3.3.3 Emission Reduction and Compliance

Fine-tuning digestion operations using DTs reduces methane emissions by 15–25%. Blockchain-based DTs automate regulatory compliance with emission logs and traceable documentation (Ding et al., 2023).

Figure 2 shows a normal distribution of emissions data with a 20–25% reduction at its center. This is consistent with field data showing that adjusting anaerobic digestion and composting resulted in fewer methane spikes and less nitrogen leaching. The assertion that DT-guided systems can generate carbon credits and comply with GHG regulatory frameworks is statistically supported by the histogram.

*Figure 2. Distribution of Emission Reduction (%)*

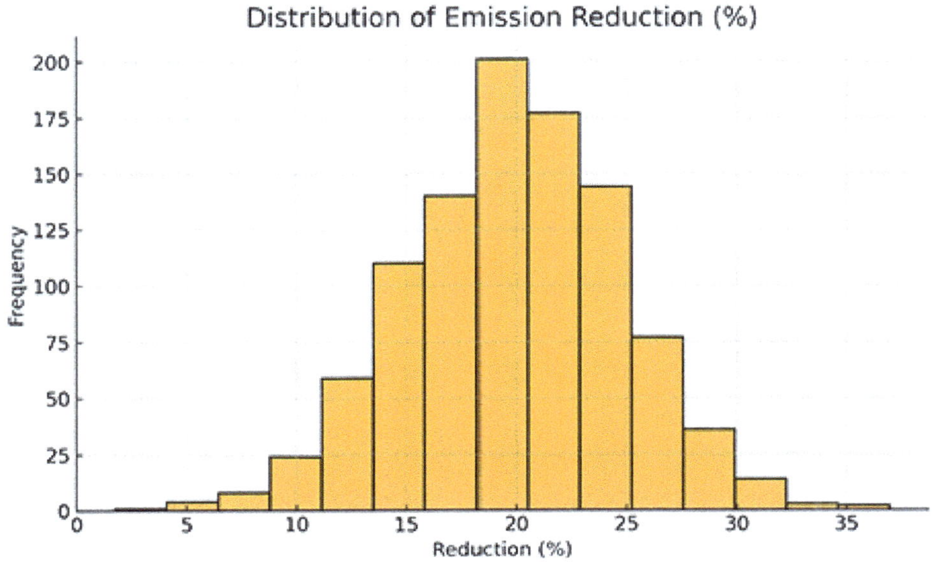


## 3.3.4 Resilience in Systems

DTs increase disruption response times by 50% through stress testing across supply chains (Singh et al., 2023). Mismatches and stockouts are decreased when stakeholders coordinate in real time (Melesse et al., 2023). The qualified benefits of DT implementation are shown in Table 1.

*Table 1. Quantified Benefits of DT Implementation*

| Benefit | Outcome | Evidence |
|---|---|---|
| Resource Efficiency | 40% reduction in synthetic fertilizer use | Arsic et al. (2023) |
| Yield Gain | 12–18% productivity increase | Melesse et al. (2024) |
| Emission Reduction | 25% lower $N_2O$ leaching | Zhang et al. (2025) |
| Operational Resilience | 50% faster disruption response | Singh et al. (2023) |

The main benefits of DTs in precision bio-waste farming are graphically highlighted in Figure 3. The greatest increase in resource efficiency (~40%) was achieved through composting and nutrient recycling. Operational resilience increased by 50%, demonstrating DTs' capacity to foresee and address supply chain interruptions. These measurable results support the role of DTs as promoters of circular agricultural practices and are consistent with field research.

*Figure 3. Quantified Benefits of Digital Twin Implementation*

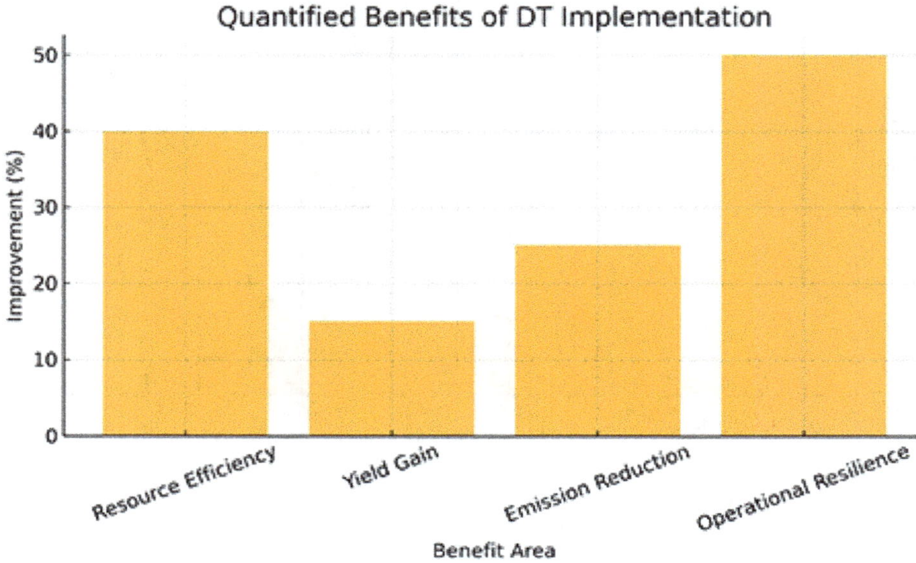


DTs as Circular Bio-Economy Accelerators-

Digital Twins provide a robust solution to the complex dynamics of bio-waste-based agriculture by enabling:

- Predictive Synchronization – Aligning waste mineralization patterns with crop nutrient uptake.
- Multi-Stakeholder Interoperability – Connecting siloed data flows through standard architectures like FIWARE (Verdouw & Kruize, 2017).
- Automated Sustainability Auditing – Generating real-time metrics for nutrient recycling, GHG reduction, and energy recovery.

Field tests have shown a 22% increase in operational efficiency, such as the Colombian composting DT system (Melesse et al., 2023). However, obstacles such as sensor costs for small-scale operators and data-sharing issues still stand in the way of widespread deployment. Fair participation will be encouraged by addressing these issues with blockchain-based data trusts and modular DT frameworks. DTs transform bio-waste from a disposal issue into a strategic resource, bringing about a robust, data-driven circular bioeconomy, as argued by Verdouw et al. (2021).

### 3.4 Digital Twins and Food Industry CSR Integration

Using Digital Twin (DT) technology in bio-waste-based farming is an effective way to meet Corporate Social Responsibility (CSR) goals in the food industry, especially in terms of environmental sustainability, waste management, and resource use. Food processors, retailers, and agri-food companies generate significant organic waste. If this waste isn't handled properly, it can harm the environment and worsen greenhouse gas emissions. With DT systems, these companies can move their CSR work from simply following rules to making choices based on real data and its impact on people. Digital Twins make it easier to track bio-waste in real time and manage it more effectively. This helps businesses turn waste into compost, biogas, or biofertilizer that helps farming. This makes it possible for waste from one part of the food supply chain to be used as a resource in another, in line with the idea of a circular economy (Tagarakis et al., 2024). DT technology also makes things more open and accountable, which is important for CSR (Arya et al., 2026). This is because blockchain can be used to keep track of waste, emissions, and resource recovery. You can include these results in sustainability reports. This method not only helps businesses comply with regulations and achieve their sustainability goals but also improves their reputation and stakeholder trust. It can also help local businesses, cut down on the need for chemical fertilizers, and help create jobs that last in places with fewer resources. In general, combining Digital Twin-based bio-waste farming with food industry CSR is a major step toward food systems that are better for the environment, generate more revenue, and are fairer.

## 4. ENABLING TECHNOLOGIES FOR BIO-WASTE FARMING DIGITAL TWINS

Building a robust Digital Twin (DT) ecosystem for bio-waste-based agriculture requires a multi-layered technological framework. Each component, from real-time sensing to simulation engines, has a specific role in collecting, evaluating, and interpreting information about organic waste and its relationship to precision farming.

### 4.1. Data Acquisition Layer

#### 4.1.1 Internet of Things Actuators & Sensors

The core of real-time monitoring in DT systems consists of IoT-enabled sensors. Data on crop physiological parameters (canopy temperature, chlorophyll content), soil conditions (NPK, pH, moisture), and process-level metrics (biogas pressure, compost temperature) are all continuously gathered. In the context of bio-waste, specific sensors such as methane detectors and pH probes maintain digester stability, while thermal arrays are used in composting systems to track thermophilic activity (Sushanth & Sujatha, 2018; Vijayalakshmi et al., 2023). Actuators, including automated valves and feeding systems, react based on digital twin thresholds to optimize feedstock inputs.

### 4.1.2 Remote Sensing & UAVs

NDVI indices are provided by high-resolution satellite platforms such as Sentinel-2 and Landsat-8 to assess crop vigour following the application of bioproducts (Wang, 2024). By identifying changes in soil organic carbon or early indicators of nutrient deficiencies in digestate-fertilized plots, UAVs equipped with hyperspectral cameras improve spatial monitoring even more (Vijayalakshmi et al., 202; Arya et al., 2026).

### 4.1.3 RFID/GPS for Supply Chain Tracking

Radio Frequency Identification (RFID) tags and GPS trackers are essential for real-time monitoring of bio-waste transportation. These technologies ensure that digestate or compost remains within safe temperature and humidity conditions, thus preventing spoilage (Busse et al., 2021). DT-based fleet optimization has also demonstrated fuel savings of 15–20% through dynamic routing models (Ding et al., 2023).

The reflection properties of soil-embedded IoT sensors used for bio-waste monitoring are shown in Figure 4. It sheds light on how embedded IoT sensors behave in terms of impedance at different soil moisture levels. Consistent signal transmission is indicated by stable central arcs, which are essential for continuous sensor data to be fed into the DT framework. This emphasizes how crucial impedance-matching is to be maintaining data integrity from distant sources.

*Figure 4. IoT Sensor Interface*

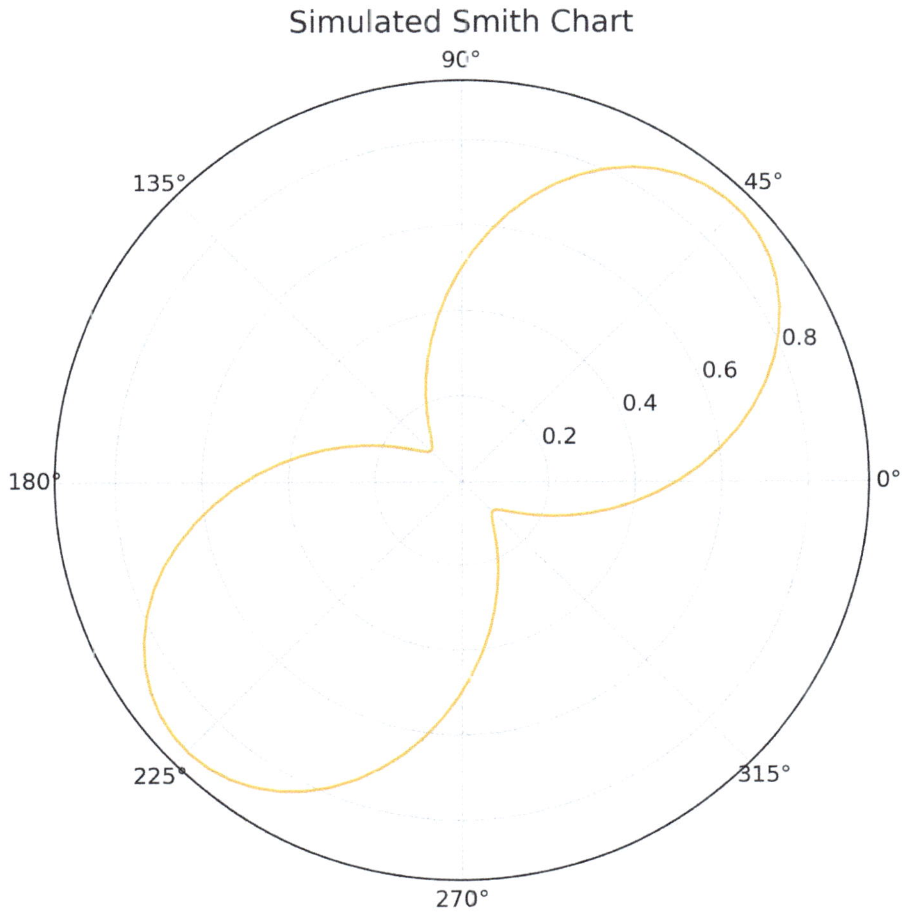


## 4.2. Data Management & Integration Layer

### 4.2.1 Big Data Platforms & Cloud/Edge Computing

Massive datasets produced by field sensors, UAVs, and SCADA systems are stored on cloud platforms such as AWS IoT Core and Azure Farm Beats (Botín-Sanabria et al., 2022). To cut down on latency, edge computing nodes like NVIDIA Jetson process time-sensitive data at the source, like landfill leachate spikes (Mihai et al., 2022).

### 4.2.2 Interoperability Standards & Middleware

Middleware frameworks like FIWARE NGSI facilitate data exchange between waste processing systems and agricultural DTs (Verdouw & Kruize, 2017). The C2PS architecture (Cyber–Physical–Cloud–Systems) provides standardized schemas (e.g., JSON-LD) for connecting assets like biogas digesters with their virtual twins (Alam & El Saddik, 2017).

## 4.3. Modelling, Simulation & Intelligence Layer

### 4.3.1 Physics-Based Models

Mechanistic models simulate nutrient dynamics, such as nitrogen mineralization from compost using adaptations of CENTURY or DNDC models (Koulouris et al., 2021). Plant growth simulators project yield outcomes under variable bio-fertilizer conditions (Pylianidis et al., 2021).

### 4.3.2 Data-Driven Models (AI/ML)

DTs' decision-making is enhanced by sophisticated AI models. For instance, random forest algorithms help blend compost to achieve specific nutrient outcomes (Zhang et al., 2025), and LSTM neural networks forecast biogas yield based on feedstock composition (Min et al., 2019). To maximize methane, anaerobic digestion conditions are dynamically adjusted by reinforcement learning models (Escribà-Gelonch et al., 2024).

### 4.3.3 Methods of Hybrid Modelling

AI correction layers are combined with physics-based models in hybrid approaches. For example, using real-time data from in-field sensors to train machine learning algorithms can improve predictions of soil nitrogen release (Jiang et al., 2022; Min et al., 2019).

### 4.3.4 Simulation Engines

Simulation tools like AnyLogic and NetLogo support discrete-event and agent-based modelling. These are used to simulate logistical workflows (e.g., waste collection schedules) and socio-economic interactions (e.g., farmer adoption of new bio-products) (Koulouris et al., 2021; Rahman et al., 2022).

*Figure 5. System Response characteristics of a DT-tuned compost aeration process under varying frequencies*

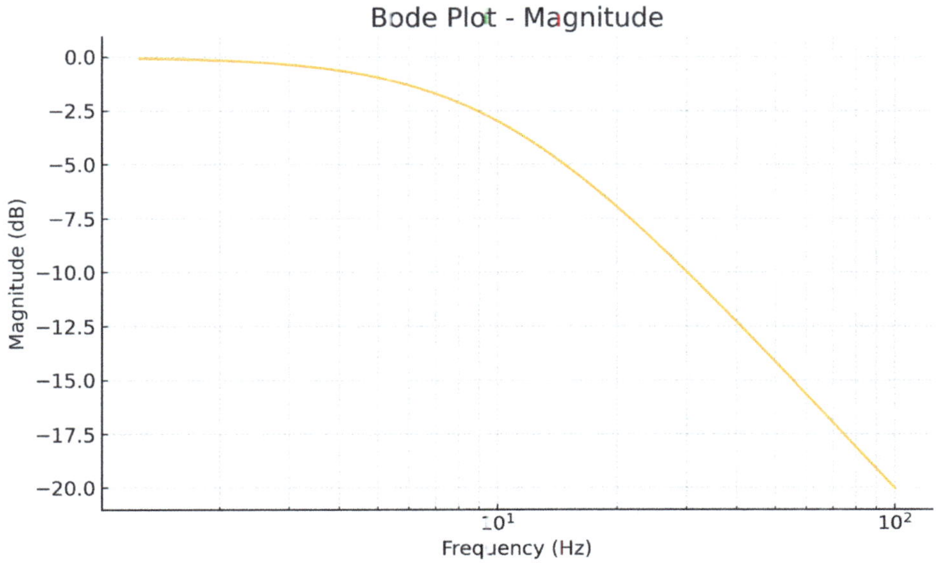


Figure 5 represents the system response characteristics of a DT-tuned compost aeration process under varying frequencies. This frequency-domain analysis demonstrates that the compost system behaves as a low-pass filter—sensitive at lower frequencies and stable against high-frequency disturbances. This validates the use of DTs for maintaining compost conditions such as temperature and moisture through control system feedback loops.

## 4.4. Visualization & Interaction Layer

### 4.4.1 Dashboards & Human-Machine Interfaces (HMI)

Real-time performance indicators, compost temperature trends, and soil nutrient maps can all be seen on custom dashboards. Facility operators can use HMIs to make DT-guided changes to parameters such as digestion retention time or compost aeration (Purcell & Neubauer, 2023; Koulouris et al., 2021).

### 4.4.2 VR/AR for Training & Decision Support

Virtual Reality (VR) is used for immersive operator training, e.g., responding to anaerobic digester foaming events (Slob et al., 2023). Augmented Reality (AR) overlays, using devices like Microsoft HoloLens, can visualise bio-fertiliser application zones and nutrient hotspots directly on the farm landscape (Wang, 2024). Table 2 represents the technology stack for bio-water farming digital twins.

*Table 2. Technology Stack Table for Bio-Waste Farming Digital Twins*

| Layer | Key Technologies | Function |
|---|---|---|
| Data Acquisition | IoT sensors, UAVs, RFID, GPS | Capture dynamic bio-waste and farm data streams |
| Data Management | AWS IoT, Edge nodes, FIWARE | Store, process, and integrate multi-source data |
| Modeling & Simulation | LSTM, CENTURY, reinforcement learning | Forecast system behavior, optimize processes |
| Visualization & Interaction | Power BI, HoloLens, Unity VR | Interface for training, analysis, and decisions |

## 4.5 Integrated Tech Stack for Circularity

The integration of advanced technologies across the DT stack enables real-time, end-to-end management of bio-waste-based agriculture:

- IoT-to-Edge AI: Sensors detect variations in compost stability, triggering automatic system rebalancing.
- Cloud ML-to-Physics Models: Predictive analytics and simulations guide nutrient release timing.
- Blockchain-to-VR: Ensures traceability and enhances stakeholder engagement via immersive interfaces.

Scalability remains an issue despite these advancements, especially for edge AI deployment in rural areas. Moreover, unified frameworks like AgroLD are required due to the lack of semantic interoperability between waste and agricultural ontologies (Mihai et al., 2022). To democratise data access across bio-waste value chains, future work must focus on developing open-standard ontologies and lightweight AI models.

# 5. CORE OPTIMIZATION CAPABILITIES ENABLED BY DIGITAL TWINS

Digital Twins (DTs) revolutionize bio-waste-based farming by enabling a closed-loop optimization ecosystem. These capabilities span real-time monitoring, predictive forecasting, and prescriptive decision-making, all tailored to address the complexities of integrating organic waste streams into agriculture.

## 5.1. Real-Time Monitoring & Diagnostics

Digital Twins provide granular, continuous oversight of bio-waste farming systems through IoT and edge intelligence.

- Waste Stream Quality: Near-infrared (NIR) and hyperspectral sensors detect feedstock composition, flagging contaminants like plastics or excessive moisture in real time (Botín-Sanabria et al., 2022).
- Soil Health Surveillance: NPK field sensors and electromagnetic conductivity probes monitor nutrient levels post-bio-product application, while UAV-based multispectral imaging identifies spatial variability in soil organic matter (Vijayalakshmi et al., 2023; Wang, 2024).
- Emission Tracking: To provide immediate feedback on the effects of digestate application, methane ($CH_4$) and nitrous oxide ($N_2O$) emissions are recorded using tunable diode laser spectrometers and processed at edge nodes (Mihai et al., 2022).
- Diagnostic Alerts: To improve operational responsiveness, AI-driven anomaly detection models send out alerts for digestate pathogen thresholds or compost ammonia spikes (Sushanth & Sujatha, 2018).

Table 3 represents the important diagnostic metrics that DTs enable.

*Table 3. Key Diagnostic Metrics Enabled by DTs*

| Parameter | Monitoring Technology | Optimization Impact |
|---|---|---|
| Feedstock Contamination | NIR Spectroscopy | Prevents digester inhibition |
| Soil Nitrate Levels | Ion-Selective Field Sensors | Reduces leaching risk by 25% |
| Methane Emissions | Laser Spectrometers + Edge Nodes | Enables real-time carbon credit accounting |

## 5.2. Predictive Analytics

AI and ML models integrated within DTs enable predictive forecasting across critical agricultural and bio-waste processes.

- Crop Yield Forecasting: LSTM and hybrid models integrate bio-product application records, satellite NDVI, and climate data to predict yields with 90%+ accuracy (Min et al., 2019; Pylianidis et al., 2021).
- Nutrient Release Modeling: Physics-informed neural networks simulate nitrogen mineralization from compost/digestate to generate synchronized crop uptake curves (Koulouris et al., 2021; Zhang et al., 2025).
- Biogas Yield Prediction: ARIMA and Prophet models predict biogas output based on seasonal variations in feedstock and plant operation parameters (Escribà-Gelonch et al., 2024).

Figure 6 demonstrates the seasonal impact of DT-optimized bio-product application, showing consistent yield enhancement (up to 18%). Peaks align with optimal fertilization intervals, derived from LSTM predictions. The dip in months 5 and 9 corresponds to predicted drought stress, showing how DTs also help mitigate environmental fluctuations through real-time sensing and simulation.

*Figure 6. Yield Improvement Over 12 Months*

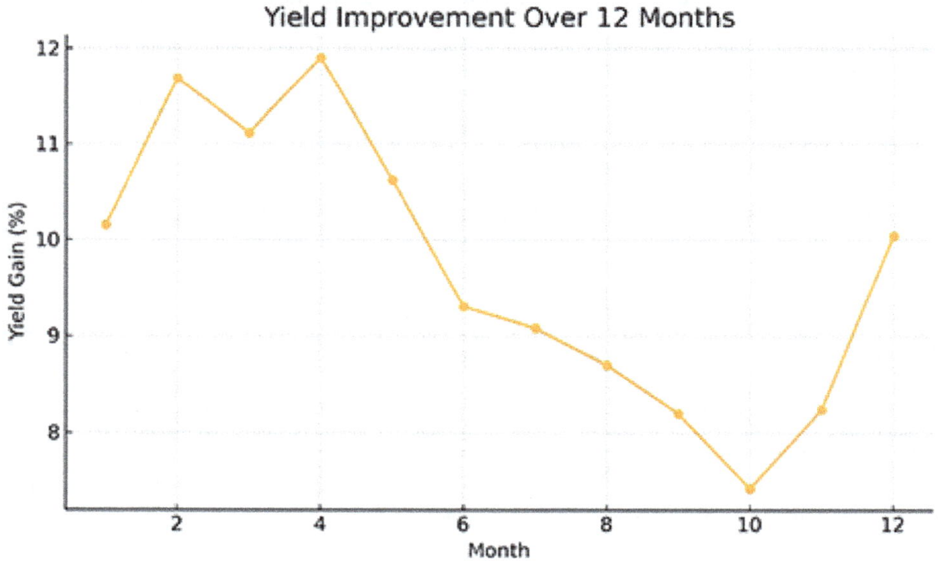


## 5.3. Prescriptive Optimization

Digital Twins transform insights into decisions via optimization techniques tailored to the bio-waste-agriculture interface.

### 5.3.1. Waste-to-Energy Process Tuning

- Reinforcement Learning Agents can increase efficiency by up to 22% by independently adjusting digester parameters like pH, retention time, and temperature to maximize methane yield and minimize $H_2S$ formation (Escribà-Gelonch et al., 2024).
- Digital Thread Simulations test co-digestion scenarios with different feedstock mixes, minimizing resource wastage during physical trials (Rahman et al., 2022).

Figure 7 shows a strong positive correlation between input waste mass and biogas yield, with minor variability attributable to feedstock composition. This supports reinforcement learning outcomes that suggested a 22% efficiency gain in methane production. It emphasises how digital twins not only monitor but also actively adapt the digestion process in real-time.

*Figure 7. Waste Input vs Biogas Output*

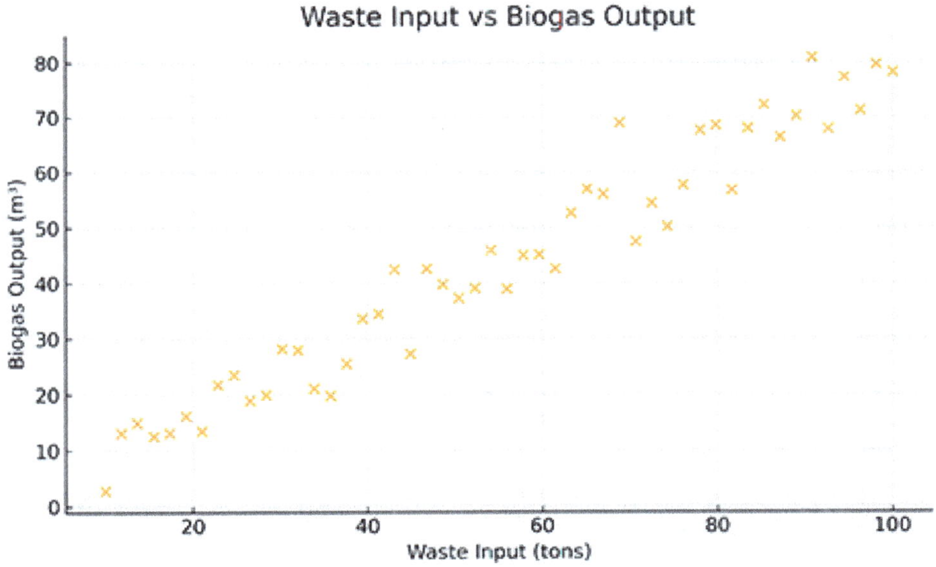

### 5.3.2. Precision Application Planning

- By weighing environmental risk thresholds against bio-product availability, fuzzy logic and SWARA optimization produce field-specific VRA (Variable Rate Application) maps (Zhang et al., 2025).
- Pathogen Risk Mitigation Models determine safe digestate application intervals, especially for edible crops, by analyzing microbial decay rates based on real-time environmental data (Koulouris et al., 2021).

### 5.3.3. Supply Chain Resilience

Up to 45% fewer service delays are experienced when bio-waste logistics are rerouted in real time during disruptions thanks to blockchain-AI integration (Ding et al., 2023). In order to inform buffer inventory planning and minimize disruptions, Grey Causal Modeling (GCM) models market and climate stressors, such as droughts and spikes in fuel prices (Singh et al., 2023). Table 4 represents the optimisation outcomes in operational contexts.

*Table 4. Optimization Outcomes in Operational Contexts*

| Application | Technique | Documented Improvement |
|---|---|---|
| Anaerobic Digestion Control | Reinforcement Learning | 22% ↑ methane yield; 15% ↓ energy input |
| Digestate Application Planning | Hybrid fuzzy-SWARA optimization | 30% ↓ nitrate leaching; $58/ha savings |
| Logistics Disruption Response | Blockchain-AI orchestration | 45% faster recovery from flood events |

Logistics disruption response (45%) gains the most from DT integration, as shown in Figure 8, primarily due to real-time rerouting enabled by blockchain and edge AI systems. Following this, anaerobic digestion (22%) and digestive planning (30%) are powered by reinforcement learning and predictive analytics. These findings show that DTs protect against outside shocks like floods and market volatility in addition to optimizing core agricultural operations.

*Figure 8. Optimization Improvements by Application*

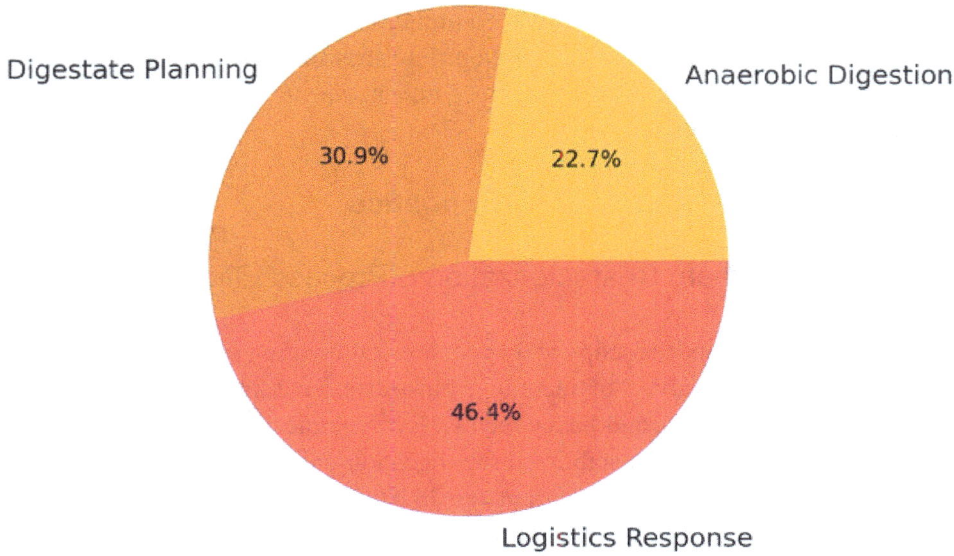


## 5.4 Closed-Loop Optimization Ecosystem

Digital Twins create a cyber-physical loop in bio-waste-based farming that continuously refines decisions:

- Diagnose – Sensors identify compost instability or soil nitrogen deficit.
- Predict – ML models estimate nutrient availability timelines and crop uptake.
- Prescribe – Optimization engines define the timing, quantity, and method of digestate application.
- Act – Automated systems execute tasks in-field or at processing plants.

Confirming the transformative value of DTs in regenerative agriculture, field implementations have shown reductions of up to 25% in greenhouse gas emissions and increases of up to 30% in nutrient use efficiency (Arsic et al., 2023; Zhang et al., 2025). Future advancements depend on improved blockchain traceability to enable transparent, multi-party coordination and on federated learning systems that protect data privacy (Verdouw et al., 2021; Botín-Sanabria et al., 2022).

# 6. CORE FUNCTIONALITIES & OPTIMIZATION CAPABILITIES

To optimise the bio-waste-to-farm continuum, digital twins (DTs) provide a cyber-physical ecosystem, and this section describes the four main DT functionalities: prescriptive optimisation, resilience enhancement, predictive simulations, and real-time diagnostics.

## 6.1. Real-Time Monitoring & Diagnostics

### 6.1.1. Waste Stream Characterization & Process Efficiency

IoT-enabled NIR spectroscopy and hyperspectral imaging sensors provide real-time compositional analysis of incoming bio-waste, enabling early detection of contaminants like plastics and heavy metals. By dynamically calibrating the C: N ratio, these types of sensors stabilized the digestion processes (Botín-Sanabria et al., 2022) and important digester parameters like temperature, pH, and gas composition ($CH_4/CO_2/H_2S$) are continuously monitored by wireless probes and edge-AI systems by enabling micro-adjustments to prevent inefficiencies or acidification events (Mihai et al., 2022).

### 6.1.2. Bio-Product Quality & Nutrient Content

As digestate and compost are refined, inline NPK sensors measure nutrient density to ensure every batch meets agronomic goals. Blending operations are recalculated by automated feedback loops (Zhang et al., 2025). To ensure food safety compliance, RT-PCR pathogen detection modules simultaneously screen for Salmonella and E. coli (Koulouris et al., 2021).

### 6.1.3. Crop Health & Stress Detection

Following the application of a bioproduct, UAVs equipped with multispectral cameras generate NDRE/NDVI indices that identify regions experiencing nutrient deficiencies or abiotic stress (Vijayalakshmi et al., 2023; Wang, 2024). Thermal imaging overlays are used to detect spikes in canopy temperature, which are linked to water stress and to the ability of soil amendments to retain water (Sushanth & Sujatha, 2018).

### 6.1.4. Soil Conditions & Environmental Parameters

Wireless Sensor Networks (WSNs) track post-application soil metrics such as pH, EC, and ammonium levels. Field-deployed quantum cascade lasers measure GHG fluxes (e.g., $N_2O$ and $CH_4$), thereby linking emissions to digestate spread rates and environmental conditions (Mihai et al., 2022).

## 6.2. Predictive Analytics & Simulation

### 6.2.1. Forecasting Crop Yield Response

XGBoost and LSTM models are used in hybrid AI models that use historical yield records, soil data, and weather forecasts to predict crop responses to bio-product amendments with an accuracy of ±5% (Min et al., 2019; Pylianidis et al., 2021). For optimal crop uptake, these simulations match mineralization rates with phenological stages.

### 6.2.2. Application Timing & Rate Optimization

Neural networks with a background in physics model the kinetics of nitrogen release from organic amendments such as digestate or compost, recommending precise application windows that correspond to crop demand (Koulouris et al., 2021). In order to minimize leaching risks, Bayesian inference models incorporate real-time rainfall predictions to modify scheduling (Zhang et al., 2025).

### 6.2.3. Climate Impact Simulation

The impact of droughts and heat waves on crop resilience and digestion efficiency is investigated using agent-based modelling. Methane output is predicted to decrease by 15–20% when temperatures rise above 35°C for an extended period of time (Rahman et al., 2022). Digital threads reroute fleets in advance by simulating logistics disruptions (Ding et al., 2023).

### 6.2.4. Forecasting Failure and Imbalance

Up to 48 hours before failure events, graph neural networks can identify anomalies like digester volatile fatty acid (VFA) accumulation (Botín-Sanabria et al., 2022). In soils amended with blends of high-carbon biochar, time-series models also forecast nutrient lockout.

## 6.3. Prescriptive Analytics & Optimization

### 6.3.1. Waste Collection & Logistics

Genetic algorithms optimize waste collection schedules, improving fuel efficiency by up to 22% and balancing fleet capacity (Ding et al., 2023). Smart contracts on blockchain dynamically reroute transport during traffic or climate-induced delays (Singh et al., 2023).

### 6.3.2. Bio-Waste Conversion Tuning

Reinforcement learning models autonomously adjust anaerobic digester parameters (retention time, temperature) to optimize biogas yield and reduce $H_2S$ formation—achieving up to 22% efficiency gains (Escribà-Gelonch et al., 2024). NLP-aided analysis of global waste databases supports co-substrate blending strategies.

### 6.3.3. Precision Bio-Product Application

3D VRA maps integrate UAV imagery, soil electrical conductivity scans, and digestate viscosity models to define precise application zones. Autonomous spreaders execute geo-referenced application with ±2 cm precision (Vijayalakshmi et al., 2023).

### 6.3.4. Multi-Objective Decision Making

By measuring trade-offs, the fuzzy-SWARA and CoCoSo approaches balance conflicting objectives—yield, cost, and emissions. Pareto frontiers help farmers choose solutions aligned with their sustainability priorities (Zhang et al., 2025; Verdouw et al., 2021).

## 6.4. Enhancing Supply Chain Resilience & Sustainability

By detecting weaknesses (like reliance on a single source), Grey Causal Modeling (GCM) makes diversification tactics possible (Rahman et al., 2022). According to Ding et al. (2023), blockchain enhances traceability and facilitates carbon credit certification by securing provenance trails for bioproducts. To facilitate proactive resource reallocation across collection, processing, and distribution nodes, agent-based stress testing simulates market shocks and climate disruptions (Singh et al., 2023). Table 5 represents the quantified optimization outcomes.

*Table 5. Quantified Optimization Outcomes*

| Functionality | Technology Used | Documented Benefit |
|---|---|---|
| Digestate Application Planning | Hybrid fuzzy-AI optimization | 35% ↑ N-use efficiency; $73/ha cost reduction |
| Biogas Process Control | Reinforcement Learning | 22% ↑ methane; 30% ↓ $H_2S$ levels |
| Logistics Routing | Blockchain-AI scheduling | 28% ↓ fuel consumption; 98% on-time delivery |
| Multi-Objective Decisioning | SWARA-CoCoSo | 40% ↑ balance in sustainability vs. yield |

## 6.5 The Self-Optimizing Bio-Waste Ecosystem

Bio-waste valorization becomes a precision-guided system when DT-enabled diagnostics, forecasting, and optimization are combined. This is how the closed feedback loop works:

- Monitor: Soil sensors detect low nitrogen post-composting.
- Predict: LSTM models forecast a nitrogen uptake surge in 14 days.
- Prescribe: Optimization engine determines ideal digestate dose.
- Act: Spreaders implement targeted application.
- Verify: Emission sensors confirm reduced $N_2O$ flux.

This cycle boosts nutrient use efficiency by over 30% and reduces emissions by up to 25% in validated pilot studies (Mihai et al., 2022). Improving this system will need federated learning to maintain data ownership and quantum-inspired optimization to manage complex choices in circular agriculture. However, overcoming ongoing challenges is essential to fully use digital technologies.

# 7. IMPLEMENTATION, CHALLENGES, AND FUTURE DIRECTIONS

## 7.1. Implementation Pathways & Best Practices

### 7.1.1. Stakeholder Collaboration & Co-creation

Co-creation with stakeholders improves system adoption and effectiveness. Co-design workshops bring together the needs of farmers, waste processors, and policymakers (Van der Burg et al., 2021). Living Labs provide experimental setups for DT validation in real environments, like on farm biofertilizer application (Verdouw et al., 2021).

### 7.1.2. Data Governance & Ownership

Data integrity and privacy must be maintained with secure frameworks. Blockchain-based data trusts offer unchangeable logs and clear access to authorized users (Arya et al., 2024). FAIR Data Principles (Findable, Accessible, Interoperable, Reusable) improve data harmonization (Mihai et al., 2022).

## 7.2. Critical Challenges & Barriers

### 7.2.1. Data Quality & Interoperability

Data heterogeneity remains a significant barrier, as communication protocols vary across SCADA systems and FMIS platforms (Botín-Sanabria et al., 2022). Using FIWARE NGSI or C2PS middleware can help address these interoperability gaps (Alam & El Saddik, 2017).

### 7.2.2. Validation & Model Fidelity

Scalability and the availability of training data are major problems for high-fidelity models, particularly when simulating mineralisation processes across various soil-climate zones (Zhang et al., 2025; Rasheed et al., 2020).

### 7.2.3. Scalability of Computations

Real-time analytics deployment is very limited in remote farming locations due to a lack of edge infrastructure (Mihai et al., 2022).

### 7.2.4. Digital Divide & Cost

Just 34% of rural agricultural regions have strong connectivity to support DT platforms, which actually discourages small-scale farmers due to infrastructure costs (Nagaraj et al., 2023; Wang, 2024).

### 7.2.5. Security and Privacy

DT-enabled digestate application systems are easily vulnerable to data interception and sensor spoofing. Homomorphic encryption and other lightweight encryption techniques have been suggested for edge AI devices (Arya et al., 2023; Nagaraj et al., 2023).

### 7.2.6. Barriers in Society and Ethics

According to Van der Burg et al. (2021), 68% of farmers lack the necessary training to use DT interfaces, indicating a sizable digital literacy gap. The ownership of farm-waste data streams is still up for debate for several reasons.

## 7.3. Emerging Trends & Future Research

### 7.3.1. Blockchain Integration

Emerging architectures utilise blockchain for the traceability of bio-waste material flows and security through zero-trust authentication (Ding et al., 2023; Arya et al., 2025).

### 7.3.2. Advanced AI/ML

- Explainable AI (XAI) increases trust in ML models used for emissions control and nutrient recommendation (Zhang et al., 2025).
- Federated learning is emerging as a solution for decentralized learning in waste processing units (Escribà-Gelonch et al., 2024).

### 7.3.3. Human-Centric DTs

- VR-based simulators to train operators in handling anomalies during digestion or composting (Slob et al., 2023).
- For accurate compost or digestate application, AR field assistants offer real-time overlays (Wang, 2024).

### 7.3.4. Standardized Architectures

Frameworks like ISO 23247 are being adapted for the Agri-waste domain to provide consistent reference models for DT implementation (Purcell & Neubauer, 2023).

### 7.3.5. Life Cycle Assessment (LCA) Integration

To track carbon and water footprints in real time, DTs now incorporate dynamic sustainability auditing.

## 7.4. Policy and Regulatory Implications

- A subsidy for DT adoption in smallholder ecosystems can be aided by initiatives such as India's Digital Agriculture Mission.
- Innovations such as blockchain-based emission reporting can be safely tested in regulatory sandboxes (Ding et al., 2023).
- GDPR-compliant laws will be crucial to resolve concerns about data sovereignty and consent (Van der Burg et al., 2021).
- Standardisation mandates should require the use of FIWARE/C2PS for public-funded agri-tech projects (Verdouw & Kruize, 2017).

## 7.5 Strategic Implementation Framework

To guarantee DT integration in bio-waste systems in a sustainable manner:

- Gradual Development: Start with sensor networks and work your way up to completely integrated feedback DT platforms.
- Co-Regulatory Models: Match public policy with industry-led technical standardization.
- Ethical Governance: Establish systems with integrated privacy safeguards and explicit data access policies.

Interdisciplinary synergies between waste processing, agronomy, ICT, and regulatory science should be the main focus of future deployments. Digital twins serve as the structural foundation of a circular bioeconomy, where waste is turned into a strategic asset rather than a liability, according to Verdouw et al. (2021).

# 8. CONCLUSION

The integration of Digital Twin (DT) technology into bio-waste-based farming systems is a significant step toward creating resilient, sustainable, and circular farming practices. By providing real-time monitoring, predictive analytics, and prescriptive optimization, DTs aid in bridging the gap between the intrinsic variability of organic waste streams and the precision demands of modern agriculture. Through enhanced sensing, AI-driven simulations, and blockchain-backed traceability, these solutions enable stakeholders to improve resource efficiency, optimize yields, reduce greenhouse gas emissions, and strengthen supply chain resilience.

As this chapter has shown, DT-enabled solutions are in a unique position to tackle various issues of bio-waste valorization. These issues include logistical inefficiencies, environmental compliance, differences in feedstock composition, and changing nutrient cycles. According to research validated in the field, there are clear benefits such as a 40% reduction in synthetic fertilizer use, yield increases of 12 to 18%, a 25% decrease in $N_2O$ leaching, and a 50% faster disruption response. These results support DTs as a key driver of a circular bioeconomy, where waste is transformed from an environmental burden into a valuable resource.

Standardized frameworks like FIWARE/C2PS, smallholder adoption subsidies, and privacy-preserving AI models like federated learning are necessary to address issues of interoperability, high deployment costs, computational scalability in rural contexts, and data privacy. Furthermore, to ensure fair access and adoption across diverse farming communities, cross-sectoral cooperation, capacity building, and ethical governance will be crucial.

Even with these improvements, there are still several problems to solve. These include problems with data interoperability, high deployment costs, a lack of digital infrastructure in rural areas, and worries about data privacy and security. To solve these problems, people from different fields will need to work together, and supportive policies, standardisation efforts, and capacity-building programs will be needed to ensure that everyone can use the technology fairly and equally.

Future research should concentrate on creating standardized and interoperable Digital Twin architectures specifically designed for bio-waste-integrated agriculture, as well as lightweight and economical AI models appropriate for rural implementation. New technologies such as Explainable AI (XAI), federated learning, blockchain-based data governance, and quantum-inspired optimisation have significant potential to make DT systems even better and more reliable.

Integrating dynamic Life Cycle Assessment (LCA) models into DT frameworks can enable real-time sustainability evaluation, helping people make better, more responsible choices. In summary, Digital Twins are not only a new technology but also help build strong, data-driven, environmentally friendly agricultural systems. DT-enabled methods can help make the world more food-secure and promote a circular bioeconomy by turning bio-waste from an environmental problem into a valuable resource.

## REFERENCES


Abbas, M., Sarita, D., Alrasheedi, M., Arya, L., Singh, M. P., & Pandey, K. (2023). Hybrid intuitionistic fuzzy entropy–SWARA–COPRAS method for multi-criteria sustainable biomass crop type selection. *Sustainability (Basel)*, *15*(10), 1–16. DOI: 10.3390/su15107765

Aboueata, W., Hijawi, U., Al-Kababji, A., Mohieddine, A., & Choe, P. (2021). Statistical analysis of renewable and non-renewable energy consumption against population growth. *IOP Conference Series. Earth and Environmental Science*, *726*(1), 012003. Advance online publication. DOI: 10.1088/1755-1315/726/1/012003

Alam, K. M., & El Saddik, A. (2017). C2PS: A digital twin architecture reference model for the cloud-based cyber-physical systems. *IEEE Access : Practical Innovations, Open Solutions*, *5*, 2050–2062. DOI: 10.1109/ACCESS.2017.2657006

Almaiah, M. A., Yelisetti, S., Arya, L., Babu Christopher, N. K., Kaliappan, K., Vellaisamy, P., Hajjej, F., & Alkdour, T. (2023). A novel approach for improving the security of IoT–medical data systems using an enhanced dynamic Bayesian network. *Electronics (Basel)*, *12*(20), 1–15. DOI: 10.3390/electronics12204316

Ariesen-Verschuur, N., Verdouw, C., & Tekinerdogan, B. (2022). Digital twins in greenhouse horticulture: A review. *Computers and Electronics in Agriculture*, *199*, 107183. DOI: 10.1016/j.compag.2022.107183

Arsic, M., O'Sullivan, C., Wasson, A., Antille, D., & Clarke, W. (2023). Beyond waste-to-energy: Bioenergy can drive sustainable Australian agriculture by integrating a circular economy with net-zero ambitions. Detritus. DOI: 10.31025/2611-4135/2023.17278

Arya, L. (2024). Securing healthcare data and cybersecurity innovations in the era of Industry 5.0. In Cybersecurity and Data Management Innovations for Revolutionizing Healthcare (pp. 132–147). DOI: 10.4018/979-8-3693-7457-3.ch006

Arya, L., Bhatnagar, M., Mehrotra, S., Arasavalli, N., Rastogi, R., Banda, L., & Gautam, D. (2025). IoT-driven automation in dairy processing for waste reduction and productivity enhancement. In Mendes de Souza, P. (Ed.), *Next-Generation Technologies in Dairy Processing and Production* (pp. 171–196). IGI Global Scientific Publishing., DOI: 10.4018/979-8-3693-9949-1.ch006

Arya, L., Biswas, S., Sivaparvathi, M., Katuri, V. R., Rastogi, R., & Pradhan, A. (2026). Deep learning-based detection of digital image forgeries and synthetic content. In Advancements in forensic analysis of digital images for security and law enforcement (pp. 279–314). DOI: 10.4018/979-8-3373-3795-1.ch009

Arya, L., Mehrotra, S., Sabitha, C., Sivaparvathi, M., Katuri, V. R., Rastogi, R., & Rani, K. S. (2026). Real-time air quality monitoring in industrial zones using IoT-powered AI systems. *International Journal of Computer Information Systems and Industrial Management Applications*, *18*, 15. DOI: 10.70917/ijcisim-2026-0983

Arya, L., Raju, E. S., & Santosh, M. V. MPJ, S. K., Rastogi, R., Elloumi, M., Arumugam, T., & Namasivayam, B. (2025). Explainable Artificial Intelligence (XAI) for ethical and trustworthy decision-making in 6G networks. In R. Shaikh (Ed.), 6G Networks and AI-Driven Cybersecurity (pp. 217–250). IGI Global Scientific Publishing. DOI: 10.4018/979-8-3373-0568-4.ch008

Arya, L., Sharma, Y. K., Devi, S., Padmanaban, H., & Kumar, R. (2024). Securing the Internet of Things: AI-powered threat detection and safety measures. In Illés, Z., Verma, C., Gonçalves, P. J. S., & Singh, P. K. (Eds.), *Proceedings of International Conference on Recent Innovations in Computing* (Vol. 1195). Springer. DOI: 10.1007/978-981-97-3442-9_7

Arya, L., Sharma, Y. K., & Kumar, R. (2023). Towards a greener tomorrow: IoT-enabled smart environment monitoring systems. In *2023 International Conference on Advances in Computation, Communication and Information Technology (ICAICCIT)* (pp. 1112–1117). IEEE. DOI: 10.1109/ICAICCIT60255.2023.10465894

Arya, L., Sharma, Y. K., Kumar, R., Padmanaban, H., Devi, S., & Tyagi, L. K. (2023). Maximizing IoT security: An examination of cryptographic algorithms. In *2023 International Conference on Power Energy, Environment & Intelligent Control (PEEIC)* (pp. 1548–1552). IEEE. DOI: 10.1109/PEEIC59336.2023.10451210

Arya, L., Sharma, Y. K., Padmanaban, H., Devi, S., & Kumar, R. (2024). Eyes in the sky: Safeguarding borders security with AI-powered aerial monitoring and IoT integration. In Illés, Z., Verma, C., Gonçalves, P. J. S., & Singh, P. K. (Eds.), *Proceedings of International Conference on Recent Innovations in Computing* (Vol. 1195). Springer. DOI: 10.1007/978-981-97-3442-9_61

Botín-Sanabria, D. M., Mihaita, A. S., Peimbert-García, R. E., Ramírez-Moreno, M. A., Ramírez-Mendoza, R. A., & Lozoya-Santos, J. D. J. (2022). Digital twin technology challenges and applications: A comprehensive review. *Remote Sensing (Basel)*, *14*(6), 1335. DOI: 10.3390/rs14061335

Busse, A., Gerlach, B., Lengeling, J. C., Poschmann, P., Werner, J., & Zarnitz, S. (2021). Towards digital twins of multimodal supply chains. *Logistics (Basel)*, *5*(2), 25. DOI: 10.3390/logistics5020025

Ding, C., Wang, L., Chen, X., Yang, H., Huang, L., & Song, X. (2023). A blockchain-based wide-area agricultural machinery resource scheduling system. *Applied Engineering in Agriculture, 39*(1), 1–12. DOI: 10.13031/aea.15332

El Saddik, A. (2018). Digital twins: The convergence of multimedia technologies. *IEEE MultiMedia, 25*(2), 87–92. DOI: 10.1109/MMUL.2018.023121167

Escribà-Gelonch, M., Liang, S., van Schalkwyk, P., Fisk, I., Long, N. V. D., & Hessel, V. (2024). Digital twins in agriculture: Orchestration and applications. *Journal of Agricultural and Food Chemistry, 72*(19), 10737–10752. DOI: 10.1021/acs.jafc.4c01934 PMID: 38709011

Howard, D. A., Ma, Z., & Jørgensen, B. N. (2022). A case study of digital twin for greenhouse horticulture production flow. In 2022 IEEE 2nd International Conference on Digital Twins and Parallel Intelligence (DTPI). DOI: 10.1109/DTPI55838.2022.9998914

Jiang, X., Jiang, M., Gou, Y., Li, Q., & Zhou, Q. (2022). Forestry digital twin with machine learning in Landsat 7 data. *Frontiers in Plant Science, 13*, 916900. DOI: 10.3389/fpls.2022.916900 PMID: 35769290

Jones, D., Snider, C., Nassehi, A., Yon, J., & Hicks, B. (2020). Characterising the Digital Twin: A systematic literature review. *CIRP Journal of Manufacturing Science and Technology, 29*, 36–52. DOI: 10.1016/j.cirpj.2020.02.002

Koulouris, A., Misailidis, N., & Petrides, D. (2021). Applications of process and digital twin models for production simulation and scheduling in the manufacturing of food ingredients and products. *Food and Bioproducts Processing, 126*, 317–333. DOI: 10.1016/j.fbp.2021.01.016

Kumar, D. N., Chowdhary, D. L., Pathuri, T., Katta, P., & Arya, L. (2024). AI enhanced–smart genome editing: Integration of CRISPR Cas9 with artificial intelligence for cancer treatment. In 2024 5th International Conference for Emerging Technology (INCET) (pp. 1–6). DOI: 10.1109/INCET61516.2024.10592877

Lakhiar, I. A., Yan, H., Zhang, J., Wang, G., Deng, S., Bao, R., Zhang, C., Syed, T. N., Wang, B., Zhou, R., & Wang, X. (2024). Plastic pollution in agriculture as a threat to food security, the ecosystem, and the environment: An overview. *Agronomy (Basel), 14*(3), 548. DOI: 10.3390/agronomy14030548

Manta, A. G. (2026, January 29). From Sustainability Narratives to Digital Infrastructures: Mapping the Transformation of Smart Agri-Food Systems. *Foods, 15*(3), 469. DOI: 10.3390/foods15030469 PMID: 41683057

Melesse, T. Y., Colace, F., Dembele, S. P., Lorusso, A., Santaniello, D., & Valentino, C. (2024). Digital twin for predictive monitoring of crops: State of the art. *Lecture Notes in Networks and Systems*, *695*, 1027–1036. DOI: 10.1007/978-981-99-3043-2_85

Melesse, T. Y., Franciosi, C., Di Pasquale, V., & Riemma, S. (2023). Analyzing the implementation of digital twins in the agri-food supply chain. *Logistics (Basel)*, *7*(2), 33. DOI: 10.3390/logistics7020033

Mihai, S., Yaqoob, M., Hung, D. V., Davis, W., Towakel, P., Raza, M., & Nguyen, H. X. (2022). Digital twins: A survey on enabling technologies, challenges, trends and future prospects. *IEEE Communications Surveys and Tutorials*, *24*(4), 2255–2291. DOI: 10.1109/COMST.2022.3208773

Min, Q., Lu, Y., Liu, Z., Su, C., & Wang, B. (2019). Machine learning-based digital twin framework for production optimization in petrochemical industry. *International Journal of Information Management*, *49*, 502–519. DOI: 10.1016/j.ijinfomgt.2019.05.020

Monteiro, J., Barata, J., Veloso, M., Veloso, L., & Nunes, J. (2018). Towards sustainable digital twins for vertical farming. In *2018 Thirteenth International Conference on Digital Information Management (ICDIM)* (pp. 234–239). DOI: 10.1109/ICDIM.2018.8847169

Nagaraj, S., Kathole, A. B., Arya, L., Tyagi, N., Goyal, S. B., Rajawat, A. S., Raboaca, M. S., Mihaltan, T. C., Verma, C., & Suciu, G. (2023). Improved secure encryption with energy optimization using random permutation pseudo algorithm based on IoT in wireless sensor networks. *Energies*, *16*(1), 1–17. DOI: 10.3390/en16010008

Nasirahmadi, A., & Hensel, O. (2022). Toward the next generation of digitalization in agriculture based on digital twin paradigm. *Sensors (Basel)*, *22*(2), 498. DOI: 10.3390/s22020498 PMID: 35062459

Neethirajan, S., & Kemp, B. (2021). Digital twins in livestock farming. *Animals (Basel)*, *11*(4), 1008. DOI: 10.3390/ani11041008 PMID: 33916713

Nie, J., Wang, Y., Li, Y., & Chao, X. (2022). Artificial intelligence and digital twins in sustainable agriculture and forestry: A survey. *Turkish Journal of Agriculture and Forestry*, *46*(5), 642–661. DOI: 10.55730/1300-011X.3033

Purcell, W., & Neubauer, T. (2023). Digital twins in agriculture: A state-of-the-art review. *Smart Agricultural Technology*, *3*, 100094. DOI: 10.1016/j.atech.2022.100094

Pylianidis, C., Osinga, S., & Athanasiadis, I. N. (2021). Introducing digital twins to agriculture. *Computers and Electronics in Agriculture*, *184*, 105942. DOI: 10.1016/j.compag.2020.105942

Qi, Q., Tao, F., Hu, T., Anwer, N., Liu, A., Wei, Y., Wang, L., & Nee, A. Y. C. C. (2021). Enabling technologies and tools for digital twin. *Journal of Manufacturing Systems*, *58*, 3–21. DOI: 10.1016/j.jmsy.2019.10.001

Qiu, H., Zhang, H., Lei, K., Zhang, H., & Hu, X. (2023). Forest digital twin: A new tool for forest management practices. *Computers and Electronics in Agriculture*, *215*, 108416. DOI: 10.1016/j.compag.2023.108416

Rahman, M. M., Nguyen, R., & Lu, L. (2022). Multi-level impacts of climate change and supply disruption events on a potato supply chain: An agent-based modeling approach. *Agricultural Systems*, *201*, 103469. DOI: 10.1016/j.agsy.2022.103469

Rasheed, A., San, O., & Kvamsdal, T. (2020). Digital twin: Values, challenges and enablers from a modeling perspective. *IEEE Access : Practical Innovations, Open Solutions*, *8*, 21980–22012. DOI: 10.1109/ACCESS.2020.2970143

Saha, A., Dabic Miletic, S., Senapati, T., Simic, V., Pamucar, D., Ala, A., & Arya, L. (2024). Fermatean fuzzy Dombi generalized Maclaurin symmetric mean operators for prioritizing bulk material handling technologies. *Cognitive Computation*, *16*(6), 3096–3121. Advance online publication. DOI: 10.1007/s12559-024-10323-y

Saha, A., Görçün, Ö. F., Pamucar, D., Arya, L., & Simic, V. (2024). Evaluation of shared micro-mobility systems for sustainable cities using a consensus-based Fermatean fuzzy multiple objective optimization. *Engineering Applications of Artificial Intelligence*, *134*, 108662. DOI: 10.1016/j.engappai.2024.108662

Saha, A., Senapati, T., Akram, M., Kahraman, C., Mesiar, R., & Arya, L. (2024). Dual probabilistic linguistic consensus reaching method for group decision making. *Granular Computing*, *9*(35), 35. Advance online publication. DOI: 10.1007/s41066-024-00458-6

Saha, A., Simic, V., Dabic-Miletic, S., Senapati, T., Pamucar, D., Arya, L., & Tirkolaee, E. B. (2025). Prioritization of AI-based material handling approaches for smart logistics in sustainable warehouses. *Environment, Development and Sustainability*. Advance online publication. DOI: 10.1007/s10668-025-06435-6

Singh, G., Rajesh, R., Daultani, Y., & Misra, S. C. (2023). Resilience and sustainability enhancements in food supply chains using digital twin technology: A grey causal modelling approach. *Computers & Industrial Engineering*, *179*, 109172. DOI: 10.1016/j.cie.2023.109172

Slob, N., Hurst, W., van de Zedde, R., & Tekinerdogan, B. (2023). Virtual reality-based digital twins for greenhouses: A focus on human interaction. *Computers and Electronics in Agriculture*, *208*, 107815. DOI: 10.1016/j.compag.2023.107815

Spyrou, O., Verdouw, C., & Hurst, W. (2023). A digital twin reference architecture for pharmaceutical cannabis production. *International Journal of Computer Integrated Manufacturing*, *37*, 1–21.

Suryani, E., Hendrawan, R. A., Muhandhis, I., & Indraswari, R. (2022). A simulation model to improve the value of rice supply chain. *Journal of Simulation*, *16*(4), 392–414. DOI: 10.1080/17477778.2020.1829118

Sushanth, G., & Sujatha, S. (2018). IoT-based smart agriculture system. In *2018 International Conference on Wireless Communications, Signal Processing and Networking (WiSPNET)* (pp. 1–4).

Symeonaki, E., Maraveas, C., & Arvanitis, K. G. (2024). Recent advances in digital twins for agriculture 5.0: Applications and open issues in livestock production systems. *Applied Sciences (Basel, Switzerland)*, *14*(2), 686. DOI: 10.3390/app14020686

Tagarakis, A. C., Benos, L., Kyriakarakos, G., Pearson, S., Sørensen, C. G., & Bochtis, D. (2024, May 14). Digital Twins in Agriculture and Forestry: A Review. *Sensors (Basel)*, *24*(10), 3117. DOI: 10.3390/s24103117 PMID: 38793969

Tao, F., Qi, Q., Wang, L., & Nee, A. Y. C. (2019). Digital twins and cyber-physical systems toward smart manufacturing and industry 4.0: Correlation and comparison. *Engineering (Beijing)*, *5*(4), 653–661. DOI: 10.1016/j.eng.2019.01.014

Van der Burg, S., Kloppenburg, S., Kok, E. J., & van der Voort, M. (2021). Digital twins in agri-food: Societal and ethical themes and questions. NJAS—Impact in Agricultural and Life Sciences, 93, 98–125.

Vargas, J. M., Castrillon, O. D., & Giraldo, J. A. (2025). Implementation and Field Validation of a Digital Twin Methodology to Enhance Production and Service Systems in Waste Management. *Applied Sciences (Basel, Switzerland)*, *15*(12), 6733. DOI: 10.3390/app15126733

Verdouw, C., Tekinerdogan, B., Beulens, A., & Wolfert, S. (2021). Digital twins in smart farming. *Agricultural Systems*, *189*, 103046. DOI: 10.1016/j.agsy.2020.103046

Verdouw, C. N., & Kruize, J. W. (2017). Digital twins in farm management: Illustrations from the FIWARE accelerators SmartAgriFood and Fractals. *7th Asian-Australasian Conference on Precision Agriculture Digital*.

Vijayalakshmi, K., Al-Otaibi, S., Arya, L., Almaiah, M. A., Anithaashri, T. P., Karthik, S. S., & Shishakly, R. (2023). Smart agricultural–industrial crop-monitoring system using UAV–IoT classification techniques. *Sustainability*, *15*(14), 11242. DOI: 10.3390/su151411242

Wang, L. (2024). Digital twins in agriculture: A review of recent progress and open issues. *Electronics (Basel)*, *13*(11), 2209. DOI: 10.3390/electronics13112209

Zhang, R., Zhu, H., Chang, Q., & Mao, Q. (2025). A comprehensive review of digital twins technology in agriculture. *Agriculture*, *15*(9), 903. DOI: 10.3390/agriculture15090903

Chapter 7

# Transforming Agricultural Waste Into Smart Geopolymer Materials for Sustainable Infrastructure

**Govind Ravish**
http://orcid.org/0009-0007-7271-5880
*MMEC, Maharishi Markandeshwar University, Mullana, India*

**Mahapara Abbass**
http://orcid.org/0000-0002-0838-2598
*MMEC, Maharishi Markandeshwar University, Mullana, India*

## ABSTRACT

*This chapter examines how agricultural residues can be transformed into high-performance geopolymer binders that address both environmental burdens and infrastructure demands. It explains the chemistry of alkali activation, the role of precursor composition, and the influence of processing conditions on mechanical, thermal, and durability behavior. The chapter highlights advanced functionalities such as self-sensing and self-healing, alongside the measurable carbon-reduction benefits demonstrated through life-cycle assessment. Case studies from transportation, marine, building, and water-management sectors illustrate real-world feasibility. By integrating material science, sustainability metrics, and implementation frameworks, the chapter articulates how waste-derived geopolymers contribute to circular-economy goals and support climate-resilient infrastructure development.*

DOI: 10.4018/979-8-2600-1438-7.ch007

## PAPER HIGHLIGHTS

1. Introduces agricultural residues as alternative raw materials for low-carbon geopolymer binders.
2. Explains alkali activation chemistry and the influence of precursor composition on material performance.
3. Demonstrates advanced properties such as self-sensing, self-healing, and high fire resistance.
4. Compares mechanical and durability properties with those of conventional concrete.
5. Presents life-cycle assessment proving 60–75% lower $CO_2$ emissions.
6. Discusses standards, case studies, and future strategies for industrial implementation.

## Abbreviations

| | |
|---|---|
| RHA | Rice Husk Ash |
| SCBA | Sugarcane Bagasse Ash |
| POFA | Palm Oil Fuel Ash |
| Si/Al | Silica-to-Alumina Ratio |
| LCA | Life Cycle Assessment |
| RSM | Response Surface Methodology |
| ANN | Artificial Neural Network |
| AI | Artificial Intelligence |
| BIM | Building Information Modeling |
| IoT | Internet of Things |
| SDG | Sustainable Development Goal |

## 1. INTRODUCTION

### 1.1 The Global Infrastructure Challenge

The twenty-first century faces a difficult balancing act: societies everywhere need to build homes, roads, bridges, and industries to support growing populations, yet these same activities must not worsen climate change. Modern construction depends heavily on Portland cement, a material that is strong and reliable but also one of the world's largest single sources of carbon dioxide emissions. Every tonne of cement produced releases approximately 0.8 to 1 tonne of $CO_2$, and because billions of tonnes are made each year, cement manufacture is responsible for roughly eight percent of total global greenhouse gas emissions (Kajaste& Hurme, 2015; Kumar et al., 2025; Mohamad et al., 2021; Olsson et al., 2023).

At the same time, the planet produces a staggering amount of agricultural waste. Billions of tonnes of residues are generated annually from crops such as rice, wheat, maize, and sugarcane (Bentsen et al., 2013; Ginni et al., 2021). Farmers often dispose of these materials through open burning or dumping, practices that pollute air and soil and release methane and carbon dioxide. Thus, while the construction industry struggles with the high carbon cost of cement, the agricultural sector battles with waste disposal. This contrast—shortage of sustainable construction materials on one hand and an oversupply of biomass residues on the other—creates a unique opportunity to connect the two through circular-economy thinking (Bachs-Herrera et al., 2023; Bragança et al., 2023).

## 1.2 Geopolymers: A Paradigm Shift in Construction Materials

Geopolymers represent a new class of materials that can help solve this problem. Unlike ordinary cement, which gains its strength from calcium-based hydration reactions, geopolymers harden through the formation of three-dimensional networks of silicon and aluminum atoms linked by oxygen. These networks arise when aluminosilicate-rich powders react with alkaline activator solutions, creating a strong and durable binder. Because the raw material does not have to be limestone, it can come from industrial or agricultural waste rich in silica and alumina (Carvalho et al., 2023; Fan et al., 2023).

The concept of geopolymers was introduced by French scientist Joseph Davidovits in the late 1970s, but their ability to use agricultural waste effectively has gained attention only in recent decades. Ashes derived from biomass residues—such as rice husk ash, sugarcane bagasse ash, and wheat-straw ash—contain large amounts of reactive silica (Duque-Acevedo et al., 2022; Šupić et al., 2021). When properly processed and activated, these ashes can form high-performance binders with properties comparable to or even superior to conventional cement. This technology therefore not only reduces carbon emissions but also transforms waste into a valuable construction resource (Ali et al., 2025; Blesson & Rao, 2023).

## 1.3 Chapter Scope and Objectives

This chapter explores how agricultural residues can be converted into smart, sustainable geopolymer materials for infrastructure development. It explains the chemistry behind their formation, the processing of agricultural wastes, and the performance of the resulting materials. The discussion covers the following major areas: the material science of ash-based geopolymers; methods for preparing and activating agricultural residues; smart properties such as self-sensing and self-healing; performance optimization through mixture design; sustainability analysis; and finally, real-world applications and implementation frameworks. By integrating all these perspectives, the chapter demonstrates how waste materials can become key building blocks for a low-carbon future. **Figure 1** presents the graphical abstract of this chapter.

## 2. AGRICULTURAL WASTE STREAMS: CHARACTERISTICS AND POTENTIAL

### 2.1 Global Agricultural Residue Production

Agriculture generates many by-products that are usually considered waste but in fact contain useful minerals. Understanding their composition and behavior is the first step in using them as geopolymer precursors (Abbass & Akhai, 2025; Abbass & Singh, 2023; Abbass & Akhai, 2025)..

#### 2.1.1 Rice Husk and Rice Husk Ash

Rice is one of the most widely cultivated crops in the world, and its processing leaves behind large volumes of husks—roughly 160 million tonnes each year. The husk accounts for about one-fifth of the paddy's weight and contains 15–20 percent silica embedded in a cellulose framework (Kaleli et al., 2020; Sanoja-López et al., 2023; Zurairah et al., 2021). When the husk is burned under controlled conditions between 500 °C and 700 °C, the organic matter is removed and the resulting rice husk ash is rich in amorphous silica (Abbas et al., 2024; Basri et al., 2021; Mostafa et al., 2020; Nasser et al., 2023). The reactivity of this silica depends strongly on how it is burned: low temperatures leave unburned carbon, while excessive heat turns it crystalline and less reactive. With careful control, RHA can reach silica contents of 85–95 percent and surface areas above 50 $m^2$ per gram, making it an excellent source of reactive silica for geopolymer production (Passuello et al., 2017; Singh & Singh, 2020; Teng et al., 2021). Because its alumina content is low, RHA is often blended with other materials that supply aluminum.

#### 2.1.2 Sugarcane Bagasse Ash

Sugarcane is another crop that produces substantial residues. After juice extraction, about one-fourth of the stalk mass remains as bagasse, which can be burned to generate energy (Matsueda & Antunes, 2024; Ungureanu et al., 2022). The combustion residue, known as sugarcane bagasse ash, contains mainly silica (55–80 percent) along with alumina, iron oxide, and minor oxides of calcium and magnesium (Capêto et al., 2023; Fredericci et al., 2014; Hipólito & Ildefonso, 2024). If the burning temperature is kept around 600–800 °C, the silica remains amorphous and highly reactive; uncontrolled burning, on the other hand, yields crystalline ash with poor activity (Adesanya et al., 2020; Cordeiro et al., 2009; Habte et al., 2025; Soares et al., 2014). Properly produced SCBA therefore offers a balanced composition suitable for direct geopolymer synthesis.

### 2.1.3 Wheat-Straw and Corn-Stover Ash

Cereal crops such as wheat and maize also leave huge amounts of residue: around 350 million tonnes of wheat straw and over 800 million tonnes of corn stover each year (Gao et al., 2022; Wang et al., 2020). When burned, these residues produce ashes containing 50–70 percent silica and 5–10 percent alumina (Wan et al., 2019). They also have relatively high levels of potassium and other alkali metals, which can influence the setting and durability of the resulting binder. Washing and controlled calcination help remove unwanted salts and improve the chemical uniformity of the ash.

### 2.1.4 Palm-Oil Biomass Waste

Palm-oil production produces multiple by-products such as palm-oil-fuel ash, palm-kernel-shell ash, and empty-fruit-bunch ash. Together, these can exceed 100 million tonnes per year in producing countries (Hassan et al., 2024; Norrrahim et al., 2022; Rubinsin et al., 2020). POFA typically contains 60–70 percent silica with moderate amounts of alumina and iron oxides (Akeke et al., 2023; Amaludin et al., 2023; Olivia et al., 2023; Toyeb et al., 2023). Complete combustion is required to remove unburned carbon, and multi-stage or fluidized-bed systems are often used to achieve consistent quality. These ashes can act as valuable geopolymer precursors once properly processed.

**Table 1** presents the characteristics, chemical makeup, reactivity factors, and application potential of major agricultural waste streams used as geopolymer precursors. It highlights availability, ideal combustion conditions, benefits, and limitations of ashes such as RHA, SCBA, wheat-straw ash, and POFA, establishing their suitability for sustainable binder production.

*Table 1. Characteristics and potential of major agricultural waste streams for geopolymer production.*

| Agricultural Residue / Ash Type | Annual Availability (Approx.) | Main Constituents (% Range) | Ideal Burning Temp (°C) | Key Reactivity Factors | Potential Benefits for Geopolymer Use | Limitations / Challenges |
|---|---|---|---|---|---|---|
| **Rice Husk / Rice Husk Ash (RHA)** | ≈160 Mt husks → 20–30 Mt ash | $SiO_2$ 85–95; $Al_2O_3$ 0.5–2; $Fe_2O_3$ <1; LOI <5 | 500–700 | Amorphous silica, high surface area > 50 $m^2/g$ | Highly reactive silica source; enhances strength & durability | Low alumina → requires blending; temperature-sensitive |
| **Sugarcane Bagasse Ash (SCBA)** | ≈200 Mt bagasse → 30–40 Mt ash | $SiO_2$ 55–80; $Al_2O_3$ 5–15; $Fe_2O_3$ 2–8; CaO 2–5 | 600–800 | Amorphous phase retention | Balanced composition; good workability and strength | Crystallization > 800 °C; variable quality |
| **Wheat-Straw / Corn-Stover Ash** | ≈1.1 billion t residue | $SiO_2$ 50–70; $Al_2O_3$ 5–10; $K_2O$ 5–10 | 550–750 | Potassium leaching control | Abundant; suitable for blended systems | High alkali → affects setting; needs washing |
| **Palm-Oil-Fuel Ash (POFA)** | >100 Mt in producing nations | $SiO_2$ 60–70; $Al_2O_3$ 5–10; $Fe_2O_3$ 4–6 | 600–850 | Complete combustion for carbon removal | Moderate Si/Al; good chemical resistance | Quality depends on firing method; requires fine grinding |
| **Other Residues (e.g., Coconut Shell, Coffee Husk Ash)** | 10–20 Mt combined | $SiO_2$ 40–60; $Al_2O_3$ 5–12; CaO 3–10 | 500–700 | Depends on organic content | Local use for regional geopolymers | Limited large-scale data; needs characterization |

## 2.2 Chemical Composition and Reactivity Requirements

For a waste material to work effectively in geopolymer formation, it must contain sufficient reactive silica and alumina, low calcium content, and minimal residual carbon (Alaneme et al., 2024; Carvalho et al., 2023; Cui et al., 2023; Huang et al., 2021; Siyal et al., 2024). Ideally, the chemical makeup should fall within the following broad ranges: silica 40–70 percent, alumina 10–30 percent, calcium oxide below 10 percent, and alkali oxides under 5 percent (Amaludin et al., 2023; Pérez et al., 2022; Tositti et al., 2023). The silica-to-alumina (Si/Al) ratio is especially important (Alaneme et al., 2024; Dehghani et al., 2021; Huang et al., 2021): values between 1.5 and 2.5 tend to give the best balance of strength and workability (Amaludin et al., 2023; Nawaz et al., 2020; Obeidy et al., 2024; Pan et al., 2024; Wang et al., 2021), while higher ratios enhance chemical resistance (Alaneme et al., 2024;

Huang et al., 2021; Nawaz et al., 2020; Vogt et al., 2021) and lower ratios lead to faster setting (Alaneme et al., 2024; Dehghani et al., 2021).

The physical form of the ash also matters. Amorphous, glassy phases dissolve more readily in alkaline solutions than crystalline ones (Bazarkhankyzy et al., 2025; Kucukgoncu&Özbayrak, 2024; Omran et al., 2023; Santi et al., 2022). Fine particle size and high surface area further improve reactivity (Bazarkhankyzy et al., 2025), as do the absence of metallic or carbon impurities (Alaneme et al., 2024; Kucukgoncu&Özbayrak, 2024; Kumble et al., 2024).

**Table 2** presents the key pre-treatment and processing technologies applied to agricultural ashes, including controlled combustion, grinding, acid leaching, and particle classification. It outlines the purpose, operating conditions, quality improvements, and process limitations that directly influence geopolymer reactivity and performance.

*Table 2. Pre-Treatment and processing technologies for agricultural ashes.*

| Processing Method | Purpose / Objective | Typical Conditions | Quality Improvements | Advantages in Geopolymer Use | Limitations / Precautions |
|---|---|---|---|---|---|
| **Controlled Combustion** | Remove organics & ensure amorphous silica | 500–800 °C for 1–3 h with air control | High $SiO_2$ reactivity; low carbon | Uniform reactive ash; enhanced strength | >800 °C causes crystallization and energy loss |
| **Fluidized-Bed / Staged Combustion** | Uniform heating & low emissions | Multi-zone (600–800 °C) air flow 1.5–2 m/s | Consistent ash quality | Scalable industrial production | High equipment cost; skilled control |
| **Mechanical Grinding / Ball Milling** | Reduce particle size & increase surface area | 2–6 h milling to 5–20 μm | Surface area ↑ to 50–60 m²/g | Faster dissolution and early strength | Over-grinding → agglomeration |
| **Sieving / Air Classification** | Uniform particle distribution | 75–150 μm mesh | Removes coarse particles | Improves packing density and flow | Finer fractions ↑ water demand |
| **Magnetic Separation** | Remove metallic contaminants | 0.3–0.6 T magnetic field | Purified chemical composition | Minimizes unwanted side reactions | Extra processing cost |
| **Acid Leaching ($HCl/H_2SO_4$)** | Remove alkalis & impurities | 0.1–1 M acid, 30–120 min | Lower $K_2O$/CaO, higher $SiO_2$ | Enhanced durability & purity | Effluent needs neutralization |
| **Water Washing / Desalination** | Eliminate soluble salts | Water:ash = 5–10:1, stir 15–30 min | Less efflorescence & better setting | Improved surface finish and bonding | Drying energy & fines loss |

continued on following page

*Table 2. Continued*

| Processing Method | Purpose / Objective | Typical Conditions | Quality Improvements | Advantages in Geopolymer Use | Limitations / Precautions |
|---|---|---|---|---|---|
| **Thermal Activation of Blends** | Homogenize multi-waste mixes | 600–750 °C for ≈ 2 h | Uniform amorphous matrix | Balanced Si/Al ratio for co-processed ash | Avoid sintering; may need re-grinding |
| **Chemical–Mechanical Activation** | Boost reactivity via acid + milling | 0.5 M acid → 3 h milling | High Si–Al dissolution rate | Superior strength geopolymers | Complex & costly process |

## 2.3 Pre-Treatment and Processing Technologies

Agricultural ashes vary widely in composition and texture, so several preparation steps are used to make them suitable for activation.

### 2.3.1 Controlled Combustion Systems

Modern technologies such as **fluidized-bed combustors** and **rotary kilns** allow uniform and precise temperature control (Maldonado-Alameda et al., 2022). Combustion temperatures between 600 °C and 800 °C are optimal: lower temperatures leave too much carbon, while higher temperatures promote crystallization of silica, which reduces reactivity (Abbas 2015; Abbas et al., 2024; Dizaji et al., 2021; Soares et al., 2014). Staged combustion, where drying, burning, and calcining occur in separate zones, further improves consistency.

### 2.3.2 Mechanical Processing

After combustion, the ash is ground and classified to achieve the right particle size. Ball-milling or other fine-grinding techniques increase surface area and expose more reactive sites (Brown & Gevaudan, 2025; Djobo et al., 2016; Habeeb & Mahmud, 2010; Sun et al., 2023). Air classification can separate fine, highly reactive particles from coarse ones, while magnetic separation removes metallic contaminants. A particle size in the range of 5–20 micrometers usually provides good reactivity without excessive energy consumption (Bouchikhi et al., 2020; Brial et al., 2022).

### 2.3.3 Chemical Treatment

Some ashes contain unwanted metallic elements that can interfere with geopolymerization. Mild acid leaching using dilute hydrochloric or sulfuric acid can remove these impurities and increase silica concentration (Chindaprasirt&Rattanasak, 2020; Rabbat et al., 2021; Sukkathanyawat et al., 2022; Yu, 2024). However, this step adds cost and produces effluent that must be neutralized, so it is used only when necessary for high-performance applications.

**Table 3** presents the chemical composition, Si/Al ratio, phase nature, and relative reactivity of various agricultural ashes. It provides a comparative assessment of their suitability for geopolymer formation, enabling selection or blending strategies to achieve optimal binder chemistry.

*Table 3. Chemical composition and reactivity requirements of agricultural ashes.*

| Ash Type | $SiO_2$ (%) | $Al_2O_3$ (%) | $Fe_2O_3$ (%) | CaO (%) | $K_2O$ + $Na_2O$ (%) | LOI (%) | Si/Al Ratio | Phase Nature | Reactivity (★ = Low →★★★★★ = High) | Geopolymer Suitability |
|---|---|---|---|---|---|---|---|---|---|---|
| **Rice Husk Ash (RHA)** | 85–95 | 0.5–2 | <1 | <1 | <2 | 1–5 | 40–80 (≈ 40–100:1) | Amorphous | ★★★★★ | Outstanding silica source; needs Al-rich blend |
| **Sugarcane Bagasse Ash (SCBA)** | 55–80 | 5–15 | 2–8 | 2–5 | 1–3 | 3–6 | 4–12 (≈ 4–8:1) | Amorphous | ★★★★☆ | Balanced binder; good strength & workability |
| **Wheat-Straw / Corn-Stover Ash** | 50–70 | 5–10 | 1–4 | 2–5 | 5–10 | 2–6 | 5–10 (≈ 5–7:1) | Semi-amorphous | ★★★☆☆ | Usable after salt removal; blended mixes preferred |
| **Palm-Oil-Fuel Ash (POFA)** | 60–70 | 5–10 | 4–6 | 3–5 | 1–3 | 3–7 | 6–10 (≈ 6–10:1) | Amorphous | ★★★★☆ | Chemically stable; acid resistant binder |
| **Coconut-Shell / Coffee-Husk Ash** | 45–65 | 5–12 | 3–8 | 3–10 | 2–4 | 4–8 | 4–8 (≈ 4–6:1) | Amorphous / semi-crystalline | ★★★☆☆ | Promising for local low-cost geopolymers |
| **Fly Ash (Class F)** *Ref.* | 50–65 | 20–30 | 5–10 | <5 | 1–2 | 1–3 | 2–3 (≈ 2–3:1) | Amorphous | ★★★★★ | Benchmark reference material for mix blending |

Key Interpretations

- Optimal **Si/Al ≈ 1.5–2.5** ensures balanced geopolymer gel formation.
- **Low LOI (< 6%)** signifies efficient combustion and higher reactivity.
- Moderate **CaO (2–5%)** aids early strength, but excess disrupts network formation.
- Combining **RHA + SCBA or POFA** achieves ideal chemical synergy for sustainable, high-performance geopolymer binders.

## 2.4 Critical Comparison of Agricultural Ash Precursors and Research Gaps

Despite many of the studies demonstrating the potential of geopolymers made from agricultural waste, the studies' findings have shown a lack of consistency. For instance, some studies have shown RHA based systems, after optimized blending, have a compressive strength of more than 70-80 MP (Alaneme et al., 2024; Nawaz et al., 2020), while other studies have shown a similar compressive strength to be 40-50 MP. The inconsistencies are often attributed to differences in the degree of amorphous silica retention (Abbas 2015; Abbas et al., 2024; Dizaji et al., 2021; Soares et al., 2014), combustion temperature, particle size (Bazarkhankyzy et al., 2025), and the control of the Si/Al ratio (Alaneme et al., 2024; Dehghani et al., 2021; Nawaz et al., 2020)

In the the research of Capêto et al. (2023), sugarcane-bagasse ash (SCBA) has been reported to be chemically balanced and is able to be used in direct geopolymerization. On the contrary, other reports, suggest that the SCBA may encounter crystallization at temperatures at or above 800°C and lose its usability (Adesanya et al. 2020, Soares et al. 2014). Geopolymers, in general, have been recognized to have regulation of chloride attack when exposed to the sea (Chiranjeevi et al. 2023, Nawaz et al. 2020). However, Pasupathy et al. (2021) and Li et al (2019) have studied certain kinds of slag that contain a higher porosity and noted that they experience a higher chloride attack when exposed to seawater over a long period of time. Due to the opposing sides to the results, it seems that refining pore structures in combination with chemistry of the precursors and the content of CaO, rather than the dissemination of the theory of geopolymer, provide long-lasting durability.

A consensus is forming for the 60-75% reduction in embodied carbon (Borges et al., 2014; Shi et al., 2021; Cong et al., 2024), increased sulfate resistance (Alahmari et al., 2023; Farhan et al., 2024), and good thermal stability (Goryunova et al., 2023; Mahmoodi et al., 2025). However, there is a considerable absence of research, especially with respect to long-term (> 5 years) field validation, a lack of standard means of classifying agricultural ash reactivity, and a lack of consensus on quality grading systems for precursor materials. The differences in chemical composition of ash, depending on soil chemistry, type of crop, method of combustion, and time of the season, are some of the most important obstacles to widespread standardization (Alaneme et al., 2024; Amaludin et al., 2023; Pérez et al., 2022).

# 3. GEOPOLYMERIZATION MECHANISMS AND MATERIAL SCIENCE

## 3.1 Fundamental Chemistry of Alkali Activation

The formation of geopolymers is based on a chemical process called *alkali activation*, in which aluminosilicate materials react with alkaline solutions (Deventer et al., 2006; Madirisha et al., 2024; Provis & Bernal, 2014; Siyal et al., 2024). When agricultural ashes such as rice husk or sugarcane bagasse ash come into contact with strong alkali solutions—usually sodium or potassium hydroxide, sometimes mixed with sodium silicate—a series of chemical reactions occur. These reactions convert the loose ash particles into a dense, stone-like material with exceptional strength and durability.

The process takes place in three main stages. The first is dissolution, where the alkali solution breaks down the silica and alumina present in the ash (Hattaf et al., 2022; Huang et al., 2021; Nana et al., 2021). The strong basic environment (pH above 12) attacks the Si–O and Al–O bonds, releasing silicate and aluminate ions into the solution. The second stage is polymerization, where these dissolved ions recombine to form a new three-dimensional network of Si–O–Al–O bonds (Ravish & Abbass, 2026; Thakur et al., 2025; Abbass et al., 2025; Samridhi et al., 2025; Goryunova et al., 2023; Nawaz et al., 2020). This process gradually turns the liquid mixture into a stiff gel. The final stage, hardening, occurs as water is expelled and the gel reorganizes into a stable solid structure.

During this transformation, alkali cations such as sodium ($Na^+$) or potassium ($K^+$) become part of the structure, balancing the charge of the aluminum atoms in the framework (Hounsi et al., 2014; Longhi et al., 2019). The proportion of silicon to aluminum strongly influences the resulting properties: higher Si/Al ratios produce denser and more chemically resistant materials, while lower ratios lead to faster setting and slightly lower ultimate strength (Alaneme et al., 2024; Dehghani et al., 2021; Juengsuwattananon et al., 2019; Nawaz et al., 2020; Pan et al., 2024).

## 3.2 Role of Agricultural Ash Composition

Different agricultural ashes behave differently during geopolymerization. Ashes that are rich in silica, such as rice husk ash, are excellent sources of reactive $SiO_2$ but lack sufficient alumina (Ngui et al., 2022; Ziegler et al., 2016). To achieve the right chemical balance, such ashes are often mixed with materials like metakaolin or fly ash, which are rich in alumina (Alaneme et al., 2023). This blending not only improves the chemistry but also enhances workability due to the spherical shape of fly ash particles.

Some ashes, such as palm-oil-fuel ash or wheat-straw ash, naturally contain both silica and alumina in favorable proportions (Hernández-Escobar et al., 2023). These materials can often be used directly without blending. They provide steady setting behavior and consistent strength development. However, minor elements in ashes—such as calcium, iron, or potassium—can affect performance (Mulapeer& Omar, 2025; Oyebisi et al., 2020; Perná et al., 2019). A small amount of calcium may accelerate early strength but too much can interfere with geopolymer formation. Alkali metals and phosphorus can cause unwanted reactions or efflorescence, while residual carbon can increase water demand. Understanding these subtle influences helps in designing effective mixtures.

### 3.3 Activator Solution Chemistry

The activator solution acts as the engine of the geopolymer reaction. Sodium hydroxide and potassium hydroxide are the most common activators, often combined with sodium or potassium silicate solution (also called water glass) (Al-Saudi et al., 2023; Arokiasamy et al., 2022; Bouchikhi et al., 2020; Nodehi&Taghvaee, 2021; Provis, 2009). The concentration of hydroxide solution usually ranges between 8 and 16 molar; stronger solutions dissolve the ash faster but may lead to excessive heat generation and cracking (Al-Saudi et al., 2023; El-Zeadani et al., 2021; Görhan&Kürklü, 2013; Koçyiğit, 2024; Nawaz et al., 2020).

Adding silicate solution supplies extra soluble silica, which helps in rapid gel formation and early strength gain (Al-Saudi et al., 2023). The ratio between silica and alkali oxide in the solution (known as the silicate modulus) must be optimized: too little silica leads to weak bonding, while too much slows down the setting. Typical ratios between 1.5 and 2.0 provide the best balance between workability and strength (Alaneme et al., 2024; Aupoil et al., 2018; Kaja et al., 2018; Nawaz et al., 2020). Researchers often use design-of-experiment techniques or even machine learning to determine the ideal activator mix for a particular type of ash.

## 4. SMART FUNCTIONALITIES IN AGRICULTURAL WASTE GEOPOLYMERS

In addition to strength and durability, modern materials are expected to be intelligent—to sense their environment, heal themselves, or respond to changes. Remarkably, agricultural waste-based geopolymers can exhibit such smart behaviors when engineered appropriately (Abbass & Singh, 2021; Abbass & Singh, 2022; Abbass & Singh, 2024; Abbass & Singh, 2023; Abbass & Singh, 2022).

## 4.1 Self-Sensing Capabilities

One of the most exciting properties of geopolymers is their ability to act as self-sensing materials. Because these materials can conduct electricity to a limited extent, changes in their internal structure—such as the formation of cracks or the application of load—can alter their electrical resistance (Biondi et al., 2020; Frandsen et al., 2021; Górski et al., 2022; Mare & Ouellet-Plamondon, 2022; Rovnaník et al., 2025). By measuring this resistance, engineers can detect stress, damage, or strain within the structure itself without using separate sensors.

This self-sensing behavior comes from two main mechanisms. The first is ionic conduction, where charged ions move through the tiny pores filled with moisture (Frandsen et al., 2021). The second is electronic conduction, which occurs if a small amount of carbon remains in the ash or if conductive fillers are added (Frandsen et al., 2021). Controlled retention of 1–3 percent carbon can improve conductivity without harming strength. The relationship between electrical resistance and strain follows a pattern similar to that of a strain gauge, allowing these materials to monitor structural health in real time.

To improve sensitivity, researchers often add conductive fillers such as carbon nanotubes, graphene, or short carbon fibers (Drabczyk et al., 2023; Górski et al., 2022). These materials form a continuous network of conductive paths within the geopolymer matrix. Even agricultural biochar—carbon obtained by pyrolyzing crop residues—can be used as a sustainable, low-cost additive for this purpose (Drabczyk et al., 2023). With proper calibration, self-sensing geopolymers can be embedded in bridges, pavements, and buildings to provide continuous health monitoring, forming part of a smart infrastructure network connected to digital systems and digital twins.

## 4.2 Self-Healing Properties

Cracking is a common problem in concrete structures, but geopolymers made from agricultural waste can repair small cracks on their own (Kadamba et al., 2024; Luhar et al., 2021; Özen et al., 2023; Rajczakowska et al., 2019). This self-healing ability occurs through several mechanisms. Some unreacted ash particles remain within the hardened material and can react later when exposed to moisture, producing new binding gel that seals fine cracks. Additionally, when calcium-bearing compounds are present, they can react with carbon dioxide from the air to form calcium carbonate crystals that block cracks (Uthayakumar et al., 2020).

Beyond these natural processes, scientists are developing engineered self-healing systems. One method uses microcapsules or hollow fibers filled with healing agents that break open when cracks form, releasing substances that polymerize and seal the gap. Another approach involves embedding special bacteria that produce calcium carbonate when activated by water (Luhar et al., 2021; Techo et al., 2024; Uthayakumar et al., 2020). These microbial systems have shown promising results in prolonging the life of concrete-like materials, and adapting them for geopolymers is an active research area.

### 4.3 Adaptive and Responsive Properties

Agricultural waste geopolymers can also be modified to regulate temperature or interact with light and electromagnetic waves. When **phase-change materials** are incorporated, the composite can absorb or release heat, helping buildings maintain stable indoor temperatures and reducing energy use (Bąk et al., 2025; Kahla et al., 2025; Łach et al., 2021; Przybek et al., 2024). When photocatalytic compounds like titanium dioxide are added, the surface can break down pollutants and remain clean under sunlight (Drabczyk et al., 2023; Strini et al., 2016).

Similarly, by controlling the carbon content or adding fine metallic particles, geopolymers can block electromagnetic interference (Maestre & Santos, 2023). This makes them suitable for sensitive environments such as hospitals, laboratories, and data centers. Thus, these materials not only replace cement but also introduce intelligent functionalities for future smart infrastructure systems.

## 5. MECHANICAL PROPERTIES AND PERFORMANCE OPTIMIZATION

### 5.1 Strength Development and Structural Performance

The primary indicator of binder performance in construction applications is compressive strength. Agricultural-waste-based geopolymers demonstrate compressive strengths comparable to or exceeding conventional Portland cement concrete. Early-age strengths within 1–3 days typically range between 20–40 MPa, while 28-day strengths commonly fall between 40–70 MPa. Under optimized curing and mix conditions, strengths exceeding 80–85 MPa have been reported (Lemougna et al., 2019).

Strength development is strongly governed by chemical balance and processing parameters. The Si/Al ratio plays a central role in defining gel structure and cross-link density; ratios between 2.0 and 2.5 generally provide optimal performance (Alaneme et al., 2024; Nawaz et al., 2020). Lower ratios accelerate setting but may reduce ultimate strength, while excessive silica content may slow polymerization.

Activator concentration significantly influences dissolution kinetics. Hydroxide molarity between 8 and 14 M is typically effective (Al-Saudi et al., 2023; Nawaz et al., 2020), though higher concentrations may generate excessive heat and induce microcracking (Kucukgoncu & Özbayrak, 2024). The water-to-solid ratio controls porosity and compaction efficiency; excessive water increases void formation, whereas insufficient water reduces workability.

Curing temperature further accelerates geopolymerization. Heat curing at 60–80 °C for 24–48 hours enhances early strength by increasing reaction kinetics (Alawi et al., 2023; Al-Saudi et al., 2023). Ambient curing remains feasible but produces slower early-age strength development (Kim et al., 2025; Statkauskas et al., 2024).

Strength enhancement strategies include hybrid precursor blending (e.g., RHA + metakaolin; SCBA + fly ash), nano-additive incorporation (nano-silica, nano-alumina), and fiber reinforcement (Abbass & Singh, 2021; Abbass & Singh, 2022; Abbass, Singh, & Aggarwal, 2023). Fibers improve crack control and post-peak ductility, increasing flexural strength to 3–8 MPa and tensile strength to 2–5 MPa.

These findings demonstrate that compressive strength in agricultural-waste geopolymers is not solely dependent on precursor availability but rather on integrated control of chemistry, activator dosage, curing regime, and microstructural refinement.

## 5.2 Durability Performance Under Aggressive Environments

Beyond strength, durability performance is critical for infrastructure longevity. Agricultural-waste-based geopolymers exhibit exceptional resistance to aggressive environments due to their dense aluminosilicate matrix (Alahmari et al., 2023; Farhan et al., 2024; Wang et al., 2023).

**Acid Resistance -** Unlike Portland cement, which contains calcium hydroxide susceptible to acid attack, geopolymers contain minimal free calcium. Exposure to sulfuric or hydrochloric acid results in strength loss typically below 10% after several months (Cui et al., 2023; Valencia-Saavedra et al., 2020), whereas OPC may lose 40–50% strength under similar conditions.

**Sulfate Resistance -** Geopolymers resist ettringite formation due to their low calcium content. Studies report negligible expansion and cracking under sulfate exposure (Alahmari et al., 2023; Farhan et al., 2024; Niveditha & Koniki, 2020).

**Chloride Penetration** - Chloride permeability values between 500–1500 coulombs classify geopolymers as low-permeability materials (Chiranjeevi et al., 2023). The refined pore structure limits ion diffusion, enhancing protection of embedded reinforcement in marine environments (Nawaz et al., 2020). However, some slag-based geopolymer systems have shown variable chloride resistance under prolonged seawater exposure (Pasupathy et al., 2021; Li et al., 2019), indicating that precursor chemistry significantly influences marine durability.

**Freeze–Thaw Performance** - When properly cured, geopolymers maintain ≥90% residual strength after 300 freeze–thaw cycles (Alahmari et al., 2023; Farhan et al., 2024). Air entrainment and low porosity (<10%) improve cyclic stability.

**Thermal and Fire Resistance** - Geopolymers retain structural integrity at temperatures up to 800–1000 °C (Goryunova et al., 2023; Mahmoodi et al., 2025; Nawaz et al., 2020). Unlike OPC, which may spall beyond 600 °C, geopolymer matrices remain dimensionally stable and exhibit lower thermal conductivity (0.3–0.6 W/m·K) (Bourbigot et al., 2021; Nkwaju et al., 2019).

Overall, durability performance consistently exceeds OPC in acidic, sulfate, chloride, and high-temperature environments.

## 5.3 Long-Term Performance and Service-Life Considerations

While short- and medium-term durability is well documented (Alahmari et al., 2023; Farhan et al., 2024; Nawaz et al., 2020), long-term service-life data beyond five to ten years remain limited. Most studies focus on accelerated laboratory exposure rather than real infrastructure monitoring.

Carbonation behavior differs from OPC systems due to lower calcium buffering capacity (Brahami et al., 2022; Cui et al., 2023). Although carbonation depth is generally modest (2–4 mm within 6–12 months), long-term pH evolution and its effect on reinforcement passivation require further investigation.

Creep and shrinkage characteristics are generally 30–40% lower than OPC (Brahami et al., 2022), yet large-scale structural monitoring over decades remains insufficiently documented. Consequently, long-term predictive models require further validation through field-scale demonstration projects.

The absence of multi-decade durability datasets represents one of the most important research gaps limiting full-scale code integration.

## 5.4 Reinforcement Compatibility and Corrosion Behavior

Steel reinforcement compatibility is a critical factor in structural design. Although chloride permeability is significantly reduced (Chiranjeevi et al., 2023), the corrosion protection mechanism differs from OPC due to lower portlandite content.

Geopolymer systems maintain high alkalinity (Mohammed et al., 2021), supporting passive film formation on steel surfaces. However, because the matrix contains less calcium hydroxide, buffering capacity against carbonation may be reduced compared with OPC (Brahami et al., 2022).

Research indicates that stress–strain behavior, elastic modulus, and mechanical compatibility remain comparable to conventional concrete (Cui et al., 2023; Mohammed et al., 2021), though elastic modulus may be slightly lower for equivalent compressive strength grades (Brahami et al., 2022).

Design implications include - aequate cover thickness in carbonation-prone environments, consideration of corrosion-resistant reinforcement in marine applications and performance-based durability modelling. While laboratory evidence supports satisfactory corrosion resistance, extended field validation remains necessary for widespread structural confidence.

**Table 4** presents the mechanical and durability performance parameters of agricultural-waste-based geopolymers, covering strength, porosity, chemical resistance, thermal stability, and microstructural integrity. It summarizes key influencing factors, optimization strategies, and comparative advantages over OPC concrete.

*Table 4. Mechanical and durability performance parameters of agricultural waste-based geopolymers.*

| Property Category | Key Factors / Variables | Typical Range / Value | Performance Behavior and Trends | Enhancement Strategies | Comparative Advantage over OPC Concrete |
|---|---|---|---|---|---|
| **Compressive Strength** | - Si/Al ratio (2.0–2.5 optimum)<br>- Activator concentration (8–14 M NaOH)<br>- Water-to-solid ratio (0.25–0.35)<br>- Curing temperature (60–80 °C, 24–48 h)<br>- Particle fineness | 20–40 MPa (3 days)<br>40–70 MPa (28 days)<br>Up to 80–90 MPa (long-term) | Strength increases with proper Si/Al balance and controlled curing. Excess alkali may cause microcracks. Higher temperature accelerates polymerization and strength gain. | - Hybrid precursor blending (RHA + metakaolin / SCBA + fly ash)<br>- Nano-additives (nano-silica, nano-alumina)<br>- Controlled curing & optimized water ratio | Equal or higher strength than OPC concrete with faster early gain; improved microstructure and reduced porosity |
| **Flexural / Tensile Strength** | - Reinforcement (natural/ synthetic fibers)<br>- Matrix homogeneity | 3–8 MPa (flexural)<br>2–5 MPa (tensile) | Fibers improve ductility and crack resistance; smoother stress transfer in fine-grained matrices | - Addition of basalt, sisal, or polypropylene fibers | 1.2–1.5× improvement in post-crack performance compared to cement concrete |
| **Density and Porosity** | - Water content<br>- Ash fineness<br>- Aggregate type | Density: 2100–2400 kg/m³<br>Porosity: 5–12% | Low water content yields dense microstructure; finer ash lowers pore connectivity | - Use of fine SCBA or POFA to fill voids<br>- Vacuum or steam curing | Lower open porosity reduces permeability and enhances durability |
| **Acid Resistance** | - Absence of $Ca(OH)_2$<br>- Aluminosilicate gel composition | Strength loss <10% after 3–6 months in 1 M $H_2SO_4$ | Cross-linked Si–O–Al bonds resist acidic degradation; minimal gypsum formation | - Use low-Ca precursors (RHA, SCBA)<br>- Add silica fume for extra densification | Outperforms OPC which loses up to 40–50% strength in same exposure |
| **Sulfate Resistance** | - CaO content <5%<br>- Dense aluminosilicate matrix | No expansion / cracking after 90 days in $MgSO_4$ | Geopolymers resist ettringite formation; maintain dimensional stability | - Controlled alkali ratio; inclusion of pozzolanic blend | Highly superior to OPC concrete (which expands under sulfate exposure) |

continued on following page

*Table 4. Continued*

| Property Category | Key Factors / Variables | Typical Range / Value | Performance Behavior and Trends | Enhancement Strategies | Comparative Advantage over OPC Concrete |
|---|---|---|---|---|---|
| **Chloride Permeability** | - Pore structure<br>- Activator ratio | 500–1500 coulombs (low permeability class) | Dense gel network limits ion diffusion; protects reinforcement | - Fine filler addition (nano-silica)<br>- Prolonged curing | Better corrosion resistance than OPC; ideal for marine or coastal environments |
| **Freeze–Thaw Resistance** | - Porosity <10%<br>- Air entrainment | ≥90% residual strength after 300 cycles | Stable structure under freezing; minimal microcracking | - Use air-entraining admixtures<br>- Hydrophobic surface treatment | Comparable or superior performance to air-entrained OPC concretes |
| **Carbonation Resistance** | - Alkalinity retention<br>- Cover thickness | Slow carbonation rate; limited depth after 6–12 months | Geopolymers have lower Ca content; $CO_2$ mainly reacts with residual alkalis | - Increase cover for reinforcement<br>- Apply surface sealers | Slightly lower than OPC due to limited buffer capacity |
| **Thermal / Fire Resistance** | - Silica-rich precursors (RHA, SCBA)<br>- Porosity & binder phase | Stable up to 800–1000 °C Conductivity: 0.3–0.6 W/m·K | Retains structural integrity; minimal spalling; may gain strength due to sintering | - Add lightweight aggregates (perlite, pumice)<br>- Controlled curing for pore uniformity | Far superior to OPC (fails at ~600 °C); excellent for tunnels, refractory elements |
| **Microstructural Integrity** | - Gel morphology<br>- Bonding of aluminosilicate matrix | Dense, uniform network; C–A–S–H and N–A–S–H gel coexistence | Refined microstructure enhances mechanical and durability synergy | - Hybrid blending and nano-reinforcement | Consistent long-term stability and self-healing potential |

Key Observations

- Strength optimization in agricultural-waste geopolymers depends primarily on *chemical balance (Si/Al ≈ 2)*, *alkali dosage*, and *curing regime.*
- Durability exceeds that of OPC due to the absence of portlandite, producing resistance to acids, sulfates, and chloride ingress.
- Fire performance is exceptional, maintaining structural integrity up to 1000 °C, making them suitable for industrial and defense infrastructure.

- Use of nano-additives and fiber reinforcement provides superior toughness, while blended ashes (e.g., RHA + SCBA) optimize cost and environmental impact.

**Table 5** presents the key optimization parameters, recommended ranges, and their functional roles in achieving maximum strength, durability, and microstructural stability in agricultural-waste-based geopolymers. It summarizes how variables such as Si/Al ratio, activator chemistry, curing regime, particle fineness, blending strategies, nano-additives, and reinforcement influence geopolymerization behavior and final performance, while also providing practical guidelines for mix design and field implementation.

*Table 5. Optimization parameters and recommended ranges for maximum strength and durability in agricultural waste-based geopolymers.*

| Optimization Parameter | Recommended Range / Value | Role in Geopolymerization | Observed Effect on Properties | Practical Recommendations |
|---|---|---|---|---|
| **Si/Al Ratio** | 1.5 – 2.5 (optimum ≈ 2.0) | Determines polymeric network cross-linking density | Low ratio (<1.5): rapid setting, lower long-term strength; High ratio (>3.0): excessive silica → incomplete polymerization | Maintain balanced Si/Al ≈ 2.0 using blended precursors (RHA + SCBA / POFA + fly ash) |
| **Alkali Activator Concentration (NaOH or KOH)** | 8 – 14 M (commonly 10 M) | Controls dissolution rate of Si and Al species | Below 6 M: incomplete activation → weak matrix; Above 14 M: thermal stress and efflorescence | Use 10–12 M for optimum strength; pre-mix activators for 24 h to stabilize |
| **Silicate to Hydroxide Ratio ($Na_2SiO_3$ / NaOH)** | 1.5 – 2.5 | Enhances Si content in activator solution, improves gel formation | Low ratio (<1.0): weak bonding; High ratio (>2.5): delayed setting | Maintain ~2.0 for balanced workability and strength |
| **Water-to-Solid Ratio (W/S)** | 0.25 – 0.35 | Influences porosity, workability, and setting time | Low W/S (<0.25): poor workability; High W/S (>0.4): porous structure, low strength | 0.30 ± 0.02 ensures optimum density and compaction |
| **Curing Temperature** | 60 – 80 °C | Accelerates geopolymerization and strength development | Below 50 °C: incomplete reaction; Above 90 °C: dehydration, cracking | 70 ± 5 °C for 24–48 h ensures early strength and dense microstructure |

continued on following page

*Table 5. Continued*

| Optimization Parameter | Recommended Range / Value | Role in Geopolymerization | Observed Effect on Properties | Practical Recommendations |
|---|---|---|---|---|
| **Curing Duration** | 24 – 72 hours (thermal) 7 – 28 days (ambient) | Affects polymer chain growth and water removal | Longer curing improves structural stability; rapid curing may cause microcracks | Combine 24 h thermal curing + 7-day ambient for high early and long-term strength |
| **Particle Fineness of Ash** | <75 µm (preferably 10–20 µm) | Controls dissolution rate and packing density | Finer particles increase reactivity and reduce voids | Use mechanical grinding for consistent particle size <20 µm |
| **Activator to Binder Ratio (A/B)** | 0.4 – 0.6 by mass | Determines alkali availability and reaction intensity | Low ratio: incomplete dissolution; High ratio: efflorescence, brittleness | Optimum ~0.5 for good strength and durability |
| **Blending Strategy (Hybrid Mixes)** | RHA + SCBA (60:40) POFA + Fly Ash (50:50) | Balances silica and alumina sources | Enhanced workability, strength > 70 MPa, and reduced porosity | Hybridization improves Si/Al ratio and packing density |
| **Nano-Additives (Nano-$SiO_2$, Nano-$Al_2O_3$)** | 1 – 3 wt.% of binder | Acts as nucleation sites and pore filler | Increases compressive strength by 15–25% and reduces water absorption | Use <2% for cost-efficiency and uniform dispersion |
| **Fiber Reinforcement (Basalt, Sisal, PP)** | 0.5 – 1.5% volume fraction | Arrests crack propagation and increases ductility | Enhances flexural and impact resistance by 20–40% | Use 1% basalt or 1.2% sisal for optimum results |
| **Aggregate Type and Gradation** | Well-graded river sand + crushed stone | Controls compaction, density, and strength transfer | Proper grading minimizes voids and enhances microstructural bonding | Follow IS 383:2016 or ASTM C33 grading standards |
| **pH of Activator Solution** | 12.5 – 13.5 | Determines ionic mobility during dissolution | pH < 12 → incomplete reaction; >13.5 → precipitation of gels | Maintain ~13.0 for controlled polymerization |
| **Additive Use (e.g., Borax, Sodium Sulfate)** | 0.1 – 0.5% by weight | Acts as setting retarder or accelerator depending on mix | Stabilizes workability; prevents flash setting at high molarity | Use small dosages; test for compatibility with ashes |
| **Cooling Regime after Curing** | Gradual air cooling (not quenching) | Reduces thermal shock and cracking | Maintains structural continuity and limits shrinkage | Allow gradual cooling over 4–6 hours before demolding |

Key Interpretations:

- The optimal geopolymer mix design requires *simultaneous control* of Si/Al ratio, alkali concentration, and curing regime.
- Hybrid blending (e.g., RHA–SCBA or POFA–fly ash) balances chemistry and improves mechanical stability.
- Nano-additives and fibers yield substantial improvements in compressive and flexural strength with marginal cost impact.
- Thermal curing (70 °C, 24–48 h) consistently delivers >70 MPa compressive strength for agricultural-waste-based binders.

Table 6 presents a detailed comparison between agricultural-waste-based geopolymer concrete and ordinary Portland cement concrete across mechanical, durability, thermal, environmental, and sustainability metrics. It highlights the superior performance and significantly lower carbon footprint of geopolymer systems.

*Table 6. Comparative Performance of agricultural-waste-based geopolymers and ordinary portland cement (OPC) concrete.*

| Property / Performance Indicator | Agricultural-Waste-Based Geopolymer Concrete (AW-GPC) | Ordinary Portland Cement (OPC) Concrete | Comparative Remarks / Key Insights |
|---|---|---|---|
| **Primary Binder Composition** | Aluminosilicate gel (N–A–S–H / C–A–S–H) from ashes such as RHA, SCBA, POFA | Calcium-silicate-hydrate (C–S–H) gel formed by hydration of clinker | Geopolymers are Ca-lean, silica-rich, and chemically more stable in aggressive environments |
| **Compressive Strength (28 days)** | 40 – 70 MPa (can exceed 80 MPa with optimized curing) | 30 – 50 MPa (typical structural concrete) | AW-GPC shows 20–40% higher strength and faster early-age development |
| **Flexural Strength** | 3 – 8 MPa (improves with fiber reinforcement) | 2 – 5 MPa | Comparable or higher; enhanced crack-bridging when fibers or nano-silica added |
| **Tensile Strength (Splitting)** | 2 – 5 MPa | 2 – 3 MPa | Slightly higher due to denser microstructure and lower shrinkage |
| **Elastic Modulus** | 25 – 35 GPa (depends on mix density) | 30 – 35 GPa | Slightly lower but adequate for design; compensated by higher strength/ductility |
| **Density** | 2100 – 2400 kg/m$^3$ | 2300 – 2500 kg/m$^3$ | Slightly lighter; enables lower dead load and better thermal insulation |

continued on following page

*Table 6. Continued*

| Property / Performance Indicator | Agricultural-Waste-Based Geopolymer Concrete (AW-GPC) | Ordinary Portland Cement (OPC) Concrete | Comparative Remarks / Key Insights |
|---|---|---|---|
| **Water Absorption** | 1 – 4% | 5 – 8% | Much lower absorption → less permeability and improved durability |
| **Porosity (Total)** | 5 – 10% | 10 – 18% | Denser matrix; improved impermeability and reduced efflorescence |
| **Acid Resistance (1 M $H_2SO_4$ / HCl)** | Strength loss < 10% after 6 months | Strength loss > 40% after 6 months | Excellent chemical resistance due to absence of portlandite ($Ca(OH)_2$) |
| **Sulfate Resistance** | No visible cracking; negligible expansion | Severe expansion and cracking due to ettringite | Outstanding performance; long-term dimensional stability |
| **Chloride Permeability (ASTM C1202)** | 500 – 1500 coulombs (Low) | 2000 – 4000 coulombs (High–Moderate) | 60–80% reduction in chloride diffusion; ideal for marine structures |
| **Freeze–Thaw Resistance** | ≥ 90% residual strength after 300 cycles | 70–85% residual strength | Superior stability under cyclic freezing and thawing |
| **Carbonation Depth (6–12 months)** | 2 – 4 mm | 4 – 8 mm | Slower carbonation but lower buffering capacity—adequate with proper cover |
| **Thermal Conductivity** | 0.3 – 0.6 W/m·K | 1.4 – 1.7 W/m·K | 2–3× better insulation; useful for energy-efficient buildings |
| **Fire Resistance (Integrity Limit)** | Stable up to 800–1000 °C; minor strength loss | Major cracking/spalling beyond 600 °C | Excellent for tunnels, industrial floors, and refractory structures |
| **Shrinkage / Creep** | 30–40% lower than OPC | Relatively high due to moisture loss and hydration heat | Reduced drying shrinkage and better dimensional stability |
| **Setting Time** | Adjustable; initial ≈ 30–60 min (ambient) | Initial ≈ 60–90 min | Comparable; can be tuned by activator concentration |
| **Curing Requirement** | Thermal curing (60–80 °C for 24–48 h) or ambient (≥ 7 days) | Moist curing for 28 days | Rapid early strength allows early demolding; less water usage |
| **Embodied $CO_2$ Emissions** | 150–250 kg $CO_2$ / t binder | 850–900 kg $CO_2$ / t binder | ~70–80% reduction in carbon footprint |
| **Energy Demand (Production)** | 1.5–2.0 GJ/t | 4.5–5.0 GJ/t | 60% energy saving due to use of waste residues |
| **Cost (Relative)** | Initially 5–10% higher (lab-scale) but competitive at scale | Conventional cost baseline | Cost parity achievable via local ash sources and industrialization |
| **Sustainability Index (Qualitative)** | ★★★★★ (Very High) | ★★☆☆☆ (Moderate) | AW-GPC aligns with circular economy & SDG 12 & 13 goals |

Key Interpretions

- Agricultural-waste-based geopolymers (AW-GPC) consistently outperform OPC concrete in strength, chemical durability, and thermal stability.
- They exhibit 60–80% lower $CO_2$ emissions and comparable or superior mechanical properties, making them ideal for green construction and climate-resilient infrastructure.
- Slight disadvantages include the need for controlled curing and alkali handling, but these are offset by longevity, sustainability, and performance gains.

*Figure 1. Comparison of Agricultural-Waste-Based Geopolymer Concrete (AW-GPC) and Ordinary Portland Cement (OPC) across key performance parameters.*

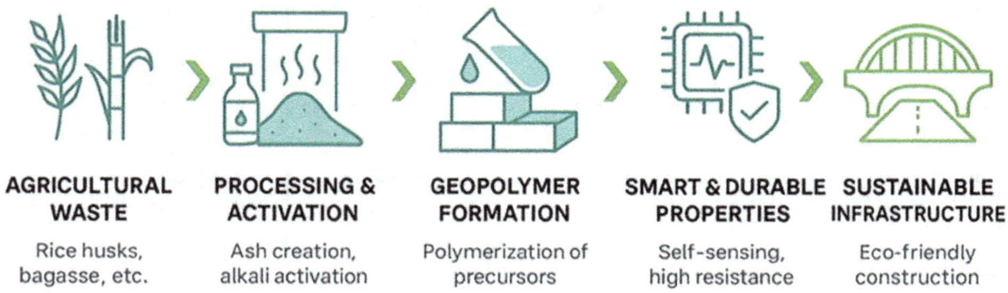


# 6. MIXTURE DESIGN AND PROCESSING TECHNOLOGIES

## 6.1 Systematic Mixture Proportion Optimization

Designing the right mixture for agricultural-waste-based geopolymers is one of the most important steps in achieving consistent performance (Alaneme et al., 2024; Matsimbe et al., 2022). Traditional mixture development relied mainly on trial and error, where researchers adjusted proportions until they achieved the desired strength and workability (Rathnayaka et al., 2024). This process, while effective in small-scale studies, consumes time and materials (Rathnayaka et al., 2024). Modern approaches now use statistical and computational tools to shorten the path to optimization.

In the traditional experimental method, the first step is to characterize the precursor material—measuring its chemical composition, fineness, and reactivity. Next comes the design of the alkaline activator: choosing between sodium or potassium systems, setting the hydroxide concentration, and selecting the silicate-to-hydroxide ratio. The liquid-to-solid ratio is then adjusted to balance flowability with final strength. Multiple trial batches are prepared and tested, and the most promising combination is refined through further iterations. Although effective, this method often misses complex interactions among variables (Matsimbe et al., 2022).

Statistical Design-of-Experiments techniques such as Response Surface Methodology or Taguchi *methods* now provide a more systematic alternative (Callai et al., 2021; Driouich et al., 2020; Lo et al., 2022; Santana et al., 2020). In RSM, selected parameters—like ash proportion, activator molarity, and liquid-to-solid ratio—are varied according to a planned experimental matrix (Quiatchon et al., 2021; Wu et al., 2023). For example, a Box-Behnken or Central Composite Design can reveal how each variable and their interactions influence compressive strength, workability, and setting time. Mathematical models derived from these experiments predict responses for untested mixtures, allowing researchers to locate an optimal composition with fewer trials. Taguchi's orthogonal array designs emphasize robustness by identifying mixtures that perform reliably even when production conditions vary (Obeidy et al., 2024; Rahman et al., 2021). Together, these tools have transformed mixture design from guesswork into quantitative optimization (Callai et al., 2021).

### 6.1.2 Machine Learning and Artificial Intelligence in Design

Recent years have seen a growing role for artificial intelligence in materials development (Jayakumar & Park, n.d.; Tanyıldızı, 2024). Machine-learning models, such as artificial neural networks, random-forest regressors, and genetic algorithms, can learn patterns from experimental data and predict properties of new mixtures (Chen et al., 2022; Gautam et al., 2024; Khan et al., 2022; Rathnayaka et al., 2024; Sharma et al., 2022; Yılmaz et al., 2024; Zou et al., 2022). Once trained on datasets containing input variables—like precursor composition and activator ratios—and outputs such as strength or setting time, these models can quickly forecast performance without laboratory testing (Abdelmongy et al., 2024).

For example, an ANN trained on hundreds of geopolymer experiments can predict compressive strength with over 95 percent accuracy (Rathnayaka et al., 2024). Genetic algorithms extend this concept by exploring countless possible combinations to find global optima that balance multiple objectives, such as high strength and low cost (Nguyen et al., 2024). These AI-based techniques are now being combined with RSM and physical modeling to form hybrid predictive systems. In essence, data science is helping transform the art of geopolymer mixture design into a science guided by algorithms.

## 6.2 Processing and Manufacturing Technologies

After the right proportions are identified, proper processing ensures that every batch performs as expected. Uniform mixing, temperature control, and correct curing are all essential.

During mixing and batching, the dry ingredients—agricultural ash, supplementary materials, and fine aggregates—are blended before the activator solution is added. Mixing time usually ranges from five to ten minutes (Santi et al., 2022). In large-scale operations, planetary or twin-shaft mixers are preferred for their efficiency and uniform dispersion (Koçyiğit, 2024). Because the alkaline reaction is exothermic, controlling temperature is crucial; pre-cooling the activator or using chilled water can prevent premature stiffening in hot climates (Leiva et al., 2019). Longer mixing durations can lead to better geopolymer chain formation (Mukhametkaliyev et al., 2022).

Workability and rheology influence how easily the fresh material can be placed (Barve et al., 2024; Muthukrishnan et al., 2020; Vītola et al., 2020). Geopolymers behave as shear-thinning fluids, meaning their viscosity decreases under shear during mixing or vibration and increases again at rest (Dong et al., 2023; Gebeyehu et al., 2021; Jiang et al., 2017; Rifaai et al., 2019). This behavior allows them to fill molds efficiently while maintaining shape afterward. Adjusting water content, particle packing, and using high-range water-reducing admixtures (especially polycarboxylate ethers adapted for high-pH systems) helps achieve smooth flow without segregation. Setting time can be controlled with small doses of retarders like citric or tartaric acid for longer workability, or accelerators such as calcium compounds for rapid construction needs (Ranjbar et al., 2020). The composition of the geopolymer and additives can also influence the initial viscosity and setting time (Christiansen et al., 2019; Santucci et al., 2019).

Casting and placement methods for geopolymers resemble those for ordinary concrete. They can be poured into molds and vibrated for compaction, or formulated as self-compacting mixes that require no vibration. For large infrastructure works, pumping systems can transport geopolymer concrete provided the mix remains workable for several hours. Emerging technologies like 3D printing use extrusion-based systems that deposit geopolymer layers one atop another (Barve et al., 2023; Hou et al., 2020; Mukhametkaliyev et al., 2022; Munir et al., 2021; Ranjbar et al., 2021; Strohle et al., 2022). Agricultural waste-derived binders are particularly suitable for this because of their rapid strength gain and adjustable rheology (Jiang et al., 2017; Lin et al., 2023; Liu et al., 2024; Wei et al., 2022).

Curing is another decisive factor. Two broad methods exist: ambient curing and heat curing (El-Zeadani et al., 2021; Rabie et al., 2022). Ambient curing, performed at room temperature and high humidity, suits on-site applications and produces good long-term strength, though initial development is slower (Kim et al., 2025; Statkauskas et al., 2024). Heat curing, usually at 60–80 °C for one or two days, greatly accelerates reaction rates and is ideal for precast elements (Alaneme et al., 2024; El-Zeadani et al., 2021; Nawaz et al., 2020; Rabie et al., 2022). Advanced approaches such as microwave curing or steam curing in sealed chambers are being explored to shorten production time while maintaining uniform quality (Hong & Kim, 2019; Statkauskas et al., 2024). The goal in all cases is to provide sufficient moisture and temperature to complete polymerization without causing cracks from drying or thermal stress.

Finally, quality control involves verifying precursor composition through X-ray fluorescence, checking particle size distribution, and monitoring key fresh and hardened properties (Dulaimi et al., 2023; Kaze et al., 2020; Kogbara et al., 2023; Kursula et al., 2023; Mashifana& Sithole, 2020). Statistical process control charts track variations in strength or setting time, allowing early correction before defects occur. Consistent production standards are essential if geopolymers are to compete with conventional cement products on a large scale.

# 7. LIFE CYCLE ASSESSMENT AND SUSTAINABILITY METRICS

## 7.1 Carbon Footprint and Energy Impacts

Assessing sustainability requires looking beyond mechanical properties to consider environmental performance across the material's life cycle. Life Cycle Assessment measures total emissions and energy use from raw-material extraction to end-of-life recycling.

In the case of Portland-cement concrete, the main impact arises from limestone calcination and fossil-fuel combustion in the kiln. Producing one tonne of cement emits about 0.9 tonnes of $CO_2$, so a cubic meter of ordinary concrete embodies roughly 350–450 kg of $CO_2$ (Turner & Collins, 2013). By contrast, agricultural-waste geopolymers avoid limestone calcination entirely (Alawi et al., 2023). The ashes used are by-products already produced in the agricultural or energy sectors (Alaneme et al., 2023). Their processing—grinding and controlled burning—adds only 0.05–0.15 kg $CO_2$ per kg of ash. The major contributor to the geopolymer's carbon footprint is the alkaline activator: sodium hydroxide and sodium silicate together emit about 1–1.5 kg $CO_2$ per kg produced. Even with these inputs, total embodied emissions for geopolymer concrete fall to around 120–200 kg $CO_2$ per $m^3$—roughly a 60–75 percent reduction compared with conventional concrete (Borges et al., 2014). Geopolymer concrete has been recognized as an environmentally friendly building material that reduces energy-intensive and emission-intensive cement use, thereby lowering environmental impact (Shi et al., 2021). Studies have shown that geopolymer concrete can reduce CO2 emissions by 72.4% compared to traditional Portland cement concrete (Borges et al., 2014), with some reporting a 44.7% lower carbon footprint for alkali-activated binary concrete (Shi et al., 2021) and up to 50% less CO2 for FA-SF geopolymer concrete (Cong et al., 2024).

Energy consumption follows a similar trend. Most energy in cement production goes into high-temperature kilns, whereas geopolymer processing operates at moderate temperatures and often uses renewable power from agricultural residues (Alawi et al., 2023). Geopolymer concrete can reduce energy consumption by 45.8% compared to Portland cement-based concrete (Borges et al., 2014). Optimization of activator dosage, transport distances, and renewable-energy integration can further shrink the footprint. Overall, agricultural-waste geopolymers deliver substantial climate benefits while turning a disposal problem into a resource.

## 7.2 Circular Economy Principles and Resource Efficiency

The concept of a circular economy emphasizes keeping materials in use for as long as possible and eliminating waste. Agricultural-waste geopolymers embody this philosophy. They transform residues that would otherwise be burned or landfilled into valuable construction inputs, thus closing material loops between agriculture, energy, and construction sectors (Alaneme et al., 2023). This innovative material, made from agricultural waste sources rich in aluminosilicate, provides a substitute for traditional cement in terms of quality and cost (Alaneme et al., 2023).

At the end of their service life, geopolymer structures can also re-enter the cycle. Crushed geopolymer concrete can serve as aggregate for new mixes or as base material in road construction. Because geopolymers are largely inert, they pose minimal leaching risks compared to industrial-waste binders. Designing for deconstruction and reuse—using mechanical rather than chemical connections—can further extend the circular chain.

Economically, while the initial material cost of geopolymers can be slightly higher due to activator expenses, savings arise through reduced maintenance, longer service life, and potential carbon-credit revenues (Alawi et al., 2023). Many studies find geopolymers to be at least cost-competitive, if not cheaper, over the long term, when accounting for total life-cycle costs (Firdous et al., 2022). Rural communities also benefit through job creation in collection, processing, and transport of agricultural wastes, turning environmental liabilities into income sources.

## 7.3 Social and Environmental Co-Benefits

The adoption of agricultural-waste geopolymers supports broader sustainability goals. For farmers, organized waste collection systems provide additional revenue streams and discourage harmful open-field burning that causes severe air pollution in many regions. Cleaner air means better health outcomes for nearby communities. Environmentally, replacing cement reduces extraction of limestone and sand, conserving landscapes and biodiversity.

At a global level, this technology contributes directly to the United Nations Sustainable Development Goals—particularly SDG 9, SDG 12, and SDG 13. By linking rural agriculture to modern infrastructure, agricultural-waste geopolymers promote inclusive and sustainable industrialization while addressing climate change and waste management challenges simultaneously.

## 7.4 Economic Feasibility and Industrial-Scale Cost Modeling

While the environmental benefits are well established (Borges et al., 2014; Shi et al., 2021; Cong et al., 2024), the industrial scale economic feasibility analysis is more complex.

When it comes to CAPEX regarding production of geopolymers using agricultural waste, expenses can be expected from the addition of units used for ash processing (combustion under control, grinding, and milling), along with units for the storage of alkalis, and units used for mixing that are resistant to high pH, and for controlled curing (Maldonado-Alameda et al., 2022; Koçyiğit, 2024). It is possible that these additional elements of infrastructure will be more than the additional expenses for more conventional batching plants during setup.

OPEX is certainly dominated more than the rest by expenses related to alkaline activators. Production of sodium hydroxide and sodium silicate is a large contributor to both material cost and embodied carbon (Alawi et al., 2023). In many of the reported designs for the mixes, activators are 40-60% of the cost of the binder. In addition, the cost of transporting the ash to the sites for collection and processing is another cost that will impact the economics of the entire operation.

However, under the circumstance of industrial scale production, cost parity can be reached when the ash is local, the transport distance is short, and when the waste-derived silicate solutions, or hybrids that contain low-alkali systems are used. For assessment horizons pertaining to life cycle (LCA), reduced maintenance and greater durability, along with possible carbon credits offer further cost savings and improved competitiveness (Firdous et al., 2022). Thus, economic sustainability also depends heavily on the supply-chain localization and activator (alkaline) optimization more than the cost of the raw materials.

## 7.5 Stakeholder Integration and Global South Implementation

Solid agricultural waste based geopolymers could benefit development in economically disadvantaged areas. Decentralized collection of ash could open rural jobs and minimize the burning of agricultural waste in open fires (Alaneme et al. 2023). Regional cooperatives could ash process using low-energy, simple, and small-scale grinding devices.

Generating profitable circular value chains along the integration of farmers, municipal authorities, builders, and small enterprises is possible. Where the waste sector is informal, ash collection systems can provide structure, formulating payment streams and ensuring quality. Localized systems improve the economic viability and reduce transport emissions.

Nonetheless, it is necessary to develop and make simple designs for low-tech systems that reduce the need for formal low-tech systems. The integration of advanced materials science with low-tech community production systems is a necessary focus for research and policy.

# 8. INFRASTRUCTURE APPLICATIONS

## 8.1 Transportation Infrastructure

The most direct and large-scale application of agricultural-waste geopolymers is in road and pavement construction. Rigid pavements made from rice-husk-ash or fly-ash-based geopolymer concrete have demonstrated compressive strengths between 35 and 50 MPa and flexural strengths around 5 MPa—sufficient for highways and rural roads (Kwunjai et al., 2020). One demonstration project built a 2.5-kilometer rural road using locally available RHA and fly ash. Although the initial cost was about 12 percent higher than a conventional concrete road, the environmental benefits and avoided waste-disposal costs more than compensated.

Geopolymer binders also serve effectively in base and sub-base layers of flexible pavements, where small amounts of activator stabilize soil or aggregate mixtures (Ikotun et al., 2024; Jallu&Saride, 2024; Jeremiah et al., 2023; Rao et al., 2024; Saba &Arairo, 2024). These stabilized layers gain early strength, reduce thickness requirements, and resist water damage better than lime-treated bases. Because setting is slower at room temperature, proper compaction and curing are essential, but construction can still proceed with local equipment.

## 8.2 Building Construction

In structural applications, geopolymer concrete performs comparably to ordinary reinforced concrete. Beams, columns, and slabs produced from sugarcane-bagasse-ash or fly-ash blends routinely reach 50 MPa compressive strength (Kumar, 2024; Mushtaq et al., 2025).

Non-structural elements such as masonry blocks, façade panels, and partition walls also benefit from the technology. Geopolymer blocks, typically cured at moderate temperatures, achieve strengths between 10 and 25 MPa—adequate for wall construction—and provide excellent fire and thermal resistance (Ngui et al., 2022). Surface-cast façade panels made with geopolymer mortar can be finished to resemble stone or exposed aggregate, maintaining color and cleanliness over decades due to their chemical stability.

## 8.3 Water and Wastewater Infrastructure

Due to chemical resistance, geopolymers are ideal for wastewater treatment facilities, storage tanks, and drainage systems that encounter acids, sulfates, or chlorides (Marathe et al., 2025). In Thailand, a wastewater treatment plant replaced deteriorated cement linings with a 20-millimeter coating of rice-husk-ash geopolymer mortar. After four years in operation, even in an environment with pH 1–2, the coating remained intact while conventional cement coatings had failed within 18 months. Geopolymer samples have shown stable behavior in corrosive environments (Nawaz et al., 2020) and metakaolin-based geopolymer composites can improve durability against acidic conditions, suggesting their use in infrastructure exposed to harsh chemical environments (Marathe et al., 2025).

For potable-water storage, geopolymer concrete offers low permeability and neutral leaching behavior when properly cured. Precast geopolymer pipes are also emerging as durable, corrosion-resistant alternatives to steel-reinforced concrete pipes, particularly in coastal areas where chloride exposure is severe (Oumar, 2025; Rihawi et al., 2025; Shahedan et al., 2024).

## 8.4 Marine and Coastal Applications

Marine environments are among the harshest for construction materials, yet geopolymer composites perform exceptionally well there. Port walls, seawalls, and offshore platforms made from sugarcane-bagasse-ash and fly-ash-based mixtures show remarkable resistance to chloride penetration and abrasion (Nawaz et al., 2020). A harbor repair project in Indonesia used such a blend for tidal-zone patching; after two years, chloride ingress was measured at less than 5 millimeters, far below the levels seen in control samples of Portland-cement concrete. Geopolymers show a more stable behavior in corrosive environments, making them suitable for marine conditions (Nawaz et al., 2020).

Precast coastal-protection units like tetrapods and dolos can also be made with geopolymer binders. They offer high density for wave dissipation, excellent durability, and a lower carbon footprint, aligning perfectly with sustainability goals for coastal infrastructure. However, it's worth noting that some studies indicate lower resistance to chloride penetration for slag-based geopolymer concrete compared to ordinary Portland cement concrete in marine environments (Pasupathy et al., 2021). The seawater environment can also inhibit geopolymerization reactions (Li et al., 2019).

### 8.5 Specialized and Emerging Applications

Beyond conventional uses, agricultural-waste geopolymers are finding roles in high-temperature structures, radiation shielding, and additive manufacturing. Their thermal stability makes them suitable for furnaces, chimneys, and fire-resistant panels (Yin et al., 2020). When loaded with heavy minerals such as barite or magnetite, they provide radiation protection for hospitals and nuclear facilities.

The combination of rapid setting and tunable rheology also enables 3D-printed geopolymer structures, from small architectural features to full-scale emergency shelters built directly from local soil and agricultural ash (Dwivedi, 2024; Mohamed et al., 2025; Sikora et al., 2025). The feasibility of employing industrial wastes in highly porous 3D-printed geopolymer lattices has been demonstrated, especially for wastewater treatment applications (Almeida et al., 2024). This capability opens a new frontier for sustainable construction, particularly in remote or disaster-affected regions where conventional materials are scarce.

## 9. STANDARDS, CODES, AND IMPLEMENTATION FRAMEWORK

### 9.1 Current Standardization Status

Although research on geopolymers has progressed rapidly, formal standards and codes are still catching up (Deventer et al., 2011). At present, most testing and design procedures for these materials borrow from existing cement-concrete standards, with necessary modifications to account for their unique chemistry (Deventer et al., 2011; Zubrod, 2013). One of the main limitations for full integration of geopolymer technology into the global concrete materials industry is the absence of technical standards (Valente et al., 2021).

Internationally, ASTM International has started to develop new performance-based standard specifications for geopolymer concrete (Zubrod, 2013). The engineering standard for the selection of geopolymer source materials is not yet available, however, existing engineering standards for agricultural or industrial waste materials used as precursors for mortar and concrete materials, such as ASTM C618-19 and ASTM C989-09, are referenced (Amaludin et al., 2023). The RILEM technical committee has also been involved in defining testing guidelines for alkali-activated materials (Deventer et al., 2011). Similar work is under way within the European Committee for Standardization and in national agencies across Australia and India. For instance, various Indian Standards are referenced in the context of construction materials (Jamwal et al., 2024; Jannat et al., 2020). These bodies are developing new terminologies, methods for assessing precursor reactivity, and durability benchmarks that accurately reflect geopolymer behavior.

At the regional level, some progress has been made. While a specific reference for Australia's Standard AS 3582.3 was not found in the search results, Indian Standards are continually being referenced and reviewed for construction materials (Jamwal et al., 2024; Jannat et al., 2020). Such developments signal growing institutional acceptance.

## 9.2 Building Codes and Design Provisions

Because building codes traditionally rely on material equivalence, structural design using geopolymer concrete currently proceeds by performance-based approval (Zubrod, 2013). Engineers demonstrate that the new material meets or exceeds the mechanical and durability requirements of conventional concrete (Zubrod, 2013). Proper standard codes that consider performance as a base for concrete evaluation may be the most suitable solution for adapting such new materials (Valente et al., 2021). Once equivalence is established—usually through compressive-strength tests, elastic-modulus data, and long-term durability studies—designs can be approved on a project-specific basis (Zubrod, 2013).

Research shows that geopolymer concretes generally possess stress-strain behavior, creep, and shrinkage characteristics comparable to or better than cement concretes (Cui et al., 2023; Zubrod, 2013), though their elastic modulus may be slightly lower for a given strength grade (Brahami et al., 2022). Data analysis has been conducted on various mechanical properties of geopolymer concrete, including compressive strength, splitting tensile strength, flexural strength, modulus of elasticity, Poisson's ratio, and strain corresponding to peak compressive stress (Mohammed et al., 2021). For design purposes, the same limit-state methods and safety factors can therefore be applied, with minor adjustments. Gradually, international organizations such as the American Concrete Institute are preparing state-of-the-art reports to provide clearer guidance and pave the way for inclusion in mainstream codes (Alaneme et al., 2024; Amaludin et al., 2023).

## 9.3 Quality Assurance and Certification

For widespread adoption, reliable quality-control systems are essential. Manufacturers of geopolymer products are encouraged to follow ISO 9001 quality-management standards, ensuring consistent chemical composition, mixing accuracy, and curing control. Independent certification through environmental product declarations can document their reduced carbon footprint.

Contractors and field engineers also require proper training. Because geopolymers are often synthesized with highly alkaline solutions, they can be corrosive and hazardous, necessitating careful handling by workers wearing appropriate protective equipment (Mobili et al., 2020; Shi et al., 2019; Wang et al., 2023). Education and training programs for engineers and contractors are essential to familiarize them with the principles and practices of geopolymer concrete production (Alaneme et al., 2024). Certification of skilled technicians will help maintain uniform quality in production and placement, boosting confidence among engineers and regulators alike.

## 9.4 Implementation Roadmap

A practical strategy for implementation begins with demonstration projects (Deventer et al., 2011). Early efforts should target low-risk applications such as pavers, blocks, and non-structural panels. Once performance data confirm durability, larger structural elements and infrastructure components can follow.

Close cooperation among stakeholders is vital (Alaneme et al., 2024). This involves farmers and agricultural cooperatives supplying raw waste, processing facilities converting it into ash, contractors and engineers using it in construction, and governments providing policy incentives. Green-procurement policies—where public projects favor low-carbon materials—can accelerate adoption. Tax benefits or carbon-credit schemes for sustainable materials would further encourage industries to shift from conventional cement to geopolymers, with carbon pricing being a potential means to level cost differences (Rintala et al., 2021).

## 9.5 Occupational Safety and Alkali Handling Protocols

Production of geopolymers means working with highly alkaline solutions. These solutions have a pH of about 12.5 to 13.5 (Alaneme et al., 2024; Nawaz et al., 2020).

Sodium and potassium hydroxides are corrosive, having occupational safety risks. Contact with these substances can cause chemical burns, and the inhalation of the fumes can cause respiratory issues.

Consequently, for the industrial scaling of geopolymers, closed mixing systems, corrosion-resistant storage tanks, personal protection equipment, spill containment systems, and effluent neutralization systems burden increased costs of construction and set-up. Contractor and plant operator training is also needed for safe shuttle and use of the equipment, and for compliance with safety regulations while at work.

Handling alkalis is dangerous and need to be done carefully, like any other chemical industry. Given this, potential dangers can cause issues with stakeholder and regulatory approvals. Flexibility in the use of Standard Operating Procedures (SOPs) to elicit safety practices is highly encouraged.

## 9.6 Regulatory and Code Adoption Barriers

Even though there have been numerous studies done on this, integration of geopolymers into regulations is still minimal (Deventer et al., 2011; Valente et al., 2021; Zubrod, 2013). Given that structural design codes have been developed for Portland cement systems, the use of geopolymers is subject to performance-based approvals (Zubrod, 2013).

The lack of a standard for the classification of precursors, the different chemistry of ashes (Amaludin et al., 2023; Alaneme et al., 2024), the absence of agreed upon durability criteria, as well as the variability of ash chemistry, is what causes reluctance on the part of insurers and regulators. Although there are certain specifications for precursor materials in ASTM C618-19 and ASTM C989-09, specific regulations for geopolymers are still being developed.

Inclusion of the geo-polymers in the codes of practice and pilot projects to prove the durability of the geo-polymers will encourage regulators to accept geo-polymers as a structural material to be used in construction. The geo-polymers will then be included in the sub-standards of the ACI and IS standards in due time. The transitional pathway is to establish performance-based design at initial stages.

# 10. FUTURE DIRECTIONS AND RESEARCH NEEDS

## 10.1 Advanced Material Development

Next-generation agricultural-waste geopolymers aim not only to replace cement but also to deliver additional functionalities. Researchers are developing self-diagnostic systems that combine conductive networks and embedded sensors to detect stress or cracks in real time (Biondi et al., 2020; Mare & Ouellet-Plamondon, 2022; Vlachakis et al., 2020, 2023). Integrating wireless data transmission with these materials can enable continuous health monitoring of bridges and buildings (Mare & Ouellet-Plamondon, 2022). Self-healing capabilities in geopolymers are also being investigated to improve long-term durability and reduce maintenance needs (Luhar et al., 2021; Özen et al., 2023).

Another frontier is adaptive materials—geopolymers that change their properties in response to environmental conditions. Examples include color-changing formulations that indicate overheating or stress, and composites that self-regulate temperature through phase-change inclusions. Future infrastructure may thus be capable of sensing, healing, and adapting like living systems.

Expanding the range of usable precursors is equally important. Beyond rice husk or bagasse ash, scientists are experimenting with under-utilized residues such as coconut shell ash (Ngui et al., 2022), coffee husk ash, and even aquatic-plant biomass. Blending agricultural wastes with industrial by-products like slag or red mud can further improve performance while maintaining sustainability (Alaneme et al., 2023; Alawi et al., 2023; Hernández-Escobar et al., 2023). Developing low-alkalinity activators—including solid "one-part" formulations or bio-derived activators—will reduce cost and safety concerns, making geopolymer production more practical for small-scale operations (Kadhim et al., 2020; Mobili et al., 2020; Omran et al., 2023; Shi et al., 2019; Wang et al., 2023).

## 10.2 Scalability and Industrialization

Large-scale use requires efficient logistics and processing infrastructure. Mapping agricultural-waste availability through geographic-information-system tools can help plan regional ash-processing centers close to major farming zones (Blanco et al., 2018; Ghani et al., 2019; Khater et al., 2022). These facilities could operate seasonally, storing processed ash for year-round supply (Wandiga, 2020). While technically challenging, overcoming regulatory, supply chain, and product confidence barriers is essential for widespread adoption (Abbas et al., 2026; Bhatia et al., 2025; Dhiman et al., 2025a; Dhiman et al., 2025b; Deventer et al., 2011).

Automation and Industry 4.0 technologies will also reshape production (Motial et al., 2024; Khan et al., 2022; Ramesh et al., 2025). AI-controlled batching plants can monitor temperature, moisture, and mix ratios in real time, automatically adjusting parameters to ensure uniformity (Khan et al., 2022; Ramesh et al., 2025). Modular, containerized manufacturing units could be deployed quickly in developing regions, offering scalable capacity without massive capital investment.

Energy efficiency is another focus. Future plants may use solar-powered kilns for ash calcination or recover waste heat from biomass power stations. Such integration would make the entire production chain virtually carbon-neutral (Sharmin et al., 2024).

## 10.3 Long-Term Performance and Durability Research

While laboratory results are impressive, long-term field data are still limited, and uncertainties regarding durability, creep, shrinkage, and resistance to environmental cycles remain (Oumar, 2025; Valente et al., 2021). Researchers are now establishing extended exposure sites in different climates to monitor geopolymer structures for decades (Law et al., 2014; Reddy et al., 2012; Wasim et al., 2021). These studies track changes in strength, porosity, and chemical composition over time, providing the evidence base needed for codes and investors to trust the technology.

Understanding reinforcement behavior is also crucial. Although the dense geopolymer matrix protects steel well, carbonation could eventually reduce alkalinity (Köenig et al., 2020; Lamaa et al., 2023; Pouhet& Cyr, 2014). Investigations into alternative reinforcements—such as stainless steel, basalt fiber, or fiber-reinforced polymer bars—will ensure corrosion-free service life in aggressive environments.

Advanced modeling using digital twins can simulate long-term degradation under variable conditions, linking physical experiments with virtual predictions (Li et al., 2025). Such approaches allow faster evaluation of durability equivalent to decades of natural aging.

## 10.4 Economic and Market Development

For commercial viability, the cost of activators must fall. For instance, the cost of sodium silicate and sodium hydroxide can significantly impact economic feasibility (You et al., 2018). Local production of sodium hydroxide from salt brine or by-product recovery from chemical industries can lower expenses (Adesanya et al., 2020). Recycling of spent activators from demolished geopolymer structures is another emerging concept. Economies of scale and automation will further narrow the price gap with Portland cement (Rintala et al., 2021). Case studies suggest that geopolymer concrete can offer economic benefits through reduced material costs for certain compositions (Oyebisi et al., 2022) and improved sustainability performance (Firdous et al., 2022).

Strategically, initial market entry should target niche sectors where performance outweighs cost—such as high-temperature (Fan, 2020; He et al., 2020; Hussain et al., 2024), marine (Nawaz et al., 2020), or chemical-resistant structures (Albitar et al., 2017; Marathe et al., 2025). As production expands, costs will decline and mainstream markets such as housing and infrastructure can follow. Public-private partnerships, green bonds, and impact-investment funds can provide the capital required for scaling.

## 10.5 Global Implementation and Social Context

Developing nations, where both agricultural residues and construction demand are abundant, stand to gain the most. Locally produced geopolymers reduce dependence on imported cement, stimulate rural economies, and provide affordable, climate-resilient infrastructure (Al-Kasassbeh et al., 2023; Verma et al., 2022). Geopolymers are recognized for their potential to contribute to sustainable development by utilizing waste materials and reducing carbon emissions (Madirisha et al., 2024; Rahimpour et al., 2024; Sbahieh et al., 2023). Training programs, technology transfer, and South-South collaboration will ensure that knowledge spreads equitably (Alaneme et al., 2024).

From a climate-adaptation standpoint, geopolymers support resilient infrastructure in flood-prone or high-temperature regions (Fan, 2020). Their low permeability resists water damage, and their thermal stability withstands wildfires. Integrating these materials into national adaptation plans can strengthen both mitigation and resilience strategies.

Cultural acceptance is equally important. Combining modern geopolymer technology with traditional building styles can foster local pride while achieving sustainability. Encouraging participation of women and community groups in waste collection and manufacturing can also create inclusive green employment.

## 10.5 Global Implementation and Social Context

Developing nations, where both agricultural residues and construction demand are abundant, stand to gain the most. Locally produced geopolymers reduce dependence on imported cement, stimulate rural economies, and provide affordable, climate-resilient infrastructure. Training programs, technology transfer, and South-South collaboration will ensure that knowledge spreads equitably.

From a climate-adaptation standpoint, geopolymers support resilient infrastructure in flood-prone or high-temperature regions. Their low permeability resists water damage, and their thermal stability withstands wildfires. Integrating these materials into national adaptation plans can strengthen both mitigation and resilience strategies.

Cultural acceptance is equally important. Combining modern geopolymer technology with traditional building styles can foster local pride while achieving sustainability. Encouraging participation of women and community groups in waste collection and manufacturing can also create inclusive green employment.

## 10.5 Global Implementation and Social Context

Developing nations, where both agricultural residues and construction demand are abundant, stand to gain the most. Locally produced geopolymers reduce dependence on imported cement, stimulate rural economies, and provide affordable, climate-resilient infrastructure (Al-Kasassbeh et al., 2023; Verma et al., 2022). Geopolymers are recognized for their potential to contribute to sustainable development by utilizing waste materials and reducing carbon emissions (Madirisha et al., 2024; Rahimpour et al., 2024; Sbahieh et al., 2023). Training programs, technology transfer, and South-South collaboration will ensure that knowledge spreads equitably (Alaneme et al., 2024).

From a climate-adaptation standpoint, geopolymers support resilient infrastructure in flood-prone or high-temperature regions (Fan, 2020). Their low permeability resists water damage, and their thermal stability withstands wildfires (Fan, 2020; He et al., 2020; Hussain et al., 2024). Integrating these materials into national adaptation plans can strengthen both mitigation and resilience strategies.

Cultural acceptance is equally important. Combining modern geopolymer technology with traditional building styles can foster local pride while achieving sustainability. Encouraging participation of women and community groups in waste collection and manufacturing can also create inclusive green employment.

## 10.6 Integration with Digital Technologies

Digital transformation is revolutionizing construction, and geopolymers fit naturally into this shift. Through Internet-of-Things networks, sensors embedded in self-sensing geopolymers can feed data into Building Information Modeling platforms, allowing engineers to track structural health and maintenance needs (Biondi et al., 2020; Mare & Ouellet-Plamondon, 2022; Vlachakis et al., 2020, 2023). Artificial-intelligence algorithms can analyze these data to predict deterioration and optimize repairs, ensuring longer service life with lower costs (Abbasset al., 2025; Abbass, Akhai et al., 2025; Wadhwa et al., 2025)

Blockchain systems may record every stage—from waste collection to finished product—ensuring traceability, authenticity, and transparent carbon accounting. Ultimately, digital and material innovations will merge, producing smart, circular, and data-driven construction ecosystems (Khan et al., 2022; Ramesh et al., 2025)..

# 11. CHALLENGES AND MITIGATION STRATEGIES

## 11.1 Technical Challenges

The main technical difficulty lies in the variability of agricultural wastes. Their chemical composition depends on crop type, soil, and combustion conditions (Alaneme et al., 2023; Alawi et al., 2023; Hernández-Escobar et al., 2023). Inconsistent inputs can lead to variable quality of ash and unpredictable strength (Alaneme et al., 2023). Establishing standardized preprocessing—such as controlled burning and particle-size regulation—will minimize this variability. Mixing ashes from different sources can also help average out differences.

Workability control is another issue. Some geopolymer mixes set too quickly, especially under warm conditions, making placement difficult. Proper selection of retarders, temperature control during mixing, and tailored activator ratios can solve this.

Although laboratory durability results are excellent, uncertainties remain about long-term performance in extreme conditions such as freeze-thaw cycles or combined chemical attacks (Oumar, 2025; Valente et al., 2021). Continuous field monitoring and accelerated testing are essential until a large body of data confirms stability over decades (Law et al., 2014; Reddy et al., 2012; Wasim et al., 2021).

## 11.2 Economic and Market Challenges

Currently, geopolymer concretes can cost slightly more per cubic meter than Portland cement concretes, mainly due to alkaline activator prices and lack of large-scale production facilities (You et al., 2018). However, life-cycle analyses show that the total cost of ownership—including maintenance and durability—often favors geopolymers (Firdous et al., 2022; Oyebisi et al., 2022; Rintala et al., 2021). Expanding production capacity, localizing activator manufacturing (Adesanya et al., 2020), and incorporating carbon-credit incentives will make them more competitive.

Market acceptance remains a barrier because the construction industry is conservative by nature. Engineers and contractors prefer familiar materials. Demonstration projects, reliable performance data, and strong certification programs will gradually build trust (Alaneme et al., 2024; Deventer et al., 2011). Once awareness spreads that geopolymers meet the same engineering standards while offering major environmental gains, acceptance will accelerate.

## 11.3 Regulatory and Environmental Challenges

The absence of comprehensive standards and clear regulatory pathways can slow adoption (Deventer et al., 2011; Valente et al., 2021; Zubrod, 2013). Engaging with code-writing bodies, sharing research results, and promoting performance-based approval processes can fill this gap (Alaneme et al., 2024; Amaludin et al., 2023).

Environmental regulations also require careful management of alkaline materials to prevent worker injury or waste contamination. Geopolymers are often synthesized with highly alkaline solutions, necessitating careful handling by workers wearing appropriate protective equipment (Mobili et al., 2020; Shi et al., 2019; Wang et al., 2023). Training, personal-protective equipment, and proper neutralization of effluents will ensure safety and compliance. Governments can assist by issuing clear guidelines for handling and storage of activators, just as they do for conventional cement additives.

## 11.4 Social and Implementation Challenges

Widespread implementation depends on human capacity. Many workers, especially in rural or developing regions, have limited exposure to new construction technologies. Establishing training centers and integrating geopolymer technology into university curricula will create a skilled workforce (Alaneme et al., 2024).

Equally important is coordination among diverse stakeholders—farmers, processors, engineers, policymakers, and communities (Alaneme et al., 2024). Collaborative frameworks and cooperative business models can align incentives. Farmers gain from selling waste; manufacturers gain raw materials; and society gains cleaner air and sustainable infrastructure. Transparent benefit-sharing will sustain participation and trust.

# 12. CONCLUSIONS AND RECOMMENDATIONS

## 12.1 Summary of Key Insights

Agricultural-waste-based geopolymers represent one of the most promising innovations for sustainable construction. They offer comparable or superior strength and durability to ordinary concrete while cutting embodied carbon by as much as 75 percent. Materials such as rice husk ash, sugarcane bagasse ash, and wheat-straw ash can be transformed—through alkali activation—into binders that resist acids, sulfates, and high temperatures far better than cement.

Beyond environmental benefits, these materials enable smart functionalities such as self-sensing and self-healing, expanding the concept of infrastructure from static to intelligent. They also create a bridge between agriculture and industry, turning waste into value and supporting rural economies. Case studies worldwide confirm that practical implementation is not only feasible but advantageous.

## 12.2 Strategic Recommendations

For researchers, priority areas include long-term durability assessment, reinforcement corrosion studies, development of low-cost activators, and standardized testing methods. Open-access data sharing and international collaboration will accelerate progress.

For industry and practitioners, gradual implementation is advisable—starting with pilot projects and expanding as experience grows. Training programs, stringent quality control, and partnerships with research institutions will ensure consistency and confidence.

For policymakers, integrating geopolymers into carbon-reduction strategies, public-procurement policies, and building codes is essential. Financial incentives for sustainable materials, combined with support for rural ash-processing units, can transform this innovation into national policy.

For the agricultural sector, organized collection and controlled combustion of residues offer new revenue streams and environmental improvements, replacing open burning with profitable recycling.

## 12.3 Vision for the Future

The future of sustainable infrastructure depends on materials that close the loop between production, use, and regeneration. Agricultural-waste geopolymers exemplify this vision. They reduce emissions, conserve resources, and embody circular-economy principles while delivering superior technical performance.

Achieving global adoption will require persistence and collaboration across all sectors. Researchers must continue refining formulations; industries must invest in production capacity; governments must provide supportive policy frameworks; and communities must embrace the environmental and economic benefits.

If pursued collectively, the waste once viewed as a burden in farmers' fields can become the foundation for the world's next generation of smart, climate-resilient infrastructure. The transformation of ash into architecture symbolizes a deeper shift—from linear consumption to regenerative creation—marking a crucial step toward a truly sustainable and intelligent built environment.

## REFERENCES


Abbas, M. A., Kwan, W. H., Samsudin, M. H., & Hai, T. (2024). Optimising factors for the production of amorphous rice husk ash via combustion process for sustainable construction: A review. *Journal of Advanced Research in Applied Mechanics*, *120*(1), 50–61. DOI: 10.37934/aram.120.1.5061

Abbas, U., Akhai, S., Abbass, M., Abass, S., Chouksey, A., & Wadhwa, A. S. (2026). Sustainable growth by navigating complexity through innovation and adaptive industrial policies. In *Industrial Policy, Innovation, and Complexity: Comparative Analysis, Trends, and Prospects* (pp. 29-82). IGI Global. https://doi.org/DOI: 10.4018/979-8-3373-1767-0.ch002

Abbass, M., Abbas, U., Jafri, R., Arif, S. M., & Akhai, S. (2025). AI and machine learning applications in sustainable smart cities. In *Sustainable Smart Cities and the Future of Urban Development* (pp. 1–32). IGI Global., DOI: 10.4018/979-8-3693-6740-7.ch001

Abbass, M., & Akhai, S. (2025). Eco-friendly geopolymer bricks synthesized from alkali-activated sugarcane bagasse ash and rice husk ash. *Industrial Crops and Products*, *233*, 121410. DOI: 10.1016/j.indcrop.2025.121410

Abbass, M., & Akhai, S. (2025). *Exploring the sustainability potential of geopolymer concrete with coal bottom ash and basalt fibres*. Multiscale and Multidisciplinary Modeling. *Experiments and Design*, *8*(3), 199. DOI: 10.1007/s41939-025-00794-3

Abbass, M., Akhai, S., Abbas, U., Jafri, R., & Arif, S. M. (2025). AI-enabled sustainable urban planning and management. In *Real-World Applications of AI Innovation* (pp. 233–260). IGI Global., DOI: 10.4018/979-8-3693-4252-7.ch012

Abbass, M., Akhai, S., Chouksey, A., Pathak, S., Abbas, U., & Abass, S. (2025). Disaster risk reduction and management with emerging technologies: Applications of IoT, AI, and data analytics for resilient urban infrastructure. In *Revolutionizing Urban Development and Governance With Emerging Technologies* (pp. 71–110). IGI Global., DOI: 10.4018/979-8-3373-1375-7.ch003

Abbass, M., Akhai, S., Verma, R., Singh, G., Singh, D., & Wani, S. A. Mechanical and Durability Properties of Sugarcane Bagasse and Cow Dung Ash-Based Sustainable Geopolymer Bricks. In *CISSC 2025* (pp. 52-64). https://doi.org/DOI: 10.1061/9780784486481.007

Abbass, M., & Singh, G. (2021). Fatigue analysis of rice husk ash and basalt fibre-based sustainable geopolymer concrete in rigid pavements. *Materials Today: Proceedings*, *45*, 5014–5022. DOI: 10.1016/j.matpr.2021.01.450

Abbass, M., & Singh, G. (2021). Rice husk ash and basalt fibre-based sustainable geopolymer concrete in rigid pavements under ambient curing conditions. In *Lecture Notes in Civil Engineering* (Vol. 143, pp. 385–397). Springer.

Abbass, M., & Singh, G. (2021). Rice husk ash and basalt fibre-based sustainable geopolymer concrete in rigid pavements: A review. In *Lecture Notes in Civil Engineering* (Vol. 143, pp. 361–372). Springer.

Abbass, M., & Singh, G. (2022). Durability of rice husk ash and basalt fibre-based sustainable geopolymer concrete in rigid pavements. *Materials Today: Proceedings, 61*, 558–570. Advance online publication. DOI: 10.1016/j.matpr.2022.02.196

Abbass, M., & Singh, G. (2022). Impact strength of rice husk ash and basalt fibre-based sustainable geopolymer concrete in rigid pavements. *Materials Today: Proceedings, 61*, 250–257. DOI: 10.1016/j.matpr.2021.09.053

Abbass, M., & Singh, G. (2022). Optimum mix design of rice husk ash-based geopolymer concrete based on workability, setting time, and compressive strength cured in ambient temperature condition. In *Lecture Notes in Civil Engineering* (Vol. 221, pp. 59–74). Springer., DOI: 10.1007/978-981-16-8433-3_7

Abbass, M., & Singh, G. (2023). *Experimental investigation of alkali-activated hybrid geopolymer concrete*. Multiscale and Multidisciplinary Modeling. *Experiments and Design, 6*(2), 235–249. DOI: 10.1007/s41939-023-00144-1

Abbass, M., & Singh, G. (2023). Experimental investigation of engineered alkali-activated fibrous geopolymer concrete. *Journal of Building Pathology and Rehabilitation, 8*(1), 1–16. DOI: 10.1007/s41024-022-00259-x

Abbass, M., & Singh, G. (2024). *Microstructural analysis of environment-friendly sustainable geopolymer concrete*. Multiscale and Multidisciplinary Modeling. *Experiments and Design, 7*(1), 301–319. DOI: 10.1007/s41939-023-00200-w

Abbass, M., Singh, G., & Aggarwal, V. (2023). Properties of rice husk ash and aluminium slag-based sustainable geopolymer bricks. In *Lecture Notes in Civil Engineering* (Vol. 338, pp. 255–267). Springer., DOI: 10.1007/978-981-99-1886-7_22

Abdelmongy, M., Iqbal, M., Farag, M. M., Yosri, A. M., Alsharari, F., & Yousef, S. E. A. S. (2024). Artificial intelligence prediction of one-part geopolymer compressive strength for sustainable concrete. *Computer Modeling in Engineering & Sciences, 141*(1), 525–543. DOI: 10.32604/cmes.2024.052505

Adesanya, E., Perumal, P., Luukkonen, T., Yliniemi, J., Ohenoja, K., Kinnunen, P., & Illikainen, M. (2020). Opportunities to improve sustainability of alkali-activated materials: A review of side-stream based activators. *Journal of Cleaner Production*, *286*, 125558. DOI: 10.1016/j.jclepro.2020.125558

Akeke, G. A., Inem, P.-E. U., Alaneme, G. U., & Nyah, E. E. (2023). Experimental investigation and modelling of the mechanical properties of palm oil fuel ash concrete using Scheffe's method. *Scientific Reports*, *13*(1), 18583. Advance online publication. DOI: 10.1038/s41598-023-45987-3

Al-Kasassbeh, S., Al-Thawabteh, J., Al-Kharabsheh, E., & Al-Tamseh, A. (2023). Influential and intellectual structure of geopolymer concrete: A bibliometric review. *Civil Engineering Journal*, *9*(9), 2330–2344. DOI: 10.28991/CEJ-2023-09-09-017

Al-Saudi, S. K. M., Géber, R., Simon, A., Kurovics, E., & Hamza, A. (2023). Comparative study of metakaolin-based geopolymer characteristics utilizing different dosages of water glass in the activator solution. *Results in Engineering*, *20*, 101469. DOI: 10.1016/j.rineng.2023.101469

Alahmari, T. S., Abdalla, T. A., & Rihan, M. A. M. (2023). Review of recent developments regarding the durability performance of eco-friendly geopolymer concrete. *Buildings (Basel, Switzerland)*, *13*(12), 3033. DOI: 10.3390/buildings13123033

Alaneme, G. U., Olonade, K. A., & Esenogho, E. (2023). Eco-friendly agro-waste based geopolymer-concrete: A systematic review. *Discover Materials*, *3*(1), 14. Advance online publication. DOI: 10.1007/s43939-023-00052-8

Alaneme, G. U., Olonade, K. A., Esenogho, E., & Lawan, M. M. (2024). Proposed simplified methodological approach for designing geopolymer concrete mixtures. *Scientific Reports*, *14*(1), 15191. Advance online publication. DOI: 10.1038/s41598-024-66093-y

Alawi, A., Milad, A., Barbieri, D. M., Alosta, M., Alaneme, G. U., & Latif, Q. B. (2023). Eco-friendly geopolymer composites prepared from agro-industrial wastes: A state-of-the-art review. *CivilEng*, *4*(2), 433–453. DOI: 10.3390/civileng4020025

Albitar, M., Ali, M. S. M., Visintin, P., & Drechsler, M. (2017). Durability evaluation of geopolymer and conventional concretes. *Construction & Building Materials*, *136*, 374–385. DOI: 10.1016/j.conbuildmat.2017.01.056

Ali, A. Y. F., Ahmed, S. A., Helal, Y., & El-Feky, M. S. (2025). Thermo-mechanical behavior and spalling resistance of alkali-activated slag versus cement mortars under rapid high-temperature exposure. *Scientific Reports*, *15*(1), 32581. Advance online publication. DOI: 10.1038/s41598-025-19301-2

Amaludin, A. E., Asrah, H., & Mohamad, H. M. (2023). A review of advances in peat soil stabilisation technology: Exploring the potential of palm oil fuel ash geopolymer as a soil stabiliser material. *Civil Engineering Journal, 9*(8), 2085–2104. DOI: 10.28991/CEJ-2023-09-08-017

Arokiasamy, P., Abdullah, M. M. A. B., Rahim, S. Z. A., Sadique, M., Yun-Ming, L., Salleh, M. A. A. M., Zainol, M. R. R. M. A., & Ghazali, C. M. R. (2022). Diverse material based geopolymer towards heavy metals removal: A review. *Journal of Materials Research and Technology, 22*, 126–156. DOI: 10.1016/j.jmrt.2022.11.100

Aupoil, J., Champenois, J., & Lacaillerie, J. (2018). Interplay between silicate and hydroxide ions during geopolymerization. *Cement and Concrete Research, 115*, 426–432. DOI: 10.1016/j.cemconres.2018.09.012

Bachs-Herrera, A., York, D., Stephens-Jones, T., Mabbett, I., Yeo, J., & Martín-Martínez, F. J. (2023). Biomass carbon mining to develop nature-inspired materials for a circular economy. *iScience, 26*(4), 106549. DOI: 10.1016/j.isci.2023.106549

Bąk, A., Łach, M., Romańska, P., Ciemnicka, J., Prałat, K., & Koper, A. (2025). Geopolymer concretes with organic phase change materials—Analysis of thermal properties and microstructure. *Materials (Basel), 18*(11), 2557. DOI: 10.3390/ma18112557

Barve, P., Bahrami, A., & Shah, S. G. (2023). Geopolymer 3D printing: A comprehensive review on rheological and structural performance assessment, printing process parameters, and microstructure. *Frontiers in Materials, 10*, 1241869. Advance online publication. DOI: 10.3389/fmats.2023.1241869

Barve, P., Bahrami, A., & Shah, S. G. (2024). A comprehensive review on effects of material composition, mix design, and mixing regimes on rheology of 3D-printed geopolymer concrete. *The Open Construction & Building Technology Journal, 18*(1), e18748368292859. Advance online publication. DOI: 10.2174/011874836829285924031306170 6

Basri, M. S. M., Mustapha, F., Mazlan, N., & Ishak, M. R. (2021). Rice-husk-ash-based geopolymer coating: Fire-retardant, optimize composition, microstructural, thermal and element characteristics analysis. *Polymers, 13*(21), 3747. DOI: 10.3390/polym13213747

Bazarkhankyzy, A., Murali, G. B., Aibuldinov, Y. K., Iskakova, Z., Kurpińska, M., Abdelgader, H. S., Avudaiappan, S., & Dixit, S. (2025). Comprehensive evaluation of impact strength and microstructural characteristics of geopolymer concrete reinforced with natural fibers of varying lengths. *Scientific Reports, 15*(1), 29624. Advance online publication. DOI: 10.1038/s41598-025-14857-5

Bentsen, N. S., Felby, C., & Thorsen, B. J. (2013). Agricultural residue production and potentials for energy and materials services. *Progress in Energy and Combustion Science*, *40*, 59–73. DOI: 10.1016/j.pecs.2013.09.003

Bhatia, B., Sharma, G., Bansal, J., Abbass, M., Akhai, S., & Kaur, P. (2025, October). AI for urban planning and management. In. AIP Conference Proceedings: Vol. 3343. *No. 1* (p. 040022). AIP Publishing LLC., DOI: 10.1063/5.0292571

Biondi, L., Perry, M., McAlorum, J., Vlachakis, C., & Hamilton, A. (2020). Geopolymer-based moisture sensors for reinforced concrete health monitoring. *Sensors and Actuators. B, Chemical*, *309*, 127775. DOI: 10.1016/j.snb.2020.127775

Blanco, I., Loisi, R. V., Sica, C., Schettini, E., & Vox, G. (2018). Agricultural plastic waste mapping using GIS: A case study in Italy. *Resources, Conservation and Recycling*, *137*, 229–242. DOI: 10.1016/j.resconrec.2018.06.008

Blesson, S., & Rao, A. U. (2023). Agro-industrial-based wastes as supplementary cementitious or alkali-activated binder material: A comprehensive review. *Innovative Infrastructure Solutions*, *8*(4), 125. Advance online publication. DOI: 10.1007/s41062-023-01096-8

Borges, P. H. R., Lourenço, T. M. de F., Foureaux, A. F. S., & Pacheco, L. S. (2014). Comparative life cycle analysis of geopolymer and Portland cement concretes. *Ambiente Construído*, *14*(2), 153. DOI: 10.1590/S1678-86212014000200011

Bouchikhi, A., Mamindy-Pajany, Y., Maherzi, W., Mercier, C., El-Moueden, H., Benzerzour, M., Peys, A., & Abriak, N.-E. (2020). Use of residual waste glass in an alkali-activated binder: Structural characterization and environmental leaching behavior. *Journal of Building Engineering*, *34*, 101903. DOI: 10.1016/j.jobe.2020.101903

Bourbigot, S., Sarazin, J., Davy, C., & Fontaine, G. (2021). Foamed geopolymers for fire protection: Burn-through testing and modeling. *Fire and Materials*, *46*(7), 1011–1019. DOI: 10.1002/fam.3048

Bragança, L., Cvetkovska, M., Askar, R., & Ungureanu, V. (2023). *Creating a roadmap towards circularity in the built environment*. Springer., DOI: 10.1007/978-3-031-45980-1

Brahami, Y., Saeidi, A., Fiset, M., & Ba, K. (2022). Effects of the type and quantity of recycled materials on physical and mechanical properties of concrete and mortar: A review. *Sustainability (Basel)*, *14*(22), 14752. DOI: 10.3390/su142214752

Brial, V., Tran, H., Sorelli, L., Conciatori, D., & Ouellet-Plamondon, C. (2022). Improvement of treated spent pot lining reactivity in cementitious material by calcination. *Developments in the Built Environment*, *12*, 100098. DOI: 10.1016/j.dibe.2022.100098

Brown, D. R. N., & Gevaudan, J. (2025). *Transforming agricultural residues into high-performance SCMs through mechanochemical activation*. https://doi.org/DOI: 10.5703/1288284318081

Callai, S. C., Tataranni, P., & Sangiorgi, C. (2021). Preliminary evaluation of geopolymer mix design applying the design of experiments method. *Infrastructures*, *6*(3), 35. DOI: 10.3390/infrastructures6030035

Capêto, A. P., Amorim, M., Sousa, S., Costa, J. R., Uribe, B. E. B., Guimarães, A. S., Pintado, M., & Oliveira, A. (2023). Fire-resistant bio-based polyurethane foams designed using by-products of sugarcane fermentation. *Waste and Biomass Valorization*, *15*(4), 2045. DOI: 10.1007/s12649-023-02274-6

Chen, K., Cheng, Y., Yu, M., Liu, L., Wang, Y., & Zhang, J. (2022). Predicting the geopolymerization process of fly-ash-based geopolymer using machine learning. *Buildings (Basel, Switzerland)*, *12*(11), 1792. DOI: 10.3390/buildings12111792

Chindaprasirt, P., & Rattanasak, U. (2020). Eco-production of silica from sugarcane bagasse ash for use as a photochromic pigment filler. *Scientific Reports*, *10*(1), 9890. Advance online publication. DOI: 10.1038/s41598-020-66885-y

Chiranjeevi, K., Abraham, M., Rath, B., & Praveenkumar, T. R. (2023). Enhancing the properties of geopolymer concrete using nano-silica: Microstructure assessment and sustainability perspective. *Scientific Reports*, *13*(1), 17302. Advance online publication. DOI: 10.1038/s41598-023-44491-y

Christiansen, C., Nielsen, K. K., & Bjørk, R. (2019). *Freeze-casting as a processing route to fabricate active magnetic regenerators for magnetic refrigeration*. Research Portal Denmark. https://local.forskningsportal.dk/local/dki-cgi/ws/cris-link?src=dtu&id=dtu-5f6fb193-e173-40d4-b67e-a9076695c205

Cong, P., Du, R., Gao, H., & Chen, Z. (2024). Comparison and assessment of carbon dioxide emissions between alkali-activated materials and OPC cement concrete. *Journal of Traffic and Transportation Engineering*, *11*(5), 918–938. DOI: 10.1016/j.jtte.2023.07.011

Cordeiro, G. C., Filho, R. D. T., & Fairbairn, E. (2009). Effect of calcination temperature on the pozzolanic activity of sugar cane bagasse ash. *Construction & Building Materials*, *23*(10), 3301–3303. DOI: 10.1016/j.conbuildmat.2009.02.013

Cui, Y., Ai, W., Tekle, B. H., Liu, M., Qu, S., & Zhang, P. (2023). State-of-the-art review on the production and bond behaviour of reinforced geopolymer concrete. *Low-Carbon Materials and Green Construction*, *1*(1), 25. Advance online publication. DOI: 10.1007/s44242-023-00027-1

de Almeida, M., Gonçalves, N. P. F., Gameiro, T., Alves, Z., Labrincha, J. A., & Novais, R. M. (2024). *Optimizing bauxite residue and biomass fly ash mixtures for 3D printing geopolymers: Promising metal sorbents for wastewater treatment*. https://doi.org/DOI: 10.2139/ssrn.4828271

de Carvalho, T. A., Gaspar, F., Marques, A. C., & Mateus, A. (2023). Evaluation of the potential of metakaolin, electric arc furnace slag, and biomass fly ash for geopolymer cement compositions. *Materials (Basel)*, *16*(7), 2741. DOI: 10.3390/ma16072741

de Carvalho, T. A., Gaspar, F., Mateus, A., & Marques, A. C. (2023). *Geopolymer cement for sustainable construction: A review*. In Sustainable Construction Materials (pp. 149–172). https://doi.org/DOI: 10.1007/978-3-031-25795-7_11

Dehghani, A., Aslani, F., & Panah, N. G. (2021). Effects of initial $SiO_2/Al_2O_3$ molar ratio and slag on fly ash-based ambient cured geopolymer properties. *Construction & Building Materials*, *293*, 123527. DOI: 10.1016/j.conbuildmat.2021.123527

Dhiman, S., Seema, S., & Akhai, S. (2025). Effects of micro-silica and ceramic tile waste on the mechanical and durability properties of M40 grade concrete. *AIP Advances*, *15*(12), 125019. Advance online publication. DOI: 10.1063/5.0308763

Dhiman, S., Seema, S., & Akhai, S. (2025). Performance evaluation of OPC 43 concrete incorporating micro silica and recycled ceramic tile waste as partial cement and coarse aggregate replacements. *Asian Journal of Civil Engineering*, 1-19. https://doi.org/DOI: 10.1007/s42107-025-01504-7

Dizaji, H. B., Zeng, T., Hölzig, H., Bauer, J., Klöß, G., & Enke, D. (2021). Ash transformation mechanism during combustion of rice husk and rice straw. *Fuel*, *307*, 121768. DOI: 10.1016/j.fuel.2021.121768

Djobo, J. N. Y., Elimbi, A., Tchakouté, H. K., & Kumar, S. (2016). Mechanical activation of volcanic ash for geopolymer synthesis: Effect on reaction kinetics and properties. *RSC Advances*, *6*(45), 39106. DOI: 10.1039/C6RA03667H

Dong, Q., Su, X., Li, X., Zhou, H., Jian, H., Bai, S., Yin, J., & You, Q. (2023). In vitro construction of lung cancer organoids by 3D bioprinting for drug evaluation. *Colloids and Surfaces. A, Physicochemical and Engineering Aspects*, *666*, 131288. DOI: 10.1016/j.colsurfa.2023.131288

Drabczyk, A., Kudłacik-Kramarczyk, S., Korniejenko, K., Figiela, B., & Furtos, G. (2023). Geopolymer nanocomposites: Novel materials for sustainable development. *Materials (Basel)*, *16*(9), 3478. DOI: 10.3390/ma16093478

Driouich, A., Chajri, F., Hassani, S. E. A. E., Britel, O., Belouafa, S., Khabbazi, A., & Chaair, H. (2020). Optimization of geopolymer mixture synthesis using metakaolin and fly ash activated by alkaline solution. *Journal of Non-Crystalline Solids*, *544*, 120197. DOI: 10.1016/j.jnoncrysol.2020.120197

Dulaimi, A., Busaltan, S. A., Mydin, M. A. O., Lu, D., Özkılıç, Y. O., Jaya, R. P., & Ameen, A. (2023). Innovative geopolymer-based cold asphalt emulsion mixture as eco-friendly material. *Scientific Reports*, *13*(1), 17380. Advance online publication. DOI: 10.1038/s41598-023-44630-5

Duque-Acevedo, M., Lancellotti, I., Andreola, F., Barbieri, L., Ureña, L. J. B., & Camacho-Ferre, F. (2022). Management of agricultural waste biomass for construction applications: Circular alternatives and sustainability analysis. *Environmental Sciences Europe*, *34*(1). Advance online publication. DOI: 10.1186/s12302-022-00655-7

Dwivedi, E. (2024). A review on development of 3D printable concrete using agro-industrial waste: Evaluation of fresh properties. *International Journal for Research in Applied Science and Engineering Technology*, *12*(7), 116–124. DOI: 10.22214/ijraset.2024.63530

El-Zeadani, M., Bompa, D. V., & Elghazouli, A. Y. (2021). Preparation and properties of rubberised geopolymer concrete: A review. *Construction & Building Materials*, *313*, 125504. DOI: 10.1016/j.conbuildmat.2021.125504

Fan, J., Liang, H., Sun, Z., & Chen, Z. (2023). Strength characteristics and mechanisms of cold mix based on geopolymerization. *Frontiers in Built Environment*, *9*. Advance online publication. DOI: 10.3389/fbuil.2023.1301126

Fan, X. (2020). A brief introduction on the research status and future prospects on geopolymer concrete. *IOP Conference Series. Earth and Environmental Science*, *508*(1), 012124. DOI: 10.1088/1755-1315/508/1/012124

Farhan, K. Z., Shihata, A. S., & Abubakar, A. (2024). Impact of pernicious chemicals on geopolymer and alkali-activated composites incorporated with different fiber types: A review. *Recent Progress in Materials*, *6*(3), 1–19. DOI: 10.21926/rpm.2403017

Firdous, R., Nikravan, M., Mancke, R., Vöge, M., & Stephan, D. (2022). Assessment of environmental, economic and technical performance of geopolymer concrete: A case study. *Journal of Materials Science*, *57*(40), 18711–18725. DOI: 10.1007/s10853-022-07820-6

Frandsen, K. M., Antonov, Y. I., Johra, H., Møldrup, P., & Jensen, R. L. (2021). *Water vapor diffusivity in bio-based building materials: New measurement method*. Research Portal Denmark.

Fredericci, C., Ett, G., Silva, G. F. B. L., Neto, J. B. F., Landgraf, F. J. G., Indelicato, R. L., & Ribeiro, T. R. (2014). Behavior of Brazilian sugarcane bagasse ash under thermal gasification. *Chemical and Biological Technologies in Agriculture*, *1*(1). Advance online publication. DOI: 10.1186/s40538-014-0015-z

Gao, Z., Alshehri, K., Li, Y., Qian, H., Sapsford, D., Cleall, P. J., & Harbottle, M. (2022). Advances in biological techniques for sustainable lignocellulosic waste utilization in biogas production. *Renewable & Sustainable Energy Reviews*, *170*, 112995. DOI: 10.1016/j.rser.2022.112995

Gautam, R., Jaiswal, R., & Yadav, U. S. (2024). *AI-enhanced data-driven approach to model the mechanical behavior of sustainable geopolymer concrete. Research Square*. https://doi.org/DOI: 10.21203/rs.3.rs-5307352/v1

Gebeyehu, A., Surapaneni, S. K., Huang, J. J., Mondal, A., Wang, V. Z., Haruna, N.-F., Bagde, A., Arthur, P., Kutlehria, S., Patel, N., Rishi, A. K., & Singh, M. (2021). Polysaccharide hydrogel-based 3D printed tumor models for chemotherapeutic drug screening. *Scientific Reports*, *11*(1), 372. Advance online publication. DOI: 10.1038/s41598-020-79325-8

Ghani, W. A. W. A. K., Salleh, M. A. M., Adam, S. N., Shafri, H. Z. M., Shaharum, S. N., Lim, K. L., Rubinsin, N. J., Lam, H. L., Hasan, A., Samsatli, S., Tapia, J. F. D., Khezri, R., Jaye, I. F. M., & Martínez-Hernández, E. (2019). Sustainable bio-economy for environment–food–energy–water nexus: Current status in Malaysia. *Food and Bioproducts Processing*, *118*, 167. DOI: 10.1016/j.fbp.2019.09.002

Ginni, G., Kavitha, S., Ravi, Y. K., & Bhatia, S. K. (2021). Valorization of agricultural residues: Different biorefinery routes. *Journal of Environmental Chemical Engineering*, *9*(4), 105435. DOI: 10.1016/j.jece.2021.105435

Görhan, G., & Kürklü, G. (2013). Influence of NaOH solution on properties of fly ash-based geopolymer mortar cured at various temperatures. *Composites. Part B, Engineering*, *58*, 371–377. DOI: 10.1016/j.compositesb.2013.10.082

Górski, M., Czulkin, P., Wielgus, N., Boncel, S., Kuziel, A. W., Kolanowska, A., & Jędrysiak, R. G. (2022). Electrical properties of carbon nanotube-reinforced geopolymer studied by impedance spectroscopy. *Materials (Basel)*, *15*(10), 3543. DOI: 10.3390/ma15103543

Goryunova, K., Gahramanli, Y., Muradkhanli, V., & Nadirov, P. (2023). Phosphate-activated geopolymers: Advantages and application. *RSC Advances, 13*(43), 30329–30345. DOI: 10.1039/D3RA05131E

Habeeb, G. A., & Mahmud, H. B. (2010). Properties of rice husk ash and its use as cement replacement material. *Materials Research, 13*(2), 185–190. DOI: 10.1590/S1516-14392010000200011

Habte, G. A., Bullo, T. A., & Ahmed, Y. (2025). Statistical optimization and eco-friendly synthesis of silica from sugarcane bagasse. *Scientific Reports, 15*(1). Advance online publication. DOI: 10.1038/s41598-025-89366-6

Hassan, M. A., Farid, M. A. A., Zakaria, M. R., Ariffin, H., Andou, Y., & Shirai, Y. (2024). Palm oil expansion in Malaysia: Policy window and biorefinery countermeasures. *Environmental Science & Policy, 153*, 103671. DOI: 10.1016/j.envsci.2024.103671

Hattaf, R., Aboulayt, A., Lahlou, N., Touhami, M. O., Gomina, M., Samdi, A., & Moussa, R. (2022). Integration of geopolymer wastes in binding matrices under acid and temperature exposure. *Polymers, 14*(5), 917. DOI: 10.3390/polym14050917

He, R., Dai, N., & Wang, Z. (2020). Thermal and mechanical properties of geopolymers exposed to high temperature: A literature review. *Advances in Civil Engineering, 2020*(1), 7532703. Advance online publication. DOI: 10.1155/2020/7532703

Hernández-Escobar, C. A., Conejo-Dávila, A. S., Vega-Ríos, A., Zaragoza-Contreras, E. A., & Farías, R. (2023). Geopolymers obtained from wheat husk native to Northern Mexico. *Materials (Basel), 16*(5), 1803. DOI: 10.3390/ma16051803

Hipólito, V. M., & Ildefonso, J. S. (2024). Functional and structural assessment of a gap-graded experimental section modified with sugarcane bagasse ash. *Scientific Reports, 14*(1). Advance online publication. DOI: 10.1038/s41598-024-67900-2

Hong, S., & Kim, H. (2019). Microwave-assisted fast strength development of coal bottom ash-based geopolymers. *Scientific Reports, 9*(1). Advance online publication. DOI: 10.1038/s41598-019-52160-2

Hou, S., Duan, Z., Xiao, J., & Ye, J. (2020). 3D-printed concrete: Performance requirements and mix design review. *Construction & Building Materials, 273*, 121745. DOI: 10.1016/j.conbuildmat.2020.121745

Hounsi, A. D., Lecomte-Nana, G. L., Djétéli, G., Blanchart, P., Alowanou, D., Kpelou, P., Napo, K., Tchangbédji, G., & Praisler, M. (2014). Influence of Na, K alkali concentration on early-age structure of kaolin-based geopolymers. *Ceramics International, 40*(7), 8953. DOI: 10.1016/j.ceramint.2014.02.052

Huang, J., Kogbara, R. B., Hariharan, N., Masad, E., & Little, D. N. (2021). State-of-the-art review of polymers used in soil stabilization. *Construction & Building Materials, 305*, 124685. DOI: 10.1016/j.conbuildmat.2021.124685

Hussain, S., Amritphale, S. S., Matthews, J. C., Paul, N., Matthews, E., & Edwards, R. (2024). Advanced solid geopolymer formulations for refractory applications. *Materials (Basel), 17*(6), 1386. DOI: 10.3390/ma17061386

Ikotun, J. O., Aderinto, G. E., Madirisha, M. M., & Katte, V. Y. (2024). Geopolymer cement in pavement applications: Bridging sustainability and performance. *Sustainability (Basel), 16*(13), 5417. DOI: 10.3390/su16135417

Jallu, M., & Saride, S. (2024). Performance of alkali-activated fly ash stabilized RAP aggregates as pavement base course. *International Journal of Geosynthetics and Ground Engineering, 10*(2). Advance online publication. DOI: 10.1007/s40891-024-00523-9

Jamwal, A., Nautiyal, A., Singh, K., Alam, S., Alselami, N. A., & Aati, K. (2024). Cow dung ash and corn stalk ash as eco-friendly concrete alternatives. *Civil Engineering Journal, 10*, 21. DOI: 10.28991/CEJ-SP2024-010-02

Jannat, N., Hussien, A., Abdullah, B. M., & Cotgrave, A. (2020). Agro and non-agro waste materials for unfired earth blocks: A review. *Construction & Building Materials, 254*, 119346. DOI: 10.1016/j.conbuildmat.2020.119346

Jayakumar, K., & Park, J. P. (n.d.). *Stimuli-responsive polymer–metal organic framework composites: Biomedical applications and design strategies.(No publication data available.)*

Jeremiah, J. J., Abbey, S. J., Booth, C. A., & Eyo, E. (2023). Viability of calcinated wastepaper sludge ash geopolymer for road pavement subgrade. *Transportation Geotechnics, 44*, 101165. DOI: 10.1016/j.trgeo.2023.101165

Jiang, T., Munguia-López, J. G., Flores-Torres, S., Grant, J., Vijayakumar, S., León-Rodríguez, A. D., & Kinsella, J. M. (2017). Bioprinting of tumor spheroids using alginate/gelatin hydrogels. *Scientific Reports, 7*(1). Advance online publication. DOI: 10.1038/s41598-017-04691-9

Juengsuwattananon, K., Winnefeld, F., Chindaprasirt, P., & Pimraksa, K. (2019). Correlation of $SiO_2/Al_2O_3$, $Na_2O/Al_2O_3$, $Na_2O/SiO_2$ ratios on phase development in metakaolin–RHA geopolymers. *Construction & Building Materials, 226*, 406. DOI: 10.1016/j.conbuildmat.2019.07.146

Kadamba, S., Blesson, S., Rao, A. U., Kamath, M., & Tantri, A. (2024). Self-healing concrete using agro-industrial waste: A critical review. *Journal of Building Pathology and Rehabilitation*, *9*(2). Advance online publication. DOI: 10.1007/s41024-024-00501-8

Kadhim, A., Sadique, M., Al-Mufti, R. L., & Hashim, K. (2020). High-calcium one-part alkali-activated cement from lime kiln dust: Long-term performance. *Journal of Building Engineering*, *32*, 101766. DOI: 10.1016/j.jobe.2020.101766

Kahla, N. B., Ghazouani, N., & Raza, A. (2025). Phase change materials in engineered geopolymer composites. *JOM*. Advance online publication. DOI: 10.1007/s11837-025-07655-x

Kaja, A. M., Lázaro, A., & Yu, Q. (2018). Effects of Portland cement on activation mechanism of Class F fly ash geopolymer cured under ambient conditions. *Construction & Building Materials*, *189*, 1113–1123. DOI: 10.1016/j.conbuildmat.2018.09.065

Kajaste, R., & Hurme, M. (2015). Cement industry greenhouse gas emissions: Management options and abatement cost. *Journal of Cleaner Production*, *112*, 4041–4052. DOI: 10.1016/j.jclepro.2015.07.055

Kaleli, M. J., Kamweru, P. K., Gichumbi, J. M., & Ndiritu, F. G. (2020). Characterization of rice husk ash from open-air burning vs furnace calcination. *Journal of Chemical Engineering and Materials Science*, *11*(2), 24–30. DOI: 10.5897/JCEMS2020.0348

Kaze, C. R., Lemougna, P. N., Alomayri, T., Assaedi, H., Adesina, A., Das, S., Lecomte-Nana, G.-L., Kamseu, E., Melo, U. C., & Leonelli, C. (2020). Laterite-based geopolymer binder cured at various temperatures: Characterization & performance. *Construction & Building Materials*, *270*, 121443. DOI: 10.1016/j.conbuildmat.2020.121443

Khan, K., Ahmad, W., Amin, M. N., Ahmad, A., Nazar, S., & Al-Faiad, M. A. (2022). Artificial intelligence strategies for strength estimation of geopolymer composites. *Polymers*, *14*(12), 2509. DOI: 10.3390/polym14122509

Khater, E.-S., Ali, S. A., Afify, M., Bayomy, M. A., & Abbas, R. S. (2022). GIS-based determination of suitable agricultural residue collection sites. *Scientific Reports*, *12*(1). Advance online publication. DOI: 10.1038/s41598-022-18850-0

Kim, K. W., Song, H., Lee, S., Lim, H.-M., & Ko, H. (2025). Accelerating ambient curing of geopolymers using metamodel-guided optimization. *Digital Discovery*, *4*(3), 653. DOI: 10.1039/D4DD00217B

Koçyiğit, Ş. (2024). Geopolymer mortars with ferrochrome slag and fly ash for sustainable construction. *Scientific Reports*, *14*(1). Advance online publication. DOI: 10.1038/s41598-024-65552-w

Köenig, A., Mahmoud, H., Baehre, O., & Dehn, F. (2020). Alkalinity impacts on performance of steel-reinforced geopolymers. *Molecules (Basel, Switzerland)*, *25*(10), 2359. DOI: 10.3390/molecules25102359

Kogbara, R. B., Al-Zubi, A., Mortada, Y., Hammoud, A., Masad, E., & Khraisheh, M. (2023). Lime-activated one-part geopolymers using construction and demolition waste. *Results in Engineering*, *21*, 101739. DOI: 10.1016/j.rineng.2023.101739

Kucukgoncu, H., & Özbayrak, A. (2024). Microstructural analysis of low-calcium fly ash-based geopolymer concrete under high temperatures. *Arabian Journal for Science and Engineering*. Advance online publication. DOI: 10.1007/s13369-024-09266-1

Kumar, N. (2024). Comparative study of geopolymer vs ordinary concrete for compressive/flexural strength and sustainability. *International Journal for Research in Applied Science and Engineering Technology*, *12*(12), 1814. DOI: 10.22214/ijraset.2024.66112

Kumar, S., Gangotra, A., & Barnard, M. (2025). *Towards net-zero cement: Policies and systems thinking*. Current Sustainable/Renewable. *Energy Reports*, *12*(1). Advance online publication. DOI: 10.1007/s40518-025-00253-0

Kumble, P., Prashant, S., & Jagadisha, H. M. (2024). Fly ash–dolomite–tile waste alkali-activated binder under ambient curing. *Emergent Materials*. Advance online publication. DOI: 10.1007/s42247-024-00772-4

Kursula, K., Illikainen, M., & Perumal, P. (2023). Recycling alkali-activated slag into artificial aggregates: Effect of particle size distribution. *Low-Carbon Materials and Green Construction*, *1*(1). Advance online publication. DOI: 10.1007/s44242-023-00031-5

Kwunjai, S., Jitsangiam, P., Suwan, T., Rinchumphu, D., Thongchua, H., Chindaprasirt, P., & Sampattagul, S. (2020). Crushed rock geopolymer as future road construction material: Strength and compaction evaluation. *Key Engineering Materials*, *841*, 171. . DOI: 10.4028/www.scientific.net/KEM.841.171

Łach, M., Pławecka, K., Bąk, A., Adamczyk, M., Bazan, P., Kozub, B., Korniejenko, K., & Lin, W. (2021). Review of solutions for the use of phase change materials in geopolymers. *Materials (Basel)*, *14*(20), 6044. DOI: 10.3390/ma14206044

Lamaa, G., Duarte, A. P. C., Silva, R. V., & de Brito, J. (2023). Carbonation of alkali-activated materials: A review. *Materials (Basel)*, *16*(8), 3086. DOI: 10.3390/ma16083086

Law, D. W., Adam, A. A., Molyneaux, T., Patnaikuni, I., & Wardhono, A. (2014). Long term durability properties of class F fly ash geopolymer concrete. *Materials and Structures*, *48*(3), 721–731. DOI: 10.1617/s11527-014-0268-9

Leiva, C., Luna-Galiano, Y., Arenas, C., Alonso-Fariñas, B., & Fernández-Pereira, C. (2019). A porous geopolymer based on aluminum-waste with acoustic properties. *Waste Management (New York, N.Y.)*, *95*, 504–512. DOI: 10.1016/j.wasman.2019.06.042

Lemougna, P. N., Nzeukou, A. N., Aziwo, B., Tchamba, A. B., Wang, K., Melo, U. C., & Cui, X. (2019). Effect of slag on the improvement of setting time and compressive strength of low reactive volcanic ash geopolymers synthesized at room temperature. *Materials Chemistry and Physics*, *239*, 122077. DOI: 10.1016/j.matchemphys.2019.122077

Li, Q., Zhao, G., Li, J., Li, S., Yan, W., Tian, X., & Ai, S. (2025). An in-situ predictive method for modulus degradation in composite structures with fatigue damage: Applications in digital twin technology. *Mechanical Systems and Signal Processing*, *237*, 113090. DOI: 10.1016/j.ymssp.2025.113090

Li, X., Rao, F., Song, S., & Ma, Q. (2019). Deterioration in the microstructure of metakaolin-based geopolymers in marine environment. *Journal of Materials Research and Technology*, *8*(3), 2747–2752. DOI: 10.1016/j.jmrt.2019.03.010

Lin, M., Tang, M., Duan, W., Xia, S., Liu, W., & Wang, Q. (2023). 3D bioprinting for tumor metastasis research. *ACS Biomaterials Science & Engineering*, *9*(6), 3116–3133. DOI: 10.1021/acsbiomaterials.3c00239

Liu, X., Shu, Y., Zhu, J., Fang, H., Su, Y., Ma, H., Li, B., Xu, J., Cheng, Y. Y., Pan, B., & Song, K. (2024). A 3D bioprinted potential colorectal tumor model based on decellularized matrix/gelatinmethacryloyl/nanoclay/sodium alginate hydrogel. *International Journal of Biological Macromolecules*, *293*, 139346. DOI: 10.1016/j.ijbiomac.2024.139346

Lo, K., Lin, W., Lin, Y., Cheng, T., & Lin, K. (2022). Synthesis metakaolin-based geopolymer incorporated with SiC sludge using design of experiment method. *Polymers*, *14*(16), 3395. DOI: 10.3390/polym14163395

Longhi, M. A., Rodríguez, E. D., Walkley, B., Zhang, Z., & Kirchheim, A. P. (2019). Metakaolin-based geopolymers: Relation between formulation, physicochemical properties and efflorescence formation. *Composites. Part B, Engineering, 182*, 107671. DOI: 10.1016/j.compositesb.2019.107671

Luhar, S., Luhar, I., & Shaikh, F. U. A. (2021). Review on performance evaluation of autonomous healing of geopolymer composites. *Infrastructures, 6*(7), 94. DOI: 10.3390/infrastructures6070094

Madirisha, M. M., Dada, O. R., & Ikotun, B. D. (2024). Chemical fundamentals of geopolymers in sustainable construction. *Materials Today Sustainability, 27*, 100842. DOI: 10.1016/j.mtsust.2024.100842

Maestre, C. V., & Santos, G. N. C. (2023). Effect of bismuth oxide nanoparticle on the EMI shielding and thermal stability of industrial waste-based geopolymer composites. *Scientific Reports, 13*(1), 1787. DOI: 10.1038/s41598-023-27623-2

Mahmoodi, O., Siad, H., Lachemi, M., & Şahmaran, M. (2025). Post-fire thermal and mechanical performance of CDW-based geopolymer composites incorporating different recycled aggregates. *Journal of Building Engineering, 114131*. Advance online publication. DOI: 10.1016/j.jobe.2025.114131

Maldonado-Alameda, À., Mañosa, J., Miro-Escola, J., Quintero-Payan, A. C., & Chimenos, J. M. (2022). Fluidised-bed incineration bottom ash as the sole precursor of alkali-activated binders: A comparison with grate incinerator bottom ash. *Construction & Building Materials, 364*, 130001. DOI: 10.1016/j.conbuildmat.2022.130001

Marathe, S., Szemiot, N., Kumar, S., & Muthu, M. (2025). Degradation potential of metakaolin-based geopolymer composites immersed in real and simulated acidic environments. *Sustainability (Basel), 17*(2), 468. DOI: 10.3390/su17020468

Mare, M. D., & Ouellet-Plamondon, C. (2022). Highly piezoresistive, self-sensing, one-part potassium-activated inorganic polymers for structural health monitoring. *Materials Today Sustainability, 20*, 100261. DOI: 10.1016/j.mtsust.2022.100261

Mashifana, T., & Sithole, T. (2020). Recovery of silicon dioxide from waste foundry sand and alkaline activation of desilicated foundry sand. *Journal of Sustainable Metallurgy, 6*(4), 700–714. DOI: 10.1007/s40831-020-00303-5

Matsimbe, J., Dinka, M. O., Olukanni, D. O., & Musonda, I. (2022). Geopolymer: A systematic review of methodologies. *Materials (Basel), 15*(19), 6852. DOI: 10.3390/ma15196852

Matsueda, Y., & Antunes, E. (2024). A review of current technologies for the sustainable valorisation of sugarcane bagasse. *Journal of Environmental Chemical Engineering, 114900*(6), 114900. Advance online publication. DOI: 10.1016/j.jece.2024.114900

Mobili, A., Tittarelli, F., & Rahier, H. (2020). One-part alkali-activated pastes and mortars prepared with metakaolin and biomass ash. *Applied Sciences (Basel, Switzerland), 10*(16), 5610. DOI: 10.3390/app10165610

Mohamad, N., Muthusamy, K., Embong, R., Kusbiantoro, A., & Hashim, M. H. (2021). Environmental impact of cement production and solutions: A review. *Materials Today: Proceedings, 48*, 741–746. DOI: 10.1016/j.matpr.2021.02.212

Mohamed, O. A., Hassan, A. M., & Abdelwahab, N. R. (2025). High-performance and durable green geopolymer based on slag/alumina sludge ash incorporating $CuFe_2O_4$ spinel nanograins for enhanced gamma radiation shielding. *International Journal of Concrete Structures and Materials, 19*(1), 87. Advance online publication. DOI: 10.1186/s40069-025-00831-y

Mohammed, A. A., Ahmed, H. U., & Mosavi, A. (2021). Survey of mechanical properties of geopolymer concrete: A comprehensive review and data analysis. *Materials (Basel), 14*(16), 4690. DOI: 10.3390/ma14164690

Mostafa, M., Salah, H., Saddek, A. B., & Shehata, N. (2020). Optimization of nano-structured/nanosized rice husk ash preparation. *Baghdad Science Journal, 17*(3), 953. DOI: 10.21123/bsj.2020.17.3(Suppl.).0953

Motia, K., Kumar, R., & Akhai, S. (2024, November). Navigating the Fourth Industrial Revolution: A Comprehensive Review of Industry 4.0 Technologies and Their Global Adoption. In *International Conference on Design and Manufacturing Technologies* (pp. 317-333). Springer Nature Singapore. https://doi.org/DOI: 10.1007/978-981-96-7659-0_28

Mukhametkaliyev, T. M., Ali, M. H., Kutugin, V., Savinova, O. V., & Vereschagin, V. I. (2022). Influence of mixing order on the synthesis of geopolymer concrete. *Polymers, 14*(21), 4777. DOI: 10.3390/polym14214777

Mulapeer, E., & Omar, A. A. (2025). Durability and mechanical performance of geopolymer mortar with partial replacement of fly ash by rice husk ash and variations in alkaline activator concentrations. *Deleted Journal, 2*(1), 82. Advance online publication. DOI: 10.1007/s44290-025-00234-8

Munir, Q., Peltonen, R., & Kärki, T. (2021). Printing parameter requirements for 3D printable geopolymer materials prepared from industrial side streams. *Materials (Basel), 14*(16), 4758. DOI: 10.3390/ma14164758

Mushtaq, A., Ali, S. S., Chaudhry, A., Sial, N. A., Aslam, M., & Batool, H. (2025). Geopolymers as supplementary cementitious materials to reduce carbon dioxide emissions. *Nature Environment and Pollution Technology, 24*(S1), 417–429. DOI: 10.46488/NEPT.2024.v24iS1.033

Muthukrishnan, S., Ramakrishnan, S., & Sanjayan, J. (2020). Effect of alkali reactions on the rheology of one-part 3D printable geopolymer concrete. *Cement and Concrete Composites, 116*, 103899. DOI: 10.1016/j.cemconcomp.2020.103899

Nana, A., Kamseu, E., Akono, A., Ngouné, J., Djobo, J. N. Y., Tchakouté, H. K., Bignozzi, M. C., & Leonelli, C. (2021). Particle size and distribution on the mechanical performance improvement of inorganic polymer composites. *Materials Chemistry and Physics, 267*, 124602. DOI: 10.1016/j.matchemphys.2021.124602

Nasser, I. M., Ibrahim, M. H. W., Zuki, S. S. M., Alshalif, A. F., Nindyawati, N., & Jaya, R. P. (2023). *Effects of milling time on nano rice husk ash particle size. E3S Web of Conferences, 445*, 1003. https://doi.org/DOI: 10.1051/e3sconf/202344501003

Nawaz, M., Heitor, A., & Sivakumar, M. (2020). Geopolymers in construction: Recent developments. *Construction & Building Materials, 260*, 120472. DOI: 10.1016/j.conbuildmat.2020.120472

Ngui, F., Muhammed, N., Mutunga, F. M., Marangu, J. M., & Kinoti, I. K. (2022). A review on selected durability parameters on performance of geopolymers containing industrial by-products, agro-wastes and natural pozzolan. *Journal of Sustainable Construction Materials and Technologies, 7*(4), 375–400. DOI: 10.47481/jscmt.1190244

Nguyen, K. L., Uddin, M., & Pham, T. M. (2024). Generative artificial intelligence and optimisation framework for concrete mixture design with low cost and embodied $CO_2$. *Construction & Building Materials, 451*, 138836. DOI: 10.1016/j.conbuildmat.2024.138836

Niveditha, M., &Koniki, S. (2020). *Effect of durability properties on geopolymer concrete – A review. E3S Web of Conferences, 184*, 1092. https://doi.org/DOI: 10.1051/e3sconf/202018401092

Nkwaju, R. Y., Djobo, J. N. Y., Nouping, J. N. F., Mejouyo, P. W. H., Nemaleu, J. G. D., & Courard, L. (2019). Iron-rich laterite-bagasse fiber-based geopolymer composite: Mechanical, durability and insulating properties. *Applied Clay Science, 183*, 105333. DOI: 10.1016/j.clay.2019.105333

Nodehi, M., & Taghvaee, V. M. (2021). Alkali-activated materials and geopolymer: A review of common precursors and activators addressing circular economy. *Circular Economy and Sustainability*, *2*(1), 165–196. DOI: 10.1007/s43615-021-00029-w

Norrrahim, M. N. F., Farid, M. A. A., Lawal, A. A., Yasim-Anuar, T. A. T., Samsudin, M. H., & Zulkifli, A. A. (2022). Emerging technologies for value-added use of oil palm biomass. *Environmental Science. Advances*, *1*(3), 259–275. DOI: 10.1039/D2VA00029F

Obeidy, N. F. A., Khalil, W. I., & Ahmed, H. K. (2024). Optimization of local modified metakaolin-based geopolymer concrete by Taguchi method. *Open Engineering*, *14*(1), 20220561. Advance online publication. DOI: 10.1515/eng-2022-0561

Olivia, M., Putri, W. R., Supit, S., Wibisono, G., & Utama, P. S. (2023). *Compressive strength and porosity of POFA blended concrete admixed with micro silica. E3S Web of Conferences, 445*, 1034. https://doi.org/DOI: 10.1051/e3sconf/202344501034

Olsson, J. A., Miller, S. A., & Alexander, M. (2023). Near-term pathways for decarbonizing global concrete production. *Nature Communications*, *14*(1), 4574. DOI: 10.1038/s41467-023-40302-0

Omran, M., Khalifeh, M., & Paiva, M. D. M. (2023). Aging and temperature effects on sustainable one-part geopolymers for well-cementing applications. *SPE Journal*, *29*(2), 843. DOI: 10.2118/217993-PA

Oumar, A. I. (2025). Review of geopolymer concrete: Reaction mechanisms, mechanical behavior, and environmental benefits. *Journal of Civil Engineering and Urbanism*, *15*(2), 40–64. DOI: 10.54203/jceu.2025.4

Oyebisi, S., Ede, A. N., Olutoge, F., & Omole, D. O. (2020). Geopolymer concrete incorporating agro-industrial wastes: Effects on mechanical properties, microstructure and mineralogical phases. *Construction & Building Materials*, *256*, 119390. DOI: 10.1016/j.conbuildmat.2020.119390

Oyebisi, S., Olutoge, F., Kathirvel, P., Oyaotuderekumor, I., Lawanson, D., Nwani, J., Ede, A. N., & Kaze, C. R. (2022). Sustainability assessment of geopolymer concrete synthesized by slag and corncob ash. *Case Studies in Construction Materials*, *17*, e01665. Advance online publication. DOI: 10.1016/j.cscm.2022.e01665

Özen, M. Y., Firdous, R., Lehmann, C. W., & Stephan, D. (2023). Effects of curing conditions on the self-healing of geopolymer paste. MATEC Web of Conferences, 378, 2017. https://doi.org/DOI: 10.1051/matecconf/202337802017

Pan, Z., Jiang, Z., Sun, X., Zhang, M., & Cao, Y. (2024). Compressive strength and isothermal calorimetry of binary and ternary geopolymer mortars at early age. *Research Square*. https://doi.org/DOI: 10.21203/rs.3.rs-5270327/v1

Passuello, A., Rodríguez, E. D., Hirt, E., Longhi, M. A., Bernal, S. A., Provis, J. L., & Kirchheim, A. P. (2017). Environmental footprint improvement of geopolymers using waste-derived activators. *Journal of Cleaner Production*, *166*, 680. DOI: 10.1016/j.jclepro.2017.08.007

Pasupathy, K., Sanjayan, J., Rajeev, P., & Law, D. W. (2021). Effect of chloride ingress in reinforced geopolymer concrete in marine environment. *Journal of Building Engineering*, *39*, 102281. DOI: 10.1016/j.jobe.2021.102281

Pérez, M. P. S., Suárez, J. A. D., & Castro-Gomes, J. (2022). Improving the behaviour of green geopolymer concrete using different hemp preservation conditions. *Minerals (Basel)*, *12*(12), 1530. DOI: 10.3390/min12121530

Perná, I., Šupová, M., Hanzlíček, T., & Špaldoňová, A. (2019). Synthesis and characterization of geopolymers based on metakaolin and high LOI straw ash. *Construction & Building Materials*, *228*, 116765. DOI: 10.1016/j.conbuildmat.2019.116765

Pouhet, R., & Cyr, M. (2014). Studies of natural and accelerated carbonation in metakaolin-based geopolymer. *Advances in Science and Technology (Owerri, Nigeria)*, 38–43. Advance online publication. . DOI: 10.4028/www.scientific.net/AST.92.38

Provis, J. L. (2009). *Activating solution chemistry for geopolymers*. In *Elsevier eBooks* (p. 50). https://doi.org/DOI: 10.1533/9781845696382.1.50

Provis, J. L., & Bernal, S. A. (2014). Geopolymers and related alkali-activated materials. *Annual Review of Materials Research*, *44*(1), 299–327. DOI: 10.1146/annurev-matsci-070813-113515

Przybek, A., Łach, M., Bogucki, R., Ciemnicka, J., Prałat, K., Koper, A., Korniejenko, K., & Masłoń, A. (2024). Energy-efficient geopolymer composites containing phase-change materials—Comparison of different contents and types. *Materials (Basel)*, *17*(19), 4712. DOI: 10.3390/ma17194712

Quiatchon, P. R. J., Dollente, I. J., Abulencia, A. B., Libre, R. G. D., Villoria, M. B. D., Guades, E. J., Promentilla, M. A. B., & Ongpeng, J. M. C. (2021). Compressive strength and setting time of low-calcium fly ash geopolymer paste using RSM. *Polymers*, *13*(20), 3461. DOI: 10.3390/polym13203461

Rabbat, C., Awad, S., Villot, A., Rollet, D., & Andrès, Y. (2021). Sustainability of biomass-based insulation materials in buildings: Current status in France, end-of-life projections and energy recovery potentials. *Renewable & Sustainable Energy Reviews*, *156*, 111962. DOI: 10.1016/j.rser.2021.111962

Rabie, M., Irshidat, M. R., & Al-Nuaimi, N. (2022). Ambient and heat-cured geopolymer composites: Mix design optimization and life cycle assessment. *Sustainability (Basel)*, *14*(9), 4942. DOI: 10.3390/su14094942

Rahimpour, H., Amini, A. B., Sharifi, F., Fahmi, A., & Zinatloo-Ajabshir, S. (2024). Facile fabrication of sustainable brick and mortar through geopolymerization of construction debris. *Scientific Reports*, *14*(1), 10914. Advance online publication. DOI: 10.1038/s41598-024-61688-x

Rahman, S. H. A., Zulkarnain, N. N., & Shafiq, N. (2021). *Experimental study and DOE statistical analysis for geopolymer matrix development for oil-well cementing*. In *Vide Leaf eBooks*. https://doi.org/DOI: 10.37247/PAMS2ED.3.2021.14

Rajczakowska, M., Habermehl-Cwirzen, K., Hedlund, H., & Ćwirzeń, A. (2019). Self-healing potential of geopolymer concrete. *Proceedings*, *6*, 6. Advance online publication. DOI: 10.3390/proceedings2019034006

Ramesh, V., Muthramu, B., & Rebekhal, D. (2025). Review of sustainability assessment of geopolymer concrete through AI-based life cycle analysis. *AI in Civil Engineering*, *4*(1), 3. Advance online publication. DOI: 10.1007/s43503-024-00045-3

Ranjbar, N., Kuenzel, C., Spangenberg, J., & Mehrali, M. (2020). Hardening evolution of geopolymers from setting to equilibrium: A review. *Cement and Concrete Composites*, *114*, 103729. DOI: 10.1016/j.cemconcomp.2020.103729

Ranjbar, N., Mehrali, M., Kuenzel, C., Gundlach, C., Pedersen, D. B., Dolatshahi-Pirouz, A., & Spangenberg, J. (2021). Rheological characterization of 3D printable geopolymers. *Cement and Concrete Research*, *147*, 106498. DOI: 10.1016/j.cemconres.2021.106498

Rao, B. N. M., Durga, C. S. S., Venkatesh, C., & Rao, T. M. (2024). Sustainable geopolymer concrete for pavements: Performance of recycled concrete aggregates in fly ash-based mixtures. *Journal of Sustainable Construction Materials and Technologies*, *9*(3), 211–220. DOI: 10.47481/jscmt.1554284

Rathnayaka, M., Karunasingha, D., Gunasekara, C., Law, D. W., Wijesundara, K. K., & Lokuge, W. (2024). Target-strength-based mix design determination for geopolymer concrete. *Archives of Civil and Mechanical Engineering*, *24*(3). Advance online publication. DOI: 10.1007/s43452-024-01002-8

Ravish, G., & Abbass, M. (2026). Engineering characteristics of agro-residue–based geopolymer concrete with fibre reinforcement. *Scientific Reports*, *16*(1), 5585. Advance online publication. DOI: 10.1038/s41598-026-36190-1

Reddy, D. V., Edouard, J.-B., & Sobhan, K. (2012). Durability of fly ash-based geopolymer structural concrete in the marine environment. *Journal of Materials in Civil Engineering*, *25*(6), 781–787. DOI: 10.1061/(ASCE)MT.1943-5533.0000632

Rifaai, Y., Yahia, A., Mostafa, A., Aggoun, S., & Kadri, E.-H. (2019). Rheology of fly ash-based geopolymer: Effect of NaOH concentration. *Construction & Building Materials*, *223*, 583–594. DOI: 10.1016/j.conbuildmat.2019.07.028

Rihawi, B., Maraş, M. M., Ekinci, E., & Kutlusoy, E. (2025). Development of fiber-reinforced eco-friendly concrete for geopolymer pipes infrastructure. *Clean Technologies and Environmental Policy*, *27*(10), 5165. DOI: 10.1007/s10098-025-03171-3

Rintala, A., Havukainen, J., & Abdulkareem, M. (2021). Cost-competitiveness of recycling-based geopolymer concretes. *Recycling*, *6*(3), 46. DOI: 10.3390/recycling6030046

Rubinsin, N. J., Daud, W. R. W., Kamarudin, S. K., Masdar, M. S., Rosli, M. I., Samsatli, S., Tapia, J. F. D., Ghani, W. A. W. A. K., Hasan, A., & Lim, K. L. (2020). Modelling and optimisation of oil palm biomass value chains and the environment–food–energy–water nexus in Peninsular Malaysia. *Biomass and Bioenergy*, *144*, 105912. DOI: 10.1016/j.biombioe.2020.105912

Saba, M., & Arairo, W. (2024). Perspective chapter: Geopolymers in civil and environmental engineering applications. In *IntechOpen eBooks*. IntechOpen., DOI: 10.5772/intechopen.1007018

Samridhi, K. J. S., Akhai, S., Abbass, M., Arif, S. M., & Pathak, S. (2025, October). Mechanical properties of graphene-reinforced cement composites: A review. In *AIP Conference Proceedings* (Vol. 3343, No. 1, p. 020026). AIP Publishing LLC. https://doi.org/DOI: 10.1063/5.0292724

Sanoja-López, K. A., Loor-Molina, N. S., & Luque, R. (2023). Rice waste feedstocks: A review of alternatives for their conversion into high-value added products. *BioResources*, *19*(1). Advance online publication. DOI: 10.15376/biores.19.1.Sanoja-Lopez

Santana, H. A., & Neto, J. (2020). Self-compacting geopolymer mixture: Dosing based on statistical mixture design and simultaneous optimization. *Construction & Building Materials*, *249*, 118677. DOI: 10.1016/j.conbuildmat.2020.118677

Santi, A., Mossini, E., Magugliani, G., Galluccio, F., Macerata, E., Lotti, P., Gatta, G. D., Vadivel, D., Dondi, D., Cori, D., Nonnet, H., & Mariani, M. (2022). Design of sustainable geopolymeric matrices for encapsulation of treated radioactive solid organic waste. *Frontiers in Materials*, *9*, 1005864. Advance online publication. DOI: 10.3389/fmats.2022.1005864

Santucci, S., Zhang, H., Sanna, S., Pryds, N., & Esposito, V. (2019). Defective ceria actuator: The influence of electrodes. *Research Portal Denmark*. https://local.forskningsportal.dk/.../dtu-ee56a4c4-e751-4751-bd93-6781666f70e4

Sbahieh, S., McKay, G., & Al-Ghamdi, S. G. (2023). Comprehensive analysis of geopolymer materials: Properties, environmental impacts, and applications. *Materials (Basel)*, *16*(23), 7363. DOI: 10.3390/ma16237363

Shahedan, N. F., Hadibarata, T., Jusoh, M. N. H., Isia, I., Bouaissi, A., Juwono, F. H., Nawawi, N. A., Kusumaningrum, H. P., Muslim, A., & Hidayat, T. (2024). Advancements in geopolymer concrete for marine infrastructure: An optimization of performance considering workability, compressive strength, capillary water absorption, porosity and chloride migration. *Civil Engineering (Shiraz)*, *49*(4), 4181–4194. DOI: 10.1007/s40996-024-01671-8

Sharma, V., Tripathi, A. K., & Mittal, H. (2022). *Technological revolutions in smart farming: Current trends, challenges & future directions*. [No publication details provided]

Sharmin, S., Biswas, W. K., & Sarker, P. K. (2024). Evaluating techno-eco-efficiency of waste clay brick powder (WCBP) in geopolymer binders. *Buildings (Basel, Switzerland)*, *14*(3), 692. DOI: 10.3390/buildings14030692

Shi, C., Qu, B., & Provis, J. L. (2019). Recent progress in low-carbon binders. *Cement and Concrete Research*, *122*, 227–250. DOI: 10.1016/j.cemconres.2019.05.009

Shi, X., Zhang, C., Liang, Y., Luo, J., Wang, X., Feng, Y., Li, Y., Wang, Q., & Abomohra, A. E. (2021). Life cycle assessment and impact correlation analysis of fly ash geopolymer concrete. *Materials (Basel)*, *14*(23), 7375. DOI: 10.3390/ma14237375

Sikora, P., Skibicki, S., Chougan, M., Szewczyk, P., Cendrowski, K., Federowicz, K., El-Khayatt, A. M., Saudi, H. A., Strzałkowski, J., Elrahman, M. A., Techman, M., Sibera, D., & Chung, S.-Y. (2025). Silica-coated admixtures of bismuth and gadolinium oxides for 3D printed concrete applications. *Construction & Building Materials*, *470*, 140563. DOI: 10.1016/j.conbuildmat.2025.140563

Singh, A., & Singh, B. (2020). Characterization of rice husk ash obtained from an industrial source. *Journal of Sustainable Cement-Based Materials*, *10*(4), 193–205. DOI: 10.1080/21650373.2020.1789010

Siyal, A. A., Mohamed, R. M. S. R., Shamsuddin, R., & Ridzuan, M. B. (2024). A comprehensive review of synthesis kinetics and formation mechanism of geopolymers. *RSC Advances*, *14*(1), 446–470. DOI: 10.1039/D3RA06205H

Soares, M. M. N. de S., & Poggiali, F. S. J. Bezerra, A. C. da S., Figueiredo, R. B., Aguilar, M. T. P., & Cetlin, P. R. (2014). The effect of calcination conditions on characteristics of sugar cane bagasse ash. *Rem—Revista Escola de Minas, 67*(1), 33–39. https://doi.org/DOI: 10.1590/s0370-44672014000100005

Statkauskas, M., Vaičiukynienė, D., & Grinys, A. (2024). Mechanical properties of low-calcium alkali-activated binder under ambient curing conditions. *Scientific Reports*, *14*(1), 13060. Advance online publication. DOI: 10.1038/s41598-024-63808-z

Strini, A., Roviello, G., Ricciotti, L., Ferone, C., Messina, F., Schiavi, L., Corsaro, D., & Cioffi, R. (2016). $TiO_2$-based photocatalytic geopolymers for nitric oxide degradation. *Materials (Basel)*, *9*(7), 513. DOI: 10.3390/ma9070513

Strohle, M., Sadique, M., Dulaimi, A., & Kadhim, M. A. (2022). Prospect and barrier of 3D concrete: A systematic review. *Innovative Infrastructure Solutions*, *8*(1), 21. Advance online publication. DOI: 10.1007/s41062-022-00975-w

Sukkathanyawat, H., Bampenrat, A., Jarunglumlert, T., & Prommuak, C. (2022). Modification of waste sugarcane bagasse fly ash for $CO_2$ capture. *Materials for Renewable and Sustainable Energy*, *11*(3), 267–276. DOI: 10.1007/s40243-022-00219-y

Sun, Q., Zhao, S., Zhao, X., Song, Y., Ban, X., & Zhang, N. (2023). Influence of different grinding degrees of fly ash on geopolymer properties. *PLoS One*, *18*(3). Advance online publication. DOI: 10.1371/journal.pone.0282927

Šupić, S., Malešev, M., Радоњанин, В., Bulatović, V., & Milović, T. (2021). Reactivity and pozzolanic properties of biomass ashes from wheat and soybean straw. *Materials (Basel)*, *14*(4), 1004. DOI: 10.3390/ma14041004

Tanyıldızı, H. (2024). Deep learning–based prediction of compressive strength of eco-friendly geopolymer concrete. *Environmental Science and Pollution Research International*, *31*(28), 41246–41263. DOI: 10.1007/s11356-024-33853-2

Techo, A., Kaewpikul, D., Sata, V., Tanapongpisit, N., Wongprasod, S., Saenrang, W., Chainakun, P., Chindaprasirt, P., & Ekprasert, J. (2024). Enhanced mechanical and self-healing properties of rice husk ash–incinerated sugarcane press mud bio-geopolymer pastes. *Scientific Reports*, *14*(1), 28121. Advance online publication. DOI: 10.1038/s41598-024-79916-9

Teng, Z., Huang, S., Xu, H., Li, N., & Zhou, Q. (2021). Preparation and properties of rice hull ash as catalysis supporter in a fluidized-bed reactor. *IOP Conference Series. Earth and Environmental Science*, *766*(1), 012080. DOI: 10.1088/1755-1315/766/1/012080

Thakur, R., Bharti, K., Abbass, M., Akhai, S., Arif, S. M., & Pathak, S. (2025, October). Insights into the thermal performance of fly ash-based geopolymer concrete. In. AIP Conference Proceedings: Vol. 3343. *No. 1* (p. 020025). AIP Publishing LLC., DOI: 10.1063/5.0292726

Tositti, L., Masi, G., Morozzi, P., Zappi, A., & Bignozzi, M. C. (2023). Cleaner, sustainable and safer: Green potential of alkali-activated materials. *Construction & Building Materials*, *409*, 133879. DOI: 10.1016/j.conbuildmat.2023.133879

Toyeb, M., Hakam, A., & Andriani, A. (2023). Strength and economic benefit of soil stabilization with palm oil fuel ash. *E3S Web of Conferences, 464*, 11001. https://doi.org/DOI: 10.1051/e3sconf/202346411001

Turner, L. K., & Collins, F. (2013). $CO_2$-equivalent emissions: A comparison between geopolymer and OPC concrete. *Construction & Building Materials*, *43*, 125–130. DOI: 10.1016/j.conbuildmat.2013.01.023

Ungureanu, N., Vlădu , V., & Biriş, S. Ş. (2022). Sustainable valorization of waste and by-products from sugarcane processing. *Sustainability (Basel)*, *14*(17), 11089. DOI: 10.3390/su141711089

Uthayakumar, M., Balamurugan, P., Korniejenko, K., Gądek, S., & Mierzwiński, D. (2020). Abrasive water jet machining of fly ash and metakaolin-based geopolymers. *MATEC Web of Conferences, 322*, 01020. https://doi.org/DOI: 10.1051/matecconf/202032201020

Valencia-Saavedra, W., de Gutiérrez, R. M., & Puertas, F. (2020). Performance of fly ash-based geopolymers exposed to acetic and sulfuric acids. *Construction & Building Materials*, *257*, 119503. DOI: 10.1016/j.conbuildmat.2020.119503

Valente, M., Sambucci, M., Chougan, M., & Ghaffar, S. H. (2021). Reducing emissions in cementitious materials: A comparison of alkali-activated materials and Portland cement composites. *Journal of Cleaner Production*, *333*, 130013. DOI: 10.1016/j.jclepro.2021.130013

van Deventer, J. S. J., Provis, J. L., & Duxson, P. (2011). Technical and commercial progress in the adoption of geopolymer cement. *Minerals Engineering*, *29*, 89–104. DOI: 10.1016/j.mineng.2011.09.009

van Deventer, J. S. J., Provis, J. L., Duxson, P., & Lukey, G. C. (2006). Reaction mechanisms in the geopolymeric conversion of inorganic waste to useful products. *Journal of Hazardous Materials*, *139*(3), 506–513. DOI: 10.1016/j.jhazmat.2006.02.044

Verma, M., Dev, N., Rahman, I., Nigam, M., Ahmed, M., & Mallick, J. (2022). Geopolymer concrete: A material for sustainable development in Indian construction industries. *Crystals*, *12*(4), 514. DOI: 10.3390/cryst12040514

Vītola, L., Pundienė, I., Pranckevičienė, J., & Bajāre, D. (2020). Effect of water content and initial temperature on rheology of metakaolin geopolymer pastes. *Sustainability*, *12*(19), 8216. DOI: 10.3390/su12198216

Vlachakis, C., Perry, M., Biondi, L., & McAlorum, J. (2020). 3D printed temperature-sensing repairs for concrete structures. *Additive Manufacturing*, *34*, 101238. DOI: 10.1016/j.addma.2020.101238

Vlachakis, C., Su, Y.-F., & Al-Tabbaa, A. (2023). Interfacial bonding effect on self-sensing coatings for infrastructure monitoring. *MATEC Web of Conferences*, *378*, 05006. https://doi.org/DOI: 10.1051/matecconf/202337805006

Vogt, O., Ukrainczyk, N., & Koenders, E. (2021). Effect of silica fume on metakaolin geopolymer sulfuric acid resistance. *Materials (Basel)*, *14*(18), 5396. DOI: 10.3390/ma14185396

Wadhwa, A. S., Abbass, M., Akhai, S., Kumar, D., & Kumar, P. (2025). Integrating Taguchi optimization for multi-criteria decision making. In *Recent Theories and Applications for Multi-Criteria Decision-Making* (pp. 125–150). IGI Global., DOI: 10.4018/979-8-3693-6502-1.ch005

Wadhwa, A. S., Akhai, S., Abbass, M., Chouksey, A., Tiwari, S., & Taneja, T. (2025). Computational intelligence-driven design and optimization of a polyurethane oil skimmer. In *Using Computational Intelligence for Sustainable Manufacturing of Advanced Materials* (pp. 445–464). IGI Global., DOI: 10.4018/979-8-3693-7974-5.ch019

Wan, K., Wang, Z., Xia, J., Vervisch, L., Domingo, P., Lv, Y., Liu, Y., He, Y., & Cen, K. (2019). Impact of HCl and $SO_2$ on potassium emissions in pulverized biomass combustion. *Fuel Processing Technology*, *193*, 19–29. DOI: 10.1016/j.fuproc.2019.04.032

Wandiga, C. A. (2020). Socio-cultural analysis criteria for BIM modeling and material passport tracking of agriwaste. *MRS Energy & Sustainability : a Review Journal*, *7*(1), 25. Advance online publication. DOI: 10.1557/mre.2020.29

Wang, H., Wu, H., Xing, Z., Wang, R., & Dai, S. (2021). Effect of Si/Al and Na/Al ratios and free water on metakaolin geopolymer strength. *Materials (Basel)*, *14*(14), 3845. DOI: 10.3390/ma14143845

Wang, H., Zhao, X., Wang, J., He, L., Zhang, A., Gao, H., Yang, J., & Liang, L. (2023). Cementation mechanism of geopolymer backfill paste with industrial solid wastes. *Materials (Basel)*, *16*(2), 480. DOI: 10.3390/ma16020480

Wang, H. T., Yang, X., Wang, M., & Qu, C. (2023). Influence of silicon-aluminium modified materials on durability of fly ash geopolymers. *Materials Science Forum*, *1103*, 139–148. DOI: 10.4028/p-0kV4eB

Wang, X., Yang, Z., Liu, X., Huang, G., Xiao, W., & Han, L. (2020). Composition characteristics of different crop straw types. *Waste Management (New York, N.Y.)*, *110*, 87–95. DOI: 10.1016/j.wasman.2020.05.018

Wasim, M., Ngo, T., & Law, D. W. (2021). Durability of geopolymer concrete: A state-of-the-art review. *Construction & Building Materials*, *291*, 123381. DOI: 10.1016/j.conbuildmat.2021.123381

Wei, X., Huang, B., Chen, K., Fan, Z., Wang, L., & Xu, M. (2022). Dot extrusion bioprinting of spatially controlled heterogeneous tumor models. *Materials & Design*, *223*, 111152. DOI: 10.1016/j.matdes.2022.111152

Wu, D., Wang, J., Tong, M., Chen, K., & Zhang, Z. (2023). Performance optimization of FA–GGBS geopolymers using RSM. *Polymers*, *15*(8), 1881. DOI: 10.3390/polym15081881

Yılmaz, Y., Çakmak, T., Kurt, Z., & Ustabaş, İ. (2024). Predicting mechanical properties in geopolymer mortars using XGBoost. *Arabian Journal for Science and Engineering*. Advance online publication. DOI: 10.1007/s13369-024-09179-z

Yin, X., Wang, X., Yuan, F., & Ding, Z. (2020). Effect of curing age on high-temperature properties of 3D-printed geopolymer mortar. *E3S Web of Conferences*, *218*, 03019. https://doi.org/DOI: 10.1051/e3sconf/202021803019

You, S., Ho, S. W., Li, T., Maneerung, T., & Wang, C. (2018). Techno-economic analysis of geopolymer production from high-Fe and high-Ca fly ash. *Journal of Hazardous Materials*, *361*, 237–245. DOI: 10.1016/j.jhazmat.2018.08.089

Yu, M. (2024). Battery components derived from silica-depleted rice hull ash. *University of Michigan—Deep Blue Repository*. https://doi.org/DOI: 10.7302/24934

Ziegler, D., Formia, A., Tulliani, J., & Palmero, P. (2016). Dense and porous geopolymers using fly ash and rice husk ash. *Materials (Basel)*, *9*(6), 466. DOI: 10.3390/ma9060466

Zou, Y., Zheng, C., Alzahrani, A., Ahmad, W., Ahmad, A., Mohamed, A. M., Khallaf, R., & Elattar, S. (2022). Evaluation of AI methods to estimate compressive strength of geopolymers. *Gels (Basel, Switzerland)*, *8*(5), 271. DOI: 10.3390/gels8050271

Zubrod, R. W. (2013). *Performance-based specification for geopolymer cement binders and supporting laboratory data*. In *ASTM International eBooks* (p. 165). https://doi.org/DOI: 10.1520/STP156620120061

Zurairah, M., Saragih, E. S., & Misdawati, M. (2021). Comparison of thermogravimetric characterization of rice husk in active carbon analyzer. *JUMPA*, *3*(2), 64–69. DOI: 10.54076/jumpa.v1i2.176

## KEY TERMS AND DEFINITIONS

**Agricultural Residue:** The by-products left after harvesting or processing crops, such as husks, bagasse, or straw, often rich in silica and alumina.

**Alkali Activation:** A chemical process where silicate and aluminate minerals dissolve in an alkaline solution, forming a cross-linked network that hardens into a solid matrix.

**Alkaline Activator:** A solution containing hydroxides and silicates of sodium or potassium used to trigger geopolymerization reactions in aluminosilicate precursors.

**Circular Economy:** A sustainable economic model focused on reducing waste and reusing resources by closing material loops between production and consumption cycles.

**Durability:** The ability of a construction material to resist environmental degradation such as acid attack, sulfate exposure, or chloride penetration over time.

**Geopolymer:** An inorganic polymer formed through the reaction of aluminosilicate materials with alkaline activators, producing a strong, durable, and low-carbon binder.

**Life Cycle Assessment (LCA):** A method used to evaluate the environmental impact of a product or process from raw-material extraction to disposal or recycling.

**Self-Healing Material:** A material that can automatically repair micro-cracks or damage through chemical, physical, or biological mechanisms.

**Self-Sensing Material:** A type of material capable of detecting its own stress, strain, or damage through changes in its electrical or physical properties.

**Sustainable Infrastructure:** Physical structures designed and constructed using materials and methods that minimize environmental impact, reduce emissions, and enhance resilience.

# Compilation of References

Abbas, U., Akhai, S., Abbass, M., Abass, S., Chouksey, A., & Wadhwa, A. S. (2026). Sustainable growth by navigating complexity through innovation and adaptive industrial policies. In *Industrial Policy, Innovation, and Complexity: Comparative Analysis, Trends, and Prospects* (pp. 29-82). IGI Global. https://doi.org/DOI: 10.4018/979-8-3373-1767-0.ch002

Abbas, M. A., Kwan, W. H., Samsudin, M. H., & Hai, T. (2024). Optimising factors for the production of amorphous rice husk ash via combustion process for sustainable construction: A review. *Journal of Advanced Research in Applied Mechanics*, *120*(1), 50–61. DOI: 10.37934/aram.120.1.5061

Abbas, M., Sarita, D., Alrasheedi, M., Arya, L., Singh, M. P., & Pandey, K. (2023). Hybrid intuitionistic fuzzy entropy–SWARA–COPRAS method for multi-criteria sustainable biomass crop type selection. *Sustainability (Basel)*, *15*(10), 1–16. DOI: 10.3390/su15107765

Abbass, M., Akhai, S., Verma, R., Singh, G., Singh, D., & Wani, S. A. Mechanical and Durability Properties of Sugarcane Bagasse and Cow Dung Ash-Based Sustainable Geopolymer Bricks. In *CISSC 2025* (pp. 52-64). https://doi.org/DOI: 10.1061/9780784486481.007

Abbas, S. A., & Zaman, A. (2024). Does digitalisation help achieve (selected) socio-economic SDGs: Evidence from emerging economies? *Sustainable Development (Bradford)*, *32*(6), 6088–6103. DOI: 10.1002/sd.3014

Abbass, M., Abbas, U., Jafri, R., Arif, S. M., & Akhai, S. (2025). AI and machine learning applications in sustainable smart cities. In *Sustainable Smart Cities and the Future of Urban Development* (pp. 1–32). IGI Global., DOI: 10.4018/979-8-3693-6740-7.ch001

Abbass, M., & Akhai, S. (2025). Eco-friendly geopolymer bricks synthesized from alkali-activated sugarcane bagasse ash and rice husk ash. *Industrial Crops and Products, 233*, 121410. DOI: 10.1016/j.indcrop.2025.121410

Abbass, M., & Akhai, S. (2025). *Exploring the sustainability potential of geopolymer concrete with coal bottom ash and basalt fibres.* Multiscale and Multidisciplinary Modeling. *Experiments and Design, 8*(3), 199. DOI: 10.1007/s41939-025-00794-3

Abbass, M., Akhai, S., Abbas, U., Jafri, R., & Arif, S. M. (2025). AI-enabled sustainable urban planning and management. In *Real-World Applications of AI Innovation* (pp. 233–260). IGI Global., DOI: 10.4018/979-8-3693-4252-7.ch012

Abbass, M., Akhai, S., Chouksey, A., Pathak, S., Abbas, U., & Abass, S. (2025). Disaster risk reduction and management with emerging technologies: Applications of IoT, AI, and data analytics for resilient urban infrastructure. In *Revolutionizing Urban Development and Governance With Emerging Technologies* (pp. 71–110). IGI Global., DOI: 10.4018/979-8-3373-1375-7.ch003

Abbass, M., & Singh, G. (2021). Fatigue analysis of rice husk ash and basalt fibre-based sustainable geopolymer concrete in rigid pavements. *Materials Today: Proceedings, 45*, 5014–5022. DOI: 10.1016/j.matpr.2021.01.450

Abbass, M., & Singh, G. (2021). Rice husk ash and basalt fibre-based sustainable geopolymer concrete in rigid pavements under ambient curing conditions. In *Lecture Notes in Civil Engineering* (Vol. 143, pp. 385–397). Springer.

Abbass, M., & Singh, G. (2022). Durability of rice husk ash and basalt fibre-based sustainable geopolymer concrete in rigid pavements. *Materials Today: Proceedings, 61*, 558–570. Advance online publication. DOI: 10.1016/j.matpr.2022.02.196

Abbass, M., & Singh, G. (2022). Impact strength of rice husk ash and basalt fibre-based sustainable geopolymer concrete in rigid pavements. *Materials Today: Proceedings, 61*, 250–257. DOI: 10.1016/j.matpr.2021.09.053

Abbass, M., & Singh, G. (2023). *Experimental investigation of alkali-activated hybrid geopolymer concrete.* Multiscale and Multidisciplinary Modeling. *Experiments and Design, 6*(2), 235–249. DOI: 10.1007/s41939-023-00144-1

Abbass, M., & Singh, G. (2023). Experimental investigation of engineered alkali-activated fibrous geopolymer concrete. *Journal of Building Pathology and Rehabilitation, 8*(1), 1–16. DOI: 10.1007/s41024-022-00259-x

Abbass, M., & Singh, G. (2024). *Microstructural analysis of environment-friendly sustainable geopolymer concrete.* Multiscale and Multidisciplinary Modeling. *Experiments and Design, 7*(1), 301–319. DOI: 10.1007/s41939-023-00200-w

Abdelmongy, M., Iqbal, M., Farag, M. M., Yosri, A. M., Alsharari, F., & Yousef, S. E. A. S. (2024). Artificial intelligence prediction of one-part geopolymer compressive strength for sustainable concrete. *Computer Modeling in Engineering & Sciences*, *141*(1), 525–543. DOI: 10.32604/cmes.2024.052505

Aboueata, W., Hijawi, U., Al-Kababji, A., Mohieddine, A., & Choe, P. (2021). Statistical analysis of renewable and non-renewable energy consumption against population growth. *IOP Conference Series. Earth and Environmental Science*, *726*(1), 012003. Advance online publication. DOI: 10.1088/1755-1315/726/1/012003

Achouch, M., Dimitrova, M., Ziane, K., Sattarpanah Karganroudi, S., Dhouib, R., Ibrahim, H., & Adda, M. (2022). On Predictive Maintenance in Industry 4.0: Overview, Models, and Challenges. In *Applied Sciences (Switzerland)* (Vol. 12, Number 16). MDPI. DOI: 10.3390/app12168081

Adebayo, T. S., Oladipupo, S. D., Kirikkaleli, D., & Adeshola, I. (2022). Asymmetric nexus between technological innovation and environmental degradation in Sweden: An aggregated and disaggregated analysis. *Environmental Science and Pollution Research International*, *29*(24), 36547–36564. DOI: 10.1007/s11356-021-17982-6

Ademi, A., & Klungseth, N. J. (2024). Advancing the understanding of sustainable business models through organizational learning. *Business Strategy and the Environment*, *33*(6), 5441–5463. DOI: 10.1002/bse.3746

Adesanya, E., Perumal, P., Luukkonen, T., Yliniemi, J., Ohenoja, K., Kinnunen, P., & Illikainen, M. (2020). Opportunities to improve sustainability of alkali-activated materials: A review of side-stream based activators. *Journal of Cleaner Production*, *286*, 125558. DOI: 10.1016/j.jclepro.2020.125558

Ajith, S., Vijayakumar, S., & Elakkiya, N. (2025). Yield prediction, pest and disease diagnosis, soil fertility mapping, precision irrigation scheduling, and food quality assessment using machine learning and deep learning algorithms. *Discover Food*, *5*(1), 67. Advance online publication. DOI: 10.1007/s44187-025-00338-1

Akberdina, V., Kuzmin, E., Kyriakopoulos, G. L., & Kumar, V. (2024). Editorial: Sustainability of digital transformation for the environment. *Frontiers in Environmental Science*, *12*(1), 1–4. DOI: 10.3389/fenvs.2024.1371047

Akeke, G. A., Inem, P.-E. U., Alaneme, G. U., & Nyah, E. E. (2023). Experimental investigation and modelling of the mechanical properties of palm oil fuel ash concrete using Scheffe's method. *Scientific Reports*, *13*(1), 18583. Advance online publication. DOI: 10.1038/s41598-023-45987-3

Alahmari, T. S., Abdalla, T. A., & Rihan, M. A. M. (2023). Review of recent developments regarding the durability performance of eco-friendly geopolymer concrete. *Buildings (Basel, Switzerland), 13*(12), 3033. DOI: 10.3390/buildings13123033

Alalawneh, A. A. F., & Alkhatib, S. F. (2021). The barriers to big data adoption in developing economies. *The Electronic Journal on Information Systems in Developing Countries, 87*(1), e12151. Advance online publication. DOI: 10.1002/isd2.12151

Alam, K. M., & El Saddik, A. (2017). C2PS: A digital twin architecture reference model for the cloud-based cyber-physical systems. *IEEE Access : Practical Innovations, Open Solutions, 5*, 2050–2062. DOI: 10.1109/ACCESS.2017.2657006

Alaneme, G. U., Olonade, K. A., & Esenogho, E. (2023). Eco-friendly agro-waste based geopolymer-concrete: A systematic review. *Discover Materials, 3*(1), 14. Advance online publication. DOI: 10.1007/s43939-023-00052-8

Alaneme, G. U., Olonade, K. A., Esenogho, E., & Lawan, M. M. (2024). Proposed simplified methodological approach for designing geopolymer concrete mixtures. *Scientific Reports, 14*(1), 15191. Advance online publication. DOI: 10.1038/s41598-024-66093-y

Alawi, A., Milad, A., Barbieri, D. M., Alosta, M., Alaneme, G. U., & Latif, Q. B. (2023). Eco-friendly geopolymer composites prepared from agro-industrial wastes: A state-of-the-art review. *CivilEng, 4*(2), 433–453. DOI: 10.3390/civileng4020025

Albert, O. O. K., Marianne, T., Jonathan, L., Nino, J. L., & Dario, C. (2020). Tracking the carbon emissions of Denmark's five regions from a producer and consumer perspective. *Ecological Economics, 177*, 106778. DOI: 10.1016/j.ecolecon.2020.106778

Albertsen, L., Richter, J. L., Peck, P., Dalhammar, C., & Plepys, A. (2021). Circular business models for electric vehicle lithium-ion batteries: An analysis of current practices of vehicle manufacturers and policies in the EU. *Resources, Conservation and Recycling, 172*, 105658. DOI: 10.1016/j.resconrec.2021.105658

Albitar, M., Ali, M. S. M., Visintin, P., & Drechsler, M. (2017). Durability evaluation of geopolymer and conventional concretes. *Construction & Building Materials, 136*, 374–385. DOI: 10.1016/j.conbuildmat.2017.01.056

Aldaya, M. M., Garrido, A., & Llamas, R. (2020). Water footprint and virtual water trade: The birth and growth of a new research field in Spain. *Water (Basel), 12*(9), 2641. Advance online publication. DOI: 10.3390/w12092641

Ali, A. Y. F., Ahmed, S. A., Helal, Y., & El-Feky, M. S. (2025). Thermo-mechanical behavior and spalling resistance of alkali-activated slag versus cement mortars under rapid high-temperature exposure. *Scientific Reports*, *15*(1), 32581. Advance online publication. DOI: 10.1038/s41598-025-19301-2

Al-Kasassbeh, S., Al-Thawabteh, J., Al-Kharabsheh, E., & Al-Tamseh, A. (2023). Influential and intellectual structure of geopolymer concrete: A bibliometric review. *Civil Engineering Journal*, *9*(9), 2330–2344. DOI: 10.28991/CEJ-2023-09-09-017

Allan, J. (2005). Virtual Water: A Strategic Resource Global Solutions to Regional Deficits. *Groundwater*, *36*(4), 545–546. DOI: 10.1111/j.1745-6584.1998.tb02825.x

Allan, J. a. (1997). *"Virtual water": a long term solution for water short Middle Eastern economies?* School of Oriental and African Studies, University of London., September., http://www.ciaonet.org/wps/aln02/

Almaiah, M. A., Yelisetti, S., Arya, L., Babu Christopher, N. K., Kaliappan, K., Vellaisamy, P., Hajjej, F., & Alkdour, T. (2023). A novel approach for improving the security of IoT–medical data systems using an enhanced dynamic Bayesian network. *Electronics (Basel)*, *12*(20), 1–15. DOI: 10.3390/electronics12204316

Alojail, M., & Khan, S. B. (2023). Impact of digital transformation toward sustainable development. *Sustainability (Basel)*, *15*(1), 1–20. DOI: 10.3390/su152014697

Al-Saudi, S. K. M., Géber, R., Simon, A., Kurovics, E., & Hamza, A. (2023). Comparative study of metakaolin-based geopolymer characteristics utilizing different dosages of water glass in the activator solution. *Results in Engineering*, *20*, 101469. DOI: 10.1016/j.rineng.2023.101469

Al-Shetwi, A. Q., Hannan, M. A., Al-Masri, H. M. K., & Sujod, M. Z. (2025). Latest advancements in smart grid technologies and their transformative role in shaping the power systems of tomorrow: An overview. *Progress in Energy*, *7*(1), 012004. DOI: 10.1088/2516-1083/ada198

Amaludin, A. E., Asrah, H., & Mohamad, H. M. (2023). A review of advances in peat soil stabilisation technology: Exploring the potential of palm oil fuel ash geopolymer as a soil stabiliser material. *Civil Engineering Journal*, *9*(8), 2085–2104. DOI: 10.28991/CEJ-2023-09-08-017

Ameer, F., Khan, M. R., Khan, I., Khan, N. R., & Keoy, K. H. (2024). Organizational resilience and green innovation for environmental performance: Evidence from manufacturing organizations. *Vision (Basel)*, 09722629241254955. Advance online publication. DOI: 10.1177/09722629241254955

An, Q., Wang, R., Wang, Y., & Pavel, K. (2024). The impact of the digital economy on sustainable development: Evidence from China. *Frontiers in Environmental Science*, *12*(1), 1–13. DOI: 10.3389/fenvs.2024.1341471

Antonelli, M., & Tamea, S. (2015). Food-water security and virtual water trade in the Middle East and North Africa. *International Journal of Water Resources Development, 31:3*(July), 326–342. DOI: 10.1080/07900627.2015.1030496

Antonelli, M., Laio, F., & Tamea, S. (2017). Water Resources, Food Security and the Role of Virtual Water Trade in the MENA Region. In *Environmental Change and Human Security in Africa and the Middle East* (pp. 199–217). DOI: 10.1007/978-3-319-45648-5_11

Ariesen-Verschuur, N., Verdouw, C., & Tekinerdogan, B. (2022). Digital twins in greenhouse horticulture: A review. *Computers and Electronics in Agriculture*, *199*, 107183. DOI: 10.1016/j.compag.2022.107183

Arner, D. W., Buckley, R. P., Zetzsche, D. A., & Veidt, R. (2020). Sustainability, FinTech and Financial Inclusion. *European Business Organization Law Review*, *21*(1), 7–35. DOI: 10.1007/s40804-020-00183-y

Arokiasamy, P., Abdullah, M. M. A. B., Rahim, S. Z. A., Sadique, M., Yun-Ming, L., Salleh, M. A. A. M., Zainol, M. R. R. M. A., & Ghazali, C. M. R. (2022). Diverse material based geopolymer towards heavy metals removal: A review. *Journal of Materials Research and Technology*, *22*, 126–156. DOI: 10.1016/j.jmrt.2022.11.100

Arsic, M., O'Sullivan, C., Wasson, A., Antille, D., & Clarke, W. (2023). Beyond waste-to-energy: Bioenergy can drive sustainable Australian agriculture by integrating a circular economy with net-zero ambitions. Detritus. DOI: 10.31025/2611-4135/2023.17278

Arya, L. (2024). Securing healthcare data and cybersecurity innovations in the era of Industry 5.0. In Cybersecurity and Data Management Innovations for Revolutionizing Healthcare (pp. 132–147). DOI: 10.4018/979-8-3693-7457-3.ch006

Arya, L., Biswas, S., Sivaparvathi, M., Katuri, V. R., Rastogi, R., & Pradhan, A. (2026). Deep learning-based detection of digital image forgeries and synthetic content. In Advancements in forensic analysis of digital images for security and law enforcement (pp. 279–314). DOI: 10.4018/979-8-3373-3795-1.ch009

Arya, L., Raju, E. S., & Santosh, M. V. MPJ, S. K., Rastogi, R., Elloumi, M., Arumugam, T., & Namasivayam, B. (2025). Explainable Artificial Intelligence (XAI) for ethical and trustworthy decision-making in 6G networks. In R. Shaikh (Ed.), 6G Networks and AI-Driven Cybersecurity (pp. 217–250). IGI Global Scientific Publishing. DOI: 10.4018/979-8-3373-0568-4.ch008

Arya, L., Bhatnagar, M., Mehrotra, S., Arasavalli, N., Rastogi, R., Banda, L., & Gautam, D. (2025). IoT-driven automation in dairy processing for waste reduction and productivity enhancement. In Mendes de Souza, P. (Ed.), *Next-Generation Technologies in Dairy Processing and Production* (pp. 171–196). IGI Global Scientific Publishing., DOI: 10.4018/979-8-3693-9949-1.ch006

Arya, L., Mehrotra, S., Sabitha, C., Sivaparvathi, M., Katuri, V. R., Rastogi, R., & Rani, K. S. (2026). Real-time air quality monitoring in industrial zones using IoT-powered AI systems. *International Journal of Computer Information Systems and Industrial Management Applications*, *18*, 15. DOI: 10.70917/ijcisim-2026-0983

Arya, L., Sharma, Y. K., Devi, S., Padmanaban, H., & Kumar, R. (2024). Securing the Internet of Things: AI-powered threat detection and safety measures. In Illés, Z., Verma, C., Gonçalves, P. J. S., & Singh, P. K. (Eds.), *Proceedings of International Conference on Recent Innovations in Computing* (Vol. 1195). Springer. DOI: 10.1007/978-981-97-3442-9_7

Arya, L., Sharma, Y. K., & Kumar, R. (2023). Towards a greener tomorrow: IoT-enabled smart environment monitoring systems. In *2023 International Conference on Advances in Computation, Communication and Information Technology (ICAICCIT)* (pp. 1112–1117). IEEE. DOI: 10.1109/ICAICCIT60255.2023.10465894

Arya, L., Sharma, Y. K., Kumar, R., Padmanaban, H., Devi, S., & Tyagi, L. K. (2023). Maximizing IoT security: An examination of cryptographic algorithms. In *2023 International Conference on Power Energy, Environment & Intelligent Control (PEEIC)* (pp. 1548–1552). IEEE. DOI: 10.1109/PEEIC59336.2023.10451210

Arya, L., Sharma, Y. K., Padmanaban, H., Devi, S., & Kumar, R. (2024). Eyes in the sky: Safeguarding borders security with AI-powered aerial monitoring and IoT integration. In Illés, Z., Verma, C., Gonçalves, P. J. S., & Singh, P. K. (Eds.), *Proceedings of International Conference on Recent Innovations in Computing* (Vol. 1195). Springer. DOI: 10.1007/978-981-97-3442-9_61

Atif, S. (2023). The role of Industry 4.0-enabled data-driven shared platform as an enabler of the product-service system in the circular economy context: A systematic literature review and future research directions. *Business Strategy & Development*, *6*(3), 275–295. DOI: 10.1002/bsd2.238

Aupoil, J., Champenois, J., & Lacaillerie, J. (2018). Interplay between silicate and hydroxide ions during geopolymerization. *Cement and Concrete Research, 115*, 426–432. DOI: 10.1016/j.cemconres.2018.09.012

Awan, U., Alshaghdali, N. O., Chotia, V., Alshaghdali, N., Sahore, N., & Walsh, S. (2025). Leveraging global knowledge integration for advancing sustainable product design and green innovation in upstream supply chains. *Journal of Knowledge Management, 29*(10), 2964–2985. DOI: 10.1108/JKM-01-2025-0101

Awan, U., Sroufe, R., & Shahbaz, M. (2021). Industry 4.0 and the circular economy: A literature review and recommendations for future research. *Business Strategy and the Environment, 30*(4), 2038–2060. DOI: 10.1002/bse.2731

Azam Khan, M. (2025). Analyzing the effects of financial inclusion on poverty and income inequality in SAARC developing nations. In *Journal of the Asia Pacific Economy* (Vol. 30, Number 3, pp. 788–811). Routledge. DOI: 10.1080/13547860.2024.2361988

Bachs-Herrera, A., York, D., Stephens-Jones, T., Mabbett, I., Yeo, J., & Martín-Martínez, F. J. (2023). Biomass carbon mining to develop nature-inspired materials for a circular economy. *iScience, 26*(4), 106549. DOI: 10.1016/j.isci.2023.106549

Bag, S., Dhamija, P., Gupta, S., & Sivarajah, U. (2021). Examining the role of procurement 4.0 towards remanufacturing operations and circular economy. *Production Planning and Control, 32*(16), 1368–1383. DOI: 10.1080/09537287.2020.1817602

Bag, S., Gupta, S., & Kumar, S. (2021). Industry 4.0 adoption and 10R advance manufacturing capabilities for sustainable development. *International Journal of Production Economics, 231*, 107844. DOI: 10.1016/j.ijpe.2020.107844

Bai, C., Dallasega, P., Orzes, G., & Sarkis, J. (2020). International Journal of Production Economics Industry 4. 0 technologies assessment : A sustainability perspective. *International Journal of Production Economics, 229*, 107776. DOI: 10.1016/j.ijpe.2020.107776

Bai, C., Zhou, H., & Sarkis, J. (2023). Evaluating Industry 4.0 technology and sustainable development goals–a social perspective. *International Journal of Production Research, 61*(23), 8094–8114. DOI: 10.1080/00207543.2022.2164375

Bąk, A., Łach, M., Romańska, P., Ciemnicka, J., Prałat, K., & Koper, A. (2025). Geopolymer concretes with organic phase change materials—Analysis of thermal properties and microstructure. *Materials (Basel), 18*(11), 2557. DOI: 10.3390/ma18112557

Balan, I. M., Trasca, T. I., Brad, I., Belc, N., Tulcan, C., Radoi, B. P., & Rinovetz, A. E. (2023). *Approaches to Limiting Food Loss and Food Waste*.

Banaitė, D. (2016). Towards circular economy: Analysis of indicators in the context of sustainable development. *Social Transformation in Contemporary Society*, *4*(9), 142–150.

Barve, P., Bahrami, A., & Shah, S. G. (2023). Geopolymer 3D printing: A comprehensive review on rheological and structural performance assessment, printing process parameters, and microstructure. *Frontiers in Materials*, *10*, 1241869. Advance online publication. DOI: 10.3389/fmats.2023.1241869

Barve, P., Bahrami, A., & Shah, S. G. (2024). A comprehensive review on effects of material composition, mix design, and mixing regimes on rheology of 3D-printed geopolymer concrete. *The Open Construction & Building Technology Journal*, *18*(1), e18748368292859. Advance online publication. DOI: 10.2174/0118748368292859240313061706

Basri, M. S. M., Mustapha, F., Mazlan, N., & Ishak, M. R. (2021). Rice-husk-ash-based geopolymer coating: Fire-retardant, optimize composition, microstructural, thermal and element characteristics analysis. *Polymers*, *13*(21), 3747. DOI: 10.3390/polym13213747

Batarseh, F. A., Kulkarni, A., Sreng, C., Lin, J., & Maksud, S. (2023). ACWA: An AI-driven cyber-physical testbed for intelligent water systems. *Water Practice & Technology*, *18*(12), 3399–3418. DOI: 10.2166/wpt.2023.197

Batlles de la Fuente, A., Franco-Garcia, L., Belmonte, L., & Plaza-Úbeda, J. (2023). *Technological Innovations Promoting Circular Economy: A Profitable Tool to Close Resource Loops*., DOI: 10.1007/978-3-031-33982-0_1

Bazarkhankyzy, A., Murali, G. B., Aibuldinov, Y. K., Iskakova, Z., Kurpińska, M., Abdelgader, H. S., Avudaiappan, S., & Dixit, S. (2025). Comprehensive evaluation of impact strength and microstructural characteristics of geopolymer concrete reinforced with natural fibers of varying lengths. *Scientific Reports*, *15*(1), 29624. Advance online publication. DOI: 10.1038/s41598-025-14857-5

Beckett, R. C., & Terziovski, M. (2025). Integrating Circular Economy Principles in Water Resilience: Implications for Corporate Governance and Sustainability Reporting. In *Journal of Risk and Financial Management* (Vol. 18, Issue 5, p. 261). DOI: 10.3390/jrfm18050261

Beltrami, M., Orzes, G., Sarkis, J., & Sartor, M. (2021). Industry 4. 0 and sustainability : Towards conceptualization and theory. *Journal of Cleaner Production*, *312*, 127733. DOI: 10.1016/j.jclepro.2021.127733

Bentsen, N. S., Felby, C., & Thorsen, B. J. (2013). Agricultural residue production and potentials for energy and materials services. *Progress in Energy and Combustion Science*, *40*, 59–73. DOI: 10.1016/j.pecs.2013.09.003

Berawi, M. A. (2019). The role of industry 4.0 in achieving Sustainable Development Goals. *International Journal of Technology*, *10*(4), 644–647. DOI: 10.14716/ijtech.v10i4.3341

Bhatia, B., Sharma, G., Bansal, J., Abbass, M., Akhai, S., & Kaur, P. (2025, October). AI for urban planning and management. In. AIP Conference Proceedings: Vol. 3343. *No. 1* (p. 040022). AIP Publishing LLC., DOI: 10.1063/5.0292571

Bian, J., Zhao, J., & Li, A. (2025). Remote sensing monitoring of mountain sustainable development goals (SDG15.4): a systematic review. In *International Journal of Digital Earth* (Vol. 18, Number 1). Taylor and Francis Ltd. DOI: 10.1080/17538947.2024.2448216

Bianchini, S., Damioli, G., & Ghisetti, C. (2023). The environmental effects of the "twin" green and digital transition in European regions. *Environmental and Resource Economics*, *84*(1), 877–918. DOI: 10.1007/s10640-022-00741-7

Biondi, L., Perry, M., McAlorum, J., Vlachakis, C., & Hamilton, A. (2020). Geopolymer-based moisture sensors for reinforced concrete health monitoring. *Sensors and Actuators. B, Chemical*, *309*, 127775. DOI: 10.1016/j.snb.2020.127775

Birkel, H., & Müller, J. M. (2021). Potentials of industry 4. 0 for supply chain management within the triple bottom line of sustainability e A systematic literature review. *Journal of Cleaner Production*, *289*, 125612. DOI: 10.1016/j.jclepro.2020.125612

Blackburn, O., Ritala, P., & Bocken, N. (2026). Circular economy platforms: A systematic review. *Business Strategy and the Environment*, *35*(2), 1123–1147. DOI: 10.1002/bse.70307

Blanco, I., Loisi, R. V., Sica, C., Schettini, E., & Vox, G. (2018). Agricultural plastic waste mapping using GIS: A case study in Italy. *Resources, Conservation and Recycling*, *137*, 229–242. DOI: 10.1016/j.resconrec.2018.06.008

Blesson, S., & Rao, A. U. (2023). Agro-industrial-based wastes as supplementary cementitious or alkali-activated binder material: A comprehensive review. *Innovative Infrastructure Solutions*, *8*(4), 125. Advance online publication. DOI: 10.1007/s41062-023-01096-8

Bocken, N., Pauw, I., Bakker, C. A., & van der Grinten, B. (2016). Product design and business model strategies for a circular economy. *J. Ind. Prod. Eng., 1015.*

Bocken, N., Boons, F., & Baldassarre, B. (2019). Sustainable business model experimentation by understanding ecologies of business models. *Journal of Cleaner Production, 208*, 1498–1512. DOI: 10.1016/j.jclepro.2018.10.159

Bon, V. (2021). *The digitalization & economic growth relationship in developing countries and the role of governance*. Scientific Annals of Economics and Business, Alexandru Ioan Cuza University. *Faculty of Economics and Business Administration, 68*(4), 481–493.

Borges, P. H. R., Lourenço, T. M. de F., Foureaux, A. F. S., & Pacheco, L. S. (2014). Comparative life cycle analysis of geopolymer and Portland cement concretes. *Ambiente Construído, 14*(2), 153. DOI: 10.1590/S1678-86212014000200011

Botín-Sanabria, D. M., Mihaita, A. S., Peimbert-García, R. E., Ramírez-Moreno, M. A., Ramírez-Mendoza, R. A., & Lozoya-Santos, J. D. J. (2022). Digital twin technology challenges and applications: A comprehensive review. *Remote Sensing (Basel), 14*(6), 1335. DOI: 10.3390/rs14061335

Bouchikhi, A., Mamindy-Pajany, Y., Maherzi, W., Mercier, C., El-Moueden, H., Benzerzour, M., Peys, A., & Abriak, N.-E. (2020). Use of residual waste glass in an alkali-activated binder: Structural characterization and environmental leaching behavior. *Journal of Building Engineering, 34*, 101903. DOI: 10.1016/j.jobe.2020.101903

Boulay, A., Hoekstra, A. Y., & Vionnet, S. (2013). Complementarities of Water-Focused Life Cycle Assessment and Water Footprint Assessment. *Environmental Science & Technology, 47*(21), 11926–11927. DOI: 10.1021/es403928f PMID: 24147821

Boulding, K. E. (1966). The Economics of Knowledge and the Knowledge of Economics. *The American Economic Review, 56*(1), 1–13.

Bourbigot, S., Sarazin, J., Davy, C., & Fontaine, G. (2021). Foamed geopolymers for fire protection: Burn-through testing and modeling. *Fire and Materials, 46*(7), 1011–1019. DOI: 10.1002/fam.3048

Bragança, L., Cvetkovska, M., Askar, R., & Ungureanu, V. (2023). *Creating a roadmap towards circularity in the built environment*. Springer., DOI: 10.1007/978-3-031-45980-1

Brahami, Y., Saeidi, A., Fiset, M., & Ba, K. (2022). Effects of the type and quantity of recycled materials on physical and mechanical properties of concrete and mortar: A review. *Sustainability (Basel), 14*(22), 14752. DOI: 10.3390/su142214752

Bravo, M. C. M., Chalezquer, C. S., & Serrano-Puche, J. (2021). Meta-framework of digital literacy: Comparative analysis of 21st century skills frameworks. *Revista Latina de Comunicacion Social, 2021*(79), 76–110. DOI: 10.4185/RLCS-2021-1508

Brears, R. (2019). *Developing the Circular Water Economy*. DOI: 10.1007/978-3-030-32575-6

Brennan, G., Tennant, M., & Blomsma, F. (2015). Business and production solutions: Closing the Loop in Kopnina, H. and Shoreman-Ouimet, E. (Eds). Sustainability: Key Issues. EarthScan. In Routledge (Ed.), *Sustainability: Key Issues* (pp. 219–239). DOI: 10.4324/9780203109496-11

Brial, V., Tran, H., Sorelli, L., Conciatori, D., & Ouellet-Plamondon, C. (2022). Improvement of treated spent pot lining reactivity in cementitious material by calcination. *Developments in the Built Environment, 12*, 100098. DOI: 10.1016/j.dibe.2022.100098

Brown, D. R. N., & Gevaudan, J. (2025). *Transforming agricultural residues into high-performance SCMs through mechanochemical activation*. https://doi.org/DOI: 10.5703/1288284318081

Busse, A., Gerlach, B., Lengeling, J. C., Poschmann, P., Werner, J., & Zarnitz, S. (2021). Towards digital twins of multimodal supply chains. *Logistics (Basel), 5*(2), 25. DOI: 10.3390/logistics5020025

Busu, C., & Busu, M. (2018). Modeling the circular economy processes at the EU level using an evaluation algorithm based on Shannon entropy. *Processes (Basel, Switzerland), 6*(11), 225. DOI: 10.3390/pr6110225

Bychkov, I. V., & Fereferov, E. S. (2022). Digital technologies for monitoring and forecasting the environmental situation in Siberia. *Herald of the Russian Academy of Sciences, 92*(1), 133–140. DOI: 10.1134/S101933162202006X

Cai, T., & Hong, Z. (2024). Exploring the structure of the digital economy through blockchain technology and mitigating adverse environmental effects with the aid of artificial neural networks. *Frontiers in Environmental Science, 12*(1), 1–14. DOI: 10.3389/fenvs.2024.1315812

Callai, S. C., Tataranni, P., & Sangiorgi, C. (2021). Preliminary evaluation of geopolymer mix design applying the design of experiments method. *Infrastructures, 6*(3), 35. DOI: 10.3390/infrastructures6030035

Camacho-Otero, J., Boks, C., & Pettersen, I. N. (2018). Consumption in the circular economy: A literature review. *Sustainability (Basel), 10*(8), 2758. DOI: 10.3390/su10082758

Cantoni, R., & Brisbois, M. C. (2024). En route to decarbonization: A periodisation of just transition in four carbon-intensive EU regions. *Geoforum*, *154*, 104061. DOI: 10.1016/j.geoforum.2024.104061

Cao, Z., & Peng, L. (2023). The impact of digital economics on environmental quality: A system dynamics approach. *SAGE Open*, *13*(4), 1–10. DOI: 10.1177/21582440231219350

Capêto, A. P., Amorim, M., Sousa, S., Costa, J. R., Uribe, B. E. B., Guimarães, A. S., Pintado, M., & Oliveira, A. (2023). Fire-resistant bio-based polyurethane foams designed using by-products of sugarcane fermentation. *Waste and Biomass Valorization*, *15*(4), 2045. DOI: 10.1007/s12649-023-02274-6

Carlos, M., Cunha, P. R., & Rodrigues, S. (2024). Enhancing circular economy practices through the adoption of digital technologies. *Business Strategy & Development*, *7*(1), e330. DOI: 10.1002/bsd2.330

Castellani, V., Beylot, A., & Sala, S. (2019). Environmental impacts of household consumption in Europe: Comparing process-based LCA and environmentally extended input-output analysis. *Journal of Cleaner Production*, *240*, 117966. DOI: 10.1016/j.jclepro.2019.117966 PMID: 31839696

Castillo-Díaz, F. J., Belmonte-Ureña, L. J., Diánez-Martínez, F., & Camacho-Ferre, F. (2024). Challenges and perspectives of the circular economy in the European Union: A comparative analysis of the member states. *Ecological Economics*, *224*, 108294. DOI: 10.1016/j.ecolecon.2024.108294

Centobelli, P., Cerchione, R., Esposito, E., Passaro, R., & Shashi, . (2021). Determinants of the transition towards circular economy in SMEs: A sustainable supply chain management perspective. *International Journal of Production Economics*, *242*, 108297. DOI: 10.1016/j.ijpe.2021.108297

Chango-Cañaveral, P. M., Quezada-Sarmiento, P. A., & Morales-Herrera, V. J. (2025). Analysis of Sustainable Development Goals (2016–2030) and Their Integration into Tourism Activities in Lago Agrio Canton, Sucumbíos Province: SDG 9 (Industry, Innovation, and Infrastructure) and SDG 15 (Life on Land). *Sustainability (Basel)*, *17*(13), 6023. Advance online publication. DOI: 10.3390/su17136023

Chauhan, C., & Singh, A. (2020). *A review of Industry 4 . 0 in supply chain management studies. 31*(5), 863–886. DOI: 10.1108/JMTM-04-2018-0105

Chen, C.-Y., Wang, S.-W., Kim, H., Pan, S.-Y., Fan, C., & Lin, Y. J. (2021). Non-conventional water reuse in agriculture: A circular water economy. *Water Research*, *199*, 117193. DOI: 10.1016/j.watres.2021.117193 PMID: 33971532

Chen, K., Cheng, Y., Yu, M., Liu, L., Wang, Y., & Zhang, J. (2022). Predicting the geopolymerization process of fly-ash-based geopolymer using machine learning. *Buildings (Basel, Switzerland), 12*(11), 1792. DOI: 10.3390/buildings12111792

Chindaprasirt, P., & Rattanasak, U. (2020). Eco-production of silica from sugarcane bagasse ash for use as a photochromic pigment filler. *Scientific Reports, 10*(1), 9890. Advance online publication. DOI: 10.1038/s41598-020-66885-y

Chiranjeevi, K., Abraham, M., Rath, B., & Praveenkumar, T. R. (2023). Enhancing the properties of geopolymer concrete using nano-silica: Microstructure assessment and sustainability perspective. *Scientific Reports, 13*(1), 17302. Advance online publication. DOI: 10.1038/s41598-023-44491-y

Christiansen, C., Nielsen, K. K., & Bjørk, R. (2019). *Freeze-casting as a processing route to fabricate active magnetic regenerators for magnetic refrigeration.* Research Portal Denmark. https://local.forskningsportal.dk/local/dki-cgi/ws/cris-link?src=dtu&id=dtu-5f6fb193-e173-40d4-b67e-a9076695c205

Chukalla, A. D., Krol, M. S., & Hoekstra, A. Y. (2015). Green and blue water footprint reduction in irrigated agriculture: Effect of irrigation techniques, irrigation strategies and mulching. *Hydrology and Earth System Sciences, 19*(12), 4877–4891. DOI: 10.5194/hess-19-4877-2015

Cong, P., Du, R., Gao, H., & Chen, Z. (2024). Comparison and assessment of carbon dioxide emissions between alkali-activated materials and OPC cement concrete. *Journal of Traffic and Transportation Engineering, 11*(5), 918–938. DOI: 10.1016/j.jtte.2023.07.011

Cordeiro, G. C., Filho, R. D. T., & Fairbairn, E. (2009). Effect of calcination temperature on the pozzolanic activity of sugar cane bagasse ash. *Construction & Building Materials, 23*(10), 3301–3303. DOI: 10.1016/j.conbuildmat.2009.02.013

Crasta, L. C., & Shailashri, V. T. (2021). A comprehensive study of talent management process adopted by tata consultancy services (TCS). International Journal of Case Studies in Business [IJCSBE]. *IT and Education, 5*(1), 267–281.

Cui, R., Wang, J., & Zhou, C. (2023). Exploring the linkages of green transformational leadership, organizational green learning, and radical green innovation. *Business Strategy and the Environment, 32*(1), 185–199. DOI: 10.1002/bse.3124

Cui, Y., Ai, W., Tekle, B. H., Liu, M., Qu, S., & Zhang, P. (2023). State-of-the-art review on the production and bond behaviour of reinforced geopolymer concrete. *Low-Carbon Materials and Green Construction, 1*(1), 25. Advance online publication. DOI: 10.1007/s44242-023-00027-1

D'Odorico, P., Carr, J., Dalin, C., Dell'Angelo, J., Konar, M., Laio, F., Ridolfi, L., Rosa, L., Suweis, S., Tamea, S., & Tuninetti, M. (2019). Global virtual water trade and the hydrological cycle: Patterns, drivers, and socio-environmental impacts. *Environmental Research Letters*, *14*(5), 053001. Advance online publication. DOI: 10.1088/1748-9326/ab05f4

D'Odorico, P., Carr, J., Laio, F., Ridolfi, L., & Vandoni, S. (2014). Feeding humanity through global food trade. *Earth's Future*, *2*(9), 458–469. Advance online publication. DOI: 10.1002/2014EF000250

Dai, J., Zhou, B., & Meng, W. (2025). The impact of digitalization on environmental sustainability: New insights from G20 nations. *Journal of Environmental Management*, *394*, 127225. DOI: 10.1016/j.jenvman.2025.127225

Dalin, C., Konar, M., Hanasaki, N., Rinaldo, A., & Rodriguez-iturbe, I. (2012). *Evolution of the Global Virtual Water Trade Network* (Issue June 2014). DOI: 10.1073/pnas.1203176109

Danladi, S., Prasad, M. S. V., Modibbo, U. M., Ahmadi, S. A., & Ghasemi, P. (2023). Attaining Sustainable Development Goals through Financial Inclusion: Exploring Collaborative Approaches to Fintech Adoption in Developing Economies. *Sustainability (Basel)*, *15*(17), 13039. Advance online publication. DOI: 10.3390/su151713039

de Almeida, M., Gonçalves, N. P. F., Gameiro, T., Alves, Z., Labrincha, J. A., & Novais, R. M. (2024). *Optimizing bauxite residue and biomass fly ash mixtures for 3D printing geopolymers: Promising metal sorbents for wastewater treatment*. https://doi.org/DOI: 10.2139/ssrn.4828271

de Carvalho, T. A., Gaspar, F., Mateus, A., & Marques, A. C. (2023). *Geopolymer cement for sustainable construction: A review*. In Sustainable Construction Materials (pp. 149–172). https://doi.org/DOI: 10.1007/978-3-031-25795-7_11

de Carvalho, T. A., Gaspar, F., Marques, A. C., & Mateus, A. (2023). Evaluation of the potential of metakaolin, electric arc furnace slag, and biomass fly ash for geopolymer cement compositions. *Materials (Basel)*, *16*(7), 2741. DOI: 10.3390/ma16072741

Debaere, P., & Konar, M. (2022). Water resources and trade: A research vision. *PLOS Water*, *1*(2), e0000010. DOI: 10.1371/journal.pwat.0000010

Dehghani, A., Aslani, F., & Panah, N. G. (2021). Effects of initial $SiO_2/Al_2O_3$ molar ratio and slag on fly ash-based ambient cured geopolymer properties. *Construction & Building Materials*, *293*, 123527. DOI: 10.1016/j.conbuildmat.2021.123527

Del Granado, P. C., Resch, G., Holz, F., Welisch, M., Geipel, J., Hartner, M., & Ramos, A. (2020). Energy transition pathways to a low-carbon Europe in 2050. *Economics of Energy & Environmental Policy*, *9*(1), 121–136.

Delpasand, M., Bozorg-Haddad, O., Goharian, E., & Loáiciga, H. A. (2023). Virtual water trade: Economic development and independence through optimal allocation. *Agricultural Water Management*, *275*, 108022. DOI: 10.1016/j.agwat.2022.108022

Demartini, M., Pinna, C., Aliakbarian, B., Tonelli, F., & Terzi, S. (2018). Soft Drink Supply Chain Sustainability: A Case Based Approach to Identify and Explain Best Practices and Key Performance Indicators. In *Sustainability* (Vol. 10, Issue 10, p. 3540). DOI: 10.3390/su10103540

Dhar, A., & Nandi, D. (2026). Exploring the Effects of Electronic Waste: A Comprehensive Study of Production, Management, and Health Risks in India. In *International Journal of Environmental Research* (Vol. 20, Number 1). Springer Science and Business Media Deutschland GmbH. DOI: 10.1007/s41742-025-00984-4

Dhiman, S., Seema, S., & Akhai, S. (2025). Performance evaluation of OPC 43 concrete incorporating micro silica and recycled ceramic tile waste as partial cement and coarse aggregate replacements. *Asian Journal of Civil Engineering*, 1-19. https://doi.org/DOI: 10.1007/s42107-025-01504-7

Dhiman, S., Seema, S., & Akhai, S. (2025). Effects of micro-silica and ceramic tile waste on the mechanical and durability properties of M40 grade concrete. *AIP Advances*, *15*(12), 125019. Advance online publication. DOI: 10.1063/5.0308763

Ding, C., Wang, L., Chen, X., Yang, H., Huang, L., & Song, X. (2023). A blockchain-based wide-area agricultural machinery resource scheduling system. *Applied Engineering in Agriculture*, *39*(1), 1–12. DOI: 10.13031/aea.15332

Dinh, L. Q. (2025). Is There a Trade-Off Between Sustainable Development Goals Achievement and Banking Profitability? Evidence From Combined Non-Parametric Methods. *Natural Resources Forum*. DOI: 10.1111/1477-8947.70036

Distefano, T., Lodi, L., & Biggeri, M. (2024). Material footprint and import dependency in EU27: Past trends and future challenges. *Journal of Cleaner Production*, *472*, 143384. DOI: 10.1016/j.jclepro.2024.143384

Dizaji, H. B., Zeng, T., Hölzig, H., Bauer, J., Klöß, G., & Enke, D. (2021). Ash transformation mechanism during combustion of rice husk and rice straw. *Fuel*, *307*, 121768. DOI: 10.1016/j.fuel.2021.121768

Djalante, R., Shaw, R., & Dewit, A. (2020). Progress in Disaster Science Building resilience against biological hazards and pandemics : COVID-19 and its implications for the Sendai Framework. *Progress in Disaster Science*, *6*, 100080. DOI: 10.1016/j.pdisas.2020.100080

Djobo, J. N. Y., Elimbi, A., Tchakouté, H. K., & Kumar, S. (2016). Mechanical activation of volcanic ash for geopolymer synthesis: Effect on reaction kinetics and properties. *RSC Advances*, *6*(45), 39106. DOI: 10.1039/C6RA03667H

Dong, Q., Su, X., Li, X., Zhou, H., Jian, H., Bai, S., Yin, J., & You, Q. (2023). In vitro construction of lung cancer organoids by 3D bioprinting for drug evaluation. *Colloids and Surfaces. A, Physicochemical and Engineering Aspects*, *666*, 131288. DOI: 10.1016/j.colsurfa.2023.131288

Drabczyk, A., Kudłacik-Kramarczyk, S., Korniejenko, K., Figiela, B., & Furtos, G. (2023). Geopolymer nanocomposites: Novel materials for sustainable development. *Materials (Basel)*, *16*(9), 3478. DOI: 10.3390/ma16093478

Driouich, A., Chajri, F., Hassani, S. E. A. E., Britel, O., Belouafa, S., Khabbazi, A., & Chaair, H. (2020). Optimization of geopolymer mixture synthesis using metakaolin and fly ash activated by alkaline solution. *Journal of Non-Crystalline Solids*, *544*, 120197. DOI: 10.1016/j.jnoncrysol.2020.120197

Duarte, R., & Yang, H. (2011). INPUT–OUTPUT AND WATER: INTRODUCTION TO THE SPECIAL ISSUE ROSA. *Economic Systems Research, 23(4)*(March 2014), 341–351. DOI: 10.1080/09535314.2011.638277

Duarte, R., Pinilla, V., & Serrano, A. (2019). Long Term Drivers of Global Virtual Water Trade: A Trade Gravity Approach for 1965–2010. *Ecological Economics, 156*(June 2017), 318–326. DOI: 10.1016/j.ecolecon.2018.10.012

Duarte, R., Pinilla, V., & Serrano, A. (2016). Understanding agricultural virtual water flows in the world from an economic perspective: A long term study. *Ecological Indicators*, *61*, 980–990. DOI: 10.1016/j.ecolind.2015.10.056

Duchin, F., & López-Morales, C. (2012). Do Water-Rich Regions Have a Comparative Advantage in Food Production? Improving the Representation of Water for Agriculture in Economic Models. *Economic Systems Research*, *24*(4), 371–389. DOI: 10.1080/09535314.2012.714746

Dulaimi, A., Busaltan, S. A., Mydin, M. A. O., Lu, D., Özkılıç, Y. O., Jaya, R. P., & Ameen, A. (2023). Innovative geopolymer-based cold asphalt emulsion mixture as eco-friendly material. *Scientific Reports*, *13*(1), 17380. Advance online publication. DOI: 10.1038/s41598-023-44630-5

Dunne, A., Multani, M., Bachus, K., Ampe, K., Goodwin-Brown, E., Shankar, A., . . . Pals, E. (2024). *Skills on a circular path: Modelling future CE scenarios and transormations in sectoral, occupational and skills structures of the Belgian Labour Market* (2024). https://lirias.kuleuven.be/retrieve/780786

Duque-Acevedo, M., Lancellotti, I., Andreola, F., Barbieri, L., Ureña, L. J. B., & Camacho-Ferre, F. (2022). Management of agricultural waste biomass for construction applications: Circular alternatives and sustainability analysis. *Environmental Sciences Europe*, *34*(1). Advance online publication. DOI: 10.1186/s12302-022-00655-7

Durkalić, D., & Ćurčić, M. (2019), Comparative analysis of debt sustainability of EU countries and EU candidates: Promethee-Gaia approach, Eastern Journal of European Studies - EJES, Vol 10 (1), 67-92, ISSN: 2068-6633, 67-92

Dwivedi, E. (2024). A review on development of 3D printable concrete using agro-industrial waste: Evaluation of fresh properties. *International Journal for Research in Applied Science and Engineering Technology*, *12*(7), 116–124. DOI: 10.22214/ijraset.2024.63530

Džajić Uršič, E., Fric, U., & Rončević, B. (2024). The Circular Economy: Recent debates and research trends. *Journal of Infrastructure. Policy and Development*, *8*(3), 2855.

Ebolor, A., Agarwal, N., & Brem, A. (2022). Fostering the Sustainable Development Goals with technologies underpinned by frugal innovation. *International Journal of Technology Management*, *88*(2–4), 155–174. DOI: 10.1504/IJTM.2022.121503

Egan, M. (2011). The Water Footprint Assessment Manual. Setting the Global Standard. In *Social and Environmental Accountability Journal* (Vol. 31, Issue 2). DOI: 10.1080/0969160X.2011.593864

El Saddik, A. (2018). Digital twins: The convergence of multimedia technologies. *IEEE MultiMedia*, *25*(2), 87–92. DOI: 10.1109/MMUL.2018.023121167

Elgadafi, A. E. (2025). Overcoming Digital Transformation Challenges in Traditional Manufacturing Industries. *International Journal for Multidisciplinary Research*, *7*(4), 52191. www.ijfmr.com. DOI: 10.36948/ijfmr.2025.v07i04.52191

Ellen MacArthur Foundation. (2013). *Towards the Circular Economy.*

El-Zeadani, M., Bompa, D. V., & Elghazouli, A. Y. (2021). Preparation and properties of rubberised geopolymer concrete: A review. *Construction & Building Materials*, *313*, 125504. DOI: 10.1016/j.conbuildmat.2021.125504

EMF (Ellen MacArthur Foundation). (2017). *Our Mission Is to Accelerate the Transition to a Circular Economy*. Ellen MacArthur Foundation. https://www.ellenmacarthurfoundation.org/

Enevoldsen, M. K., Ryelund, A. V., & Andersen, M. S. (2007). Decoupling of industrial energy consumption and CO2-emissions in energy-intensive industries in Scandinavia. *Energy Economics*, *29*(4), 665–692. DOI: 10.1016/j.eneco.2007.01.016

Escribà-Gelonch, M., Liang, S., van Schalkwyk, P., Fisk, I., Long, N. V. D., & Hessel, V. (2024). Digital twins in agriculture: Orchestration and applications. *Journal of Agricultural and Food Chemistry*, *72*(19), 10737–10752. DOI: 10.1021/acs.jafc.4c01934 PMID: 38709011

Eskiyerli, M. H., & Dondrup, M. (2025). Circularity in motion: The circular knowledge management model for international joint ventures in small and medium-sized enterprises. *Journal of Circular Economy*, *2*(1), 1–32. DOI: 10.55845/IEZW9337

European Commission. (2015). *Closing the Loop - an EU Action Plan for the Circular Economy, Com(2015) 614 Communication from the Commission to the European Parliament, the Council, the European Economic and Social Committee and the Committee of the Regions*.

European commission. (2020), EU Circular Economy Action Plan, https://eur-lex.europa.eu/legal-content/EN/TXT/HTML/?uri=CELEX:52020DC0098

European Environment Agency. (2023). *Consumption footprint and circular economy, 8th Environment Action Programme*, https://www.eea.europa.eu/en/analysis/publications/monitoring-progress-towards-8th-eap-objectives/indicators/25-consumption-footprint-based-on-life-cycle-assessment-in-europe/@@download/file

European Environment Agency. (2025), National circular economy policies, Countries with national adopted CE Strategies, Roadmaps, Action plans. https://www.eea.europa.eu/en/circularity/thematic-metrics/enabling/national-circular-economy-policies

Eurostat, (2025), Circular economy, Database, https://ec.europa.eu/eurostat/web/circular-economy/database

Fader, M., Gerten, D., Thammer, M., Heinke, J., Lotze-Campen, H., Lucht, W., & Cramer, W. (2011). Internal and external green-blue agricultural water footprints of nations, and related water and land savings through trade. *Hydrology and Earth System Sciences*, *15*(5), 1641–1660. DOI: 10.5194/hess-15-1641-2011

Fan, J., Liang, H., Sun, Z., & Chen, Z. (2023). Strength characteristics and mechanisms of cold mix based on geopolymerization. *Frontiers in Built Environment*, *9*. Advance online publication. DOI: 10.3389/fbuil.2023.1301126

Fan, X. (2020). A brief introduction on the research status and future prospects on geopolymer concrete. *IOP Conference Series. Earth and Environmental Science*, *508*(1), 012124. DOI: 10.1088/1755-1315/508/1/012124

Farhan, K. Z., Shihata, A. S., & Abubakar, A. (2024). Impact of pernicious chemicals on geopolymer and alkali-activated composites incorporated with different fiber types: A review. *Recent Progress in Materials*, *6*(3), 1–19. DOI: 10.21926/rpm.2403017

Feng, K., Chapagain, A., Suh, S., Pfister, S., & Hubacek, K. (2011). Comparison of bottom-up and top-down approaches to calculating the water footprints of nations. *Economic Systems Research*, *23*(4), 371–385. DOI: 10.1080/09535314.2011.638276

Feng, K., Hubacek, K., Siu, Y. L., & Li, X. (2014). The energy and water nexus in Chinese electricity production: A hybrid life cycle analysis. *Renewable & Sustainable Energy Reviews*, *39*, 342–355. DOI: 10.1016/j.rser.2014.07.080

Ferreira, J. J., Tuma, F., Veiga, P. M., & Vrontis, D. (2025). The interplay of corporate entrepreneurship, knowledge acquisition, knowledge-based resources and SME performance. *International Studies of Management & Organization*, *55*(2), 141–164. DOI: 10.1080/00208825.2024.2385232

Finkbeiner, M., Inaba, A., Tan, R., Christiansen, K., & Klüppel, H.-J. (2006). The New International Standards for Life Cycle Assessment: ISO 14040 and ISO 14044. *The International Journal of Life Cycle Assessment*, *11*(2), 80–85. DOI: 10.1065/lca2006.02.002

Firdous, R., Nikravan, M., Mancke, R., Vöge, M., & Stephan, D. (2022). Assessment of environmental, economic and technical performance of geopolymer concrete: A case study. *Journal of Materials Science*, *57*(40), 18711–18725. DOI: 10.1007/s10853-022-07820-6

Firoz, A. K., Zo, H., & Chiravuri, A. (2021). Digital transformation and environmental sustainability: A review and research agenda. *Sustainability (Basel)*, *13*(3), 1530. Advance online publication. DOI: 10.3390/su13031530

Fracasso, A. (2014). A gravity model of virtual water trade. *Ecological Economics*, *108*, 215–228. DOI: 10.1016/j.ecolecon.2014.10.010

Fracasso, A., Sartori, M., & Schiavo, S. (2016). Determinants of virtual water flows in the Mediterranean. *The Science of the Total Environment, 543*, 1054–1062. https://doi.org/https://doi.org/10.1016/j.scitotenv.2015.02.059. DOI: 10.1016/j.scitotenv.2015.02.059 PMID: 25708715

Fragkiadakis, K., Fragkos, P., & Paroussos, L. (2020). Low-carbon R&D can boost EU growth and competitiveness. *Energies, 13*(19), 5236. DOI: 10.3390/en13195236

Frandsen, K. M., Antonov, Y. I., Johra, H., Møldrup, P., & Jensen, R. L. (2021). *Water vapor diffusivity in bio-based building materials: New measurement method.* Research Portal Denmark.

Fredericci, C., Ett, G., Silva, G. F. B. L., Neto, J. B. F., Landgraf, F. J. G., Indelicato, R. L., & Ribeiro, T. R. (2014). Behavior of Brazilian sugarcane bagasse ash under thermal gasification. *Chemical and Biological Technologies in Agriculture, 1*(1). Advance online publication. DOI: 10.1186/s40538-014-0015-z

FUJII. T., & RAY, R. (2021). Singapore as a Sustainable City: Past, present, and the future. In *The Singapore Economy: Dynamism and Inclusion*. DOI: 10.4324/9780429266584-5

Fura, B., Karasek, A., & Hysa, B. (2025). Statistical assessment of digital transformation in European Union countries under sustainable development goal 9. *Quality & Quantity, 59*(1), 937–972. DOI: 10.1007/s11135-024-01972-0

Gao, Z., Alshehri, K., Li, Y., Qian, H., Sapsford, D., Cleall, P. J., & Harbottle, M. (2022). Advances in biological techniques for sustainable lignocellulosic waste utilization in biogas production. *Renewable & Sustainable Energy Reviews, 170*, 112995. DOI: 10.1016/j.rser.2022.112995

García-Muiña, F. E., González-Sánchez, R., Ferrari, A. M., & Settembre-Blundo, D. (2018). The paradigms of Industry 4.0 and circular economy as enabling drivers for the competitiveness of businesses and territories: The case of an Italian ceramic tiles manufacturing company. *Social Sciences (Basel, Switzerland), 7*(12), 255. DOI: 10.3390/socsci7120255

García-Navarro, J., & Poltronieri, O. C. C. (2024). Circular economy and GHG emissions, current situation. In *Circular economy on energy and natural resources industries: new processes and applications to reduce, reuse and recycle materials and decrease greenhouse gases emissions* (pp. 1–18). Springer International Publishing. DOI: 10.1007/978-3-031-56284-6_1

Gariba, M. I., Arthur, E. E., & Odei, S. A. (2024). Assessing the impact of public digitalization on sustainability: The mediating role of technological innovation in the context of the EU. *Discover Sustainability*, *5*(1), 1–10. DOI: 10.1007/s43621-024-00397-x

Garmaroodi, M. S. S., Farivar, F., Haghighi, M. S., Shoorehdeli, M. A., & Jolfaei, A. (2021). AquaFeL-PSO: A Monitoring System for Water Resources using Autonomous Surface Vehicles based on Multimodal PSO and Federated Learning. *IEEE Internet of Things Journal*, *8*(13), 10280–10287. DOI: 10.1109/JIOT.2020.3034311

Gautam, R., Jaiswal, R., & Yadav, U. S. (2024). *AI-enhanced data-driven approach to model the mechanical behavior of sustainable geopolymer concrete. Research Square*. https://doi.org/DOI: 10.21203/rs.3.rs-5307352/v1

Gebeyehu, A., Surapaneni, S. K., Huang, J. J., Mondal, A., Wang, V. Z., Haruna, N.-F., Bagde, A., Arthur, P., Kutlehria, S., Patel, N., Rishi, A. K., & Singh, M. (2021). Polysaccharide hydrogel-based 3D printed tumor models for chemotherapeutic drug screening. *Scientific Reports*, *11*(1), 372. Advance online publication. DOI: 10.1038/s41598-020-79325-8

Geissdoerfer, M., Savaget, P., Bocken, N. M., & Hultink, E. J. (2017). The Circular Economy–A new sustainability paradigm? *Journal of Cleaner Production*, *143*, 757–768. DOI: 10.1016/j.jclepro.2016.12.048

Gerbens-Leenes, P. W., Hoekstra, A. Y., & Bosman, R. (2018). The blue and grey water footprint of construction materials: Steel, cement and glass. *Water Resources and Industry, 19*(April 2017), 1–12. DOI: 10.1016/j.wri.2017.11.002

Ghani, W. A. W. A. K., Salleh, M. A. M., Adam, S. N., Shafri, H. Z. M., Shaharum, S. N., Lim, K. L., Rubinsin, N. J., Lam, H. L., Hasan, A., Samsatli, S., Tapia, J. F. D., Khezri, R., Jaye, I. F. M., & Martínez-Hernández, E. (2019). Sustainable bio-economy for environment–food–energy–water nexus: Current status in Malaysia. *Food and Bioproducts Processing*, *118*, 167. DOI: 10.1016/j.fbp.2019.09.002

Ghisellini, P., Cialani, C., & Ulgiati, S. (2016). A review on circular economy: The expected transition to a balanced interplay of environmental and economic systems. *Journal of Cleaner Production*, *114*, 11–32. DOI: 10.1016/j.jclepro.2015.09.007

Ghobakhloo, M., Iranmanesh, M., Grybauskas, A., Vilkas, M., & Petraitė, M. (2021). Industry 4.0, innovation, and sustainable development: A systematic review and a roadmap to sustainable innovation. *Business Strategy and the Environment*, *30*(8), 4237–4257. DOI: 10.1002/bse.2867

Ginni, G., Kavitha, S., Ravi, Y. K., & Bhatia, S. K. (2021). Valorization of agricultural residues: Different biorefinery routes. *Journal of Environmental Chemical Engineering*, *9*(4), 105435. DOI: 10.1016/j.jece.2021.105435

Göçoğlu, V., Ayan, D., & Demirkol, A. (2025). Climate Change Adaptation Strategies in Vulnerable Countries Through the SDG 13: A Cross-Sectoral Analysis. *Sustainable Development*. Advance online publication. DOI: 10.1002/sd.70254

Goel, A., Masurkar, S., & Pathade, G. R. (2024). An overview of digital transformation and environmental sustainability: Threats, opportunities, and solutions. *Sustainability (Basel)*, *16*(24), 1–13. DOI: 10.3390/su162411079

Görhan, G., & Kürklü, G. (2013). Influence of NaOH solution on properties of fly ash-based geopolymer mortar cured at various temperatures. *Composites. Part B, Engineering*, *58*, 371–377. DOI: 10.1016/j.compositesb.2013.10.082

Górski, M., Czulkin, P., Wielgus, N., Boncel, S., Kuziel, A. W., Kolanowska, A., & Jędrysiak, R. G. (2022). Electrical properties of carbon nanotube-reinforced geopolymer studied by impedance spectroscopy. *Materials (Basel)*, *15*(10), 3543. DOI: 10.3390/ma15103543

Goryunova, K., Gahramanli, Y., Muradkhanli, V., & Nadirov, P. (2023). Phosphate-activated geopolymers: Advantages and application. *RSC Advances*, *13*(43), 30329–30345. DOI: 10.1039/D3RA05131E

Grybaitė, V., & Burinskienė, A. (2024). Assessment of circular economy development in the EU countries based on SAW method. *Sustainability (Basel)*, *16*(21), 9582. DOI: 10.3390/su16219582

Gupta, A., & Ruebush, E. (2019). *AquaSight: Automatic Water Impurity Detection Utilizing Convolutional Neural Networks*.

Gupta, M., Sharma, B., & Singh, A. K. (2025). Impact of digital technologies on tourist arrival in selected economies. In Lytras, M., Alkhaldi, A., & Ordóñez de Pablos, P. (Eds.), *Harnessing AI, Blockchain, and Cloud Computing for Enhanced e-Government Services* (pp. 441–474). IGI Global Scientific Publishing., DOI: 10.4018/979-8-3693-7678-2.ch014

Guth, D., & Herák, D. (2025). Modern Water Treatment Technology Based on Industry 4.0. *Sensors (Basel)*, *25*(6), 1925. Advance online publication. DOI: 10.3390/s25061925

Haas, W., Krausmann, F., Wiedenhofer, D., & Heinz, M. (2015). How circular is the global economy?: An assessment of material flows, waste production, and recycling in the European Union and the world in 2005. *Journal of Industrial Ecology, 19*(5), 765–777. DOI: 10.1111/jiec.12244

Habeeb, G. A., & Mahmud, H. B. (2010). Properties of rice husk ash and its use as cement replacement material. *Materials Research, 13*(2), 185–190. DOI: 10.1590/S1516-14392010000200011

Habte, G. A., Bullo, T. A., & Ahmed, Y. (2025). Statistical optimization and eco-friendly synthesis of silica from sugarcane bagasse. *Scientific Reports, 15*(1). Advance online publication. DOI: 10.1038/s41598-025-89366-6

Hahladakis, J. N. (2025). From Local Actions to Global Impact: Overcoming Hurdles and Showcasing Sustainability Achievements in the Implementation of SDG12. *Sustainability (Basel), 17*(15), 7106. Advance online publication. DOI: 10.3390/su17157106

Hantoko, D., Li, X., Pariatamby, A., & Yoshikawa, K. (2020). *Challenges and practices on waste management and disposal during COVID-19 pandemic*. (January).

Hariyani, D., Hariyani, P., & Mishra, S. (2025). Digital technologies for the sustainable development Goals. *Green Technologies and Sustainability, 3*(3), 100202. DOI: 10.1016/j.grets.2025.100202

Hartley, K., Van Santen, R., & Kirchherr, J. (2020). Policies for transitioning towards a circular economy: Expectations from the European Union (EU). *Resources, Conservation and Recycling, 155*, 104634. DOI: 10.1016/j.resconrec.2019.104634

Hassan, M. A., Farid, M. A. A., Zakaria, M. R., Ariffin, H., Andou, Y., & Shirai, Y. (2024). Palm oil expansion in Malaysia: Policy window and biorefinery countermeasures. *Environmental Science & Policy, 153*, 103671. DOI: 10.1016/j.envsci.2024.103671

Hattaf, R., Aboulayt, A., Lahlou, N., Touhami, M. O., Gomina, M., Samdi, A., & Moussa, R. (2022). Integration of geopolymer wastes in binding matrices under acid and temperature exposure. *Polymers, 14*(5), 917. DOI: 10.3390/polym14050917

He, G., Jiang, H., & Zhu, Y. (2024). The effect of digital technology development on the improvement on environmental governance capacity: A case study of China. *Ecological Indicators, 165*(1), 1–12. DOI: 10.1016/j.ecolind.2024.112162

Hegab, H., Shaban, I., Jamil, M., & Khanna, N. (2023). Toward sustainable future: Strategies, indicators, and challenges for implementing sustainable production systems. *Sustainable Materials and Technologies*, *36*, e00617. DOI: 10.1016/j.susmat.2023.e00617

He, R., Dai, N., & Wang, Z. (2020). Thermal and mechanical properties of geopolymers exposed to high temperature: A literature review. *Advances in Civil Engineering*, *2020*(1), 7532703. Advance online publication. DOI: 10.1155/2020/7532703

Hermawan, J., Wijaya, L. I., & Rianawati, A. (2025). Digital Transformation for Economic Growth and SDG 8 Alignment in Southeast Asia: A Bibliometric Analysis and Systematic Literature Review with ADO-TCM Framework. *Journal of Lifestyle and SDGs Review*, *5*(2), e04052. DOI: 10.47172/2965-730X.SDGsReview.v5.n02.pe04052

Hernández-Escobar, C. A., Conejo-Dávila, A. S., Vega-Ríos, A., Zaragoza-Contreras, E. A., & Farías, R. (2023). Geopolymers obtained from wheat husk native to Northern Mexico. *Materials (Basel)*, *16*(5), 1803. DOI: 10.3390/ma16051803

Hervey, G. (2018). Ranking how EU countries do with the circular economy. *POLITICO's circular economy*. https://www.politico.eu/article/ranking-how-eu-countries-do-with-the-circular-economy/

Hipólito, V. M., & Ildefonso, J. S. (2024). Functional and structural assessment of a gap-graded experimental section modified with sugarcane bagasse ash. *Scientific Reports*, *14*(1). Advance online publication. DOI: 10.1038/s41598-024-67900-2

Hoekstra, A., Chapagain, A., Aldaya, M., & Mekonnen, M. (2011). *The Water Footprint Assessment Manual*. DOI: 10.4324/9781849775526

Hoekstra, A. Y. (2017). Water Footprint Assessment in Supply Chains. *Springer Series in Supply Chain Management*, *4*, 65–85. DOI: 10.1007/978-3-319-29791-0_4

Hoekstra, A. Y., & Chapagain, A. K. (2007). Water footprints of nations: Water use by people as a function of their consumption pattern. *Water Resources Management*, *21*(1), 35–48. DOI: 10.1007/s11269-006-9039-x

Hoekstra, A., & Hung, P. Q. (2002). Virtual water trade: A quantification of virtual water flows between nations in relation to international crop trade. *Water Science and Technology*, *49*, 203–209.

Hoekstra, A., & Mekonnen, M. (2012). The Water Footprint of Humanity. *Proceedings of the National Academy of Sciences of the United States of America*, *109*(9), 3232–3237. DOI: 10.1073/pnas.1109936109 PMID: 22331890

Hong, S., & Kim, H. (2019). Microwave-assisted fast strength development of coal bottom ash-based geopolymers. *Scientific Reports*, *9*(1). Advance online publication. DOI: 10.1038/s41598-019-52160-2

Hong, Z., & Xiao, K. (2024). Digital economy structuring for sustainable development: The role of blockchain and artificial intelligence in improving supply chain and reducing negative environmental impacts. *Scientific Reports*, *14*(1), 1–10. DOI: 10.1038/s41598-024-53760-3

Hoppe, J., Hinder, B., Rafaty, R., Patt, A., & Grubb, M. (2023). Three decades of climate mitigation policy: What has it delivered? *Annual Review of Environment and Resources*, *48*(1), 615–650. DOI: 10.1146/annurev-environ-112321-103821

Hounsi, A. D., Lecomte-Nana, G. L., Djétéli, G., Blanchart, P., Alowanou, D., Kpelou, P., Napo, K., Tchangbédji, G., & Praisler, M. (2014). Influence of Na, K alkali concentration on early-age structure of kaolin-based geopolymers. *Ceramics International*, *40*(7), 8953. DOI: 10.1016/j.ceramint.2014.02.052

Hou, S., Duan, Z., Xiao, J., & Ye, J. (2020). 3D-printed concrete: Performance requirements and mix design review. *Construction & Building Materials*, *273*, 121745. DOI: 10.1016/j.conbuildmat.2020.121745

Howard, D. A., Ma, Z., & Jørgensen, B. N. (2022). A case study of digital twin for greenhouse horticulture production flow. In 2022 IEEE 2nd International Conference on Digital Twins and Parallel Intelligence (DTPI). DOI: 10.1109/DTPI55838.2022.9998914

Huang, C., Wang, C., Rani, T., & Rehman, S. A. U. (2024). Digitalization's role in shaping climate change, renewable energy, and technological innovation for achieving sustainable development in top Asian countries. *Energy & Environment*, *0*(0), 0958305X241258799. Advance online publication. DOI: 10.1177/0958305X241258799

Huang, D., Zhou, Z., Zhang, Z., Dai, Q., Lu, H., Li, Y., & Huang, Y. (2025). Land Use/Land Cover Remote Sensing Classification in Complex Subtropical Karst Environments: Challenges, Methodological Review, and Research Frontiers. *Applied Sciences (Basel, Switzerland)*, *15*(17), 9641. DOI: 10.3390/app15179641

Huang, J., Kogbara, R. B., Hariharan, N., Masad, E., & Little, D. N. (2021). State-of-the-art review of polymers used in soil stabilization. *Construction & Building Materials*, *305*, 124685. DOI: 10.1016/j.conbuildmat.2021.124685

Huang, Y. C., Yang, M. L., & Chiu, M. H. (2026). Digital transformation as an enabler of organizational green learning orientation and ambidextrous green innovation: Organizational information processing perspectives. In *Multidisciplinary Social Networks Research* (pp. 468–481). Springer., DOI: 10.1007/978-3-032-09945-7_40

Hussain, M., Abdullah, M., Ashraf, M. N., Shaheen, A., Farooqi, Z. U. R., Abbas, A., & Tariq, Y. (2025). World food hunger in 2050 and nano solutions: probabilities and prospects based on plant based food. In *Nanomaterials for Enhanced Plant-Based Food Production* (pp. 11–21). Academic Press. DOI: 10.1016/B978-0-443-23688-4.00010-5

Hussain, S., Amritphale, S. S., Matthews, J. C., Paul, N., Matthews, E., & Edwards, R. (2024). Advanced solid geopolymer formulations for refractory applications. *Materials (Basel), 17*(6), 1386. DOI: 10.3390/ma17061386

IAEG, U. (2016). *Final list of proposed Sustainable Development Goal indicators.*

Ikotun, J. O., Aderinto, G. E., Madirisha, M. M., & Katte, V. Y. (2024). Geopolymer cement in pavement applications: Bridging sustainability and performance. *Sustainability (Basel), 16*(13), 5417. DOI: 10.3390/su16135417

Ilnytskyy, D., Drobotiuk, O., & Andrusyk, V. (2024, June). Sustainable Development through Green Innovations: Economic Strategies of China and the EU Compared. In *Proceedings of the International Conference on Economics And Social Sciences* (Vol. 6, No. 1, pp. 412-525). Bucharest University of Economic Studies, Romania. DOI: 10.24818/ICESS/2024/048

Inthavong, P., Rehman, K. U., Masood, K., Shaukat, Z., Hnydiuk-Stefan, A., & Ray, S. (2023). Impact of organizational learning on sustainable firm performance: Intervening effect of organizational networking and innovation. *Heliyon, 9*(5), e16177. DOI: 10.1016/j.heliyon.2023.e16177 PMID: 37251908

Irannezhad, M., Ahmadi, B., Liu, J., Chen, D., & Matthews, J. H. (2022). Global water security: A shining star in the dark sky of achieving the sustainable development goals. *Sustainable Horizons, 1*(September 2021), 100005. DOI: 10.1016/j.horiz.2021.100005

ISO 14040. (2006). *Environmental Management - Life Cycle Assessment - Principles and Framework (ISO 14040:2006), Geneva, Switzerland.*

ISO 14044. (2006). *Environmental Management—Life Cycle Assessment—Requirements and Guidelines* (Vol. 2006).

Istrate, R., Tulus, V., Grass, R. N., Vanbever, L., Stark, W. J., & Guillén-Gosálbez, G. (2024). The environmental sustainability of digital content consumption. *Nature Communications, 15*(1), 24–37. DOI: 10.1038/s41467-024-47621-w

IWA. (2016). *Water Utility Pathways in a Circular Economy*. https://nextgenwater.eu/wp-content/uploads/2018/10/IWA_Circular_Economy_screen-1.pdf

Jackson, T. T. A.-T. T. -. (2016). *Prosperity without growth : foundations for the economy of tomorrow* (Second edition NV-1 online resource : illustrations (black and white)). Routledge. https://doi.org/ LK - https://worldcat.org/title/969665612

Jacob, J. (2025). A Background History of the Sustainable Development Goals. *Sustainable Development (Bradford), 33*(3), 3747–3759. DOI: 10.1002/sd.3317

Jaiswal, R., Gupta, S., & Gupta, S. K. (2025). The impending disruption of digital nomadism: Opportunities, challenges, and research agenda. *World Leisure Journal, 67*(1), 74–104. DOI: 10.1080/16078055.2024.2346091

Jallu, M., & Saride, S. (2024). Performance of alkali-activated fly ash stabilized RAP aggregates as pavement base course. *International Journal of Geosynthetics and Ground Engineering, 10*(2). Advance online publication. DOI: 10.1007/s40891-024-00523-9

Jamwal, A., Nautiyal, A., Singh, K., Alam, S., Alselami, N. A., & Aati, K. (2024). Cow dung ash and corn stalk ash as eco-friendly concrete alternatives. *Civil Engineering Journal, 10*, 21. DOI: 10.28991/CEJ-SP2024-010-02

Jannat, N., Hussien, A., Abdullah, B. M., & Cotgrave, A. (2020). Agro and non-agro waste materials for unfired earth blocks: A review. *Construction & Building Materials, 254*, 119346. DOI: 10.1016/j.conbuildmat.2020.119346

Jawahir, I. S., & Bradley, R. (2016). Technological elements of circular economy and the principles of 6R-based closed-loop material flow in sustainable manufacturing. *Procedia CIRP, 40*, 103–108. DOI: 10.1016/j.procir.2016.01.067

Jayakumar, K., & Park, J. P. (n.d.). *Stimuli-responsive polymer–metal organic framework composites: Biomedical applications and design strategies.(No publication data available.)*

Jeremiah, J. J., Abbey, S. J., Booth, C. A., & Eyo, E. (2023). Viability of calcinated wastepaper sludge ash geopolymer for road pavement subgrade. *Transportation Geotechnics, 44*, 101165. DOI: 10.1016/j.trgeo.2023.101165

Jiang, T., Munguia-López, J. G., Flores-Torres, S., Grant, J., Vijayakumar, S., León-Rodríguez, A. D., & Kinsella, J. M. (2017). Bioprinting of tumor spheroids using alginate/gelatin hydrogels. *Scientific Reports*, *7*(1). Advance online publication. DOI: 10.1038/s41598-017-04691-9

Jiang, X., Jiang, M., Gou, Y., Li, Q., & Zhou, Q. (2022). Forestry digital twin with machine learning in Landsat 7 data. *Frontiers in Plant Science*, *13*, 916900. DOI: 10.3389/fpls.2022.916900 PMID: 35769290

Jones, D., Snider, C., Nassehi, A., Yon, J., & Hicks, B. (2020). Characterising the Digital Twin: A systematic literature review. *CIRP Journal of Manufacturing Science and Technology*, *29*, 36–52. DOI: 10.1016/j.cirpj.2020.02.002

Juengsuwattananon, K., Winnefeld, F., Chindaprasirt, P., & Pimraksa, K. (2019). Correlation of $SiO_2/Al_2O_3$, $Na_2O/Al_2O_3$, $Na_2O/SiO_2$ ratios on phase development in metakaolin–RHA geopolymers. *Construction & Building Materials*, *226*, 406. DOI: 10.1016/j.conbuildmat.2019.07.146

K., V. K., K., S., Kandasamy, J., Govindan, K., Sankaranarayanan, B., & Reddy, K. N. (2023). Barriers to the adoption of digital technologies in a functional circular economy network. *Operations Management Research, 16*(3), 1541–1561. DOI: 10.1007/s12063-023-00375-y

Kadamba, S., Blesson, S., Rao, A. U., Kamath, M., & Tantri, A. (2024). Self-healing concrete using agro-industrial waste: A critical review. *Journal of Building Pathology and Rehabilitation*, *9*(2). Advance online publication. DOI: 10.1007/s41024-024-00501-8

Kadhim, A., Sadique, M., Al-Mufti, R. L., & Hashim, K. (2020). High-calcium one-part alkali-activated cement from lime kiln dust: Long-term performance. *Journal of Building Engineering*, *32*, 101766. DOI: 10.1016/j.jobe.2020.101766

Kahla, N. B., Ghazouani, N., & Raza, A. (2025). Phase change materials in engineered geopolymer composites. *JOM*. Advance online publication. DOI: 10.1007/s11837-025-07655-x

Kaja, A. M., Lázaro, A., & Yu, Q. (2018). Effects of Portland cement on activation mechanism of Class F fly ash geopolymer cured under ambient conditions. *Construction & Building Materials*, *189*, 1113–1123. DOI: 10.1016/j.conbuildmat.2018.09.065

Kajaste, R., & Hurme, M. (2015). Cement industry greenhouse gas emissions: Management options and abatement cost. *Journal of Cleaner Production*, *112*, 4041–4052. DOI: 10.1016/j.jclepro.2015.07.055

Kakwani, N. S., & Kalbar, P. P. (2020). Review of Circular Economy in urban water sector : Challenges and opportunities in India. *Journal of Environmental Management, 271*(August 2019). DOI: 10.1016/j.jenvman.2020.111010

Kaleli, M. J., Kamweru, P. K., Gichumbi, J. M., & Ndiritu, F. G. (2020). Characterization of rice husk ash from open-air burning vs furnace calcination. *Journal of Chemical Engineering and Materials Science, 11*(2), 24–30. DOI: 10.5897/JCEMS2020.0348

Kandpal, V., Jaswal, A., Santibanez Gonzalez, E. D., & Agarwal, N. (2024). Challenges and opportunities for sustainable energy transition and circular economy. *Sustainable Energy Transition: Circular Economy and Sustainable Financing for Environmental, Social and Governance (ESG) Practices*, 307-324.

Kara, A., Zhou, H., & Zhou, Y. (2021). Achieving the United Nations' sustainable development goals through financial inclusion: A systematic literature review of access to finance across the globe. *International Review of Financial Analysis, 77*, 101833. DOI: 10.1016/j.irfa.2021.101833

Karanam, R. K., Addimulam, S., Ahmmed, S., & Natakam, V. M. (2024). The Role of Digital Transformation in Achieving Sustainability Goals: A Preview of SAC 2024 (2.0). *Journal of Computing and Digital Technologies, 2*(1). https://americandigits.comhttps://americandigits.com/

Kartal, M. T., Mukhtarov, S., Depren, Ö., Ayhan, F., & Ulussever, T. (2025). How Can SDG-13 Be Achieved by Energy, Environment, and Economy-Related Policies? Evidence From Five Leading Emerging Countries. *Sustainable Development (Bradford), 33*(4), 5110–5133. DOI: 10.1002/sd.3391

Kasinathan, P., Pugazhendhi, R., Elavarasan, R. M., Ramachandaramurthy, V. K., Ramanathan, V., Subramanian, S., Kumar, S., Nandhagopal, K., Raghavan, R. R. V., Rangasamy, S., Devendiran, R., & Alsharif, M. H. (2022). Realization of Sustainable Development Goals with Disruptive Technologies by Integrating Industry 5.0, Society 5.0, Smart Cities and Villages. *Sustainability (Basel), 14*(22), 15258. Advance online publication. DOI: 10.3390/su142215258

Kaze, C. R., Lemougna, P. N., Alomayri, T., Assaedi, H., Adesina, A., Das, S., Lecomte-Nana, G.-L., Kamseu, E., Melo, U. C., & Leonelli, C. (2020). Laterite-based geopolymer binder cured at various temperatures: Characterization & performance. *Construction & Building Materials, 270*, 121443. DOI: 10.1016/j.conbuildmat.2020.121443

Khan, K., Ahmad, W., Amin, M. N., Ahmad, A., Nazar, S., & Al-Faiad, M. A. (2022). Artificial intelligence strategies for strength estimation of geopolymer composites. *Polymers, 14*(12), 2509. DOI: 10.3390/polym14122509

Khan, N. R., Ameer, F., Bouncken, R. B., & Covin, J. G. (2023). Corporate sustainability entrepreneurship: The role of green entrepreneurial orientation and organizational resilience capacity for green innovation. *Journal of Business Research, 169*, 114296. DOI: 10.1016/j.jbusres.2023.114296

Khater, E.-S., Ali, S. A., Afify, M., Bayomy, M. A., & Abbas, R. S. (2022). GIS-based determination of suitable agricultural residue collection sites. *Scientific Reports, 12*(1). Advance online publication. DOI: 10.1038/s41598-022-18850-0

Kim, D., Steinbach, S., & Zurita, C. (2025). Virtual Water Trade and Economic Integration: The Role of Trade Agreements in Global Water Redistribution. *Applied Economic Perspectives and Policy, 47*(5), 1998–2018. https://doi.org/https://doi.org/10.1002/aepp.70021. DOI: 10.1002/aepp.70021

Kim, K. W., Song, H., Lee, S., Lim, H.-M., & Ko, H. (2025). Accelerating ambient curing of geopolymers using metamodel-guided optimization. *Digital Discovery, 4*(3), 653. DOI: 10.1039/D4DD00217B

Kirchherr, J., Reike, D., & Hekkert, M. (2017). Conceptualizing the circular economy: An analysis of 114 definitions. *Resources, Conservation and Recycling, 127*, 221–232. https://doi.org/https://doi.org/10.1016/j.resconrec.2017.09.005. DOI: 10.1016/j.resconrec.2017.09.005

Kirchherr, J., & van Santen, R. (2019). Research on the circular economy: A critique of the field. *Resources, Conservation and Recycling, 151*, 104480. DOI: 10.1016/j.resconrec.2019.104480

Koçyiğit, Ş. (2024). Geopolymer mortars with ferrochrome slag and fly ash for sustainable construction. *Scientific Reports, 14*(1). Advance online publication. DOI: 10.1038/s41598-024-65552-w

Köenig, A., Mahmoud, H., Baehre, O., & Dehn, F. (2020). Alkalinity impacts on performance of steel-reinforced geopolymers. *Molecules (Basel, Switzerland), 25*(10), 2359. DOI: 10.3390/molecules25102359

Kogbara, R. B., Al-Zubi, A., Mortada, Y., Hammoud, A., Masad, E., & Khraisheh, M. (2023). Lime-activated one-part geopolymers using construction and demolition waste. *Results in Engineering, 21*, 101739. DOI: 10.1016/j.rineng.2023.101739

Korhonen, J., Honkasalo, A., & Seppälä, J. (2018). Circular Economy: The Concept and its Limitations. *Ecological Economics*, *143*, 37–46. https://doi.org/https://doi.org/10.1016/j.ecolecon.2017.06.041. DOI: 10.1016/j.ecolecon.2017.06.041

Korhonen, J., Nuur, C., Feldmann, A., & Birkie, S. E. (2018). Circular economy as an essentially contested concept. *Journal of Cleaner Production*, *175*, 544–552. https://doi.org/https://doi.org/10.1016/j.jclepro.2017.12.111. DOI: 10.1016/j.jclepro.2017.12.111

Koulouris, A., Misailidis, N., & Petrides, D. (2021). Applications of process and digital twin models for production simulation and scheduling in the manufacturing of food ingredients and products. *Food and Bioproducts Processing*, *126*, 317–333. DOI: 10.1016/j.fbp.2021.01.016

Krishnan, J., Mondal, S., & SEM, I. (2012). Financial inclusion. Emerging Strategies For Sustainable Growth & Competence, 716.

Kuang, Y., Fan, Y., Bin, J., & Fan, M. (2024). Impact of the digital economy on carbon dioxide emissions in resource-based cities. *Scientific Reports*, *14*(1), 1–16. DOI: 10.1038/s41598-024-66005-0

Kucukgoncu, H., & Özbayrak, A. (2024). Microstructural analysis of low-calcium fly ash-based geopolymer concrete under high temperatures. *Arabian Journal for Science and Engineering*. Advance online publication. DOI: 10.1007/s13369-024-09266-1

Kulakovskaya, A., Knoeri, C., Radke, F., & Blum, N. U. (2023). Measuring the economic impacts of a circular economy: An evaluation of indicators. *Circular Economy and Sustainability*, *3*(2), 657–692. DOI: 10.1007/s43615-022-00190-w PMID: 37408852

Kumar, D. N., Chowdhary, D. L., Pathuri, T., Katta, P., & Arya, L. (2024). AI enhanced–smart genome editing: Integration of CRISPR Cas9 with artificial intelligence for cancer treatment. In 2024 5th International Conference for Emerging Technology (INCET) (pp. 1–6). DOI: 10.1109/INCET61516.2024.10592877

Kumar, N. (2024). Comparative study of geopolymer vs ordinary concrete for compressive/flexural strength and sustainability. *International Journal for Research in Applied Science and Engineering Technology*, *12*(12), 1814. DOI: 10.22214/ijraset.2024.66112

Kumar, S., Gangotra, A., & Barnard, M. (2025). *Towards net-zero cement: Policies and systems thinking*. Current Sustainable/Renewable. *Energy Reports*, *12*(1). Advance online publication. DOI: 10.1007/s40518-025-00253-0

Kumble, P., Prashant, S., & Jagadisha, H. M. (2024). Fly ash–dolomite–tile waste alkali-activated binder under ambient curing. *Emergent Materials*. Advance online publication. DOI: 10.1007/s42247-024-00772-4

Kursula, K., Illikainen, M., & Perumal, P. (2023). Recycling alkali-activated slag into artificial aggregates: Effect of particle size distribution. *Low-Carbon Materials and Green Construction*, *1*(1). Advance online publication. DOI: 10.1007/s44242-023-00031-5

Kwunjai, S., Jitsangiam, P., Suwan, T., Rinchumphu, D., Thongchua, H., Chindaprasirt, P., & Sampattagul, S. (2020). Crushed rock geopolymer as future road construction material: Strength and compaction evaluation. *Key Engineering Materials*, *841*, 171. . DOI: 10.4028/www.scientific.net/KEM.841.171

Łach, M., Pławecka, K., Bąk, A., Adamczyk, M., Bazan, P., Kozub, B., Korniejenko, K., & Lin, W. (2021). Review of solutions for the use of phase change materials in geopolymers. *Materials (Basel)*, *14*(20), 6044. DOI: 10.3390/ma14206044

Lahane, S., Patel, B., Kant, R., & Malviya, R. K. (2026). Evaluating Industry 4.0 implementation obstacles and solutions for the medical waste reverse logistics system. *International Journal of Logistics Research and Applications*, 1–29. DOI: 10.1080/13675567.2026.2615203

Lakhiar, I. A., Yan, H., Zhang, J., Wang, G., Deng, S., Bao, R., Zhang, C., Syed, T. N., Wang, B., Zhou, R., & Wang, X. (2024). Plastic pollution in agriculture as a threat to food security, the ecosystem, and the environment: An overview. *Agronomy (Basel)*, *14*(3), 548. DOI: 10.3390/agronomy14030548

Lamaa, G., Duarte, A. P. C., Silva, R. V., & de Brito, J. (2023). Carbonation of alkali-activated materials: A review. *Materials (Basel)*, *16*(8), 3086. DOI: 10.3390/ma16083086

Lant, C. (2003). Commentary. *Water International*, *28*(1), 113–115. DOI: 10.1080/02508060.2003.9724813

Lasseur, N. M. C. G., Holstead, K., & Huitema, D. (2025). How is the governance of circular economy of water organized? A systematic review of the literature. *Ecology and Society*, *30*(3), art36. Advance online publication. DOI: 10.5751/ES-16390-300336

Law, D. W., Adam, A. A., Molyneaux, T., Patnaikuni, I., & Wardhono, A. (2014). Long term durability properties of class F fly ash geopolymer concrete. *Materials and Structures*, *48*(3), 721–731. DOI: 10.1617/s11527-014-0268-9

Leal Filho, W., Vidal, D. G., Chen, C., Petrova, M., Dinis, M. A. P., Yang, P., Rogers, S., Álvarez-Castañón, L., Djekic, I., Sharifi, A., & Neiva, S. (2022). An assessment of requirements in investments, new technologies, and infrastructures to achieve the SDGs. *Environmental Sciences Europe*, *34*(1), 58. Advance online publication. DOI: 10.1186/s12302-022-00629-9

Lee, H., Zhang, Y., Zhang, H., & Liu, X. (2023). Challenges and opportunities of utilizing design thinking in the industry 4. 0 era : Based on the case study of industry wastewater treatment system development project process. *Journal of Innovation and Entrepreneurship*, *12*(1), 56. Advance online publication. DOI: 10.1186/s13731-023-00315-x

Leiva, C., Luna-Galiano, Y., Arenas, C., Alonso-Fariñas, B., & Fernández-Pereira, C. (2019). A porous geopolymer based on aluminum-waste with acoustic properties. *Waste Management (New York, N.Y.)*, *95*, 504–512. DOI: 10.1016/j.wasman.2019.06.042

Lemougna, P. N., Nzeukou, A. N., Aziwo, B., Tchamba, A. B., Wang, K., Melo, U. C., & Cui, X. (2019). Effect of slag on the improvement of setting time and compressive strength of low reactive volcanic ash geopolymers synthesized at room temperature. *Materials Chemistry and Physics*, *239*, 122077. DOI: 10.1016/j.matchemphys.2019.122077

Lenzen, M., Moran, D., Kanemoto, K., Foran, B., Lobefaro, L., & Geschke, A. (2012). International trade drives biodiversity threats in developing nations. *Nature*, *486*(7401), 109–112. DOI: 10.1038/nature11145 PMID: 22678290

Lieder, M., & Rashid, A. (2015). Towards Circular Economy implementation: A comprehensive review in context of manufacturing industry. *Journal of Cleaner Production*, *115*, 36–51. Advance online publication. DOI: 10.1016/j.jclepro.2015.12.042

Lin, M., Tang, M., Duan, W., Xia, S., Liu, W., & Wang, Q. (2023). 3D bioprinting for tumor metastasis research. *ACS Biomaterials Science & Engineering*, *9*(6), 3116–3133. DOI: 10.1021/acsbiomaterials.3c00239

Li, Q., Zhao, G., Li, J., Li, S., Yan, W., Tian, X., & Ai, S. (2025). An in-situ predictive method for modulus degradation in composite structures with fatigue damage: Applications in digital twin technology. *Mechanical Systems and Signal Processing*, *237*, 113090. DOI: 10.1016/j.ymssp.2025.113090

Li, S., Hu, K., & Kang, X. (2024). Impact of financial technologies, digitalization, and natural resources on environmental degradation in G-20 countries: Does human resources matter? *Resources Policy*, *93*, 105041. DOI: 10.1016/j.resourpol.2024.105041

Liu, J., Williams, J. R., Zehnder, A. J. B., & Yang, H. (2007). GEPIC - modelling wheat yield and crop water productivity with high resolution on a global scale. *Agricultural Systems*, *94*(2), 478–493. DOI: 10.1016/j.agsy.2006.11.019

Liu, W. (2023). The digital economy and environmental pollution: New evidence based on the support of logistics development. *Journal of Cleaner Production*, *427*, 139210. DOI: 10.1016/j.jclepro.2023.139210

Liu, X., Shu, Y., Zhu, J., Fang, H., Su, Y., Ma, H., Li, B., Xu, J., Cheng, Y. Y., Pan, B., & Song, K. (2024). A 3D bioprinted potential colorectal tumor model based on decellularized matrix/gelatinmethacryloyl/nanoclay/sodium alginate hydrogel. *International Journal of Biological Macromolecules*, *293*, 139346. DOI: 10.1016/j.ijbiomac.2024.139346

Li, X., Rao, F., Song, S., & Ma, Q. (2019). Deterioration in the microstructure of metakaolin-based geopolymers in marine environment. *Journal of Materials Research and Technology*, *8*(3), 2747–2752. DOI: 10.1016/j.jmrt.2019.03.010

Lo, K., Lin, W., Lin, Y., Cheng, T., & Lin, K. (2022). Synthesis metakaolin-based geopolymer incorporated with SiC sludge using design of experiment method. *Polymers*, *14*(16), 3395. DOI: 10.3390/polym14163395

Lo, M., Sonetti, G., & Rosso, M. (2024). Investigating digital technologies' implementation in circular businesses: Evidence from the going circular path. *Journal of Management & Organization*, *30*(3), 421–451. DOI: 10.1017/jmo.2023.60

Longhi, M. A., Rodríguez, E. D., Walkley, B., Zhang, Z., & Kirchheim, A. P. (2019). Metakaolin-based geopolymers: Relation between formulation, physicochemical properties and efflorescence formation. *Composites. Part B, Engineering*, *182*, 107671. DOI: 10.1016/j.compositesb.2019.107671

Lopez-Vargas, A., Fuentes, M., & Vivar, M. (2020). Challenges and opportunities of the internet of things for global development to achieve the united nations sustainable development goals. *IEEE Access: Practical Innovations, Open Solutions*, *8*, 37202–37213. DOI: 10.1109/ACCESS.2020.2975472

Lowan-Trudeau, G. (2023). Digital technologies and environmental education. *The Journal of Environmental Education*, *54*(1), 1–7. DOI: 10.1080/00958964.2022.2152413

Luhar, S., Luhar, I., & Shaikh, F. U. A. (2021). Review on performance evaluation of autonomous healing of geopolymer composites. *Infrastructures*, *6*(7), 94. DOI: 10.3390/infrastructures6070094

Luković, M., Kostić, M., Dudić, B., Spalević, V., & Pantović, D. (2024). Perceptions of mountain ecosystem services in Golija-Studenica Biosphere Reserve, Serbia: Latent transformation from sustainable towards regenerative tourism. *Eco.Mont*, *16*(2), 4–15. DOI: 10.1553/eco.mont-16-2s4

Lu, Q., Shen, Y., & Yu, K. (2024). Digital transformation of enterprises under the pressure of air pollution. *Applied Economics*, *1*(1), 1–12. DOI: 10.1080/00036846.2024.2385755

Luwedde, J., & Nakazi, F. (2024). In Mhlanga, D., & Ndhlovu, E. (Eds.), *Implications of Russia-Ukraine War on Uganda's Fertilizer and Wheat Supply BT - The Russia-Ukraine Conflict and Development in Africa: Implications for Sustainable Development* (pp. 315–323). Springer Nature Switzerland., DOI: 10.1007/978-3-031-63333-1_19

Mabkhot, M. M., Ferreira, P., Maffei, A., Podržaj, P., Mądziel, M., Antonelli, D., Lanzetta, M., Barata, J., Boffa, E., Finžgar, M., Paśko, Ł., Minetola, P., Chelli, R., Nikghadam-Hojjati, S., Wang, X. V., Priarone, P. C., Litwin, P., Stadnicka, D., Lohse, N., & Lupi, F. (2021). Mapping industry 4.0 enabling technologies into united nations sustainability development goals. *Sustainability (Switzerland)*, *13*(5), 1–35. DOI: 10.3390/su13052560

Machkour, B., & Abriane, A. (2020). Industry 4.0 and its implications for the financial sector. *Procedia Computer Science*, *177*, 496–502. DOI: 10.1016/j.procs.2020.10.068

Madiha, Z. (2025). Technological Innovation in the Banking and Financial Sector: Risks and Challenges. In *Innovating Cost-Efficient and Scalable Business Models in the Digital Era* (pp. 299–342). IGI Global. DOI: 10.4018/979-8-3373-2120-2.ch010

Madirisha, M. M., Dada, O. R., & Ikotun, B. D. (2024). Chemical fundamentals of geopolymers in sustainable construction. *Materials Today Sustainability*, *27*, 100842. DOI: 10.1016/j.mtsust.2024.100842

Maestre, C. V., & Santos, G. N. C. (2023). Effect of bismuth oxide nanoparticle on the EMI shielding and thermal stability of industrial waste-based geopolymer composites. *Scientific Reports*, *13*(1), 1787. DOI: 10.1038/s41598-023-27623-2

Mahmoodi, O., Siad, H., Lachemi, M., & Şahmaran, M. (2025). Post-fire thermal and mechanical performance of CDW-based geopolymer composites incorporating different recycled aggregates. *Journal of Building Engineering*, *114131*. Advance online publication. DOI: 10.1016/j.jobe.2025.114131

Maldonado-Alameda, À., Mañosa, J., Miro-Escola, J., Quintero-Payan, A. C., & Chimenos, J. M. (2022). Fluidised-bed incineration bottom ash as the sole precursor of alkali-activated binders: A comparison with grate incinerator bottom ash. *Construction & Building Materials*, *364*, 130001. DOI: 10.1016/j.conbuildmat.2022.130001

Malik, R. A., Wani, M. A., & Gani, S. (2025). Unveiling the dynamics of sustainable development: A holistic examination of green organizational learning, innovation, and performance in Indian SMEs. *Business Strategy & Development*, *8*(1), e70060. DOI: 10.1002/bsd2.70060

Malynovska, Y., Bohomaz, P., Mats, Y., & Parashchyn, O. (2025). Digital Business Transformation: Key Challenges for Modern Managers. *European Journal of Economics and Management*, *11*(2), 21–28. DOI: 10.46340/eujem.2025.11.2.3

Manta, A. G. (2026, January 29). From Sustainability Narratives to Digital Infrastructures: Mapping the Transformation of Smart Agri-Food Systems. *Foods*, *15*(3), 469. DOI: 10.3390/foods15030469 PMID: 41683057

Marathe, S., Szemiot, N., Kumar, S., & Muthu, M. (2025). Degradation potential of metakaolin-based geopolymer composites immersed in real and simulated acidic environments. *Sustainability (Basel)*, *17*(2), 468. DOI: 10.3390/su17020468

Mare, M. D., & Ouellet-Plamondon, C. (2022). Highly piezoresistive, self-sensing, one-part potassium-activated inorganic polymers for structural health monitoring. *Materials Today Sustainability*, *20*, 100261. DOI: 10.1016/j.mtsust.2022.100261

Maresova, P., Soukal, I., Svobodova, L., Hedvicakova, M., Javanmardi, E., Selamat, A., & Krejcar, O. (2018). Consequences of industry 4.0 in business and economics. In *Economies* (Vol. 6, Number 3). MDPI Multidisciplinary Digital Publishing Institute. DOI: 10.3390/economies6030046

Markard, J., Raven, R., & Truffer, B. (2012). Sustainability transitions: An emerging field of research and its prospects. *Research Policy*, *41*(6), 955–967. DOI: 10.1016/j.respol.2012.02.013

Mashifana, T., & Sithole, T. (2020). Recovery of silicon dioxide from waste foundry sand and alkaline activation of desilicated foundry sand. *Journal of Sustainable Metallurgy*, *6*(4), 700–714. DOI: 10.1007/s40831-020-00303-5

Matsimbe, J., Dinka, M. O., Olukanni, D. O., & Musonda, I. (2022). Geopolymer: A systematic review of methodologies. *Materials (Basel)*, *15*(19), 6852. DOI: 10.3390/ma15196852

Matsueda, Y., & Antunes, E. (2024). A review of current technologies for the sustainable valorisation of sugarcane bagasse. *Journal of Environmental Chemical Engineering, 114900*(6), 114900. Advance online publication. DOI: 10.1016/j.jece.2024.114900

Mazur-Wierzbicka, E. (2021). Circular economy: Advancement of European Union countries. *Environmental Sciences Europe, 33*(1), 111. DOI: 10.1186/s12302-021-00549-0

Medeiros, T. G. B. T., de Medeiros, J. F., Kolling, C., Duarte Ribeiro, J. L., & Morea, D. (2023). Redesign in the textile industry: Proposal of a methodology for the insertion of circular thinking in product development processes. *Journal of Cleaner Production, 397*, 136588. DOI: 10.1016/j.jclepro.2023.136588

Mekonnen, M. M., Kebede, M. M., Demeke, B. W., Carr, J. A., Chapagain, A., Dalin, C., Debaere, P., D'Odorico, P., Marston, L., Ray, C., Rosa, L., & Zhuo, L. (2024). Trends and environmental impacts of virtual water trade. *Nature Reviews. Earth & Environment, 5*(12), 890–905. DOI: 10.1038/s43017-024-00605-2

Melece, L. (2016). Challenges and opportunities of circular economy and green economy. *Engineering for Rural Development, 25*, 1162–1169.

Melesse, T. Y., Colace, F., Dembele, S. P., Lorusso, A., Santaniello, D., & Valentino, C. (2024). Digital twin for predictive monitoring of crops: State of the art. *Lecture Notes in Networks and Systems, 695*, 1027–1036. DOI: 10.1007/978-981-99-3043-2_85

Melesse, T. Y., Franciosi, C., Di Pasquale, V., & Riemma, S. (2023). Analyzing the implementation of digital twins in the agri-food supply chain. *Logistics (Basel), 7*(2), 33. DOI: 10.3390/logistics7020033

Meng, B., Fang, Y., Guo, J., & Yaxiong, Z. (2017). Measuring China ' s domestic production networks through Trade in Value-added perspectives. *Economic Systems Research, 29*(January), 48–65. DOI: 10.1080/09535314.2017.1282435

Merrett, S. (1997). *Introduction To The Economics Of Water Resources: An International Perspective* (Routledge (ed.); 1st Editio). 10.4324/9780203645390

METI. (2004). *Handbook on Resource Recycling Legislation and 3R Initiatives.*

Mhlanga, D. (2021). Artificial intelligence in the industry 4.0, and its impact on poverty, innovation, infrastructure development, and the sustainable development goals: Lessons from emerging economies? *Sustainability (Basel), 13*(11), 5788. Advance online publication. DOI: 10.3390/su13115788

Mhlanga, D. (2022). Human-Centered Artificial Intelligence: The Superlative Approach to Achieve Sustainable Development Goals in the Fourth Industrial Revolution. *Sustainability (Basel), 14*(13), 7804. Advance online publication. DOI: 10.3390/su14137804

Mihai, S., Yaqoob, M., Hung, D. V., Davis, W., Towakel, P., Raza, M., & Nguyen, H. X. (2022). Digital twins: A survey on enabling technologies, challenges, trends and future prospects. *IEEE Communications Surveys and Tutorials*, *24*(4), 2255–2291. DOI: 10.1109/COMST.2022.3208773

Min, Q., Lu, Y., Liu, Z., Su, C., & Wang, B. (2019). Machine learning-based digital twin framework for production optimization in petrochemical industry. *International Journal of Information Management*, *49*, 502–519. DOI: 10.1016/j.ijinfomgt.2019.05.020

Mirabi, M., Javan, K., Darestani, M., & Karrabi, M. (2025). Integrating Circular Economy and Life Cycle Assessment in Virtual Water Management: A Case Study of Food Consumption Across Economic Classes in Iran. *Sustainability (Basel)*, *17*(6), 1–16. DOI: 10.3390/su17062743

Mishra, H., & Maheshwari, P. (2020). Achieving sustainable development goals through Fourth Industrial Revolution: An Indian perspective. *Indian Journal of Commerce & Management Studies*, *XI*(2), 63. DOI: 10.18843/ijcms/v11i2/06

Mishra, R., Singh, R. K., & Song, M. (2025). Managing tensions in resilience development: A paradox theory perspective on the role of digital transformation. *Journal of Enterprise Information Management*, *38*(1), 127–151. DOI: 10.1108/JEIM-08-2022-0271

Miyake, K. K. (2024). Abolition-democracy and the future of climate change. *Environment and Planning. E, Nature and Space*, *7*(6), 2365–2385. DOI: 10.1177/25148486241287028

Mobili, A., Tittarelli, F., & Rahier, H. (2020). One-part alkali-activated pastes and mortars prepared with metakaolin and biomass ash. *Applied Sciences (Basel, Switzerland)*, *10*(16), 5610. DOI: 10.3390/app10165610

Mohamad, N., Muthusamy, K., Embong, R., Kusbiantoro, A., & Hashim, M. H. (2021). Environmental impact of cement production and solutions: A review. *Materials Today: Proceedings*, *48*, 741–746. DOI: 10.1016/j.matpr.2021.02.212

Mohamed, O. A., Hassan, A. M., & Abdelwahab, N. R. (2025). High-performance and durable green geopolymer based on slag/alumina sludge ash incorporating $CuFe_2O_4$ spinel nanograins for enhanced gamma radiation shielding. *International Journal of Concrete Structures and Materials*, *19*(1), 87. Advance online publication. DOI: 10.1186/s40069-025-00831-y

Mohammed, A. A., Ahmed, H. U., & Mosavi, A. (2021). Survey of mechanical properties of geopolymer concrete: A comprehensive review and data analysis. *Materials (Basel)*, *14*(16), 4690. DOI: 10.3390/ma14164690

Molu, G. G., & Luketero, S. (2025). Influence of prepaid smart water metering on performance of community water projects in Marsabit County, Kenya. *International Academic Journal of Information Sciences and Project Management*, *3*(7), 351–369.

Monteiro, J., Barata, J., Veloso, M., Veloso, L., & Nunes, J. (2018). Towards sustainable digital twins for vertical farming. In *2018 Thirteenth International Conference on Digital Information Management (ICDIM)* (pp. 234–239). DOI: 10.1109/ICDIM.2018.8847169

Mora-Contreras, R., Ormazabal, M., Jaca, C., & Santos, J. (2025). Revealing the effects of circular economy, eco-innovation and Industry 4.0 on sustainability performance and competitive advantage in manufacturing companies. *Sustainable Development (Bradford)*, *33*(4), 3255–3278. DOI: 10.1002/sd.70075

Morseletto, P. (2020). Targets for a circular economy. *Resources, Conservation and Recycling*, *153*, 104553. DOI: 10.1016/j.resconrec.2019.104553

Morseletto, P., Mooren, C. E., & Munaretto, S. (2022). Circular Economy of Water: Definition, Strategies and Challenges. *Circular Economy and Sustainability*, *2*(4), 1463–1477. DOI: 10.1007/s43615-022-00165-x

Mostafa, M., Salah, H., Saddek, A. B., & Shehata, N. (2020). Optimization of nanostructured/nanosized rice husk ash preparation. *Baghdad Science Journal*, *17*(3), 953. DOI: 10.21123/bsj.2020.17.3(Suppl.).0953

Motia, K., Kumar, R., & Akhai, S. (2024, November). Navigating the Fourth Industrial Revolution: A Comprehensive Review of Industry 4.0 Technologies and Their Global Adoption. In *International Conference on Design and Manufacturing Technologies* (pp. 317-333). Springer Nature Singapore. https://doi.org/DOI: 10.1007/978-981-96-7659-0_28

Mroz, B. (2010). Consumerism vs. sustainability: The emergence of new consumer trends in Poland. *International Journal of Economic Policy in Emerging Economies*, *3*(1), 1–15. DOI: 10.1504/IJEPEE.2010.032791

Mukhametkaliyev, T. M., Ali, M. H., Kutugin, V., Savinova, O. V., & Vereschagin, V. I. (2022). Influence of mixing order on the synthesis of geopolymer concrete. *Polymers, 14*(21), 4777. DOI: 10.3390/polym14214777

Mulapeer, E., & Omar, A. A. (2025). Durability and mechanical performance of geopolymer mortar with partial replacement of fly ash by rice husk ash and variations in alkaline activator concentrations. *Deleted Journal, 2*(1), 82. Advance online publication. DOI: 10.1007/s44290-025-00234-8

Munir, Q., Peltonen, R., & Kärki, T. (2021). Printing parameter requirements for 3D printable geopolymer materials prepared from industrial side streams. *Materials (Basel), 14*(16), 4758. DOI: 10.3390/ma14164758

Murthy, A., Galli, A., Madeira, C., & Moreno Pires, S. (2023). Consumer attitudes towards fish and seafood in portugal: Opportunities for footprint reduction. *Sustainability (Basel), 15*(2), 1363. DOI: 10.3390/su15021363

Mushtaq, A., Ali, S. S., Chaudhry, A., Sial, N. A., Aslam, M., & Batool, H. (2025). Geopolymers as supplementary cementitious materials to reduce carbon dioxide emissions. *Nature Environment and Pollution Technology, 24*(S1), 417–429. DOI: 10.46488/NEPT.2024.v24iS1.033

Muthukrishnan, S., Ramakrishnan, S., & Sanjayan, J. (2020). Effect of alkali reactions on the rheology of one-part 3D printable geopolymer concrete. *Cement and Concrete Composites, 116*, 103899. DOI: 10.1016/j.cemconcomp.2020.103899

Mwansa, G., Ngandu, M. R., & Mkwambi, Z. (2025). Bridging the digital divide: Exploring the challenges and solutions for digital exclusion in rural South Africa. *Discover Global Society, 3*(1), 54. Advance online publication. DOI: 10.1007/s44282-025-00189-2

Nagaraj, S., Kathole, A. B., Arya, L., Tyagi, N., Goyal, S. B., Rajawat, A. S., Raboaca, M. S., Mihaltan, T. C., Verma, C., & Suciu, G. (2023). Improved secure encryption with energy optimization using random permutation pseudo algorithm based on IoT in wireless sensor networks. *Energies, 16*(1), 1–17. DOI: 10.3390/en16010008

Nana, A., Kamseu, E., Akono, A., Ngouné, J., Djobo, J. N. Y., Tchakouté, H. K., Bignozzi, M. C., & Leonelli, C. (2021). Particle size and distribution on the mechanical performance improvement of inorganic polymer composites. *Materials Chemistry and Physics, 267*, 124602. DOI: 10.1016/j.matchemphys.2021.124602

Nasirahmadi, A., & Hensel, O. (2022). Toward the next generation of digitalization in agriculture based on digital twin paradigm. *Sensors (Basel), 22*(2), 498. DOI: 10.3390/s22020498 PMID: 35062459

Nasser, I. M., Ibrahim, M. H. W., Zuki, S. S. M., Alshalif, A. F., Nindyawati, N., & Jaya, R. P. (2023). *Effects of milling time on nano rice husk ash particle size. E3S Web of Conferences, 445*, 1003. https://doi.org/DOI: 10.1051/e3sconf/202344501003

Nastasi, B., Markovska, N., Puksec, T., Duić, N., & Foley, A. (2022). Renewable and sustainable energy challenges to face for the achievement of Sustainable Development Goals. *Renewable & Sustainable Energy Reviews, 157*, 112071. DOI: 10.1016/j.rser.2022.112071

Nawaz, M., Heitor, A., & Sivakumar, M. (2020). Geopolymers in construction: Recent developments. *Construction & Building Materials, 260*, 120472. DOI: 10.1016/j.conbuildmat.2020.120472

Nazibudin, N. A., Sabri, S. A. M., & Manaf, L. A. (2025). Aligning with sustainable development goals (SDG) 12: A systematic review of food waste generation in Malaysia. In *Cleaner Waste Systems* (Vol. 10). Elsevier B.V. DOI: 10.1016/j.clwas.2025.100205

Neeraja, kalluri, Gupta, T., Vaish, A., Kumar Gowda B N, V., & Purohit, P. (2024). The impact of artificial intelligence on human resource functions: a case study of Tata Consultancy Services (TCS) In India. *Frontiers in Health Informatics, 13*(8). www.healthinformaticsjournal.comwww.healthinformaticsjournal.com

Neethirajan, S., & Kemp, B. (2021). Digital twins in livestock farming. *Animals (Basel), 11*(4), 1008. DOI: 10.3390/ani11041008 PMID: 33916713

Neri, A., Cagno, E., Negri, M., & Bassani, C. A. (2024). The relationship between digital technologies and the circular economy: A systematic literature review and a research agenda. *R & D Management, 54*(4), 671–694. DOI: 10.1111/radm.12715

Ngui, F., Muhammed, N., Mutunga, F. M., Marangu, J. M., & Kinoti, I. K. (2022). A review on selected durability parameters on performance of geopolymers containing industrial by-products, agro-wastes and natural pozzolan. *Journal of Sustainable Construction Materials and Technologies, 7*(4), 375–400. DOI: 10.47481/jscmt.1190244

Nguyen, K. L., Uddin, M., & Pham, T. M. (2024). Generative artificial intelligence and optimisation framework for concrete mixture design with low cost and embodied $CO_2$. *Construction & Building Materials, 451*, 138836. DOI: 10.1016/j.conbuildmat.2024.138836

Nie, J., Wang, Y., Li, Y., & Chao, X. (2022). Artificial intelligence and digital twins in sustainable agriculture and forestry: A survey. *Turkish Journal of Agriculture and Forestry, 46*(5), 642–661. DOI: 10.55730/1300-011X.3033

Nika, C. E., Vasilaki, V., Expósito, A., & Katsou, E. (2020). Water Cycle and Circular Economy: Developing a Circularity Assessment Framework for Complex Water Systems. *Water Research*, *187*, 116423. DOI: 10.1016/j.watres.2020.116423 PMID: 32979579

Niveditha, M., &Koniki, S. (2020). *Effect of durability properties on geopolymer concrete – A review. E3S Web of Conferences, 184*, 1092. https://doi.org/DOI: 10.1051/e3sconf/202018401092

Nkwaju, R. Y., Djobo, J. N. Y., Nouping, J. N. F., Mejouyo, P. W. H., Nemaleu, J. G. D., & Courard, L. (2019). Iron-rich laterite-bagasse fiber-based geopolymer composite: Mechanical, durability and insulating properties. *Applied Clay Science*, *183*, 105333. DOI: 10.1016/j.clay.2019.105333

Nodehi, M., & Taghvaee, V. M. (2021). Alkali-activated materials and geopolymer: A review of common precursors and activators addressing circular economy. *Circular Economy and Sustainability*, *2*(1), 165–196. DOI: 10.1007/s43615-021-00029-w

Norrrahim, M. N. F., Farid, M. A. A., Lawal, A. A., Yasim-Anuar, T. A. T., Samsudin, M. H., & Zulkifli, A. A. (2022). Emerging technologies for value-added use of oil palm biomass. *Environmental Science. Advances*, *1*(3), 259–275. DOI: 10.1039/D2VA00029F

Nowak-Marchewka, K., Osmólska, E., & Stoma, M. (2025). Progress and Challenges of Circular Economy in Selected EU Countries. *Sustainability (Basel)*, *17*(1), 320. DOI: 10.3390/su17010320

Obeidy, N. F. A., Khalil, W. I., & Ahmed, H. K. (2024). Optimization of local modified metakaolin-based geopolymer concrete by Taguchi method. *Open Engineering*, *14*(1), 20220561. Advance online publication. DOI: 10.1515/eng-2022-0561

Ocelík, V., Kolk, A., & Ciulli, F. (2023). Multinational enterprises, Industry 4.0 and sustainability: A multidisciplinary review and research agenda. *Journal of Cleaner Production*, *413*, 137434. Advance online publication. DOI: 10.1016/j.jclepro.2023.137434

Odey, G., Adelodun, B., Kim, S. H., & Choi, K. S. (2021). Conflicting Drivers of Virtual Water Trade: A Review Based on the "virtual Water Concept.". *Water Economics and Policy*, *7*(3), 2150011. Advance online publication. DOI: 10.1142/S2382624X21500119

OECD. (2025), The Circular Economy in Cities and Regions of the European Union, OECD Urban Studies, OECD Publishing,Paris, DOI: 10.1787/e09c21e2-en

OECD. (2026). The OECD Going Digital Measurement Roadmap 2026. OECD Digital Economy Paper, 382. [Online]. https://www.oecd.org/content/dam/oecd/en/publications/reports/2026/03/the-oecd-going-digital-measurement-roadmap-2026_590c5900/b455e132-en.pdf

OECD. 2025, Resource efficiency and circular economy, https://www.oecd.org/en/topics/resource-efficiency-and-circular-economy.html

Oelze, N., Hoejmose, S. U., Habisch, A., & Millington, A. (2016). Sustainable development in supply chain management: The role of organizational learning for policy implementation. *Business Strategy and the Environment*, *25*(4), 241–260. DOI: 10.1002/bse.1869

Olanrewaju, V. O., Gyamfi, B. A., Ozsahin, I., & Adebayo, T. S. (2025). Achieving SDGs 7, 8, and 13: Balancing policy uncertainty with renewable energy demand. *Environmental Sciences Europe*, *37*(1), 97. Advance online publication. DOI: 10.1186/s12302-025-01133-6

Olivia, M., Putri, W. R., Supit, S., Wibisono, G., & Utama, P. S. (2023). *Compressive strength and porosity of POFA blended concrete admixed with micro silica. E3S Web of Conferences, 445*, 1034. https://doi.org/DOI: 10.1051/e3sconf/202344501034

Olsson, J. A., Miller, S. A., & Alexander, M. (2023). Near-term pathways for decarbonizing global concrete production. *Nature Communications*, *14*(1), 4574. DOI: 10.1038/s41467-023-40302-0

Omol, E. J. (2024). Organizational digital transformation: from evolution to future trends. In *Digital Transformation and Society* (Vol. 3, Number 3, pp. 240–256). Emerald Publishing. DOI: 10.1108/DTS-08-2023-0061

Omran, M., Khalifeh, M., & Paiva, M. D. M. (2023). Aging and temperature effects on sustainable one-part geopolymers for well-cementing applications. *SPE Journal*, *29*(2), 843. DOI: 10.2118/217993-PA

Oumar, A. I. (2025). Review of geopolymer concrete: Reaction mechanisms, mechanical behavior, and environmental benefits. *Journal of Civil Engineering and Urbanism*, *15*(2), 40–64. DOI: 10.54203/jceu.2025.4

Oyebisi, S., Ede, A. N., Olutoge, F., & Omole, D. O. (2020). Geopolymer concrete incorporating agro-industrial wastes: Effects on mechanical properties, microstructure and mineralogical phases. *Construction & Building Materials*, *256*, 119390. DOI: 10.1016/j.conbuildmat.2020.119390

Oyebisi, S., Olutoge, F., Kathirvel, P., Oyaotuderekumor, I., Lawanson, D., Nwani, J., Ede, A. N., & Kaze, C. R. (2022). Sustainability assessment of geopolymer concrete synthesized by slag and corncob ash. *Case Studies in Construction Materials, 17*, e01665. Advance online publication. DOI: 10.1016/j.cscm.2022.e01665

Özen, M. Y., Firdous, R., Lehmann, C. W., & Stephan, D. (2023). Effects of curing conditions on the self-healing of geopolymer paste. MATEC Web of Conferences, 378, 2017. https://doi.org/DOI: 10.1051/matecconf/202337802017

Pace, L. A. (2020). Eco-innovation in Malta: EIO country profile 2018-2019, 1-40.

Pakuła, N., Łapniewska, Z., & Dutra, C. J. (2025). Comparative measurements of circular economy performance among European countries: Reviewing approaches and limitations. *Journal of Environmental Management, 375*, 124414. DOI: 10.1016/j.jenvman.2025.124414 PMID: 39904241

Pantović, D., Bošković, N., & Petrović, T. (2022). Measuring Convergence in Tourism Competitiveness of Natural and Cultural Resources: A Case of the Balkans and Eastern Europe. *Ekonomický časopis,* 910 (70/2022), 703 – 722.

Pantović, D., Kostić, M., Veljović, S., Luković, M. (2023a). Evaluation Model of Environmental Sustainable Competitive Tourism Based on Entropy, *Problemy Ekorozwoju/ Problems of Sustainable Development*, 18(2): 193-203.

Pantovic, D., Chaichi, K., & Pavlović, S. (2024). Contribution of tourism to economic development in selected European countries. *BizInfo (Blace) Journal of Economics. Management and Informatics, 15*(2), 83–89.

Pantovic, D., Fedajev, A., & Milošević, I. (2023). Monetary and fiscal policies in the EU. Is there a difference between EMU and non-EMU members? *Acta Oeconomica, 73*(1), 85–100. DOI: 10.1556/032.2023.00006

Pan, Z., Jiang, Z., Sun, X., Zhang, M., & Cao, Y. (2024). Compressive strength and isothermal calorimetry of binary and ternary geopolymer mortars at early age. *Research Square*. https://doi.org/DOI: 10.21203/rs.3.rs-5270327/v1

Pappas, I. O., Mikalef, P., Dwivedi, Y. K., Jaccheri, L., & Krogstie, J. (2023). Responsible Digital Transformation for a Sustainable Society. In *Information Systems Frontiers* (Vol. 25, Number 3, pp. 945–953). Springer. DOI: 10.1007/s10796-023-10406-5

Passuello, A., Rodríguez, E. D., Hirt, E., Longhi, M. A., Bernal, S. A., Provis, J. L., & Kirchheim, A. P. (2017). Environmental footprint improvement of geopolymers using waste-derived activators. *Journal of Cleaner Production, 166*, 680. DOI: 10.1016/j.jclepro.2017.08.007

Pasupathy, K., Sanjayan, J., Rajeev, P., & Law, D. W. (2021). Effect of chloride ingress in reinforced geopolymer concrete in marine environment. *Journal of Building Engineering*, *39*, 102281. DOI: 10.1016/j.jobe.2021.102281

Pauliuk, S. (2018). Critical appraisal of the circular economy standard BS 8001:2017 and a dashboard of quantitative system indicators for its implementation in organizations. *Resources, Conservation and Recycling*, *129*, 81–92. DOI: 10.1016/j.resconrec.2017.10.019

Pearce, D., & Turner, R. (1989). Economics of natural resources and the environment. In *Johns Hopkins University Press*. DOI: 10.56021/9780801839863

Pérez, M. P. S., Suárez, J. A. D., & Castro-Gomes, J. (2022). Improving the behaviour of green geopolymer concrete using different hemp preservation conditions. *Minerals (Basel)*, *12*(12), 1530. DOI: 10.3390/min12121530

Pérez-Martínez, J., Hernandez-Gil, F., Miguel, G. S., Ruiz, D., & Arredondo, M. T. (2023). Analysing associations between digitalization and the accomplishment of the sustainable development goals. *The Science of the Total Environment*, *857*(3), 1–12. DOI: 10.1016/j.scitotenv.2022.159700

Perná, I., Šupová, M., Hanzlíček, T., & Špaldoňová, A. (2019). Synthesis and characterization of geopolymers based on metakaolin and high LOI straw ash. *Construction & Building Materials*, *228*, 116765. DOI: 10.1016/j.conbuildmat.2019.116765

Personal, M., Archive, R., & Ibrahim, M. (2020). *Munich Personal RePEc Archive Impact of Technological Innovation on Energy Efficiency in Industry 4 . 0 Era : Moderation of Shadow Economy in Sustainable Development.* (104842), 0–32.

Pfister, S., Boulay, A. M., Berger, M., Hadjikakou, M., Motoshita, M., Hess, T., Ridoutt, B., Weinzettel, J., Scherer, L., Döll, P., Manzardo, A., Núñez, M., Verones, F., Humbert, S., Buxmann, K., Harding, K., Benini, L., Oki, T., Finkbeiner, M., & Henderson, A. (2017). Understanding the LCA and ISO water footprint: A response to Hoekstra (2016) "A critique on the water-scarcity weighted water footprint in LCA. *Ecological Indicators*, *72*, 352–359. DOI: 10.1016/j.ecolind.2016.07.051 PMID: 30344449

Pham, T. T., Kuo, T. C., Tseng, M. L., Tan, R. R., Tan, K., Ika, D. S., & Lin, C. W. (2019). Industry 4.0 to accelerate the circular economy: A case study of electric scooter sharing. *Sustainability (Basel)*, *11*(23), 6661. DOI: 10.3390/su11236661

Pina, A., Ferrão, P., Fournier, J., Lacarrière, B., & Le Corre, O. (2019). ScienceDirect ScienceDirect Industry 4. 0 Technology Implementation Impact to Industrial Technology Implementation Impact to Industrial Sustainable Energy in Indonesia : A Model Conceptualization Sustainable Energy in Indonesia : A Model Conceptualizatio. *Energy Procedia*, *156*, 227–233. DOI: 10.1016/j.egypro.2018.11.133

Polyviou, A., Venters, W., & Pouloudi, N. (2023). Distant but close: Locational, relational and temporal proximity in cloud computing adoption. *Journal of Information Technology*, *0*(0), 1–23. DOI: 10.1177/02683962231186161

Pouhet, R., & Cyr, M. (2014). Studies of natural and accelerated carbonation in metakaolin-based geopolymer. *Advances in Science and Technology (Owerri, Nigeria)*, 38–43. Advance online publication. . DOI: 10.4028/www.scientific.net/AST.92.38

Prieto-Sandoval, V., Jaca, C., & Ormazabal, M. (2018). Towards a consensus on the circular economy. *Journal of Cleaner Production*, *179*, 605–615. DOI: 10.1016/j.jclepro.2017.12.224

Provis, J. L. (2009). *Activating solution chemistry for geopolymers*. In *Elsevier eBooks* (p. 50). https://doi.org/DOI: 10.1533/9781845696382.1.50

Provis, J. L., & Bernal, S. A. (2014). Geopolymers and related alkali-activated materials. *Annual Review of Materials Research*, *44*(1), 299–327. DOI: 10.1146/annurev-matsci-070813-113515

Przybek, A., Łach, M., Bogucki, R., Ciemnicka, J., Prałat, K., Koper, A., Korniejenko, K., & Masłoń, A. (2024). Energy-efficient geopolymer composites containing phase-change materials—Comparison of different contents and types. *Materials (Basel)*, *17*(19), 4712. DOI: 10.3390/ma17194712

Purcell, W., & Neubauer, T. (2023). Digital twins in agriculture: A state-of-the-art review. *Smart Agricultural Technology*, *3*, 100094. DOI: 10.1016/j.atech.2022.100094

Pylianidis, C., Osinga, S., & Athanasiadis, I. N. (2021). Introducing digital twins to agriculture. *Computers and Electronics in Agriculture*, *184*, 105942. DOI: 10.1016/j.compag.2020.105942

Qian, Y., Tian, X., Geng, Y., Zhong, S., Cui, X., Zhang, X., Moss, D. A., & Bleischwitz, R. (2019). Driving Factors of Agricultural Virtual Water Trade between China and the Belt and Road Countries. *Environmental Science & Technology*, *53*(10), 5877–5886. DOI: 10.1021/acs.est.9b00093 PMID: 31013057

Qing, Z., Dan, M., & Xin, H. (2023). Digital transformation and firms' pollution emissions. *Technological Forecasting and Social Change*, *197*(1), 1–12. DOI: 10.1016/j.techfore.2023.122910

Qi, Q., Tao, F., Hu, T., Anwer, N., Liu, A., Wei, Y., Wang, L., & Nee, A. Y. C. C. (2021). Enabling technologies and tools for digital twin. *Journal of Manufacturing Systems*, *58*, 3–21. DOI: 10.1016/j.jmsy.2019.10.001

Qiu, H., Zhang, H., Lei, K., Zhang, H., & Hu, X. (2023). Forest digital twin: A new tool for forest management practices. *Computers and Electronics in Agriculture*, *215*, 108416. DOI: 10.1016/j.compag.2023.108416

Qudrat-Ullah, H. (2025). A Thematic Review of AI and ML in Sustainable Energy Policies for Developing Nations. In *Energies* (Vol. 18, Number 9). Multidisciplinary Digital Publishing Institute (MDPI). DOI: 10.3390/en18092239

Quiatchon, P. R. J., Dollente, I. J., Abulencia, A. B., Libre, R. G. D., Villoria, M. B. D., Guades, E. J., Promentilla, M. A. B., & Ongpeng, J. M. C. (2021). Compressive strength and setting time of low-calcium fly ash geopolymer paste using RSM. *Polymers*, *13*(20), 3461. DOI: 10.3390/polym13203461

Rabbat, C., Awad, S., Villot, A., Rollet, D., & Andrès, Y. (2021). Sustainability of biomass-based insulation materials in buildings: Current status in France, end-of-life projections and energy recovery potentials. *Renewable & Sustainable Energy Reviews*, *156*, 111962. DOI: 10.1016/j.rser.2021.111962

Rabie, M., Irshidat, M. R., & Al-Nuaimi, N. (2022). Ambient and heat-cured geopolymer composites: Mix design optimization and life cycle assessment. *Sustainability (Basel)*, *14*(9), 4942. DOI: 10.3390/su14094942

Rafey, A., & Siddiqui, F. Z. (2023). A review of plastic waste management in India – challenges and opportunities. *International Journal of Environmental Analytical Chemistry*, *103*(16), 3971–3987. DOI: 10.1080/03067319.2021.1917560

Rahimpour, H., Amini, A. B., Sharifi, F., Fahmi, A., & Zinatloo-Ajabshir, S. (2024). Facile fabrication of sustainable brick and mortar through geopolymerization of construction debris. *Scientific Reports*, *14*(1), 10914. Advance online publication. DOI: 10.1038/s41598-024-61688-x

Rahman, S. H. A., Zulkarnain, N. N., & Shafiq, N. (2021). *Experimental study and DOE statistical analysis for geopolymer matrix development for oil-well cementing*. In *Vide Leaf eBooks*. https://doi.org/DOI: 10.37247/PAMS2ED.3.2021.14

Rahman, M. M., Nguyen, R., & Lu, L. (2022). Multi-level impacts of climate change and supply disruption events on a potato supply chain: An agent-based modeling approach. *Agricultural Systems*, *201*, 103469. DOI: 10.1016/j.agsy.2022.103469

Rajczakowska, M., Habermehl-Cwirzen, K., Hedlund, H., & Ćwirzeń, A. (2019). Self-healing potential of geopolymer concrete. *Proceedings*, *6*, 6. Advance online publication. DOI: 10.3390/proceedings2019034006

Raman, R., Sreenivasan, A., Ma, S., Patwardhan, A., & Nedungadi, P. (2023). Green Supply Chain Management Research Trends and Linkages to UN Sustainable Development Goals. *Sustainability (Basel)*, *15*(22), 15848. Advance online publication. DOI: 10.3390/su152215848

Ramesh, V., Muthramu, B., & Rebekhal, D. (2025). Review of sustainability assessment of geopolymer concrete through AI-based life cycle analysis. *AI in Civil Engineering*, *4*(1), 3. Advance online publication. DOI: 10.1007/s43503-024-00045-3

Ranjbar, N., Kuenzel, C., Spangenberg, J., & Mehrali, M. (2020). Hardening evolution of geopolymers from setting to equilibrium: A review. *Cement and Concrete Composites*, *114*, 103729. DOI: 10.1016/j.cemconcomp.2020.103729

Ranjbar, N., Mehrali, M., Kuenzel, C., Gundlach, C., Pedersen, D. B., Dolatshahi-Pirouz, A., & Spangenberg, J. (2021). Rheological characterization of 3D printable geopolymers. *Cement and Concrete Research*, *147*, 106498. DOI: 10.1016/j.cemconres.2021.106498

Rao, B. N. M., Durga, C. S. S., Venkatesh, C., & Rao, T. M. (2024). Sustainable geopolymer concrete for pavements: Performance of recycled concrete aggregates in fly ash-based mixtures. *Journal of Sustainable Construction Materials and Technologies*, *9*(3), 211–220. DOI: 10.47481/jscmt.1554284

Rasheed, A., San, O., & Kvamsdal, T. (2020). Digital twin: Values, challenges and enablers from a modeling perspective. *IEEE Access : Practical Innovations, Open Solutions*, *8*, 21980–22012. DOI: 10.1109/ACCESS.2020.2970143

Rathnayaka, M., Karunasingha, D., Gunasekara, C., Law, D. W., Wijesundara, K. K., & Lokuge, W. (2024). Target-strength-based mix design determination for geopolymer concrete. *Archives of Civil and Mechanical Engineering*, *24*(3). Advance online publication. DOI: 10.1007/s43452-024-01002-8

Ravish, G., & Abbass, M. (2026). Engineering characteristics of agro-residue–based geopolymer concrete with fibre reinforcement. *Scientific Reports*, *16*(1), 5585. Advance online publication. DOI: 10.1038/s41598-026-36190-1

Razzouki, A., Ridaoui, M., Oudgou, M., & Boudhar, A. (2025). Econometric Analysis of Climate Change Impacts on Agricultural Output in the MENA Region. In *Economies* (Vol. 13, Issue 12, p. 340). DOI: 10.3390/economies13120340

Reddy, D. V., Edouard, J.-B., & Sobhan, K. (2012). Durability of fly ash-based geopolymer structural concrete in the marine environment. *Journal of Materials in Civil Engineering*, *25*(6), 781–787. DOI: 10.1061/(ASCE)MT.1943-5533.0000632

Rehman, A., Saba, T., Kashif, M., Fati, S. M., Bahaj, S. A., & Chaudhry, H. (2022). A Revisit of Internet of Things Technologies for Monitoring and Control Strategies in Smart Agriculture. *Agronomy (Basel)*, *12*(1), 1–21. DOI: 10.3390/agronomy12010127

Rehman, S. U., Kraus, S., Shah, S. A., Khanin, D., & Mahto, R. V. (2021). Analyzing the relationship between green innovation and environmental performance in large manufacturing firms. *Technological Forecasting and Social Change*, *163*, 120481. DOI: 10.1016/j.techfore.2020.120481

Remeikienė, R., Gasparėnienė, L., & Bankauskienė, J. (2025). Assessment of the circular economy indicators in the EU Member States. *Discover Sustainability*, *6*(1), 1–19. DOI: 10.1007/s43621-024-00719-z

Ridaoui, M., Razzouki, A., Oudgou, M., & Boudhar, A. (2025). Revisiting agricultural policies in Morocco through the lens of virtual water trade: a literature review. *Frontiers in Water, Volume 7-2025*. https://doi.org/10.3389/frwa.2025.1717928

Ridaoui, M., Razzouki, A., Ouhbi, H., Oudgou, M., & Boudhar, A. (2025). Exploring the Dynamics of Virtual Water Trade in Crop Products Between Morocco and the European Union. *Water (Basel)*, *17*(18), 2664. DOI: 10.3390/w17182664

Rifaai, Y., Yahia, A., Mostafa, A., Aggoun, S., & Kadri, E.-H. (2019). Rheology of fly ash-based geopolymer: Effect of NaOH concentration. *Construction & Building Materials*, *223*, 583–594. DOI: 10.1016/j.conbuildmat.2019.07.028

Rihawi, B., Maraş, M. M., Ekinci, E., & Kutlusoy, E. (2025). Development of fiber-reinforced eco-friendly concrete for geopolymer pipes infrastructure. *Clean Technologies and Environmental Policy*, *27*(10), 5165. DOI: 10.1007/s10098-025-03171-3

Rintala, A., Havukainen, J., & Abdulkareem, M. (2021). Cost-competitiveness of recycling-based geopolymer concretes. *Recycling*, *6*(3), 46. DOI: 10.3390/recycling6030046

Robbins, Lord. (1984). An Essay on the Nature and Significance of Economic Science. *An Essay on the Nature and Significance of Economic Science*. DOI: 10.1007/978-1-349-17510-9

Rubinsin, N. J., Daud, W. R. W., Kamarudin, S. K., Masdar, M. S., Rosli, M. I., Samsatli, S., Tapia, J. F. D., Ghani, W. A. W. A. K., Hasan, A., & Lim, K. L. (2020). Modelling and optimisation of oil palm biomass value chains and the environment–food–energy–water nexus in Peninsular Malaysia. *Biomass and Bioenergy*, *144*, 105912. DOI: 10.1016/j.biombioe.2020.105912

Saba, M., & Arairo, W. (2024). Perspective chapter: Geopolymers in civil and environmental engineering applications. In *IntechOpen eBooks*. IntechOpen., DOI: 10.5772/intechopen.1007018

Sachs, J. D. (2015). *The age of sustainable development*. Columbia University Press. DOI: 10.7312/sach17314

Sadiq, M., Pham Thi, T. D., Nguyen, C. M., & Do, H. D. (2025). Sustainable entrepreneurship and knowledge management: Role of green information technology in building sustainable entrepreneurial ecosystems. *Journal of Innovation & Knowledge*, *10*(3), 100689. DOI: 10.1016/j.jik.2025.100689

Saha, A., Dabic Miletic, S., Senapati, T., Simic, V., Pamucar, D., Ala, A., & Arya, L. (2024). Fermatean fuzzy Dombi generalized Maclaurin symmetric mean operators for prioritizing bulk material handling technologies. *Cognitive Computation*, *16*(6), 3096–3121. Advance online publication. DOI: 10.1007/s12559-024-10323-y

Saha, A., Görçün, Ö. F., Pamucar, D., Arya, L., & Simic, V. (2024). Evaluation of shared micro-mobility systems for sustainable cities using a consensus-based Fermatean fuzzy multiple objective optimization. *Engineering Applications of Artificial Intelligence*, *134*, 108662. DOI: 10.1016/j.engappai.2024.108662

Saha, A., Senapati, T., Akram, M., Kahraman, C., Mesiar, R., & Arya, L. (2024). Dual probabilistic linguistic consensus reaching method for group decision making. *Granular Computing*, *9*(35), 35. Advance online publication. DOI: 10.1007/s41066-024-00458-6

Saha, A., Simic, V., Dabic-Miletic, S., Senapati, T., Pamucar, D., Arya, L., & Tirkolaee, E. B. (2025). Prioritization of AI-based material handling approaches for smart logistics in sustainable warehouses. *Environment, Development and Sustainability*. Advance online publication. DOI: 10.1007/s10668-025-06435-6

Samridhi, K. J. S., Akhai, S., Abbass, M., Arif, S. M., & Pathak, S. (2025, October). Mechanical properties of graphene-reinforced cement composites: A review. In *AIP Conference Proceedings* (Vol. 3343, No. 1, p. 020026). AIP Publishing LLC. https://doi.org/DOI: 10.1063/5.0292724

Samuel, G., Lucivero, F., & Somavilla, L. (2022). The environmental sustainability of digital technologies: Stakeholder practices and perspectives. *Sustainability (Basel)*, *14*(7), 1–14. DOI: 10.3390/su14073791

Sandström, V., Lehikoinen, E., & Peltonen-Sainio, P. (2018). Replacing Imports of Crop Based Commodities by Domestic Production in Finland: Potential to Reduce Virtual Water Imports. *Frontiers in Sustainable Food Systems*, *2*(October), 1–13. DOI: 10.3389/fsufs.2018.00067

Sanoja-López, K. A., Loor-Molina, N. S., & Luque, R. (2023). Rice waste feedstocks: A review of alternatives for their conversion into high-value added products. *BioResources*, *19*(1). Advance online publication. DOI: 10.15376/biores.19.1.Sanoja-Lopez

Santana, H. A., & Neto, J. (2020). Self-compacting geopolymer mixture: Dosing based on statistical mixture design and simultaneous optimization. *Construction & Building Materials*, *249*, 118677. DOI: 10.1016/j.conbuildmat.2020.118677

Santi, A., Mossini, E., Magugliani, G., Galluccio, F., Macerata, E., Lotti, P., Gatta, G. D., Vadivel, D., Dondi, D., Cori, D., Nonnet, H., & Mariani, M. (2022). Design of sustainable geopolymeric matrices for encapsulation of treated radioactive solid organic waste. *Frontiers in Materials*, *9*, 1005864. Advance online publication. DOI: 10.3389/fmats.2022.1005864

Santucci, S., Zhang, H., Sanna, S., Pryds, N., & Esposito, V. (2019). Defective ceria actuator: The influence of electrodes. *Research Portal Denmark*. https://local.forskningsportal.dk/.../dtu-ee56a4c4-e751-4751-bd93-6781666f70e4

Saraji, M. K., & Torabi, M. (2025). Progress toward a circular economy: A comparative analysis of EU member states. *Sustainability*, *17*(18), 1–21.

Sbahieh, S., McKay, G., & Al-Ghamdi, S. G. (2023). Comprehensive analysis of geopolymer materials: Properties, environmental impacts, and applications. *Materials (Basel)*, *16*(23), 7363. DOI: 10.3390/ma16237363

Seekell, D. A., D'Odorico, P., & Pace, M. L. (2011). Virtual water transfers unlikely to redress inequality in global water use. *Environmental Research Letters*, *6*(2), 024017. Advance online publication. DOI: 10.1088/1748-9326/6/2/024017

Selim, A. M., & ElGohary, A. S. (2020). Public–private partnerships (PPPs) in smart infrastructure projects: The role of stakeholders. *HBRC Journal*, *16*(1), 317–333. DOI: 10.1080/16874048.2020.1825038

Shabeer, M. G., & Rasul, F. (2025). Aligning innovation and information with development: A comparative analysis of developed and developing nations. *Environment, Development and Sustainability*, *27*(6), 14305–14319. DOI: 10.1007/s10668-024-04478-9

Shahedan, N. F., Hadibarata, T., Jusoh, M. N. H., Isia, I., Bouaissi, A., Juwono, F. H., Nawawi, N. A., Kusumaningrum, H. P., Muslim, A., & Hidayat, T. (2024). Advancements in geopolymer concrete for marine infrastructure: An optimization of performance considering workability, compressive strength, capillary water absorption, porosity and chloride migration. *Civil Engineering (Shiraz)*, *49*(4), 4181–4194. DOI: 10.1007/s40996-024-01671-8

Shannon, C. E. (1948). A mathematical theory of communication. *The Bell System Technical Journal*, *27*(3), 379–423. DOI: 10.1002/j.1538-7305.1948.tb01338.x

Sharma, V., Tripathi, A. K., & Mittal, H. (2022). *Technological revolutions in smart farming: Current trends, challenges & future directions*. [No publication details provided]

Sharmin, S., Biswas, W. K., & Sarker, P. K. (2024). Evaluating techno-eco-efficiency of waste clay brick powder (WCBP) in geopolymer binders. *Buildings (Basel, Switzerland)*, *14*(3), 692. DOI: 10.3390/buildings14030692

Sheng, T. J. I., Islam, M. S., Misran, N., Baharuddin, M. H., Arshad, H., Chowdhury, M. E. H., Rmili, H., & Islam, M. T. (2020). An Internet of Things Based Smart Waste Management System Using LoRa and Tensorflow Deep Learning Model. *IEEE Access : Practical Innovations, Open Solutions*, *8*, 148793–148811. DOI: 10.1109/ACCESS.2020.3016255

Shen, Y., Yang, Z., & Zhang, X. (2023). Impact of digital technology on carbon emissions: Evidence from Chinese cities. *Frontiers in Ecology and Evolution*, *11*(1), 1–17. DOI: 10.3389/fevo.2023.1166376

Shi, C., Qu, B., & Provis, J. L. (2019). Recent progress in low-carbon binders. *Cement and Concrete Research*, *122*, 227–250. DOI: 10.1016/j.cemconres.2019.05.009

Shi, X., Zhang, C., Liang, Y., Luo, J., Wang, X., Feng, Y., Li, Y., Wang, Q., & Abomohra, A. E. (2021). Life cycle assessment and impact correlation analysis of fly ash geopolymer concrete. *Materials (Basel)*, *14*(23), 7375. DOI: 10.3390/ma14237375

Shpak, N., Melnyk, O., Horbal, N., Ruda, M., & Sroka, W. (2021, March). Assessing the implementation of the circular economy in the EU countries. *Forum Scientiae Oeconomia*, *9*(1), 25–39.

Siddique, K., Saleem, A. R., Arslan, M., & Afzal, M. (2025). file:///C:/Users/Smart-Com/Downloads/sensors-25-01925.pdf. *Sustainability (Switzerland), 17*(13), 1–21. DOI: 10.3390/su17136226

Siekmann, F., Schlör, H., & Venghaus, S. (2023). Linking sustainability and the Fourth Industrial Revolution: A monitoring framework accounting for technological development. *Energy, Sustainability and Society, 13*(1), 26. Advance online publication. DOI: 10.1186/s13705-023-00405-4

Sikder, M., Wang, C., Yao, X., Huai, X., Wu, L., Yeboah, F. K., Wood, J., Zhao, Y., & Dou, X. (2022). The integrated impact of GDP growth, industrialization, energy use, and urbanization on $CO_2$ emissions in developing countries: Evidence from the panel ARDL approach. *The Science of the Total Environment, 837*, 155795. DOI: 10.1016/j.scitotenv.2022.155795

Sikora, P., Skibicki, S., Chougan, M., Szewczyk, P., Cendrowski, K., Federowicz, K., El-Khayatt, A. M., Saudi, H. A., Strzałkowski, J., Elrahman, M. A., Techman, M., Sibera, D., & Chung, S.-Y. (2025). Silica-coated admixtures of bismuth and gadolinium oxides for 3D printed concrete applications. *Construction & Building Materials, 470*, 140563. DOI: 10.1016/j.conbuildmat.2025.140563

Simicevic, V. (2025). Unemployment in Croatia: Trends and Challenges in the Digital Age (2010-2024). *Croatian Regional Development Journal, 6*(1), 1–17. DOI: 10.2478/crdj-2025-0001

Singh, A. K., & Jyoti, B. (2023). Empirical evidence from different income group countries on the interdependency between digitalization and economic development. In Patricia Ordóñez de Pablos and Xi Zhang (Eds.), 5G, Artificial Intelligence, and Next Generation Internet of Things: Digital Innovation for Green and Sustainable Economies, (pp. 44-85). IGI Global. DOI: DOI: 10.4018/978-1-6684-8634-4.ch003

Singh, A. K. (2025). Importance of digital technologies in economic sector of selected countries. In Ahmadi, A., Mna, A., & Slimani, A. (Eds.), *Renewable Energy and the Economic Welfare of Society* (pp. 335–370). IGI Global Scientific Publishing., DOI: 10.4018/979-8-3693-7580-8.ch015

Singh, A. K., Issac, J., & Narayanan, K. G. S. (2019). Measurement of environmental sustainability index and its association with socio-economic indicators in selected Asian economies: An empirical investigation. *International Journal of Environment and Sustainable Development, 18*(1), 57–100. DOI: 10.1504/IJESD.2019.098641

Singh, A. K., Kumar, S., & Gupta, M. (2024). Relationship between digitalization and environmental sustainability in selected countries. In Yıldırım, S., Yıldırım, D., Demirtaş, I., & Kandpal, V. (Eds.), *Green Transition Impacts on the Economy, Society, and Environment* (pp. 83–107). IGI Global., DOI: 10.4018/979-8-3693-3985-5.ch006

Singh, A. K., Sharma, A. K., & Jyoti, B. (2023). Does economic development have a causal relationship with environmental degradation? Experience from different income group countries. In Sart, G. (Ed.), *Considerations on Education for Economic, Social, and Environmental Sustainability* (pp. 300–333). IGI Global., DOI: 10.4018/978-1-6684-8356-5.ch015

Singh, A. K., & Srinivasan, S. (2026). Environmental degradation influencing factors in different income groups countries. In Köktaş, A., & Gölçek, A. (Eds.), *Inequality and Environmental Degradation in a Prosperity-Driven World* (pp. 149–186). IGI Global Scientific Publishing., DOI: 10.4018/979-8-3373-1862-2.ch006

Singh, A., & Singh, B. (2020). Characterization of rice husk ash obtained from an industrial source. *Journal of Sustainable Cement-Based Materials, 10*(4), 193–205. DOI: 10.1080/21650373.2020.1789010

Singh, G., Rajesh, R., Daultani, Y., & Misra, S. C. (2023). Resilience and sustainability enhancements in food supply chains using digital twin technology: A grey causal modelling approach. *Computers & Industrial Engineering, 179*, 109172. DOI: 10.1016/j.cie.2023.109172

Singh, S., & Goyal, M. K. (2025). A review of India's water policy and implementation toward a sustainable future. *Journal of Water and Climate Change, 16*(2), 493–510. DOI: 10.2166/wcc.2025.560

Siyal, A. A., Mohamed, R. M. S. R., Shamsuddin, R., & Ridzuan, M. B. (2024). A comprehensive review of synthesis kinetics and formation mechanism of geopolymers. *RSC Advances, 14*(1), 446–470. DOI: 10.1039/D3RA06205H

Slob, N., Hurst, W., van de Zedde, R., & Tekinerdogan, B. (2023). Virtual reality-based digital twins for greenhouses: A focus on human interaction. *Computers and Electronics in Agriculture, 208*, 107815. DOI: 10.1016/j.compag.2023.107815

Smol, M., Adam, C., & Preisner, M. (2020). Circular economy model framework in the European water and wastewater sector. *Journal of Material Cycles and Waste Management, 22*(3), 682–697. DOI: 10.1007/s10163-019-00960-z

Smol, M., Kulczycka, J., & Avdiushchenko, A. (2017). Circular economy indicators in relation to eco-innovation in European regions. *Clean Technologies and Environmental Policy, 19*(3), 669–678. DOI: 10.1007/s10098-016-1323-8

Smol, M., Kulczycka, J., Henclik, A., Gorazda, K., & Wzorek, Z. (2015). The possible use of sewage sludge ash (SSA) in the construction industry as a way towards a circular economy. *Journal of Cleaner Production, 95*, 45–54. DOI: 10.1016/j.jclepro.2015.02.051

Soares, M. M. N. de S., & Poggiali, F. S. J. Bezerra, A. C. da S., Figueiredo, R. B., Aguilar, M. T. P., & Cetlin, P. R. (2014). The effect of calcination conditions on characteristics of sugar cane bagasse ash. *Rem—Revista Escola de Minas, 67*(1), 33–39. https://doi.org/DOI: 10.1590/s0370-44672014000100005

Šobić, Lj., Bošković, N., & Pantović, D. (2023). Entrepreneurial elements in rural tourism - findings from PLS-SEM. *Economics of Agriculture, 70*(2), 521–535.

Spyrou, O., Verdouw, C., & Hurst, W. (2023). A digital twin reference architecture for pharmaceutical cannabis production. *International Journal of Computer Integrated Manufacturing, 37*, 1–21.

Stahel, W. R. (1982). *The product life factor. An Inquiry into the Nature of Sustainable Societies. The Role of the Private Sector*. Houston Area Research Centre.

Stankevičienė, J., Nikanorova, M., & Çera, G. (2020). Analysis of green economy dimension in the context of circular economy: The case of Baltic sea region. *E+M. Ekonomie a Management, XXIII*(1), 4–18. DOI: 10.15240/tul/001/2020-1-001

Statkauskas, M., Vaičiukynienė, D., & Grinys, A. (2024). Mechanical properties of low-calcium alkali-activated binder under ambient curing conditions. *Scientific Reports, 14*(1), 13060. Advance online publication. DOI: 10.1038/s41598-024-63808-z

Strini, A., Roviello, G., Ricciotti, L., Ferone, C., Messina, F., Schiavi, L., Corsaro, D., & Cioffi, R. (2016). $TiO_2$-based photocatalytic geopolymers for nitric oxide degradation. *Materials (Basel), 9*(7), 513. DOI: 10.3390/ma9070513

Strohle, M., Sadique, M., Dulaimi, A., & Kadhim, M. A. (2022). Prospect and barrier of 3D concrete: A systematic review. *Innovative Infrastructure Solutions, 8*(1), 21. Advance online publication. DOI: 10.1007/s41062-022-00975-w

Su, B., Heshmati, A., Geng, Y., & Yu, X. (2013). A review of the circular economy in China: Moving from rhetoric to implementation. *Journal of Cleaner Production, 42*, 215–227. DOI: 10.1016/j.jclepro.2012.11.020

Suh, S., & Huppes, G. (2005). Methods for life cycle inventory of a product. *Journal of Cleaner Production, 13*(7), 687–697. DOI: 10.1016/j.jclepro.2003.04.001

Sukkathanyawat, H., Bampenrat, A., Jarunglumlert, T., & Prommuak, C. (2022). Modification of waste sugarcane bagasse fly ash for $CO_2$ capture. *Materials for Renewable and Sustainable Energy, 11*(3), 267–276. DOI: 10.1007/s40243-022-00219-y

Sun, Q., Zhao, S., Zhao, X., Song, Y., Ban, X., & Zhang, N. (2023). Influence of different grinding degrees of fly ash on geopolymer properties. *PLoS One, 18*(3). Advance online publication. DOI: 10.1371/journal.pone.0282927

Šupić, S., Malešev, M., Радоњанин, В., Bulatović, V., & Milović, T. (2021). Reactivity and pozzolanic properties of biomass ashes from wheat and soybean straw. *Materials (Basel), 14*(4), 1004. DOI: 10.3390/ma14041004

Suryani, E., Hendrawan, R. A., Muhandhis, I., & Indraswari, R. (2022). A simulation model to improve the value of rice supply chain. *Journal of Simulation, 16*(4), 392–414. DOI: 10.1080/17477778.2020.1829118

Sushanth, G., & Sujatha, S. (2018). IoT-based smart agriculture system. In *2018 International Conference on Wireless Communications, Signal Processing and Networking (WiSPNET)* (pp. 1–4).

Swarna, M. F. M., Khan, S., Ramalingam, P., & Reddy, A. (2024). Role of HR Analytics in People Management: Challenges and Opportunities in the Indian IT/ITeS Space. In *HR Analytics* (pp. 1–23). Fundamentals and Applications.

Symeonaki, E., Maraveas, C., & Arvanitis, K. G. (2024). Recent advances in digital twins for agriculture 5.0: Applications and open issues in livestock production systems. *Applied Sciences (Basel, Switzerland), 14*(2), 686. DOI: 10.3390/app14020686

Tagarakis, A. C., Benos, L., Kyriakarakos, G., Pearson, S., Sørensen, C. G., & Bochtis, D. (2024, May 14). Digital Twins in Agriculture and Forestry: A Review. *Sensors (Basel), 24*(10), 3117. DOI: 10.3390/s24103117 PMID: 38793969

Tamea, S., Laio, F., & Ridolfi, L. (2016). Global effects of local food-production crises: A virtual water perspective. *Scientific Reports, 6*(May 2015), 1–14. DOI: 10.1038/srep18803

Tamea, S., Carr, J. A., Laio, F., & Ridolfi, L. (2014). Drivers of the virtual water trade. *Water Resources Research, 50*(1), 17–28. DOI: 10.1002/2013WR014707

Taneja, S., Bansal, N., & Ozen, E. (2024). What was, is and will be: A bibliometric analysis of European Green Deal (EGD). *International Journal of Technology Management & Sustainable Development, 23*(1), 85–104. DOI: 10.1386/tmsd_00086_1

Tanyıldızı, H. (2024). Deep learning–based prediction of compressive strength of eco-friendly geopolymer concrete. *Environmental Science and Pollution Research International*, *31*(28), 41246–41263. DOI: 10.1007/s11356-024-33853-2

Tao, F., Qi, Q., Wang, L., & Nee, A. Y. C. (2019). Digital twins and cyber-physical systems toward smart manufacturing and industry 4.0: Correlation and comparison. *Engineering (Beijing)*, *5*(4), 653–661. DOI: 10.1016/j.eng.2019.01.014

Tao, J., Cai, M. M., & Wang, Q. J. (2025). Impact of digital economy on environmental performance among worldwide countries: Role of emerging technologies and energy consumption. *Journal of Environmental Management*, *395*, 127860. DOI: 10.1016/j.jenvman.2025.127860

Tazhibayev, A., Utepbergenov, I., & Skliarova, I. (2025). Development of Customer-Focused Automated Systems for Transformer Design and Manufacturing: A Comprehensive Review. In *Journal of Computational and Cognitive Engineering* (Vol. 4, Number 3, pp. 251–266). Bon View Publishing Pte Ltd. DOI: 10.47852/bonviewJCCE52025158

Techo, A., Kaewpikul, D., Sata, V., Tanapongpisit, N., Wongprasod, S., Saenrang, W., Chainakun, P., Chindaprasirt, P., & Ekprasert, J. (2024). Enhanced mechanical and self-healing properties of rice husk ash–incinerated sugarcane press mud biogeopolymer pastes. *Scientific Reports*, *14*(1), 28121. Advance online publication. DOI: 10.1038/s41598-024-79916-9

Teng, Z., Huang, S., Xu, H., Li, N., & Zhou, Q. (2021). Preparation and properties of rice hull ash as catalysis supporter in a fluidized-bed reactor. *IOP Conference Series. Earth and Environmental Science*, *766*(1), 012080. DOI: 10.1088/1755-1315/766/1/012080

Thomas, P., & Davis, N. (2018). The fourth industrial revolution: Shaping new era. *Journal of International Affairs*, *72*(1), 17–22. DOI: 10.2307/26588339

Tian, X., Geng, Y., Sarkis, J., & Zhong, S. (2018). Trends and features of embodied flows associated with international trade based on bibliometric analysis. *Resources, Conservation and Recycling, 131*(September 2017), 148–157. DOI: 10.1016/j.resconrec.2018.01.002

Tiwari, S. P. (2025). The implications of artificial intelligence in management consulting: A risk and barrier assessment. In *Multidisciplinary Reviews* (Vol. 8, Number 8). Malque Publishing. DOI: 10.31893/multirev.2025244

Tositti, L., Masi, G., Morozzi, P., Zappi, A., & Bignozzi, M. C. (2023). Cleaner, sustainable and safer: Green potential of alkali-activated materials. *Construction & Building Materials*, *409*, 133879. DOI: 10.1016/j.conbuildmat.2023.133879

Toyeb, M., Hakam, A., & Andriani, A. (2023). Strength and economic benefit of soil stabilization with palm oil fuel ash. *E3S Web of Conferences, 464*, 11001. https://doi.org/DOI: 10.1051/e3sconf/202346411001

Tripathi, S., Bachmann, N., Brunner, M., Rizk, Z., & Jodlbauer, H. (2024). Assessing the current landscape of AI and sustainability literature: Identifying key trends, addressing gaps and challenges. *Journal of Big Data*, *11*(1), 65. Advance online publication. DOI: 10.1186/s40537-024-00912-x

Truong, T. C. (2022). The impact of digital transformation on environmental sustainability. *Advances in Multimedia*, *2022*(1), 1–12. DOI: 10.1155/2022/6324325

Turner, L. K., & Collins, F. (2013). $CO_2$-equivalent emissions: A comparison between geopolymer and OPC concrete. *Construction & Building Materials*, *43*, 125–130. DOI: 10.1016/j.conbuildmat.2013.01.023

Umoru, U., Ogundana, O. M., Mangena, M., & Udeozor, V. (2026). Informal Institutions and Multinationals' Drive Towards Sustainable Development Goals (SDGs): A Dark-Side Perspective. *Business Ethics, the Environment & Responsibility*, *35*(1), 75–98. DOI: 10.1111/beer.12773

UN. (2015). *Transforming Our World: The 2030 Agenda for SustainableDevelopment*. Springer., DOI: 10.1007/978-3-031-07461-5_1

Ungureanu, N., Vlădu , V., & Biriş, S. Ş. (2022). Sustainable valorization of waste and by-products from sugarcane processing. *Sustainability (Basel)*, *14*(17), 11089. DOI: 10.3390/su141711089

United Nations Development Programme (UNDP). (2023). [Online]. https://www.undp.org/press-releases/digital-technologies-directly-benefit-70-percent-sdg-targets-say-itu-undp-and-partners

United Nations Development Programme (UNDP). (2026). Digitalization for sustainability. [Online]. https://www.unep.org/topics/digital-transformations/digitalization-sustainability

Uthayakumar, M., Balamurugan, P., Korniejenko, K., Gądek, S., & Mierzwiński, D. (2020). Abrasive water jet machining of fly ash and metakaolin-based geopolymers. *MATEC Web of Conferences, 322*, 01020. https://doi.org/DOI: 10.1051/matecconf/202032201020

Valencia-Saavedra, W., de Gutiérrez, R. M., & Puertas, F. (2020). Performance of fly ash-based geopolymers exposed to acetic and sulfuric acids. *Construction & Building Materials*, *257*, 119503. DOI: 10.1016/j.conbuildmat.2020.119503

Valente, M., Sambucci, M., Chougan, M., & Ghaffar, S. H. (2021). Reducing emissions in cementitious materials: A comparison of alkali-activated materials and Portland cement composites. *Journal of Cleaner Production*, *333*, 130013. DOI: 10.1016/j.jclepro.2021.130013

Vallino, E., Ridolfi, L., & Laio, F. (2020). Measuring economic water scarcity in agriculture: A cross-country empirical investigation. *Environmental Science & Policy*, *114*, 73–85. DOI: 10.1016/j.envsci.2020.07.017

Vallino, E., Ridolfi, L., & Laio, F. (2021). Trade of economically and physically scarce virtual water in the global food network. *Scientific Reports*, *11*(1), 1–19. DOI: 10.1038/s41598-021-01514-w PMID: 34815433

Van der Burg, S., Kloppenburg, S., Kok, E. J., & van der Voort, M. (2021). Digital twins in agri-food: Societal and ethical themes and questions. NJAS—Impact in Agricultural and Life Sciences, 93, 98–125.

van Deventer, J. S. J., Provis, J. L., & Duxson, P. (2011). Technical and commercial progress in the adoption of geopolymer cement. *Minerals Engineering*, *29*, 89–104. DOI: 10.1016/j.mineng.2011.09.009

van Deventer, J. S. J., Provis, J. L., Duxson, P., & Lukey, G. C. (2006). Reaction mechanisms in the geopolymeric conversion of inorganic waste to useful products. *Journal of Hazardous Materials*, *139*(3), 506–513. DOI: 10.1016/j.jhazmat.2006.02.044

Vanham, D., Hoekstra, A. Y., & Bidoglio, G. (2013). Potential water saving through changes in European diets. *Environment International*, *61*, 45–56. DOI: 10.1016/j.envint.2013.09.011 PMID: 24096041

Vargas, J. M., Castrillon, O. D., & Giraldo, J. A. (2025). Implementation and Field Validation of a Digital Twin Methodology to Enhance Production and Service Systems in Waste Management. *Applied Sciences (Basel, Switzerland)*, *15*(12), 6733. DOI: 10.3390/app15126733

Verdouw, C. N., & Kruize, J. W. (2017). Digital twins in farm management: Illustrations from the FIWARE accelerators SmartAgriFood and Fractals. *7th Asian-Australasian Conference on Precision Agriculture Digital.*

Verdouw, C., Tekinerdogan, B., Beulens, A., & Wolfert, S. (2021). Digital twins in smart farming. *Agricultural Systems*, *189*, 103046. DOI: 10.1016/j.agsy.2020.103046

Verma, M., Dev, N., Rahman, I., Nigam, M., Ahmed, M., & Mallick, J. (2022). Geopolymer concrete: A material for sustainable development in Indian construction industries. *Crystals*, *12*(4), 514. DOI: 10.3390/cryst12040514

Viegas, M., Mello, C. J., & Pires, S. M. (2023). Contributions to a more sustainable model of food production and consumption in Portugal: An opportunity to reduce the ecological footprint of food. *Progress in Industrial Ecology*, *16*(4), 280–299. DOI: 10.1504/PIE.2023.135570

Vijayalakshmi, K., Al-Otaibi, S., Arya, L., Almaiah, M. A., Anithaashri, T. P., Karthik, S. S., & Shishakly, R. (2023). Smart agricultural–industrial crop-monitoring system using UAV–IoT classification techniques. *Sustainability*, *15*(14), 11242. DOI: 10.3390/su151411242

Vikranth, K., & Prasad, K. K. (2019). Sustained Policies on Technical and Operational aspects of IT Industry-A Case Study of Tata Consultancy Limited. *SRINIVAS PUBLICATION International Journal of Applied Engineering and Management Letters(IJAEML) A Refereed International Journal of Srinivas University*, *3*(2), 2581–7000. DOI: 10.5281/zenodo.3597751

Vītola, L., Pundienė, I., Pranckevičienė, J., & Bajāre, D. (2020). Effect of water content and initial temperature on rheology of metakaolin geopolymer pastes. *Sustainability*, *12*(19), 8216. DOI: 10.3390/su12198216

Vlachakis, C., Su, Y.-F., & Al-Tabbaa, A. (2023). Interfacial bonding effect on self-sensing coatings for infrastructure monitoring. *MATEC Web of Conferences, 378*, 05006. https://doi.org/DOI: 10.1051/matecconf/202337805006

Vlachakis, C., Perry, M., Biondi, L., & McAlorum, J. (2020). 3D printed temperature-sensing repairs for concrete structures. *Additive Manufacturing*, *34*, 101238. DOI: 10.1016/j.addma.2020.101238

Vogt, O., Ukrainczyk, N., & Koenders, E. (2021). Effect of silica fume on metakaolin geopolymer sulfuric acid resistance. *Materials (Basel)*, *14*(18), 5396. DOI: 10.3390/ma14185396

Voulvoulis, N. (2018). Water reuse from a circular economy perspective and potential risks from an unregulated approach. *Current Opinion in Environmental Science & Health*, *2*, 32–45. DOI: 10.1016/j.coesh.2018.01.005

Wadhwa, A. S., Abbass, M., Akhai, S., Kumar, D., & Kumar, P. (2025). Integrating Taguchi optimization for multi-criteria decision making. In *Recent Theories and Applications for Multi-Criteria Decision-Making* (pp. 125–150). IGI Global., DOI: 10.4018/979-8-3693-6502-1.ch005

Wadhwa, A. S., Akhai, S., Abbass, M., Chouksey, A., Tiwari, S., & Taneja, T. (2025). Computational intelligence-driven design and optimization of a polyurethane oil skimmer. In *Using Computational Intelligence for Sustainable Manufacturing of Advanced Materials* (pp. 445–464). IGI Global., DOI: 10.4018/979-8-3693-7974-5.ch019

Wandiga, C. A. (2020). Socio-cultural analysis criteria for BIM modeling and material passport tracking of agriwaste. *MRS Energy & Sustainability : a Review Journal*, *7*(1), 25. Advance online publication. DOI: 10.1557/mre.2020.29

Wang, H. T., Yang, X., Wang, M., & Qu, C. (2023). Influence of silicon-aluminium modified materials on durability of fly ash geopolymers. *Materials Science Forum*, *1103*, 139–148. DOI: 10.4028/p-0kV4eB

Wang, H., Wu, H., Xing, Z., Wang, R., & Dai, S. (2021). Effect of Si/Al and Na/Al ratios and free water on metakaolin geopolymer strength. *Materials (Basel)*, *14*(14), 3845. DOI: 10.3390/ma14143845

Wang, H., Zhao, X., Wang, J., He, L., Zhang, A., Gao, H., Yang, J., & Liang, L. (2023). Cementation mechanism of geopolymer backfill paste with industrial solid wastes. *Materials (Basel)*, *16*(2), 480. DOI: 10.3390/ma16020480

Wang, L. (2024). Digital twins in agriculture: A review of recent progress and open issues. *Electronics (Basel)*, *13*(11), 2209. DOI: 10.3390/electronics13112209

Wang, L., Liu, S., & Xiong, W. (2022). The impact of digital transformation on corporate environment performance: Evidence from China. *International Journal of Environmental Research and Public Health*, *9*(19), 12–24. DOI: 10.3390/ijerph191912846

Wang, Q. J., Zhu, Y. J., Zhang, Y., & Chang, C. P. (2025). Impact of digital economy on energy efficiency: Role of emerging technologies such as AI. *Energy Economics*, *150*, 108840. DOI: 10.1016/j.eneco.2025.108840

Wang, R., & Ding, C. (2023). Bilateral impact of digital economy on air pollution: Emissions increase and reduction effects. *Frontiers in Environmental Science*, *11*(1), 1–18. DOI: 10.3389/fenvs.2023.1134334

Wang, X., Yang, Z., Liu, X., Huang, G., Xiao, W., & Han, L. (2020). Composition characteristics of different crop straw types. *Waste Management (New York, N.Y.)*, *110*, 87–95. DOI: 10.1016/j.wasman.2020.05.018

Wang, Y. B., Liu, D., Cao, X. C., Yang, Z. Y., Song, J. F., Chen, D. Y., & Sun, S. K. (2017). Agricultural water rights trading and virtual water export compensation coupling model: A case study of an irrigation district in China. *Agricultural Water Management*, *180*, 99–106. DOI: 10.1016/j.agwat.2016.11.006

Wang, Z., Li, T., Liang, W., Fu, B., Li, J., & Yan, J. (2024). Uncovering the structure and evolution of global virtual water and agricultural land network. *Sustainable Production and Consumption*, *51*, 599–611. DOI: 10.1016/j.spc.2024.08.017

Wan, K., Wang, Z., Xia, J., Vervisch, L., Domingo, P., Lv, Y., Liu, Y., He, Y., & Cen, K. (2019). Impact of HCl and $SO_2$ on potassium emissions in pulverized biomass combustion. *Fuel Processing Technology*, *193*, 19–29. DOI: 10.1016/j.fuproc.2019.04.032

Wasim, M., Ngo, T., & Law, D. W. (2021). Durability of geopolymer concrete: A state-of-the-art review. *Construction & Building Materials*, *291*, 123381. DOI: 10.1016/j.conbuildmat.2021.123381

Wasiu Dauda, B., Duru, G. O., Olagoke, M. F., & Patrick Egbon, E. (2024). Optimizing Operational Efficiency through Digital Supply Chain Transformation in U.S. Manufacturing. *International Journal of Advances in Engineering and Management*, *6*(11), 343–358. DOI: 10.35629/5252-0611343358

WBCSD. (2010). Vision 2050. In *The New Agenda for Business*.

Weiland, S., Hickmann, T., Lederer, M., Marquardt, J., & Schwindenhammer, S. (2021). The 2030 agenda for sustainable development: Transformative change through the sustainable development goals? In *Politics and Governance* (Vol. 9, Number 1, pp. 90–95). Cogitatio Press. DOI: 10.17645/pag.v9i1.4191

Wei, X., Huang, B., Chen, K., Fan, Z., Wang, L., & Xu, M. (2022). Dot extrusion bioprinting of spatially controlled heterogeneous tumor models. *Materials & Design*, *223*, 111152. DOI: 10.1016/j.matdes.2022.111152

WHO & UNICEF. (2024). Progress on Household Drinking Water, Sanitation and Hygiene 2000-2024. In *UNICEF journal*. https://www.eea.europa.eu/publications/industrial-waste-water-treatment-pressures%0Ahttp://files/558/Rapport EEA Industrial waste water treatment – pressures on Europe's environment.pdf

Wichelns, D. (2004). The policy relevance of virtual water can be enhanced by considering comparative advantages. *Agricultural Water Management*, *66*(1), 49–63. DOI: 10.1016/j.agwat.2003.09.006

Wichelns, D. (2015). Virtual Water and Water Footprints: Overreaching Into the Discourse on Sustainability, Efficiency, and Equity. *Water Alternatives*, *8*, 396–414.

Wiedmann, T. (2009). A first empirical comparison of energy Footprints embodied in trade - MRIO versus PLUM. *Ecological Economics*, *68*(7), 1975–1990. DOI: 10.1016/j.ecolecon.2008.06.023

Winans, K., Kendall, A., & Deng, H. (2017). The history and current applications of the circular economy concept. *Renewable & Sustainable Energy Reviews*, *68*, 825–833. DOI: 10.1016/j.rser.2016.09.123

Wong, X., Kang, W., Kim, J., Xu, Y., & Wang, A. (2025). The criticality of the digital economy in environmental sustainability: Fresh insights from a wavelet-based quantile-on-quantile approach. *Sustainability (Basel)*, *17*(2), 1–17. DOI: 10.3390/su17020622

World Bank (WB). (2025). "Digital Progress and Trends Report 2025: Strengthening AI Foundations." Overview booklet. World Bank, Washington, DC. [Online]. https://openknowledge.worldbank.org/server/api/core/bitstreams/d2ac1ea9-b70e-4080-b5de-8b31098e992f/content

World Economic Forum (WEM). (2024). Least-developed countries can aid sustainable digital transformation through e-wastage management. [Online]. https://www.weforum.org/stories/2024/11/least-developed-countries-sustainable-ewaste-management/

World Economic Forum. (2015). *Global Risks 2015; World Economic Forum: Geneva, Switzerland*. http://www3.weforum.org/docs/WEF_Global_Risks_2015_Report15.pdf

Wu, D., Wang, J., Tong, M., Chen, K., & Zhang, Z. (2023). Performance optimization of FA–GGBS geopolymers using RSM. *Polymers*, *15*(8), 1881. DOI: 10.3390/polym15081881

Xiao, D., Xu, J., & Li, Q. (2024). The "double-edged sword" effect of air quality information disclosure policy– empirical evidence based on the digital transformation of Chinese listed companies. *Energy Economics*, *133*(1), 10–21. DOI: 10.1016/j.eneco.2024.107513

Xu, J., She, S., & Liu, W. (2022). Role of digitalization in environment, social and governance, and sustainability: Review-based study for implications. *Frontiers in Psychology*, *13*(1), 1–15. DOI: 10.3389/fpsyg.2022.961057

Yang, H., Pfister, S., & Bhaduri, A. (2013). Accounting for a scarce resource: Virtual water and water footprint in the global water system. *Current Opinion in Environmental Sustainability*, *5*(6), 599–606. DOI: 10.1016/j.cosust.2013.10.003

Yang, H., Wang, L., Mikayilov, F., & Zehnder, A. (2006). Virtual water trade: An assessment of water use efficiency in the international food trade. *Hydrology and Earth System Sciences*, *10*(3), 443–454. Advance online publication. DOI: 10.5194/hess-10-443-2006

Yang, J., Wang, Y., Tang, C., & Zhang, Z. (2024). Can digitalization reduce industrial pollution? roles of environmental investment and green innovation. *Environmental Research*, *240*(1), 117442. DOI: 10.1016/j.envres.2023.117442

Yılmaz, Y., Çakmak, T., Kurt, Z., & Ustabaş, İ. (2024). Predicting mechanical properties in geopolymer mortars using XGBoost. *Arabian Journal for Science and Engineering*. Advance online publication. DOI: 10.1007/s13369-024-09179-z

Yin, X., Wang, X., Yuan, F., & Ding, Z. (2020). Effect of curing age on high-temperature properties of 3D-printed geopolymer mortar. *E3S Web of Conferences*, *218*, 03019. https://doi.org/DOI: 10.1051/e3sconf/202021803019

Yin, Y., Luan, X., Sun, S., Wang, Y., Wu, P., & Wang, X. (2021). Environmental impact of grain virtual water flows in China: From 1997 to 2014. *Agricultural Water Management*, *256*, 107127. DOI: 10.1016/j.agwat.2021.107127

Yoo, S.-H., Kim, T., Im, J.-B., & Choi, J.-Y. (2012). Estimation of the international virtual water flow of grain crop products in Korea. *Paddy and Water Environment -. Paddy and Water Environment*, *10*(2), 83–93. Advance online publication. DOI: 10.1007/s10333-011-0267-1

Young, J. C. (2020). Environmental colonialism, digital indigeneity, and the politicization of resilience. *Environment and Planning. E, Nature and Space*, *4*(2), 230–251. DOI: 10.1177/2514848619898098

You, S., Ho, S. W., Li, T., Maneerung, T., & Wang, C. (2018). Techno-economic analysis of geopolymer production from high-Fe and high-Ca fly ash. *Journal of Hazardous Materials*, *361*, 237–245. DOI: 10.1016/j.jhazmat.2018.08.089

Yuan, H., Li, X., & Zhong, S. (2024). The impact of digital economy on environmental pollution: Evidence from 267 cities in China. *PLoS One*, *19*(1), 1–10. DOI: 10.1371/journal.pone.0297009

Yu, M. (2024). Battery components derived from silica-depleted rice hull ash. *University of Michigan—Deep Blue Repository*. https://doi.org/DOI: 10.7302/24934

Zeb, A., Shuhai, N., & Ullah, O. (2025). Socioeconomic determinants of ecological footprints: Bridging the gap between developed and developing nations. *Environment, Development and Sustainability*. Advance online publication. DOI: 10.1007/s10668-025-06081-y

Zeleny, M., & Cochrane, J. L. (1982). Multiple criteria decision making McGraw-Hill New York, 34.

Zetzsche, D. A., Buckley, R. P., Arner, D. W., & Barberis, J. N. (2017). Regulating a Revolution: From Regulatory Sandboxes to Smart Regulation. SSRN *Electronic Journal, 23*(1). DOI: 10.2139/ssrn.3018534

Zhang, J., Liang, F., & Gao, P. (2024). Can big data reduce urban environmental pollution? Evidence from China's digital technology experimental zone. *PLoS One*, *20*(1), 1–11. DOI: 10.1371/journal.pone.0288429

Zhang, L., Ling, J., & Lin, M. (2022). Artificial intelligence in renewable energy: A comprehensive bibliometric analysis. *Energy Reports*, *8*, 14072–14088. DOI: 10.1016/j.egyr.2022.10.347

Zhang, R., Zhu, H., Chang, Q., & Mao, Q. (2025). A comprehensive review of digital twins technology in agriculture. *Agriculture*, *15*(9), 903. DOI: 10.3390/agriculture15090903

Zhang, Y., Li, M., Dong, J., Yang, H., Van Zwieten, L., Lu, H., Alshameri, A., Zhan, Z., Chen, X., Jiang, X., Xu, W., Bao, Y., & Wang, H. (2021). A critical review of methods for analyzing freshwater eutrophication. *Water (Basel)*, *13*(2), 225. DOI: 10.3390/w13020225

Zhang, Z., Chen, L., Li, J., & Ding, S. (2024). Digital economy development and carbon emissions intensity – mechanisms and evidence from 72 countries. *Scientific Reports*, *18*(14), 1–19. DOI: 10.1038/s41598-024-78831-3

Zhang, Z., Ding, Z., Geng, Y., Pan, L., & Wang, C. (2023). The impact of digital economy on environmental quality: Evidence from China. *Frontiers in Environmental Science*, *11*(1), 1–17. DOI: 10.3389/fenvs.2023.1120953

Zhong, R., Chen, A., Zhao, D., Mao, G., Zhao, X., Huang, H., & Liu, J. (2023). Impact of international trade on water scarcity: An assessment by improving the Falkenmark indicator. *Journal of Cleaner Production*, *385*, 135740. DOI: 10.1016/j.jclepro.2022.135740

Zhuo, L., Mekonnen, M. M., & Hoekstra, A. Y. (2016). The effect of inter-annual variability of consumption, production, trade and climate on crop-related green and blue water footprints and inter-regional virtual water trade: A study for China (1978-2008). *Water Research*, *94*, 73–85. DOI: 10.1016/j.watres.2016.02.037 PMID: 26938494

Ziegler, D., Formia, A., Tulliani, J., & Palmero, P. (2016). Dense and porous geopolymers using fly ash and rice husk ash. *Materials (Basel)*, *9*(6), 466. DOI: 10.3390/ma9060466

Zisopoulou, K., Zisopoulos, D., & Panagoulia, D. (2022). Water Economics: An In-Depth Analysis of the Connection of Blue Water with Some Primary Level Aspects of Economic Theory I. *Water (Basel)*, *14*(1), 103. Advance online publication. DOI: 10.3390/w14010103

Zou, S., Ju, H., & Zhang, J. (2025). Water Quality Management in the Age of AI: Applications, Challenges, and Prospects. *Water (Basel)*, *17*(11), 1641. DOI: 10.3390/w17111641

Zou, Y., Zheng, C., Alzahrani, A., Ahmad, W., Ahmad, A., Mohamed, A. M., Khallaf, R., & Elattar, S. (2022). Evaluation of AI methods to estimate compressive strength of geopolymers. *Gels (Basel, Switzerland)*, *8*(5), 271. DOI: 10.3390/gels8050271

Zubrod, R. W. (2013). *Performance-based specification for geopolymer cement binders and supporting laboratory data*. In *ASTM International eBooks* (p. 165). https://doi.org/DOI: 10.1520/STP156620120061

Zurairah, M., Saragih, E. S., & Misdawati, M. (2021). Comparison of thermogravimetric characterization of rice husk in active carbon analyzer. *JUMPA*, *3*(2), 64–69. DOI: 10.54076/jumpa.v1i2.176

Буряк, М. О., Лисенко, С. М., & Шевченко, Р. О. (2024). Siemes Digital Transformation Case Study Towards Organizational Scale And Success In Electrical Engineering Industry. *Управління Змінами Та Інновації*, (11), 57–65. DOI: 10.32782/CMI/2024-11-9

# About the Contributors

**Syed Abdul Rehman Khan** completed his postdoctoral fellowship at Tsinghua University. Dr. Khan is currently associated with Business Research and Consultancy Limited in the United Kingdom. Dr. Khan has consistently received recognition as one of the world's top 2% highly cited scholars. His impressive portfolio includes nearly 200 high-level academic research articles and 11 published academic books related to the circular economy and green business practices. Additionally, he has led numerous research funding projects. Prof. Khan is a sought-after keynote speaker, invited speaker, and conference chair, having participated in over 70 international academic conferences. His expertise and influence in the field are unparalleled.

**Zhang Yu** is associated with Yunnan University of Finance and Economics. She has expertise in artificial intelligence, Circular Economy, Sustainable Development, Closed-loop Supply Chain, and Sustainability aspects in business operations. Dr. Zhang has published 150+ peer reviewed articles in well-known international journals, including SCI and SSCI. Dr. Zhang also has published 9 books related to the circular economy, waste management, and environmental sustainability in business management field.

**Muhammad Tanveer** is a top 2% Scientist of the World (Stanford Ranking). He is a researcher and academic at the College of Business, Imam Mohammad Ibn Saud Islamic University (IMSIU), Riyadh, Saudi Arabia. His expertise includes management, sustainability, and emerging technologies, with a focus on Green HRM, AI, Corporate Performance, and Sustainable Development Goals. He has authored high-impact publications and is committed to advancing knowledge through research, mentorship, and collaboration.

***

**Mahapara Abbass** is a distinguished academician and researcher in structural and sustainable engineering, with expertise in low-carbon materials, geopolymer concrete, and AI-enabled applications in urban and infrastructure systems. Her professional contributions include teaching at UG and PG levels, supervising M.Tech and Ph.D. research scholars, and mentoring innovation-driven projects. Recognized among Emerging Global Researchers (2025) in sustainable materials and AI-driven engineering, Dr. Abbass has published numerous research papers in SCI, SCIE, and Scopus-indexed journals, authored several academic books, and secured multiple design and utility patents. A respected reviewer, technical expert, and research mentor, she continues to advance sustainable construction, smart materials, and technology-driven engineering solutions.

**Leena Arya** is a Professor at the Department of Computer Science and Engineering at Koneru Lakshmaiah Education Foundation Deemed to be University, Vaddeswaram, a 22nd NIRF Ranking University in Guntur, AP, India. She completed her Ph.D. from IIT Roorkee in 2012. She has published over 70 research papers in Scopus and SCI-indexed international journals. She led a research project for the Department of Science and Technology (DST), New Delhi, as Principal Investigator under the Women Scientists Scheme (WOS-A). She has been granted a UK design and Australian Government Innovation patents. She has been a reviewer of many prestigious international journals and conferences. Her research area includes wireless communication, the Internet of Things (IoT), network security, and artificial intelligence.

**Khayrilla Kurbonov** is a faculty member in the Department of Finance and Tourism at Termez University of Economics and Service, Termez, Uzbekistan. He is engaged in teaching and academic activities related to finance, tourism management, and economic development. His academic interests include financial analysis, tourism economics, destination management, and sustainable tourism practices. He is committed to integrating theoretical knowledge with practical applications to enhance students' professional competencies. Khayrilla Kurbonov also contributes to departmental and institutional initiatives focused on curriculum development, academic quality enhancement, and strengthening industry–academia linkages in finance and tourism education.

**Mohamed Oudgou** is a Moroccan academic and researcher specializing in the fields of corporate finance, entrepreneurship, and innovation. He currently holds the position of Professor (accredited to supervise research, HDR) at Sultan Moulay Slimane University (USMS) in Béni Mellal, specifically within the National School of Trade and Management (ENCG). His research is characterized by an analytical and quantitative approach, frequently employing regression models and advanced statistical tools to address complex economic issues. With numerous publications in international journals (such as Risks, Journal of Open Innovation, and Water), he is an active contributor to research on the Moroccan economic development model.

**Danijela Pantović**, PhD is an Associate Professor at the Faculty of Hotel Management and Tourism in Vrnjačka Banja, University of Kragujevac, in the narrow scientific field of General Economics. She teaches courses in Cultural Tourism, Fundamentals of Hospitality and Tourism, EU Tourism and Cultural Tourism and Gastronomic Heritage. Her research interests include economics and tourism economics, economic convergence, cultural and rural tourism. She has extensive research experience in these fields and has published over 70 scientific papers, as well as 2 monographs and 2 university textbooks. She is proficient in the use of analytical and software tools such as SPSS, Visual PROMETHEE, Smart PLS and Microsoft Office. Also, Danijela has successfully completed a professional course in Dashboard for Circular Economy. Since 2018, she has been serving as the Technical Editor of the scientific journal Economics of Agriculture (ISSN 0352-3462). In addition, she has delivered lectures at international institutions, including the Faculty of Tourism and Hospitality Management in Opatija, Croatia and the Faculty of Tourism and Hotel Management in Kotor, Montenegro.

**Ravi Rastogi** received his Ph.D. in Computer Science and Engineering in December 2011 from Uttarakhand Technical University, Dehradun, Uttarakhand, India. MS in Computer Science degree in September 2005 from Fairleigh Dickinson University, Teaneck, New Jersey, USA. He is working as a Professor in the Department of Computer Science and Engineering, JIMS Engineering Management Technical Campus, Greater Noida, India. He had worked at various Universities, Koneru Lakshmaiah Education Foundation Deemed to be a university, Andhra Pradesh, India and Bisha University, KSA and Galgotias University, Greater Noida, India and Sharda University, Greater Noida, India and Jaypee University of Information and Technology, Solan, India. He was a database developer for Microsoft, Seattle, USA, and ING, Philadelphia, USA. His research interests are interconnection networks, stable matching problems, data mining and intelligence in systems, the Internet of Things, and cloud computing. Refereed International Journal publications are 23 and Refereed International Conference Publications are 8.

**Govind Ravish** is a research scholar at the Department of Civil Engineering, Maharishi Markandeshwar Engineering College, Maharishi Markandeshwar (Deemed to be University), Mullana (Ambala) – 133207, Haryana, IndiaAdditionally, he has also served as faculty in engineering colleges like CGC Mohali, Punjab and SDDIET Panchkula, Haryana.

**Sadia Saeed** is a dedicated Lecturer in the Department of Accounting and Finance at the National University of Modern Languages (NUML), Islamabad. With over 16 years of teaching experience, she has consistently demonstrated excellence in academia through her commitment to student development, curriculum enhancement, and academic research. Dr. Saeed teaches a diverse range of courses, including Risk Management, Financial Reporting, Financial Accounting, and other finance-related subjects at both undergraduate and graduate levels. Her teaching philosophy emphasizes critical thinking, practical application, and fostering a dynamic learning environment that prepares students for the evolving demands of the financial sector. Dr. Saeed has made significant contributions to research, with numerous publications in reputable national and international journals. Her scholarly work spans various areas of accounting and finance, reflecting her broad expertise and dedication to advancing knowledge in the field. She has also co-authored several book chapters, contributing to academic literature and supporting the professional development of students.

**Sadia Shaheen** earned her Ph.D. degree from Capital University of Technology, Pakistan. She is working as Assistant Professor at Government College University, Faisalabad. She has published several papers in the domain of human behavior and leadership. Her interest areas are organizational cronyism, organizational changes, employee behaviors, and attitudes.

**Ajay K. Singh** is working as an Associate Professor (Research) in the Department of Humanities and Social Science, Graphic Era (Deemed to be University) Dehradun. He has worked as Assistant Professor (Economics) in the School of Liberal Arts & Management, DIT University Dehradun for 6 years. He did Post-Doctorate Research with EDI of India, Ahmedabad, Gujarat (India). He received MPhil (Economics) from DAVV Indore (India), and PhD (Economics) from IIT Indore (India. He has published several research papers in the diversified area such as climate change, agricultural productivity, assessment of food security; estimation of GFSI, development of environmental sustainability index (ESI) and its association with socio-economic indicators; measurement and determinants of entrepreneurship ecosystem, and dimension of sustainable development and its interlinkages with economic development.

**Srinivasan Vasan** is an Assistant Professor in the Department of Humanities and Social Sciences at Graphic Era (Deemed to be University), with 14 years of teaching and field expertise. He has served in the Ministry of Health and Family Welfare, as a Guest Faculty, and as a Mobilization Training Specialist with the State Government. Recently, he contributed to a tuberculosis project funded by GFATM and USAID. He has published 60 papers, with 20 more under peer review in UGC-CARE and SCOPUS journals.

**Kamal Kant Verma** is a Professor at the School of Computer Science and Engineering, IILM University. With over 18.5 years of teaching and research experience, he has worked various reputed universities, including Lovely Professional University Phagwara, COER University Roorkee, VIT Bhopal University, Quantum University Roorkee, and Vidya College of Engineering Meerut. He specializes in Bloom's taxonomy, teaching pedagogy, curriculum development, and student mentoring, having served as DRC Chairperson, Academic Council member, and member of NAAC committees. Dr. Verma earned his Ph.D. in Computer Science and Engineering from Uttarakhand Technical University, Dehradun, along with an M.Tech in CSE and a B.Tech in IT. He has published 36+ research papers in reputed journals and conferences, including SCI/SCIE and Scopus-indexed publications, authored two books (one funded by Training and Learning bureau, Ministry of Education, AICTE New Delhi), and filed 8+ patents. His research interests include Video and Image Processing, Deep Learning, Human Activity Recognition, Gesture Recognition, EEG Signal Classification, and Autonomous Driving Detection etc. He has supervised 8+ M.Tech scholars and is currently guiding 6 Ph.D. scholars on cutting-edge topics. An active member of IEEE, CSI, and ISTE, Dr. Verma has attended numerous FDPs at IITs/NITs/NITTTR and has organized several academic courses during his career.

**Sehar Zulfiqar** is a senior lecturer in management at Birmingham City University, UK. Before taking up this role, she served as a research fellow at the Corvinus University of Budapest, Hungary. She holds a PhD in human resource management from the University of Debrecen, Hungary. She has vast experience teaching various business courses to graduate and undergraduate students in Pakistan. Her research interests include organizational behaviour, knowledge management, sustainability, and corporate social responsibility. Her research mainly focuses on understanding how and when individual and organisational factors affect human behaviour in the workplace. Her work has been presented and published at international conferences and journals. She is also a frequent reviewer of various renowned peer-reviewed journals.

# Index

## A



## B



## C



## D



## E

## F



## G



## I



## K



## L



## M



## O



## P



## R

## S



## T



## V



## W



## X

www.ingramcontent.com/pod-product-compliance
Lightning Source LLC
LaVergne TN
LVHW060005031026
849161LV00025B/1436